The Public and the Private

The Public and the Private

Issues of Democratic Citizenship

Edited by

Gurpreet Mahajan
in collaboration with
Helmut Reifeld

Konrad
-Adenauer-
Stiftung

Sage Publications
New Delhi • Thousand Oaks • London

First published in 2003 by

Sage Publications India Pvt Ltd
B-42, Panchsheel Enclave
New Delhi 110 017

Sage Publications Inc   **Sage Publications Ltd**
2455 Teller Road   6 Bonhill Street
Thousand Oaks, California 91320   London EC2A 4PU

Published by Tejeshwar Singh for Sage Publications India Pvt Ltd, typeset in 10/12 Esprit Book, by S.R. Enterprises, New Delhi and printed at Chaman Enterprises, New Delhi.

Library of Congress Cataloging-in-Publication Data

The public and the private: Issues of democratic citizenship edited by Gurpreet Mahajan in collaboration with Helmut Reifeld.
    p.   cm.
    Includes bibliographical references and index.
    1. Democracy. 2. Democratization. 3. Individualism. 4. Community. 5. Public interest. I. Mahajan, Gurpreet. II. Reifeld, Helmut.
JC423.P8836   2003   323'.01—dc21   2003008749

ISBN: 0-7619-9702-4 (US-Hb)   81-7829-178-9 (India-Hb)

Sage Production Team: Kamini Karlekar, Sayantani Dasgupta, Shweta Vachani, Radha Dev Raj and Santosh Rawat

Contents

Preface

Controversies about the relation and the distinctions between the public and the private sphere are finding a lot of attention in India as well as in Europe. How can the borderline between the public and the private sphere be understood, described and accepted? Where does the public sphere, mainly associated with the state, end and where does the private sphere, mainly associated with the family, begin? What constitutes and what are the main features of both spheres? Why, how and since when have the two to be distinguished? Questions of this kind are very often asked when the relation between the society and the state has to be fought out and when the legitimacy of the state is at stake.

The German *Konrad Adenauer Foundation* is trying already for quite some time to bring together scholars from both India and Germany, in order to encourage exchange and promote discussion. A workshop under the title of 'The Public and the Private. Democratic Citizenship in a Comparative Perspective' was held at the India Habitat Centre between 2 and 4 November 2000. It was initiated and organized by the Konrad Adenauer Foundation as part of a series of workshops focused on India in a programme called 'Dialogue on Values'. This workshop could not have been realized, however, without the collaboration of Professor Gurpreet Mahajan from the Jawaharlal Nehru University, New Delhi. Her excellent knowledge of the topic as well as of other experts updated the project, gave it a specific focus and turned it into a real comparative and intercultural dialogue.

Thus, the articles in this book emanated from the common interest among the participants to find a new approach for dialogue in the areas of values related to the public-private divide. In order to be fruitful, such a dialogue has to be based on a mutual consensus of interest in the dialogue itself. By its very nature it has to be a process where one does not merely state and restate one's final conclusions but is willing to negotiate the differences of points of view. The articles of this book were written with the idea of raising questions and exploring the possible implications. They seek to promote and carry forward the spirit of dialogue rather than end it with a final statement. In this respect the present book not only provides some useful information about South Asia but also hopes to contribute to the promotion of a world-wide process of dialogue.

Many words of thanks have to be expressed, as inputs have come from many sides, in the process of preparation as well as of publication. Most of the organizational and administrative problems have been solved by Manu Emmanuel and the process of publication was carefully handled by Omita Goyal and the copy editors. Our special gratitude, however, should go to those, who not only presented a paper and participated in the discussion, but who made the effort to revise their paper in the light of these discussions. Their effort is reflected in this book. Nevertheless, we owe our greatest thanks to Professor Gurpreet Mahajan. For her quick, precise and efficient collaboration the Konrad Adenauer Foundation is particularly grateful. Without her expertise and judgement, the book would not have come out as it did.

New Delhi, October 2002   Helmut Reifeld

INTRODUCTION

The Public and the Private: Two Modes of Enhancing Democratization

Gurpreet Mahajan

I

Concepts, as Wittgenstein reminds us, are context specific. This does not imply that the meaning of a concept varies from person to person or from one text to another. It rather suggests that a concept must be understood in relation to a totality that is historically and structurally specific. In different contexts and milieus, concepts acquire different meaning and value. Consequently, it is by referring to the institutional and ideological practices that configure a given totality that we can understand any particular concept. We need to be attentive to this methodological insight while dealing with such concepts as the public and the private. This is necessary for the terms public and private have been in currency for a long period of time. Within the western political tradition itself they have been in use for at least twenty-five centuries. However, despite this prolonged usage, these concepts have received a new and fairly distinct meaning in the modern world. Indeed they have gained a fresh significance in relation to the idea of democratic citizenship, and it is this dimension of the public and private that deserves greater attention in the contemporary scenario.

The idea of public and private figured in an important way in the writings of Aristotle. Writing in Athens, 4th century B.C., he made a distinction between *oikos* and *polis*. The former indicated the world of the Household and comprised of three distinct relationships—namely, that of husband and wife, parent and child, and master and slave. For Aristotle, the Household represented the private domain of which the master was the unquestioned supreme head. 'The reproduction of life, the labour of the slaves, and the service of the women went on under the aegis of the master's domination; birth and death took place in his shadow, and the realm of necessity and transitoriness remained immersed in the obscurity of the private sphere' (Habermas 1989: 3). The *oikos* was thus the arena in which the master ruled in accordance with his judgement. The slaves were his property and as someone who is naturally superior to all others in the family, his authority was complete. In contrast to this the *polis* symbolized the public political domain. In it decisions were collectively arrived at, albeit by those few who were designated as citizens. In the ancient city state of Athens, citizenship was a privilege conferred only upon a few people who constituted the 'masters', the leisure class in society. Slaves (who were approximately 1/3rd of the population of Athens) resident foreigners and women were all excluded from the category of citizens. Thus, while the public denoted a collectivity that was engaged in deliberating upon the political affairs of the state, the collectivity was by no means the entire adult population of the city-state. Only one class of people had the right to participate in the *polis*, and it is they alone who constituted the public and interacted in the public sphere.

Even in Republican Rome, where the liberty of the citizens was a greatly extolled virtue, the social and political systems were anchored in the idea of differential privileges. Neither the Greeks nor the Romans accept the possibility of a world where individuals were equal and free to determine their own destiny. In the Homeric world morality and virtue were closely linked to the social role that the individual is performing. Each role, be that of a master or a parent, a teacher or a citizen, had a specific purpose that was defined within a given social order, and it is this that defined the moral injunctions. Even when Aristotle challenged this vision and spoke of man apart from all his roles, he did not think of a moral vocabulary created by the self. He dissociated morality from a specific role and social circumstance and linked it instead to the essential human nature. What constituted good life was still pre-given, albeit it was defined by the goals that help to realize that human *telos*. Within this understanding of human existence, the idea of the private and public that prevailed in each of these historical epochs was significantly different from contemporary conceptions of the same. At the most obvious level these concepts were accompanied by notions of the self and the collective that were radically different. One needs therefore to reflect upon the specificity of the modern conception of the private and public, and recognize that this point of view is not simply an extension of the perspectives that existed in the pre-modern civilizations.

Perhaps the most important aspect of the modern conception is that the public and private here exist as complementary entities. Indeed they constitute two modes of enhancing democratic citizenship. To put it in another way, in the modern world the private and the public serve the same end. Both represent moments in the process of democratization, and embody attributes that are essential to the existence of a democratic polity. At the same time, the public and the private are defined in relation to the ongoing process of democratization. It is therefore hardly surprising that at various stages of the process, boundaries of the private and the public are drawn differently. As the polity becomes more democratic the private arena gets reconstituted in a way that the public permeates it without eclipsing the space for the expression of individual difference and creativity. What is significant is that the sphere of the public and private are continuously re-articulated in a manner that the two reinforce each other. The mutuality and the inter-linking of the public and private in the contemporary world needs to be emphasized for most analyses begin by postulating a sharp, and fairly unbridgeable, wall between the two.

II

The popular belief that the private and the public are two separate spheres, with discrete boundaries and distinct logic is primarily a legacy of early liberalism. It has been further strengthened by the emergence of a centralized state. Expressing the belief that a minimalist state is necessary for protecting the freedom of the individual, early liberals attempted to carve out a sphere in which the state would not enter. In this connection they separated the home from the state, private industry from public corporations, self-regulating markets from state controlled economy. John Stuart Mill gave this perspective a more systematic form by making a distinction between that 'part of a person's life which concerns only himself and that which concerns others' (Mill 1971: 98). The former, in his view, constituted the realm of the private and must be left to the free will of the individual. The latter, by comparison, fell within the domain of the public and the state could well intervene and regulate these kinds of action. The proposed distinction between self and other regarding actions has since been questioned and most liberals accept that almost all actions impact upon others in one way or another. Yet despite this, early liberal attempts to build a rigid wall between the private from the public continue to rule the popular imagination. In everyday life people customarily begin by dissociating the private from the public and assume that these two domains have distinct boundaries that limit each other. The private, as it were, marks an area from which the public is, or must be, kept out and *vice-versa*, the public necessarily marks the absence of the private.

Divisions of this kind, that have become second-nature to most people, have little analytical value. To understand the particularity of the public and private in the modern world we need therefore to challenge this dichotomous mode of representation. Indeed the importance of these two concepts can best be appreciated if we see the idea of the public and the private as two parallel modes of enhancing democracy. Only when we give up the idea of the private and public as two competing zones, zealously guarding their respective territories, can we understand the importance of these two ideas.

Rigid separation between the public and the private could exist in a context where all persons were not seen as being equally free or autonomous. Within the framework of differential privileges and natural superiority of some individuals, a few areas always remained under the exclusive jurisdiction of the dominant sections. These areas, commonly identified as the private sphere, were sheltered from the scrutiny of the public. Within the liberal framework, where the private was also carefully separated and sheltered from the public, the former, associated with the home and the beliefs of the individual, were placed outside the purview of state regulations. Even though this was intended or at least justified, in the name of protecting individual freedom from state coercion, it helped to shelter the home or family from the concern of justice that prevailed in the public arena. Feminist scholarship, for much of the 20th century, pointed to the injustices that ensued from this liberal perspective. Placing the family in the realm of the private and a personal protected patriarchal privileges. The separation of the private from the public meant that the issue of unequal or unfair treatment within the family remained untouched (see, Okin 1979 and Pateman 1988). Hence, in the interest of justice and democratization, they strongly advocated that affairs of the family also be opened to public examination.

What surfaced from these feminist and other interventions, is that in a democratic polity the public and the private cannot simply be located in opposition to one another. They must interpenetrate. While the norms of fairness in the private sphere are shaped by the public, the latter, in particular system of law and accountability must allow free and equal persons to have a sphere of the private—a sphere in which individuals can exercise their choices freely and create a subjective moral vocabulary. The public too is redefined and reconstituted in these circumstances. It is no longer a gathering of persons who are bound together by bonds of kinship or commitment to some notion of common good. Instead the public surfaces as a domain in which all persons are free and equal: a political and social realm, located outside the family, in which individuals enter and participate giving expression to their separate interests and engagements. The private and the public thus, interpenetrate as two complementary elements in the process of democratization.

In the context of modern democratic polities, the operative principle of the private is individual freedom and the guiding norms of the public are equality, collective deliberation and accountability. The private, one needs to underline, does not refer to a specific area of human existence. Indeed, as democratization advances what is identified as the private sphere changes significantly. However, at each point the private continues to signify an arena in which an autonomous self charters her own destiny. To put it another way, the idea of the private coincides with, if not expresses, the emergence of the individual as an autonomous, self-governing person. On the one hand, the attempt to separate the individual from all other collectivities creates space for the articulation of a private sphere. On the other, the recognition of the self as a self-determining individual with the capacity to reason allows critical appraisal of all received knowledges and beliefs. Endowed with rationality the individual can, it is believed, question inheritances, challenge tradition and make independent choices. The realm in which the individual exercises such freedom represents the domain of the private.

Three points need to be stressed with regard to the notion of the private that prevails in modern democracies. First, the notion of autonomous, self-governing persons, who are by nature equal, forms the basis of the modern notion of the private. Demarcation of the private constitutes a moment in the development of the idea of individualism; and liberal individualism is the condition in which the modern notion of a private sphere flourishes. In ancient Greece, Aristotle used the notion of public and private but the latter was not a sphere of independent action or freedom. The master was the acknowledged superior and, for this reason, it remained a domain where his will reigned supreme. In the absence of any notion of free and equal individuals, the private remains a sphere of arbitrary authority and discretion of the master. On all matters pertaining to the family as well as the fate of the slave it is the master who alone is free to act as he deems best. It is only when the ideology of individualism takes root and all persons are seen as being equal and free that the private emerges as the domain of individual freedom anchored in the principle of rights rather than privileges.

Second, as a sphere of individual freedom the private is not a realm characterized by the absence of the public. It is primarily in societies marked by different privileges rather than equal rights that the private is defined as that which is determined 'by the silence of the Law' (Hobbes 1974: 271). More importantly, when the private is identified as a sphere that is not constituted by the authority of the political sovereign, then this domain is open to the vagaries of the dominant few. Writing about such private entities, Thomas Hobbes states: 'Private Bodies Regular, and Lawful, are those that are constituted without Letters, or other written Authority, saving the Laws common to all other Subjects. And because they are united in one Person Representative, they are held to be Regular; such as are all Families, in which the Father, or Master **ordereth** the whole Family. For he obligeth his Children, and Servants, as farre as Law permitteth, though not further, because none of them are bound to obedience in those actions, which the Law hath forbidden to be done. In all other actions, during the time they are under domestique government, they are **subject to their Fathers, and Masters, as to their immediate Sovereigns'** (Ibid.: 285. Emphasis added).

The private sphere remains unquestionably a domain in which the fathers and the masters govern so long as the idea of all persons being equal in liberty does not take root. In the modern democratic context, when the principle of equal liberty of all individuals is seriously considered, the family and the various relationships that it encompasses are radically redefined. In place of the rule of the husband over the wife or of parents over their children, the law has to step in to guarantee the rights of women and children. The family becomes a domain of free and equal individuals, a sphere which accommodates the various members as private persons, only when the public guides the private. In sharp contrast to this, the private is assiduously guarded against any incursions from the outside in hierarchical societies where rights are unequally distributed. In modern democracies the public, through the instrument of law, aims to establish conditions in which equal rights of all persons are protected in every sphere: in the family as well as in the workplace. As such nothing is sheltered from public scrutiny. But what is equally important is that the law also lays down the boundaries within which individuals are free to make choices. In other words, the law provides a general framework of rights that cannot, or must not, be violated. The delineation of inviolable conditions, at the same time, creates space within which individuals are free to choose and pursue their own private goals, so long as they do not violate the rights of others. The private is thus prefigured by the public in democratic polities and the two operate in conjunction rather than irreconcilable opposition.

Since the incursions of the State are frequently associated with the eclipse of the private it is necessary to reiterate that in a democracy the law exists to facilitate freedom in the private domain. What poses a threat to individual freedom is the exercise of arbitrary power. The actions of the State or public authority that either sidestep the rights of individuals or impose some substantive good, are the two most important sources of discrimination in a democracy. The private domain, and with it individual freedom, are therefore best protected not by creating a rigid divide between the private and the public, but by making all spheres of human action open to the concerns of equal citizenship. And this requires that the private and the public must exist in tandem with each other.

Third, the notion of the private finds a coherent expression only in the 19th century. Although long before this political philosophers, from Marsilius of Padua to John Locke, speak of the individual, there are few attempts to demarcate a sphere of private action in which individuals have the liberty to determine their own destiny. Indeed most things, from religious beliefs and scientific knowledge to family are governed by the dictates of the Church and/or the ruler. Several theorists plead for freedom of conscience, in particular for the right to interpret the scriptures and challenge the doctrine and liturgy of the Established and Unified Roman Catholic Church. However, religion continues to be guided and controlled by the Church: the established Roman Catholic Church or the various recognized National Churches. As a result, even freedom of religious beliefs and religious practices does not exist in any meaningful way. Under these circumstances political philosophers like John Locke associate freedom and tolerance with the right of the churches to determine the nature of religious beliefs independent from state interference and the right of the magistrate to regulate some aspects of religious life which do not constitute the essentials of religion (Locke 1967 and Bainton 1978).

The point is that the individual surfaces but nothing akin to a private domain, in which the self is the supreme legislator, emerges till about the 19th century. It is around this time that individuals are able to carve a small space in which they can make their own choices, so long as they do not violate the rights of other citizens. Gradually when the private sphere emerges it is hardly surprising that religious beliefs are among the first few things to be located in this domain. The freedom of conscience is over the next century expanded to include the liberty to make moral and aesthetic choices. It is also perhaps necessary to note that even though the private sphere is at first demarcated to stave off interference by political and religious institutions, it is subsequently reinforced to shelter the individual from what John Stuart Mill called, the 'tyranny of the majority' (Mill 1971: 9). The boundaries of the private are further extended by the advocates of *laissez-faire*. To favour free enterprise they place the market in the sphere of the private. In all these different configurations of the domain of the private, the attempt is primarily to create space for individual action but it becomes evident soon that the market too needs to be regulated so that individuals can exercise their choices in a fair manner.

In the process of delineating the sphere of the private the boundaries of the self get more narrowly defined. At first, individuation results in the separation of the person from the community and subsequently the boundaries are drawn to exclude others except the nuclear family. Eventually the space within the home is reconfigured to create a private sphere for each of its members. A room is set aside to meet the visitors and people who are outside of the nuclear family; another, usually referred to as the living room, is used as a place where the members of the family meet and interact with one another; and then there are bedrooms. Each marks the private space of an individual and in a manner of speaking, it excludes all others, even other members of the family. The bedroom signifies a space in which the self prevails; others must seek permission to enter or to rummage through the contents of the room.

The restructuring of the home is just an example to illustrate that with modernity and democratization the private is identified as a domain in which the individual is perceived as being an autonomous agent. When freedom is linked to the individual, the family like any other collectivity comes to be viewed as a unit comprising of several separate persons, all equally free, with rights of their own. As a consequence, the private is defined, as Hannah Arendt suggests, against the social rather than the political. Indeed, the latter plays an important role in enhancing the sphere of the private. It is only when the basic rights of all persons are protected that the private comes into existence in the modern world. The presence of law, and with it of public authority, is not therefore antithetical to the existence or interests of the private. Its presence does not indicate the erosion of the public. On the contrary, publicly defined law can, and is expected to, enhance freedom. Like the rules of grammar, it exists to provide a framework within which individuals can choose what they wish to say or do. The private, in this sense, co-exists with the public and is inextricably linked with it.

The public signifies a body of citizens but what distinguishes this body in modern democracies is that it is *not* based on ties of kinship, community or class. Unlike other pre-modern societies, in contemporary democracies the public is constituted by people of diverse classes, castes, religions and races. It is, in other words, inclusive and, at least in principle, open to all categories of people, irrespective of their identity and gender. Collective deliberations by citizens existed even in Ancient Greek city-states. In Athens, for instance, people who had the rights of citizenship frequently met in the market-place to determine the common good that the State must pursue. Similarly in India too, there were caste panchayats which decided on various community matters collectively. However each of these institutions were only partially open. In Athens only the masters were citizens. Men of Greek origin, who had leisure and supposedly rationality to deliberate, were given the right to participate in the affairs of the State. Caste panchayats likewise comprised of people belonging to the same social identity. In sharp contrast to all such arrangements, the modern concept of public includes people, both men and women, of different social identities. Citizenship rights are granted equally to all persons without regard to their specific social identity. An inclusive and open public of this kind has emerged through prolonged struggles of diverse groups that were previously excluded. It is therefore of recent provenance but nevertheless represents the single most important attribute of the idea of public in our times.

The association of public with that which is open to people of all categories is so central to democracy that the term public is usually prefixed to spaces that are not exclusive. Thus, we speak of public parks, public building, public meetings to suggest that these entities or gatherings are accessible to persons of all identities. In contrast to these public places we have several associations in society which are exclusive. Some clubs may only allow gays and others may open their membership only to women or members of a specific caste or religion. Associations of these kinds may perform valuable functions: they may generate solidarity in the social arena or even help to articulate collective group interests. Yet, irrespective of the functions they perform, there remains, in a democratic context, a fairly sharp difference between these groups or associations and those that are represented as being public in nature. Indeed as democratization occurs the public sphere is extended as more and more social spaces become inclusive and open to all persons.

This distinction between groups that are primarily exclusive and those that are open and inclusive, is crucial to an understanding of democracy as well to our conception of the public. Since pre-modern and non-democratic polities were characterized by a series of exclusions and political and social privileges were linked to group memberships, institutions became public in character only when social identities and estates-based distribution of rights was challenged. And, along with that institutions came to represent the views of the people instead of addressing them as subjects.

The transition from subjects to citizens occurred gradually as institutions became representative of public opinion and accountable to the body of citizens. Some notion of publicity and representation existed even in the Middle Ages. But at that time, as Habermas points out, '*publicness* (or *publicity*) *of representation* was not constituted as a social realm, that is, as a public sphere: rather it was something like a status attribute' (Habermas 1989: 7). The incumbent or the Lord 'displayed himself, presented himself as an embodiment of some sort of "higher" power'. ...The staging of publicity involved in representation was wedded to personal attributes such as insignia (badges and arms), dress (clothing and coiffure), demeanor...' (Ibid.: 7–8). In other words, publicity was associated with display and visibility, and this 'attained its ultimate pure form at the French and Burgundian courts in the fifteenth century' (Ibid.: 9). While various forms of visual displays continue even in present days, the public-ness has taken on a new meaning in modern democracies. It is now linked to political communication, legitimation and accountability of authority—aspects that were absent from previous bodies.

A variety of formal and informal institutions facilitate the expression of public opinion, debate and communication from the citizens to the state functionaries. In 17th-and-18th century Europe, coffeehouses, salons, literary societies, libraries, concert halls, opera houses and, above all, journals and a commercial press, played a crucial role. While many of these were initially instruments that were used to convey the messages and notifications of the monarch, they gradually became vehicles for expressing the sentiments and opinions of the literati and the new class of bourgeoisie. Perhaps the most significant contribution was that they created an avenue for the expression of opinion that did not originate in the Court or the Church. Through the press there emerged a group of individuals who were addressing each other and discussing issues that were of common concern. The medium of newsletters and journals thus generated, what has often been described as, public opinion. At the very least these spaces cultivated, and even encouraged, the spirit of public debate: aspects that would subsequently be cherished in democracy.

Habermas, whose study of the evolution of the public sphere in Europe, pays particular attention to these social forums of discussion, sees these avenues as an instance of the public making use of its reason. For him these channels help to make government and administration into a 'public affair' (Ibid.: 24). Collective discussions, albeit by a class of people who had access to these forums and were admitted to the salons, transformed the subject. According to Habermas, these engagements meant that the subject was no longer a passive receiver of regulations. Citizens had to be viewed instead as reasoning subjects, interrogating the ruler and articulating their own demands. Within Habermasian analysis the emergence of these channels for the formation of 'the public will' are placed alongside the formal structures of participation, legitimation and accountability of political authority. However, in popular accounts the latter dimension is frequently lost and relegated into the background. As a consequence, the emergence of the public is associated with the presence of these multiple forums of debate and discussion in society. It is in this context that one needs to reiterate that coffeehouses, lending libraries and salons do play an important role but their presence is not enough for the emergence of a public sphere, even in Western Europe. Nor is the presence of these institutions an adequate indicator of the existence of democratic citizenship. It is the process of secularization and democratization that accompanies the proliferation of these social entities that makes a crucial difference and yields a public sphere in which public opinions are formed, expressed and contested.

A culture of collective discussion was not altogether absent before the 17th century. But what was distinctive of the salons of the 17th and 18th centuries was that they were not functioning around the monarch. Nor were they mere instruments for the expression of the will of the ruler or of the church. In it '[T]ranscending the barriers of social hierarchy, the bourgeoisie met...with the socially prestigious but politically uninfluential—nobles as "common" human beings' (Habermas 1989: 34). It is equally important to recall that the decisive element of these social gatherings was 'not so much the political equality of the members but their exclusiveness in relation to the political realm of absolutism as such: social equality was possible at first only as equality outside the state. The coming together of private people into a public was therefore anticipated in secret, as a public sphere still existing largely behind closed doors' (Ibid.).

The public sphere is constituted eventually as diverse opinions step out of these closed gatherings. In particular, when people of different social identities participate and have the opportunity to influence public opinion and shape the affairs of the state. Historically political equality has been an important pre-condition for the emergence of a public in the modern democratic world. Formal equality is however not enough, and for all persons to have a fair degree of, if not equal, access in the public political arena, it needs to be supplemented by social and material equality. In the absence of the latter large masses of people are likely to remain outside the public sphere. In the process of democratization therefore, the effort has been to expand the public sphere by making it truly universal and accessible to people of all identities living within the nation-state.

Collective deliberations and participation by citizens is without doubt a central part of the notion of the public in modern democracies. The only qualification being that formal institutions of debate and negotiations should be open to people of all social identities. That is, no one should be excluded from them on account of their caste, colour, religion, race or even gender. Institutions of representative democracy based on the idea of universal adult franchise were deeply valued as they were intended to perform this task. However, with the deepening of democratic sentiment, citizens are today asking for a more direct and active role in decision making. Indirect participation through political parties and electoral processes offer, in their view, a very limited space for the incorporation of public opinion in the affairs of the state. Since this space has in recent times been further eclipsed by the highly bureaucratic and centralized state machinery, the public sphere is sought to be strengthened through a decentralized system of administration and involvement of people in governing themselves, at least at the local level.

The recent emphasis on citizen initiatives, local self-government and the greater role of social institutions has been inspired by these assessments of the modern leviathan. In fact it is in this context that the public sphere is increasingly being represented as a domain in which citizens participate directly. That is, not merely through representative political institutions, but through associations and community structures that exist in society. This model of participatory democracy, as it emerged in America, envisaged greater role for 'new' communities that were not built upon ascribed identities but around neighborhoods (see, Barber 1984). However, in India and many other countries it has been translated into a plea for activating existing social bodies and community structures. It is argued that through a variety of institutions that exist in society, for example, caste groups, religious bodies and even voluntary associations and non-governmental organizations, citizens could directly participate in decision making. These institutions could provide avenues by which citizens could engage with each other and arrive at a consensus by mutual consultation and debate.

The idea of a rationally motivated consensus is indeed central to the modern notion of the public but it is doubtful whether such a consensus is likely to be achieved by empowering traditional community structures. In a highly stratified society, such as India, traditional communities may well be an effective means of communicating and reaching out to large numbers of people. Yet, given the existing pattern of social inequalities, strengthening community structures may well be a means of reinforcing the voice of the privileged sections within the community. What is perhaps even more important is that in the context of modern democracy, it is equality and not participation that is the defining feature of the public sphere. The public sphere represents an arena in which people of all categories and identities participate as equal partners. Therefore the mere existence or proliferation of associations or active involvement of communities in the political process is not enough. Participation needs to be accompanied by respect for the equal rights of all persons. In the absence of the latter, participatory consensus may be another means of imposing the will of the majority over the minority.

The public sphere emerges in the process of democratization, and vice-versa, the presence of an arena in which equal freedom of all persons is protected through a system of rights is the single most important indicator of democracy. Participation gains special meaning in this situation as it provides an avenue through which every one can exercise their rights and be counted in the political process. One might also add here that the public represents a body of citizens, who form a collective unit on account of sharing a commitment to the same political ideal: namely, equal rights for all persons. In a democracy citizenship is dissociated from kinship; as such the members of the public are/must be linked by political bonds that are much wider than those that connect the members of an ascriptive community. But in the formation of the nation-states in Europe, a concerted effort was made, through policies on language and religion, to weld together the public into a single community. The belief that a national community, with a shared identity, is essential for the unity of a country has since been echoed in different societies in Asia and elsewhere.

The project of constructing a national community around the history of a particular group or the identity of a specific community has been, and continues to be, a means of excluding some groups from the public domain. In the process of democratization societies are gradually becoming more sensitive to these, more subtle, forms of discrimination. There is increasingly a realization that democratic citizenship can be effectively realized when the ethics of equality governs the political domain as well as the patterns of interaction between citizens in the family as well as the rest of society. The construction of a public as a **collective** body of citizens rather than a **community** of citizens sharing a social identity, or a substantive notion of good, is an important step in realizing this goal. It is only when the public emerges as a body of private persons bound together by mutual recognition of each other's rights that it is possible to speak of distributive justice and freedom as opposed to simply charity and benevolence.

The public thus coexists with the private in a democracy. Instead of being antithetical to the existence of the private its presence makes it possible for individuals to have a private world. Consequently, the public and the private need to be studied in conjunction with each other; indeed they can best be defined in relation to each other. In the modern world the private and the public constitute two complementary modes of democratization. While the creation of a public creates a collective body of citizens who otherwise belong to different communities of birth, the private heralds the presence of the individual as an autonomous citizen. It is when citizenship is dissociated from community identity that the public emerges as a body of equal citizens; and it is when the notion of equality of all persons is seriously considered that it becomes possible to speak of the private sphere for the individual. Indeed it is only with the emergence of this democratic understanding of the public that rights and freedom of people within the family becomes a matter of collective concern. The private and the public thus act in tandem to ensure greater degree of freedom and equality for all members of the polity. One might even say that it is when the public and the private operate in this conjunctive relationship, rather than as two distinct and exclusive domains, that democratic citizenship gets enhanced.

III

In this volume, the discussion on the question of private and public is divided into three sections. The first interrogates the distinction that is commonly drawn between these two spheres and enunciates more creative ways of thinking about the co-presence of the private and the public in the modern, democratic world. The second airs concern about the diminishing space for the individual. It seeks to retrieve the private by challenging some of the ways in which the public impinges upon and defines the private. The third explores issues that have arisen from the redefinition of the public in the context of globalization. In particular, it scrutinizes the notion of governance and the proposed role of the state and other voluntary associations in society. Reflections upon the private and the public are, in each case, informed by the concern for democratic citizenship. Indeed, they deliberate upon the nature of democratic citizenship and discuss the diverse aspects of the private and the public with a view to enhancing equal citizenship.

The first two essays, by Andre Beteille and Dipankar Gupta, challenge the popular conceptions of the private and the public and articulate frameworks within which the complementarity of these two concepts in a democracy may be apprehended. Their formulations gain significance against the background of a whole body of literature in which the public and the private are invariably seen as irreconcilable opposites, representing two separate domains of activity. The distinction between the private and the public has ofcourse been queried before. While some theorists have pointed to the difficulties of culling out distinct domains, others have shown the dangers of affirming this distinction. Over the last two decades, the feminists have been the severest critics of the private-public distinction on the ground that it shelters gender discrimination. By placing the home and the family in the private domain, they maintain, it leaves these spheres outside of the general concern for justice.

The contribution by Beteille explores a different line of argumentation while critiquing the widely accepted distinction between the private and the public. Andre Beteille argues that in the modern era, the public and the private complement each other as each limits the interventions of the community in the life of the individual. In a pre-modern society there is no real notion of private space, particularly of a space against one's own caste and sub-caste. However, as we move to the modern world, the idea of private gains a social value. An attempt is made here to carve a sphere for the individual in which even the members of one's own caste are kept out. When the private becomes a distinct social category, we have the emergence of the notion of the public. As the public becomes a social category, it too acts to keep the community out. It restricts the latter by prescribing special channels for regulating the personal and collective life of the individual. When, for instance, the public regulates the home and the family, spheres which traditionally belong to the private, it intervenes in a way that minimizes the space for the community in the internal affairs of the family.

The realization that in a modern democracy no sphere of life is completely shielded from the interventions of the public has yielded considerable anxiety about the fate of the individual. Most social theorists fear that the increasing incursions of the state, through the majesty of the law, are likely to restrict individual freedom and, with it, creativity and individuality. Can we have a notion of the public, which can in principle penetrate all spheres of life, including the family, and yet retain the idea of the private and the freedom that goes with it? Dipankar Gupta in his paper addresses just this dilemma. He shows that the presence of the public does not spell the end of individual differences, creativity or autonomy. When the public is seen not as a separate domain or set of institutions but primarily as a regime of injunctions that clearly spell out in a standardized fashion what cannot be done, there is still room for individuals to decide what can be done. The private, in this framework, emerges as the world of choices and, within it, freedom is respected and upheld so long as it does not transgress the regime of injunctions. For Gupta, in the modern world, the public is as active indoors as it is outdoors. One's home is no longer one's castle to do what one pleases. It follows then that the public and the private are not governed by antithetical principles; rather they reaffirm each other. The public defines the boundaries by specifying what is unacceptable and therefore not permitted. However, within that ambience it leaves considerable room for individuals to decide and choose what they would like to do. Individuality thus emerges not in the absence of the public but through it. Infact the public provides the conditions that enhance democratic citizenship for all.

Gupta's argument that the concept of private and public needs to be rescued from such popular antinomies as, indoors-outdoors, family-state, secretive and non-secretive, is reinforced in a different way by Ute Frevert. Looking at the experiences of Europe in the 19th century, she points to the many ways in which the world of the private and the public were intertwined in everyday life. A person's private life, in the family and society, shaped his interests in the public sphere; and *vice-versa*, the family, seen as the sphere of the private, served an important public function. It was expected to teach future citizens all those values that could prepare them for public life. Ute Frevert also points to another dimension of the concept of public that is frequently missed in contemporary debates. She argues that the public was, at least in Europe, constituted by the attitudes, norms and interests of the middle classes. It is the middle classes that defined its content, and it is they who prescribed social roles both within the family as also outside of it. Ute reminds us of the class origins of the public, and her analysis implicitly points to the crucial role played by the middle classes in creating what was subsequently termed as the collective and shared world of the public. They were the first to demand participatory rights and to form parties and associations.

While Ute Frevert explores the cultural and social identity of the middle classes in Europe, and more particularly Germany, T.N. Madan looks at the different meanings that the notion of public and private take on, particularly in non-western settings and terrains. He points to situations where the public and the private are deliberately separated. Indeed, people themselves make these distinctions in everyday life as they distinguish between the personal, the collective and the political. However, at other times (for instance, in traditional Japanese society), the public may be continuous with, rather than in contradistinction to, the private. Hence, we may find different patterns of interaction between the private and public—from overlaps and mergers to antagonism and contradistinction. By examining some of the ways in which the concept of the private and the public are used Madan shows that the private is not entirely passive or subordinate to the public. The latter may infact be sustained and legitimized by values that originate in private life. One needs to take cognizance therefore of this complexity and realize that in a democracy the private and the public also frame a middle ground in the form of civil society: a space for citizens initiatives and actions.

Madan suggests, quite appropriately, that civil society expresses the dialectic of the private and the public. After all citizens enter civil society in their individual capacity. They bring with them their separate interests. At the same time, as Hegel reminds us, civil society is characterized by a shared ethic which penetrates and regulates the actions of the individuals and the associations or institutions that they form. Civil society is therefore a sphere of freedom and restraint and it is this that forms the condition of civility in modern life. Over the years, specially with the growing disillusionment with the state and its ability to either generate a set of shared public values or effect transformation, the public has been increasingly associated with institutions of civil society, and the latter are almost always placed in opposition to the state. This characterization of the public is perhaps most strikingly evident in Habermas' work on the 'Structural Transformation of the Public Sphere'. Here, Habermas associates the public sphere with the emergence of certain institutions in society: institutions that lie outside the domain of the church and the state, and play a crucial role in moulding and articulating independent public opinion.

Margrit Pernau both extends and interrogates the Habermasian reading of the public sphere. She undertakes a study of 19th century Delhi to show that institutions similar of those that have been identified with the public sphere in Europe may also be found in India. There are ofcourse significant differences in the way the boundary of the public and the private is drawn in Europe and Delhi. In the Islamic tradition, the public is differentiated from that which is commonplace. It is often a symbol of nobility, power and special status. Likewise, the private frequently includes the domain of religion and religious institutions. Indeed, after colonization, religion is a sphere in which men dominate and structure the affairs of the family. The bourgeoisie as a social class are also absent in Delhi. Nevertheless, there do exist independent forums of debate and discussions: forums, such as Mushairas, where public concerns are spoken about in a situation of considerable equality. We also have a literary public constituted increasingly by the print medium.

Pernau's study reveals, at least indirectly, the limits of defining the public sphere in terms of the presence of forums of discussion and opinion formation. Such forums, as her paper points out, exist even in non-democratic contexts and they often function without any reference to democratic citizenship. The public sphere acts as an expression of democracy when it is defined as a universal sphere, open and accessible to people of all categories, irrespective of their ascribed social identity. Gail Ombedt's paper argues that the anti-caste movements in India recognized this dimension and they played a crucial role in creating such an open public domain. In a colonized society where there was no real equality in the political domain, the imagined Indian identity was derived from the cultural traditions of ancient India. However, a national community constructed along these lines, and defined largely in spiritual terms, could not provide a sense of belonging to all groups. The anti-caste movements challenged these constructions of the nation and attempted to create a truly universal public sphere: a sphere in which different groups are equally represented and each enjoys real rather than formal equality.

The creation of a universal and open public sphere anchored in the principle of equality for all is without doubt an essential requirement of democracy. Indeed, in most democratic polities it is assumed that the state and the law would not only affirm this principle, they would act to ensure that equality for all is the operative norm of social and political life. It is this expectation that has transformed the state, from a law and order maintaining machinery to one that is responsible for ensuring equal citizenship. The functioning of the state along with the steady expansion of its spheres of activity have however come under attack in the last quarter of the 20th century. The second section in this book gives expression to some of these misgivings about the state and the growing incursions of the public domain in the lives of the people. Most of the papers in this unit make a case for limiting the state and protecting the private from being engulfed by the logic of the public.

Looking at some of the reformist agendas initiated by the state as well as associations in society, Rajeev Dhavan underlines the need for exercising some caution for the sake of protecting the freedom to define ourselves. Modern law, he argues, claims mastery over the entire universe. It presents itself as the sovereign and stakes its supremacy over all existing custom and other legal orders. In its reformist incarnation it goes further by evolving a theory of public interest and welfare to ensure that every aspect of social life falls within its purview. Although the law does make a distinction between the public and the private sphere, this distinction is not sacro-sanct and over the years there have been a number of corrective interventions in the private domain. Under the circumstances we need to 'recover a great deal of lost ground to reverse the undue and hasty passion with which modernity claimed the world in its own image for its own sake'.

The paper by Neera Chandhoke also expresses disquiet about modernity. She speaks of the phenomena of 'homelessness' and, against that experience, underlines the need to transform the public and civil society into a more warm and hospitable habitat. Homelessness, in her view, is a major consequence of capitalist modernity. In different ways, theorists from Hegel to Marx, Freud and Simmel to Heidegger and Foucault, documented this dimension and pointed to the alienation that comes with relinquishing the familiar. Chandhoke invokes Adam Smith's notion of sympathy to rise above our self-interests and self-oriented desires and feel for others. Whether individuals can successfully empathize with things that they have themselves never experienced? Whether placing ourselves in the other person's shoes will eventually give individuals the much-needed sense of belonging is an open question, however, the phenomenon of homelessness, that Neera Chandhoke speaks of, may well explain the more recent emphasis on building solidarities in the public sphere.

The paper by Patricia Uberoi expresses anxiety about the way in which the rationale of the public is being extended to the sphere of family and marriage—areas that are seen as being constitutive of the private. She accepts that the feminist critique of the private-public distinction was prompted by the concern for justice and gender equality. Nevertheless, recent attempts to apply the bargaining approach to intra-family affairs and contract approach to the issue of marriage leave many questions unanswered. While these approaches allow concerns of equality to enter into the discussion of domestic work, function distribution and violence within the family, Uberoi maintains that these misunderstand the nature of family and marriage. In particular, she challenges the view endorsed by the bargaining approach that family exists because individuals, despite the conflict of interests, find cooperation within this setting more beneficial than non-cooperation. Uberoi wishes to accommodate the possibility of individuals acting altruistically and it is from this vantage-point that she questions the usurpation of the private by the rationale of self-interest that dominates the market and many other areas of public life.

In the debates on democracy in India the public is frequently associated with the state and the private with individual liberty. This is most starkly evident among civil rights activists and votaries of civil society. Both sets of writers challenge the preponderance of the state in the public sphere and attempt to carve a space where actions of the state are subordinated to the rights and demands of the people. In the present volume the papers by Clauspeter Hill and Aswini K. Ray reflect this point of view. Addressing the issue of democratic citizenship from the perspective of the civil and democratic rights movements they emphasize the need to recast the public in the language of rights. Priority to rights would, they maintain, limit the state as well as protect the liberty of the individual—the latter being central to the existence of the private.

Clauspeter Hill discusses the structure of basic rights guaranteed by the German Constitution and the role they have played in the emergence of the private and public sphere. Rights, according to Hill, provide the framework necessary for sustaining the private sphere against the incursions of the state. In fact they serve three important functions: namely, protecting individual liberty, creating conditions that enable citizens to live a life of dignity and participating in the affairs of the state. Guaranteeing of these rights is however possible only when there are specific organizational and legal structures. The right to liberty, for instance, requires an independent judiciary and an autonomous press. The enunciation of basic rights in the absence of accompanying institutional structures can therefore never be enough.

Aswini K. Ray affirms the centrality of basic rights in the articulation of democratic citizenship. Like Hill, Ray maintains that rights are necessary not only for protecting the liberty of the individual but also for curtailing the arbitrary power of the state. However, analyzing the specific history of India and her struggles against colonialism, he argues that the narrow social base of democratic concerns has seriously curtailed individual rights here. In a country where the nation as a community struggled against colonial rule, the individual and her rights as a citizen were never the central concern. This along with the presence of an elaborate coercive machinery of the state and weak institutions of conflict resolution, have posed serious hurdles in building a secular nation-state. He further points to the redefinition of the public in the post-emergency period and the role of non-governmental organizations and civil rights groups in curtailing state repression and enhancing the rights of the citizens.

Along with the concern for state repression and the terror unleashed by it there is today a deep anxiety about corruption in the public domain. L.C. Jain raises this issue in his paper by postulating two models: one popularized by Robert Clive and the other advocated by Mahatma Gandhi. The former justified the siphoning of public funds to private accounts while the latter vehemently opposed this. Indeed Gandhi saw the distinction between public and private meaningless for individuals engaged in public life. Through the exemplary action of Gandhi, Jain reminds us that public accountability requires that we initiate an internal monitor and accept the need for an equity compass. This is perhaps an appropriate reminder in present-day India, however since the check by one's inner moral self is self imposed, it may be equally necessary to think also of institutional arrangements by which the same goal may be well served.

The last section of the book analyzes the understanding of the public that has emerged in the context of liberalization. On the one hand, it discusses the assault on the public sector and the accompanying plea to subject the economic sphere to the logic of the market. On the other, it reflects upon the idea of governance that discusses whether the institutions of 'civil society' are likely to strengthen the public sphere and make it more democratic. In contemporary India the institutional structure traditionally associated with the public is being significantly altered. If in the social arena greater emphasis is being placed on non-state associations and organizations, in the economic sphere hopes are increasingly being pinned on the efficiency of the market. Private control of public goods is being strongly advocated and in this context the role of the state is being debated. The papers by Arjun Sengupta and Kuldeep Mathur intervene in this debate and address questions that are inextricably linked to the issue of privatization as it has come to be defined in India.

Arjun K. Sengupta draws attention to the role of the public sector in a market economy. While contemporary writings are replete with assertions of government and public sector failures, he reminds us that markets also fail. Besides, having a market or an economy in which markets determine individual activity does not mean that the market is competitive. One needs to begin by recognizing the many different kinds of markets that do exist in actuality, but even more importantly, to note that the state is necessary in every market economy. It is necessary to protect the freedom to negotiate and to reconcile the 'preference functions' of actors. For Sengupta it is not necessary for the state to engage in production economy, but it must nevertheless provide 'public goods' and 'merit goods', such as, health care and education, and create physical and social infrastructure.

Kuldeep Mathur analyzes the different internal and external compulsions that have resulted in the recent attempts to restructure public enterprises in India. Shortly after independence the public sector was created to augment a more rational allocation of resources, and to ensure, through systematic state planning, greater equity and social justice. However, over the years, the assessment of the public sector, including its non-profit motivation, have been significantly revised. The declining faith in the public sector has in turn affirmed the neo-liberal agenda and the policies of privatization, although these have, according to him, progressed at a slow pace, perhaps on account of the vested interests of the civil servants themselves.

The call for reforming the public sector is today accompanied by the belief that public goods cannot be effectively delivered by the bureaucratic machinery of the state. Indeed, this understanding has led a rethinking of the role of the state in social and economic life as well as a strong plea for strengthening non-state, non-governmental organizations in society. The last two papers in this volume focus on this new agenda of 'good governance' to see whether it can fulfil the hope of greater democratization. The paper by Harsh Sethi takes a close look at some of the forums involved in partnering the state and effecting social and economic transformation. Taking cognizance of the significance of non-governmental organizations in articulating citizens interests and the difficulties that they face in battling state bureaucracy and local interests, he points out that the nature of these organizations has changed considerably in the last decade and-a-half. Since many international donors have changed their policy and decided to support private voluntary agencies to ensure good governance, there has been a massive expansion of the 'grassroots market'. There is a 'new breed' of actors, who often hegemonize the voice of the people in a way that has become unrecognizable to the subjects themselves. We therefore have a strange paradox. While the space for these NGOs has increased there are almost no sustained struggles against the new policy regimen. The efforts towards social transformation may, in the era of globalization, require a shift in focus: from blanket opposition to the state, to a more constructive collaboration with the state.

Sarah Joseph makes sense of the re-definition of the public in the discourse on governance by examining two conceptions of citizenship: the liberal democratic and the civic republican tradition. The liberal tradition values individual autonomy and defines citizenship in terms of equal civil and political rights for all members. The civic republican tradition underlines the need to form a national political community around shared public norms and conceptions of good life. The liberal and republican traditions thus constitute two competing visions of democratic citizenship. However, in the recent past, the concern for good governance accompanied by the desire to activate citizenship by creating greater participation of citizens in public affairs, has prompted a fresh interest in the civic republican tradition. While the civic republican tradition assumes that increased participation of citizens directly in the decision-making process will enhance democracy, Joseph questions whether a more active role of the citizen, as it is envisioned within the framework of good governance, is likely to ensure greater inclusiveness and equality. For her, the language of civic activism and stakeholders suggests that the government will become more accountable, but one needs to note that these measures may actually remove several key areas of policy from political decision making. While it is likely to provide more opportunities for organized interests and lobbies it may leave the individual more powerless. What is perhaps equally important is that it may strengthen and exploit existing relations of power instead of changing them in any significant way.

At a time when the slogan of good governance is coming with a mistrust of the ability of the state to manage public goods and a greater reliance on non-governmental organization for performing these tasks, the anxieties expressed by Joseph and Sethi merit serious consideration. They point not only to the need to re-think strategies of social transformation but also hint that the state has an important role to play in this regard. This is significant because the state is today under attack both from rights-based movements as well as participatory models of democracy. While the former seek to enhance the space for individual liberty by limiting the actions of the state, the latter see voluntary citizens groups of various kinds as articulators of the public. While both debate the role and importance of different institutions in defining the public domain, what needs to be emphasized is that in a democracy the public expresses the principle of equality. To the extent that an institution acknowledges the equality of all persons and acts to make equality of opportunity a reality, it is constitutive of the public. The public, in other words, does not simply signify the collective; it betokens a specific kind of collectivity—one which acknowledges and respects the rights of other citizens. Likewise, the private does not signal the absence of the collective or the presence of the atomized individual self. It indicates individualism and the emergence of an autonomous, self-directing and rights-bearing self. It is by appreciating the centrality of the idea of freedom and equality that we can understand the dialectic of the private and the public, and the role they play in enhancing democratic citizenship.

REFERENCES

Bainton, Roland H. 1978. *The Travail of Religious Liberty*. Philadelphia: Westminster Press.

Barber, Benjamin. 1984. *Strong Democracy: Participatory Politics for a New Age*. Berkeley: University of California Press.

Habermas, Jurgen. 1989. *The Structural Transformation of the Public Sphere: An Inquiry into the Category of Bourgeois Society*. Massachussetts: Polity Press.

Hobbes, Thomas. 1974. *Leviathan*. Edited by C.B. MacPherson. Harmondsworth, Middlesex: Penguin Books.

Locke, John. 1967. *Two Tracts on Government*. Edited by P. Abrams. Cambridge: Cambridge University Press.

Mill, John Stuart. 1971. *On Liberty, Representative Government and Subjection of Women: Three Essays*. London: Oxford University Press.

Okin, Susan Moller. 1979. *Women in Western Political Thought*. Princeton, New Jersey: Princeton University Press.

Pateman, Carole. 1988. *The Sexual Contract*. Stanford: Stanford University Press.

PART I

CONCEPTUALIZING THE PUBLIC AND THE PRIVATE

1

The Public as a Social Category

André Béteille

Private faces in public places
Are wiser and nicer
Than public faces in private places.

W.H. Auden

The term 'public' has many and diverse meanings. In the western historical tradition, the term—and its offshoot the 'republic'—has been in use since classical antiquity and no doubt there are corresponding terms in other historical traditions such as the Islamic, the Indian and the Chinese. It has undergone modification, elaboration and differentiation in the course of its evolution from ancient to modern times and its diffusion from one social environment to another. The various meanings of the term flow easily into one another and it is difficult to keep them strictly apart. Therefore it is important to specify the context of its discussion here in order to minimize the confusion of meanings. The sense in which we use the term when we compare and contrast monarchy, aristocracy and republic is not the same as the one in which we use it when we contrast the public with the private.

The context of the present discussion is provided by the emphasis on democracy, citizenship and, I would like to add, civil society. The idea of the public has a specific significance in the context of democratic society and politics and it is that significance which I will make the focus of the present essay. If it is obvious that democratic society must value the public, it is equally obvious that it must respect the private. Thus in modern societies the public and the private become linked together and it is difficult to conceive of the one in isolation from the other. The two are distinct yet they are inseparable, somewhat like an object and its shadow.

It follows from the above that we may speak of the public in at least two different ways. We may use the term in the substantive or empirical sense to mean all the members of the community or the society as a whole: in this inclusive sense the public becomes co-terminous with society itself. But the same term may also be used in an analytical or normative sense to refer to a particular sphere or domain of activity to which a particular significance or value is socially assigned. In the second sense the term is no longer identical with society as a whole, for that includes and values the private as well as the public.

Given the context of the present discussion, I will dwell on the second, analytical and normative sense of the term. It seems to me that in that sense the term 'public' stands for a historical and not a universal category of social experience. It is present and valued in some societies and not in all. As a distinctive domain of social action, it has a significant presence in modern democratic societies but not in every kind of society.

Why does it make sense to speak of a distinctive public domain in modern France but not in a tribal community? After all, we can speak in either case of the people or the community as a whole, and perhaps more easily in the case of a tribal community than of a modern nation-state. But it is only in the second and not the first case that we can speak of a public domain that is distinct from the private. The public becomes a distinct social category only when the legitimacy of the private comes to be socially acknowledged. Where it is difficult to distinguish the one from the other, the public has an uncertain existence as a social category; we may then speak of the community rather than the public.

What I wish to stress is that the public and the private are both social categories and that it will be a mistake to treat only the public and not the private as one. The respect for privacy is a social fact but it is not equally developed in all societies; where it is poorly developed, as in peasant communities, what is commonly encountered is secrecy rather than privacy. In those societies in which both the public and the private are acknowledged as fundamental social values, the same individual is expected to act in both domains, for instance as a citizen in the public domain and as a householder in the private.

The separation of private and public is a part of the differentiation of societies which is a long-term evolutionary tendency. This has to be understood in its proper perspective. To say that differentiation is a long-term evolutionary tendency is not to mean that every society becomes differentiated to the same extent or in the same way. On the contrary, evolution in the strict sense is a process of *divergent* development. This means two things: first, that each society is likely to be more differentiated internally in later than in earlier phases; and secondly, that we find more types of society as we move from the past to the present.

If we look at the world in which we live and at our own times, we are likely to be struck by convergence more than divergence in the development of human society and culture. It is a truism among anthropologists that diffusion contributes as much to the development of society and culture as does evolution. Technical know-how, ideas, beliefs, values and institutions grow as much by the unfolding of their own inner potential as by diffusion, adaptation and accretion. This has been the case in India since time immemorial and Irawati Karve (1961) has pointed to the special significance of accretion in the Indian cultural tradition. The point to be noted here is that any given society may become internally differentiated not only by virtue of its own internal dynamic but also through the process of accretion. Material and non-material elements of culture travel from one corner of the world to another with unprecedented rapidity today but it will be rash to conclude from this that human societies are becoming more homogeneous or more alike.

*

If we take a long-range view of the development of mankind, it will be difficult to deny that past societies were less differentiated than present ones. Economics, politics, kinship and religion enjoy less institutional autonomy in tribal and peasant communities than in industrial societies. It is not surprising that private and public are less clearly differentiated in the former than in the latter. It is well known that in tribal communities life is lived largely in the open, and the individual who seeks to withdraw from the community to live his own life is regarded as a deviant if not a sorcerer or a witch.

The separation of the economic domain from that of family and kinship is far more marked in modern than in pre-modern societies. This does not mean that the two domains were inter-linked in the same way or to the same extent in all societies of the past. Pre-modern societies differed greatly among themselves in their systems of kinship and affinity.

Indeed, there were great variations within India itself. There were patri-lineal and matrilineal communities; communities which allowed po-lygyny and those which allowed polyandry; communities which pre-ferred cross-cousin marriage and those which preferred parallel-cousin marriage, and yet others which allowed neither. But in all these commu-nities the claims and obligations of kinship seeped into economic, po-litical and religious activities in a variety of different ways.

The separation of work and home first began in the west, particu-larly in the Protestant countries, at the dawn of the modern age. Perhaps the seeds of separation were already present in England, Scotland, Holland and other Protestant nations, and what was latent became manifest with the growth of capitalist enterprise and industrial organi-zation. As the new economic order extended its influence to other parts of the world, it began to alter in one way or another the relation-ship between work and home there as well.

The differentiation of the economic domain from the general social matrix has been a subject of much discussion and debate. Louis Dumont (1977: 33) opened his discussion of the subject with the following words: 'The modern era has witnessed the emergence of a new mode of consid-eration of human phenomena and the carving out of a separate domain, which are currently evoked for us by the words, *economics*, the *economy*'. It does not follow from this that the economic domain becomes discon-nected from the rest of society, but only that it begins to be thought of as a distinct domain to which a distinct social value comes to be assigned.

The differentiation of the economic from the political domain has not taken the same course in all industrially advanced societies, not to speak of the industrially backward ones. This becomes clear when we compare the trajectories of the United States and the Soviet Union for the better part of the 20th century (Aron 1962). The decline of social-ism in eastern Europe might appear to strengthen the argument in favour of the autonomy of the economic domain, but the last word on the sub-ject has not been said as yet. In India too, the balance between the 'public' and the 'private' sectors is altering, but no matter where the balance is struck, the need for making a clear distinction between the two has come to be generally acknowledged by now.

When we talk of the differentiation of the economic from the politi-cal domain, we are dealing with questions not only of fact but also of value, not just with what people undergo but, in addition, with what they desire and seek to bring about. The regulation of economic life by political authority—and its deregulation—has become more conscious, more planned, and, in that sense, more 'rational' in modern times. But the political regulation of economic life cannot reverse entirely the tendencies that are the unintended consequences of the everyday actions of millions of ordinary persons.

The differentiation of the religious domain from other domains of society is a long-term historical tendency to which the term 'secularization' has generally been applied. This tendency was analyzed in a classic study in the mid-sixties by M.N. Srinivas (1966), and he attributed its operation to a variety of acts, both intended and unintended but mainly the latter. The historical tendency towards secularization may be accelerated, slowed down or reversed by the conscious actions of intellectuals and ideologues. Just as some ideologues favour greater political regulation of economic life, so too others favour closer regulation of political life by religion.

In speaking of the long-term tendency towards the differentiation of economics and politics, of religion and politics—or of the private and the public—we must not underestimate the strength of the ideologies that set themselves consciously against such differentiation. The course of human history is a disorderly movement in which there are currents as well as counter-currents. At the time of independence there was some consensus about the political regulation of economic life whereas now deregulation appears to enjoy greater favour. By contrast, intellectuals then seemed by and large to favour the separation of religion and politics whereas now more of them appear to be in favour of bringing them closer together. Long-term evolutionary tendencies can tell us little about what may happen in the next decade or two.

*

I would now like to return to the observation that the public emerges as a significant social category only when a distinct social value is assigned to privacy and the private. Societies which lack a well-formed idea of privacy are unlikely to assign much significance to the public in the sense adopted here. There is abundant ethnographic evidence to show that the idea of the private is at best weakly developed in many societies. It is more difficult to show this in the case of the public because there is no society in which the public in the substantive sense of 'all the members of the community taken together' is absent. Yet in the sense that I would like to give to the term, the public is not identical with the community; in some respects it is its opposite.

If in the modern world there is a particular institutional setting reserved for the private, it is the family or the home. The home and the outside world serve as metaphors for the private and the public. At the same time, family and home are not and have not been insulated from the outside world to the same extent in all societies or at all times. The historical process of this insulation marks an important chapter in the development of the idea of privacy.

In many modern western societies the elementary family comprising parents and unmarried children accounts for the better part of kinship. Within the elementary family the obligations of kinship—between spouses, between parents and children and between siblings—are strong and intense. Outside it those obligations tend to be weak and undefined and they easily fade away. No doubt there are variations according to class, race and religion. But the boundaries of the middle-class western family are extremely well marked and they may not be infringed even by other relatives such as cousins, uncles and nephews who might elsewhere be regarded as near.

The western family system had acquired a set of distinctive, not to say unique, social characteristics by the beginning of the 18th century, i.e., before the age of capital and before the age of industry (Laslett 1972, 1977). It is possible that they contributed something important to the emergence of the 'private' and the 'individual' as significant social values. Outside the west and before the 20th century, these characteristics were in evidence to some extent, and in their own distinctive forms, only in Japan.

In other societies the elementary family lacks the clear definition that it had acquired in the west by the time of the industrial and the democratic revolutions. In both India and China it was embedded in a wider system of kinship and marriage and the home was not insulated to nearly the same extent as in the west. This is still true by and large in rural communities throughout the world.

The Japanese anthropologist Chie Nakane has recorded her surprise on finding how porous the boundaries of the home were in a Bengali village where she went to do fieldwork. She had hardly settled into the village when a young unmarried woman took her in hand and showed her not only her own home but also the homes of many of her relatives.

As soon as we entered a house, the young and the old, men and women, gathered round me and warm conversation flowed as I was offered coconut juice and other drinks. Then she began to show me round every corner of the house, including storerooms and the kitchen, without asking permission of the mistress of the household, as if it was her own home (Nakane 1975: 19).

As an ethnographer Nakane was of course delighted, but as a Japanese she was dismayed by the disregard for boundaries.

The action of Nakane's young friend would be interpreted very differently in different cultures. In the west it would be viewed as a gross violation of privacy. But in the Bengali village, the issue was not of privacy but hospitality, and there hospitality overrides privacy, at least among relatives and with regard to any special friend a relative might bring. Were the mistress of the house to deny access to her kitchen and her storeroom to her young relative, it would indicate that either she had some secret to hide—and there are plenty of secrets in a village home—or that there was bad blood between the two families.

In the Indian village, although the ties of kinship extend far and wide, they cannot extend indefinitely. They have to stop short at the boundaries of caste. But then the ties of caste extend beyond the village and they might extend quite far. Through repeated intermarriage all members of a subcaste become related to each other or at least have to be treated as if they were. To invoke the right of privacy against a member of one's own caste or subcaste might be to incur the opprobrium of the community. Do intra-caste interactions fall within the private or the public domain? Where obligations to communities of birth are far-reaching, the distinction between the private and the public is likely to be tenuous.

In China, the major morphological divisions of society are those of clan rather than caste (Hsu 1963). Whereas a caste is an endogamous division, a clan is exogamous. Hence at least in principle the obligations of kinship could extend much further in China than in India. The obligations of clanship are to this day used extensively both on the mainland and overseas, and for linking mainland and overseas Chinese. Again, the question we asked about caste has to be asked about clan: Are actions governed by the norms of clanship to be regarded as private or as public?

It is difficult to determine exactly when in the transition to the modern age the idea of the home as the bastion of privacy and the private came to be established. Historical evidence suggests that the home was not viewed in the same way in western Europe everywhere and at all times. In his study of childhood, Philippe Ariès has presented some interesting material about the use of space in the European home before the 18th century. He observes:

It is easy to imagine the promiscuity which reigned in these rooms where nobody could be alone, which one had to cross to reach any of the communicating rooms, where several couples and several groups of boys or girls slept together (not to speak of the servants, of whom at least some must have slept beside their masters, setting up beds which were still collapsible in the room or just outside the door), in which people foregathered to have their meals, to receive their friends or clients, and sometimes to give alms to beggars (Ariès 1962: 395).

It is true that Ariès was speaking here of the houses of notables; but it is unlikely that privacy would have been more highly valued among the peasantry in the period he was describing.

*

Where the distinction between the private and the public has become a part of common sense, if the domestic stands as the metaphor for the private, the political stands as the metaphor for the public. The public faces mentioned in the epigraph above almost certainly refer to politicians for whom Auden rarely concealed his allergy.

Not only does the political system become progressively differentiated from other social systems, but that system itself becomes internally differentiated. There are variations from one society to another in how politics actually operates, and also in how its agents think it operates and should operate. The same term has different meanings even in neighbouring countries. The French have only one term for what in English is described by two separate terms, 'politics' and 'policy' (Aron 1965: 21–22). When Max Weber spoke of Politik als Beruf, or Politics as a Vocation, he had both politics and policy in mind. He believed that politics in both senses of the term belonged to the public domain, and he certainly did not assign a wholly negative meaning to it.

Politics and kinship are not differentiated to the same extent in all societies. In some societies they are scarcely differentiated at all in either practice or principle. Lewis Henry Morgan wrote in the 19th century that the earliest societies were organized on the basis of kinship and not territory, and that territory only gradually replaced kinship as the basis of political organization (Morgan 1985). There was a kernel of truth in this observation although it came to be discredited later because Morgan did not have a clear enough understanding of the relation between kinship and locality. All societies are territorially organized, but in some the local group is in effect an extended kin group.

Morgan's observations were refined and extended in the 20th century by Meyer Fortes (1970) whose analysis of the relationship between kinship, territory and politics stands as a landmark. In the simpler societies studied by Fortes, kinship has a domestic or familial dimension, but it also has a politico-jural dimension. He tried to develop a technique whereby the two dimensions of kinship which the actor traverses easily and effortlessly may be separated analytically.

Fortes used the Australian Aborigines as his example of what he called the 'kinship polity'. To be sure, the Australian Aborigines provide the extreme example of the interpenetration of kinship and politics—of the private and the public—but a study of the example throws light on the emergence of the private and the public as distinct domains. In the kinship polity, the boundaries of the politico-jural domain are co-extensive with those of the domain of kinship: 'The jural domain and the familial domain are coterminous, unified by the common body of norms and the overriding ethic of generosity' (Fortes 1970: 110). There are in such societies no separate norms regulating the 'private' and the 'public'.

In the case of segmentary tribes with well-marked lineages, one may make a distinction in principle between the lineage system based on genealogy and the political system based on territory (Evans-Pritchard 1940). Evans-Pritchard's classic study of the Nuer of East Africa showed how political order was maintained in such a system in the absence of any centralized authority vested in chief, council or court. But even here, although the territorial system is distinct from the genealogical, 'political' relations between territorial sections are expressed typically in terms of relations between the lineage segments of the dominant clan. This led Dumont to question whether it was at all valid to speak of a 'political system' in the case of the Nuer: 'The so-called political system has neither head nor tongue: it expresses itself almost exclusively in the language of clans, of lineages, of ancestral myths' (Dumont 1971: 71, my translation).

Besides segmentary tribes there are of course tribal chiefdoms as well as tribal states. Whereas there are no constituted authorities in a kinship polity or even in a segmentary political system, there are chiefs, counsellors, headmen and so on in the tribal chiefdom and even more so in the tribal state. But although chiefs and headmen perform political functions, these are by no means the only functions they perform.

Even at the highest point of the socio-political pyramid, 'household' and 'office' are never clearly separated. The chief cannot deny the claims of his kinsmen on his cattle and his granary on the ground that they are his 'private' wealth; nor can he say that they constitute 'public' wealth in the disposal of which he cannot favour his kin (Gluckman 1955).

When we move from tribe to peasantry, the picture is not very different. Peasant communities have been described as 'part-societies' and 'part-cultures' (Redfield 1956). This is because, though relatively isolated and self-sufficient, they have links of one kind or another with centres of civilization. Both in medieval Europe and until recent times in China and the Islamic world, everyday life in the community was governed by its own internal rhythm. Peasant communities were relatively homogeneous and undifferentiated in most parts of the world, though never quite like 'so many potatoes in a sack of potatoes'. The Indian village, as we know, was stratified on the basis of caste, but that is different from the kind of institutional differentiation I have been speaking of so far. At any rate, the subordination of the individual to the group—village, caste and joint family—was no less marked in India than in other agrarian communities.

*

I have used the distinction between the home and the outside world to illustrate the distinction between the private and the public. But is there any society in which the home—or the privileged site of the private, wherever it may lie—is insulated completely from the outside world? This is clearly impossible, because the same individual has necessarily to act in both domains. Here I may refer to the distinction between the sacred and the profane as formulated by Durkheim (1915). The sacred and the profane are distinct and must ordinarily be kept apart; yet there has to be communication between them in socially prescribed ways. (It must be noted that whereas the opposition between sacred and profane is universal, that between private and public is not.)

It is generally acknowledged in modern western societies that the relations between husband and wife or between parents and children are their private affair. This does not mean that they are outside the reach of the law; the divorce court and the juvenile court are very much within the public domain. What it does mean perhaps is that the neighbourhood or the community should not intercede in the internal affairs of the family. Private affairs may be publicly regulated but only through specified channels and in prescribed ways.

In agrarian societies generally, disputes within the home are legitimate concerns of the neighbourhood and the community. One may say that the diffuse sanctions exercised by the community act against disputes within the home reaching the point of crisis where only a legal settlement is possible. In the typical Indian village, elders feel free to advise and even to discipline younger members of the community on matters that would in other societies be regarded as private. In all these matters, distinctions of caste and gender have to be kept in mind of course, but these distinctions do not correspond to the one between the private and the public. Here it is important to distinguish the community not only from the private but also from the public. In rural society how the elders of the community think and feel is certainly important: but is that the same thing as public opinion?

Apart from the diffuse sanctions of the community, there are more specific mechanisms for the settlement of disputes. In rural India, these mechanisms took two main forms: the village panchayat and the caste panchayat. The village panchayat was probably less common and less active than is generally presumed. Caste panchayats, on the other hand, were often active and vigorous, although not all castes had equally effective panchayats. What have been regarded as village panchayats were in effect often panchayats of the dominant caste of the village. Such bodies, no matter how effective, were very different from what would be regarded as public organs in a modern democracy.

Returning to the home and other domains of modern society that may properly be regarded as private, we have seen that they cannot be kept outside the reach of the law: this is because the private no less than the public is a part of society, being both defined and regulated by it. While it is true that all aspects of modern societies, both 'public', and 'private', are regulated by law, it is also true that the differentiation of society is accompanied by the differentiation of law. It was Durkheim's profound insight that societies based on what he called the division of labour (but what it may be better to describe as the differentiation of institutions) are characterized by legal systems that are enormously more complex than the legal systems of societies based on mechanical solidarity, in other words on clan, caste and community.

The emergence in the 18th and 19th centuries of what in English is known as 'civil society' and in German as 'Bürgerlichegesellschaft' was accompanied by far-reaching innovations in the legal system. Civil society is impossible in the absence of a differentiated legal system with its great variety of laws: administrative, commercial, contract, patent, procedural and so on. But while there is an increase in the volume and variety of laws, the initiative for legal action passes more and more from the state or the community to the individual or private party. In Durkheim's language, there is a displacement of repressive law by resti- tutive law.

The law of contract, and even more the idea of contract, provided the basis for the free and unfettered pursuit of private interests by other- wise unrelated individuals to their mutual advantage. Individuals be- came free to enter into contracts that they considered to be to their advantage without consideration of birth, station or rank. Bernard de Mandeville's phrase about 'private vices, public benefits'—meant ironi- cally for the orderly pursuit of private interests—was ceasing to be viewed as a vice or a mark of dishonor as it had been in the earlier social code (Hirschman 1977). This sense of the transition from one kind of order to a different one was captured in Sir Henry Maine's dictum that the movement of progressive societies has hitherto been 'a movement *from Status to Contract*' (Maine 1950: 141).

Is it possible to have a society that is based solely on contractual relations between private parties without the state or other public insti- tutions casting any shadow on them? The prospect of such a society lurked behind Adam Smith's idea of the invisible hand and Herbert Spencer's idea of contractual solidarity. In a brilliant polemic against Spencer and the English utilitarians, Durkheim (1933) demolished the idea of a social order, no matter how much freedom it gave to private parties, without any regulation by public institutions. Private and pub- lic, Durkheim would argue, are not enemies of each other, they are mutually reinforcing; differentiation does not weaken the fabric of society, it strengthens it.

A particular contract may be a private matter between two individu- als, but the law of contracts, which alone makes it binding, belongs in the public domain. A contract is private in the sense that I am free to enter or not enter into it and to choose the person with whom to enter into it, without leave of my clan, caste or community. It is public in the sense that no contract is valid unless it meets the requirements of the law of contracts which exists independently of the parties to the contract. With the increase in the number and variety of contracts, there has been a corresponding elaboration of the law of contracts.

The value placed on privacy or the private grows along with the value placed on the individual or person. De Tocqueville had underlined the central part played by the growing social recognition of the individual in the passage from an aristocratic to a democratic society: 'Individualism is a novel expression to which a novel idea has given birth' (Tocqueville 1956: II, 98). It signalled the replacement of a social order based on the privileges and disabilities of estates (or castes) by one based on the rights and duties of individuals as citizens. It is my argument that the emancipation of the individual from clan, caste and community is crucial to the modern conception of not only the private but also the public.

I have argued that the private and the public are complementary categories and that they are held together by the value placed on the individual as citizen. Citizenship is both an individualizing and a universalizing concept, and the progress of democracy is intimately linked to the enlargement of citizenship.

Citizenship is an individualizing concept in the sense that its entitlements are the entitlements of the individual irrespective of 'religion, race, caste, sex or place of birth'. These entitlements are diminished by the arbitrary exercise of the coercive power of the state. But they may also be stunted by the bondage of the individual to clan, caste and community. In India the individual has been for centuries subordinated to the group: village, caste and joint family. While the subordination of the individual to the group was not unique to India, it was carried further here than perhaps in any other society known in history. Before independence it was the colonial state that appeared as the main obstacle to the growth of citizenship. Today that role has been taken over by the demands of caste and community.

The enlargement of citizenship may be understood in two senses. Firstly, hitherto excluded sections of society are granted citizenship which in that sense becomes more inclusive. In a purely formal sense, the extension of the franchise provides a good example of this. If we look at the history of western democracies in the last two hundred years, we will find that initially the franchise was restricted by property, gender and race. At first citizens were drawn from a small and exclusive section of society and from the democratic point of view it was this section that constituted the political public. In 19th century America, women and Blacks did not form a part of the political public. As the franchise became extended in the 20th century, citizenship became enlarged and the public more inclusive.

I have used a purely formal criterion of citizenship to illustrate my point about the public becoming more and more inclusive. What took two hundred years and more in the West was accomplished overnight in India where subjects were transformed into citizens with the adoption of a republican constitution. But while all Indians are in a purely formal sense citizens under its constitution the public in any politically meaningful sense of the term is still highly restricted. The disabilities of subjecthood have been removed, but the abilities essential for effective citizenship have not been created. There has been a quantitative enlargement of citizenship without much qualitative advance.

The enlargement of citizenship in Britain from the 18th century to the 20th was traced in a landmark study by the sociologist T. H. Marshall (1977). He saw this enlargement not so much in terms of an increase in numbers as of the addition of new rights from one phase to the next. In the 18th century citizenship was defined in terms of civil rights; to these were added political rights in the 19th century and social rights in the 20th. Marshall himself realized that the enlargement of citizenship did not follow a smooth or uniform course, and a later commentator has pointed out that 'full' or 'substantive' citizenship is still some distance away (Lockwood 1992). Nevertheless, the enlargement of citizenship, both quantitatively and qualitatively, has made the public in Britain far more inclusive now than it was in the 18th century, and inclusive in a more meaningful sense than it is in India.

It hardly needs to be emphasized that the substance of citizenship is outside the reach of millions of Indians. Apart from the divisions of caste and community referred to earlier, society is deeply stratified by income, occupation and education. Poverty, hunger, disease and illiteracy are widespread. If there is a public domain in which decisions relating to the major institutions of society are made, it is inaccessible to many Indians.

This brings us back to the substantive concept of the public, the public not as a domain of activity distinct from the private, but as the 'people', as all the members of the society or nation taken together. Is there any society in which the public in the sense of the people as a whole acts effectively and meaningfully in a single, homogeneous and undifferentiated public domain? This certainly does not happen in either India or the United States, and it is difficult to see how it can possibly happen in any large and complex modern society. The idea of the equal participation in the political process of all members of the public may be the dream of the political philosopher but it has very little foundation in sociological reality.

Is the idea of the public, in either the analytical or the substantive sense, incompatible with social differentiation and social stratification?

Were it so, it would be unviable from the start. I have argued that all modern societies are internally differentiated and they are in general more differentiated than societies of the past. They are also stratified in terms of income, esteem and power. But social stratification is not the same thing as social exclusion. Pre-modern societies, whether in India or in Europe, accepted social exclusion based on caste, creed and gender in both practice and principle. Discrimination based on race, caste and gender is incompatible with citizenship; stratification based on income, occupation and education is not.

When T. H. Marshall made the case for the enlargement of citizenship he certainly did not expect that it would lead to the elimination of social class in the sense of inequalities of income, occupation and education. He recognized that *both* citizenship *and* social class were central features of modern liberal democracies. The two acted contrapuntally, class as a force for inequality and citizenship as a force for equality. It is hard to believe that the equalizing tendency of citizenship will eliminate social classes, but it is reasonable to expect it to mitigate class distinctions and to keep their excesses under control. All citizens do not have to be equal in every respect for each of them to be able to look forward to a dignified social existence.

I have said that citizenship is a universalizing concept. I must insist, as I have done in an earlier work (Béteille 1994), that universality is not the same thing as equality even though the two are frequently confused. Universality requires that certain basic facilities and capabilities be placed within the reach of all members of society without consideration of individual merit or individual need; in short, that they be made universally available. It is not concerned, at least not directly, with the distribution of benefits in society as a whole, say for instance, disparities of income or esteem between managers and civil servants or between different ranks of civil servants. Under certain circumstances, universality may be more effectively secured through measures that increase rather than decrease income differentials at certain levels of the occupational system.

Apart from the opposition of public and private, I have tried to distinguish between public and community, particularly the community of birth based on race, caste and clan. There is another distinction that I would like to consider in the end, and that is the distinction between public and mass. Civil society in the liberal democratic conception is a society of publics; it is not a mass society. The liberal critique of totalitarian regimes is that under such regimes the public is transformed into a mass. The anxiety about mass society goes beyond the critique of fascism or communism; with some it is a critique of the homogenizing tendency that they see as inherent in the age of technology.

C. Wright Mills (1956: 298–324) had warned against 'the transformation of public into mass' in the United States in a work that received wide attention in the fifties and sixties. According to him, this would be the outcome of the emergence of a strong power elite which secured increasing control over the instruments of coercion as well as the instruments of communication. The more cohesive and unified the elite became, the more fragmented and impotent the masses would become. He contrasted the society of publics that had prevailed in the USA in the 19th century with the mass society that was emerging in the 20th.

A crucial distinction between public and mass, according to Mills, lay in the dominant modes of communication characteristic of each. Opinion formation through discussion characterizes a society of publics whereas in a mass society opinion is formed by the media, and 'the publics become mere *media markets*' (Ibid.: 304, emphasis in original). He argued that control of these markets became increasingly concentrated in the hands of the very persons who also controlled the instruments of coercion. Mills was not alone in pointing to the debilitating effects of the mass media in the operation of the democratic process.

Mills's argument about the transformation of public into mass was strongly coloured by a romantic notion of society and politics in 19th century America. He simply assumed that active and vigorous communities of public had existed in the past and were being undermined in his time. He did not ask what positions women, blacks and other excluded sections of society occupied in the communities of public in 19th century America. Modern means of communication no doubt alter the operation of the political process. But the role of the media and of modern technology more generally should not be viewed in only a negative light. Certainly in post-independence India both the print and the electronic media have given hitherto excluded sections of society a better sense of the larger political process and a better chance of participating in it than they had in the past. They have contributed to the enlargement of the public, although the enlarged public of today cannot have the same character as the 'communities of public', real or imagined, that existed in the 19th century.

A mass society is the antithesis of a society of publics in so far as the former tends to be homogenized whereas the latter is internally differentiated. But the enlargement of the public through the expansion of citizenship need not lead to the homogenization of society. The effective functioning of a democratic polity requires the presence of appropriate institutions to link citizens to each other and to mediate between citizens and the state. A democratic state and democratic citizenship cannot be sustained in the absence of open and secular institutions that are very different from the communities of birth which were so prominent in the societies of the past.

When the state becomes too powerful it penetrates into the institutions of society and either stultifies them or absorbs them within itself. When institutions lose their autonomy there is little to stand between citizen and state in a society in which the old communities of birth have lost their vitality: this is the transformation of public into mass. This is what happened in the Soviet Union under Stalin, in Germany under Hitler and in Italy under Mussolini. In the fifties and sixties many began to fear that this would also happen in the western democracies as a result of the runaway expansion of technology.

The system of differentiated institutions by which a society of publics is sustained is the outcome of a long and complex historical process. It is an open question how far such institutions can be replicated in the different parts of the world under historical conditions that are very different from those under which they first emerged. In countries like India they have to contend for space in the political arena with other social formations anchored in kinship and religion.

There is no reason to believe or to expect that the enlargement of citizenship—and through it of the public—will take the same course in India as in the West. We have seen that the purely quantitative enlargement of citizenship has been dramatic, but this has happened without much meaningful or qualitative advance. It would be unwise to dismiss as trivial the creation of a more inclusive citizenry in the last 50 years. But we cannot disregard the deepening tension created by the disjunction between the quantitative increase in citizenship and its lack of qualitative advance.

Compared to the West, the pace of political expansion appears to be forced. More and more persons participate not only in elections but also in demonstrations, rallies, stoppages and closures. When a city is brought to a halt by the call for a *bandh*, it is difficult to decide whether we are dealing with public participation or mass participation. It has now become difficult to ignore the wear and tear caused by these forms of participation to the institutions of civil society that provide substance to democratic citizenship.

There is no doubt that the restricted public that existed at the time of Independence has been enlarged in the last fifty years and that this is irreversible. However the process of making an exclusive public more inclusive in a relatively short span of time has been accompanied by extensive mobilization on the basis of caste and community, often in the name of equality and social justice. While this leads to the strengthening of caste and community, at least in the short run, it is doubtful that it contributes much to the qualitative advance of citizenship. If the qualitative advance of citizenship has to surrender to caste and community, it will not augur well for the growth of a political public even when the surrender is made for the sake of substantive equality.

REFERENCES

Ariès, Philippe. 1962. *Centuries of Childhood: A Social History of Family Life.* New York: Vintage Books.
Aron, Raymond. 1962. *Dix-huit leçons sur la société industrielle.* Paris: Gallimard.
_____. 1965. *Democratie et totalitarisme.* Paris: Gallimard.
Béteille, André. 1994. 'Equality and Universality', *Cambridge Anthropology,* vol. 17, no. 1, pp. 1–12.
Dumont, Louis. 1971. *Introduction à deux théories d'anthropologie sociale.* Paris: Mouton.
_____. 1977. From *Mandeville to Marx: The Genesis and Triumph of Economic Ideology.* Chicago: University of Chicago Press.
Durkheim, Émile. 1915. *The Elementary Forms of the Religious Life.* London: George Allen and Unwin.
_____. 1933. *The Division of Labour in Society.* Glencoe: The Free Press.
Evans-Pritchard, E.E. 1940. *The Nuer: A Description of the Modes of Livelihood and Political Institutions of a Nilotic People.* Oxford: Clarendon Press.
Fortes, Meyer. 1970. *Kinship and the Social Order: The Legacy of Lewis Henry Morgan.* London: Routledge and Kegan Paul.
Gluckman, Max. 1955. *The Judicial Process among the Barotse of Northern Rhodesia.* Manchester: Manchester University Press.
Hirschman, Albert O. 1977. *The Passions and the Interests: Political Arguments for Capitalism before its Triumph.* Princeton: Princeton University Press.
Hsu, Francis L. K. 1963. *Clan, Caste and Club.* Princeton: Van Nostrand.
Karve, Irawati. 1961. *Hindu Society: An Interpretation.* Poona: Deshmukh Prakashan.
Laslett, Peter (ed). 1972. *Household and Family in Past Times.* Cambridge: Cambridge University Press.
_____. 1977. *Family Life and Illicit Love in Earlier Generations.* Cambridge: Cambridge University Press.

Lockwood, David. 1992. *Solidarity and Schism: 'The Problem of Disorder' in Durkheimian and Marxist Sociology*. Oxford: Clarendon Press.

Maine, Henry Sumner. 1950. *Ancient Law: Its Connection with the Early History of Society and its Relation to Modern Ideas*. London: Oxford University Press.

Marshall, T. H. 1977. *Class, Citizenship and Social Development*. Chicago: University of Chicago Press.

Mills, C. Wright. 1956. *The Power Elite*. New York: Oxford University Press.

Morgan, Lewis Henry. 1985. *Ancient Society*. Tucson: University of Arizona Press.

Nakane, Chie. 1975. 'Fieldwork in India: A Japanese Experience,' in André Béteille and T. N. Madan (eds), *Encounter and Experience: Personal Accounts of Fieldwork*. Delhi: Vikas, pp. 13–26.

Redfield, Robert. 1956. *Peasant Society and Culture: An Anthropological Approach to Civilization*. Chicago: University of Chicago Press.

Srinivas, M. N. 1966. *Social Change in Modern India*. Berkeley: University of California Press.

Tocqueville, Alexis de. 1956. *Democracy in America*. New York: Alfred Knopf, 2 vols.

2

The Domesticated Public: Tradition, Modernity and the Public/Private Divide

Dipankar Gupta

I

The understanding of public and private is usually conflated with open and closed, or indoors and outdoors. Thus Michel de Certeau writes that the private space is equal to the domestic space where one can withdraw to heal and recuperate from the ravages of the public world which is out there in the open (de Certeau 1988: 146). The private place is a 'place for the body' (Ibid.) to heal and embrace with 'family and kin' (Ibid.: 147). The private is really 'home sweet home' (Ibid.: 148).

This notion of public and private is fairly widespread and the only reason to question it is because it does not help us to understand the specifics of the modern condition. There was always an indoors and an outdoors. There are things that people do behind walls and closed doors and there are things that are done in the open. If what is customarily done indoors is taken out on the streets then that would entail embarrassment and even 'shame'. That is as much true of modern societies as it is of pre-modern societies.

It cannot be said either that the items that should be performed indoors have always remained the same. In modern cities bodily functions are performed within a specific portion of the house, but this is not true of earlier times. Going to the bathroom, for example, was not exclusively a 'private' affair in pre-industrial cities. In 17th century Europe it was quite common for an entire family to walk naked from their home down the street to the baths (Elias 1978: 164). People of eminence were known to issue instructions to their subordinates while performing what we would today consider the most intimate of bodily ablutions (see Lofland 1985: 35). Such an unconcern for the naked body would be clearly shocking in modern times.

Further, pre-industrial cities, specialists inform us, were characterized by cramped houses. People spent more time socializing, eating, drinking, and even sleeping (weather permitting) outside rather than inside (Ibid.: 40). Such a state of affairs would instantly offend contemporary sensibilities. Just because more time was spent outdoors than indoors, did not make pre-industrial societies more 'public'.

On the other hand, in contemporary western societies, there is a greater exhibition of sexual attraction in the presence of others than would have been permissible in the past. Even today, in countries like India, such passionate demonstrations would be severely looked down upon. Thus, while some things were done outdoors in the past but are done only intramurally today, so also there were several things that were done only behind closed doors in the past, but are today performed in the open.

It should be obvious by now that public and private cannot be equated with outside and inside respectively. If public and private are to be relevant for understanding and analysing contemporary societies, it is necessary to appreciate the specific characteristics they have acquired over the past five hundred years and more. This will also tell us a lot about the specifics of the modern condition and the diacritics of the modern individual.

II

The terms 'public' and 'private' emerged in England before they did in France. It was probably first recorded in the English language around 1470. Public meant the 'common good', while private stood for the privilege that those in high government positions enjoyed (Sennet 1978: 16). The terms public and private were employed rather frequently in France from around the 17th and 18th centuries. During that period in France the term public referred primarily to audience for plays (Ibid.).

Public therefore came to mean the life that one passed outside the warm circle of family and friends. This is the sense in which the terms public and private are understood in popular parlance even today.

It is important to note the importance of the French meaning given to the term 'public'. According to Richard Sennet, arguably one of the most perceptive scholars on the subject, if the term public meant audience for plays, there is a historical tale behind it. Eighteenth-century France was the era of cafes, parks and opera houses that were open to all those who could afford to go there. One could watch a play simply by buying tickets to it, quite contrary to the earlier practice whereby 'aristocratic patrons distributed places' (Ibid.: 17). In other words, urban facilities were slowly radiating outwards from a small, select stratum of the nobility and aristocracy to a wider number of people who did not quite belong to this elite circle, but were not exactly rabble either. Walking in public parks for relaxation and exercise was possible for the first time for those who were hitherto confined to the boxed quarters characteristic of pre-industrial houses. The non-elite people could thus approximate in some fashion the life styles of the superior classes. For example, before the era of public parks, it was only the aristocrats who had the privilege of 'walking in their *private* gardens, or giving an evening at the theater' (Ibid.: 17; emphasis mine). Salon culture grew after Louis XIV as the centre of gravity gradually shifted from the king's *palais* to *l'hotels* of counts and to *maisons* of financiers (Elias 1983: 79).

Thus, the words 'public' and 'private' have been in use for nearly five centuries. But it is necessary to make at least one additional comment at this stage before we launch into the specifics of the public-private distinction that exists in modern societies. Private was still the zone epitomized by the family, while the public realm was one that was claimed by demands of civility. Thus 'while man made himself in public, he realized his nature in the private realm, above all in the experiences within the family' (Sennet 1978: 18–19). Consequently, to be in public was like a 'hardship' posting. The etiquette demanded by the court was borne unwillingly even by the nobility (Elias 1983: 87) Gradually, public was seen as the immoral domain, while the private world was a virtuous one. Obviously, therefore, the two were often in conflict, but the 18th century steadfastly refused to 'prefer one over the other, but held the two in a state of equilibrium' (Sennet 1978: 18).

This is where the crucial distinction lies between modern conceptions of the public and the private and those that were evident in the 18th century. Modern industrial societies do not hold the distinction between the private and the public as if they were forces antithetical to each other. This does not mean that there is no longer a distinction between indoors and outdoors, nor that there is no sense of shame and embarrassment in the modern condition. What has changed is that the public informs private lives more critically than it could have been envisioned, even till as late as the early years of this century. The view that all that is base, common, or non-virtuous lay in the public domain characterized the thinking of those who had not quite seen modernity in a full blown fashion. Tonnies, for instance, mourned the passing away of the *gesellschaft* and with it foresaw a situation where all strive crassly for their personal advantage and compete viciously against one another. Even Georg Simmel shared this point of view. In his paper 'The Metropolis and Mental Life' he complained that cities bred alienation and impersonality. Recalling Max Weber's 'iron cage', Simmel lamented the fact that people now only interacted with one another on the basis of impersonal rules. In the metropolis, even formal justice was characterized by 'an inconsiderate hardness' (Simmel 1978: 150). All in all a metropolitan life was 'a retrogression in the culture of the individual with reference to spirituality, delicacy, and idealism' (Ibid.). This is why Edward Shils clubbed Tonnies, Simmel, Spengler, Schaler and Bergson together as those who bemoaned the arrival of the ruinous modern society (Shils 1981: 19). What really turned them against modernity was largely the belief that the public was a non-virtuous domain that only caged people and stifled their initiatives. This is in stark contrast to Hobhouse who came a few decades after Simmel, and for whom advance in modern times was exemplified by mutuality, efficiency and freedom. This is the spirit with which I approach the conception of tradition and modernity in this paper.

III

Hegel had said somewhere in the *Philosophy of Right* that in the past monarchs and potentates were free, but that did not mean that the others in those societies were also free. The unfreedom of the traditional condition arose because what the ruling class could do with abandon was prohibited for the other classes (Hegel 1945). Norbert Elias' study of the court society details the many idiosyncrasies that Louis XIV indulged in (Elias 1983: 19). In other words, for the term public and private to make an appearance, there must be a certain element of universal law at work. We do know that in India tradition sanctioned different forms of punishment for the same crime depending on the caste of the offender. Even in absolutist states of Europe that were a far cry from either the Turkish courts of the Byzantium or the caste society of India, there was a clearly granted disproportionate privilege to the ruling classes. In Aristocratic France, for example, a man could be sentenced to death for a simple theft from the house of an important person (Ibid. 1983: 48). When Absolutist Europe took recourse to Roman Law it did it for selective advantage. As Perry Anderson comments, 'the enhancement of private property from below was matched by the increase of public authority from above, embodied in the discretionary power of the royal ruler.... The Roman Law was the most powerful intellectual weapon available for their typical programme of territorial integration and administrative centralism' (Anderson 1979: 28).

If this was true of absolutism one can well imagine the idiosyncrasies that were prevalent in the parcellized sovereignties that characterized feudal and proto-feudal formations. In these societies there is very little that the superior classes could not do to the subordinate people. Arbitrary levying of taxes, loot, pillage, confining subjects to land, rescinding of allodial property, were some of the common features of these traditional societies. To this one must still add the many physical assaults and humiliating encumberances that the ruling classes imposed on the ruled. There was therefore a sanctioned and authorized inbuilt inequality in tradition. For the purposes of this paper I will assume this to be the traditional condition without any further finessing of details.

Under these circumstances the idea of the public and private is impossible to derive other than of that of outside and inside. Minimally, the notion of public requires popular accountability in political life. This too may not be enough once we come to contemporary times. For the term public to gain its modern resonance there must be a substratum of equality on which perhaps structures of inequality could be built (Marshall 1964: 88). The public really comes into its own with the advent of universal citizenship. This is what firmly anchors the distinction between private and public to modern times.

One can therefore plot a kind of historical progression. If tradition, in an unmarked sense, did not know of such terms as public and private, then it was primarily because there was a clear asymmetry between the superior and subordinate classes. Once these terms begin to get used with some degree of frequency we still find the presence of the absolutist powers of the royal ruler and the inordinate advantages that members of the nobility enjoyed over the rest. The pre-industrial city did not quite experience absolutism, but here too it was not as if everybody enjoyed equal rights. It is only with the coming of industrial capitalism that a fundamental transformation takes place and through the medium of citizenship substantive equality of status is given to all. No longer are merchants, or those without property exempt from enjoying certain privileges. This was not quite true even in pre-industrial cities. Very often Jews were segregated 'like a troop of lepers' (Lofland 1985: 50). It was as if 'there were cities within cites' (Ibid.). In 17th- and 18th-century China foreign merchants were barred from the city and they were lodged in quarters specifically designated for them (Ibid.). Even in terms of business and commerce, for which the pre-industrial city prided itself, what a seller could sell was fixed by law. Retailers were also disallowed from distributing handbills showing a fixed price for their goods (Sennet 1978: 147, 142).

If all of this sounds both foreign and offensive to contemporary ears then it is on account of the fact that we have moved far ahead in terms of our understanding of the public and the private. When the terms public and private first came to be used, the distinction between the two was absolute. This state of affairs persisted right up to the culmination of industrial capitalism. In the past there was the public world which had its own set of rules and then there was the private world with its own set of rules. If the two were not consonant with each other it did not really make any difference. In fact, they were meant to be that way.

Before the advent of industrial capitalism and modernity, the public and the private were seen as two different zones of life with divergent rules. The public world did not penetrate the private world and vice versa. It is only when they began to be mutually penetrative that Tonnies, Spengler and Simmel began to lament the demise of tradition. It is hard to understand why they should have felt that way. Commerce was restricted, differential privileges prevailed, and there was a clearly articulated belief that all people were not equal.

It is worthwhile noting, however, what follows when public and private are clearly separated from each other. It can perhaps be argued that once the heydays of the Roman Empire were over, the *res publica* became more and more bloodless and inanimate. The Romans found in the private a new kind of emotional outlet. This was primarily through the medium of mysticism and other worldliness. What the Romans may have done is to seek 'another principle to set against the public' (Ibid. 1978: 4). Whether or not this is true may be debatable, but this seems to be the case whenever the public and the private are clearly segregated from each other as they were in pre-modern times. Public life, in such circumstances, shows little consideration for the sensitivities and conveniences of others. Francis Trollope writes about pre-industrial Cincinnati where rubbish was heaped in the middle of the street, not right nor left, and it was left to pigs to perform the 'Herculean service' of polishing them off (Lofland 1985: 37–38).

What remains to be done is to self-consciously detail the features of the modern understanding of the public and the private.

IV

A dominant characteristic of modern times is the mutual interpenetration of the public and the private. In this sense Hegel perhaps was one of the first modern thinkers of Europe. In *Philosophy of Right* Hegel said quite bluntly: 'One of the blackest marks against Roman legislation is the law whereby children were treated by their fathers as slaves' (Hegel 1945: 118). So much for the so-called modern strains in Roman law.[1] According to him the family was also a sphere where the ethical spirit prevails. For Hegel: 'Children are potentially free and their life directly embodies nothing save potential freedom. Consequently they are not *things* and cannot be the property of their parents or others. In respect of his relation to the family, the child's education has the positive aim of instilling ethical principles into him...' (Ibid.: 117; emphasis mine). The aim of socializing children is to make sure that they are 'educated to freedom of personality, and have come of age, they become recognized as persons in the eyes of the law...' (Ibid.: 118). This is why Hegel appreciatively quoted a Pythagorean who said that the best education one can give to one's child is to '(m)ake him a citizen of a state with good laws' (Ibid.: 109).

Likewise marriage too is based on ethical authority and is 'against the mere whims of hostile disposition or the accident of purely passing mood...' (Ibid.). Hegel could not have been more specific on this issue when he said: 'It is in the actual conclusion of a marriage, i.e. in the wedding, that the essence of the tie is expressed and established beyond dispute as something ethical, raised above the contingency of feeling and private inclination' (Ibid.: 113).[2] To remind the reader quickly, Hegel believed that the ethic of freedom, or the ethical life, should pulsate in the family, in civil society and in the State (Ibid.: 36). It is not as if the State alone should uphold the ethic of freedom while the family can do what it wants.

The family for Hegel was not a clearly segregated zone where one can be 'natural'. Marriage and the raising of children are determined by ethical principles. The child is a citizen in the making and it is the job of the family to hasten and secure this process. The private/public distinction that is so often upheld as pure opposites, is dissolved in Hegel's treatment of the ethics of freedom. In my view, Hegel was actually describing the modern condition.

From this first step it is now possible to go further down the road in detailing how the public and private relate to each other in modern societies. It is not as if the terms public and private have lost their distinctive meanings because they are no longer pure opposites, but that they gain their resonance at a different level in which they mutually influence and reinforce each other.

To be able to appreciate this, it is necessary once again to delve into the issue of ethics that Hegel was the first to initiate for modern times. For Hegel ethical life is a general condition of existence. Only 'when societies and communities are uncivilized' that ethical life appears 'as a private choice or the natural genius of an exceptional individual' (Ibid.: 108). What Hegel called 'uncivilized' in a rather bold fashion, we prefer to term as 'unmodern', or 'traditional'.

Ethical life, as a general condition of existence outside 'private choice' or 'natural genius', is possible only when the ethic of freedom guarantees a substratum of equality between members of a society. As ethics cannot be kept away from the domain of the family, much less the civil society, likewise in an ethical society there cannot be different sets of rules or laws for different categories and classes. An individual in a modern society is governed by ethical considerations and cannot look to the family as the fount of a contrary (or more virtuous) set of wisdom and morality. The private is no longer a place one can hide. In the modern condition the public is inside the home as well—hence the title of this paper 'The Domesticated Public.'

Once ethical life is understood as a general condition of social existence then a consideration of the *'other'* becomes a paramount concern. It is therefore not at all surprising that a long line of scholars beginning from Charles Cooley to George Herbert Mead to Martin Buber to Alfred Schutz to Talcott Parsons to Habermas, all recognize the importance of the 'other'. The 'other' is central in the construction of the self, in the determination of norms, as well as in the very process of communication itself. It is for this reason that all of them can be considered as theorists of modernity as well as contributors, in one form or the other, to a modern construction of the public and the private.

In my view it was Emmanuel Levinas who most forcefully brought to our recognition how closely ethics is entwined with a concern for the other. For Levinas the 'other' is an object of understanding and an interlocutor at the same time (Levinas 1998: 6). Further, Levinas argues that a person is 'individuated' by a sense of responsibility for the other (Ibid.: 108). This is a very critical point. A person gains as an individual, not by indulgence, whim, superior intelligence, heroism, or virtue, but by responsibility for the other. The other is crucial for the development of the self.

Such a point of view must necessarily privilege inter-subjectivity (Ibid.: 86). Inter-subjectivity can become a viable phenomenon only in modern societies which break down barriers of natural distinctions and constantly strains to minimize, if not eradicate, the privileges/ disprivileges of birth. Inter-subjectivity would be completely meaningless in a traditional society, under absolutism, and considerably constrained even in a pre-industrial city. A member of the warrior caste cannot be inter-subjective with respect to a person of the peasant community, nor a merchant with a member of the nobility, nor a Jew with a gentile. The pre-modern individual is thus not individuated by a concern for the other. Modern ethics, *pace* Levinas, would be absent in such settings. In fact, it is a flagrant unconcern for the 'other' that makes tradition so different from modernity.

This is the right place to distinguish courtesy from ethics. Courtesy, as the term suggests, is about courtly manners marked significantly by deference to those of superior rank. There were rules regarding where to dispose of leftovers at a dining table, who should dip bread first into the common soup bowl, where should the servants stand, who one can throw one's half gnawed bones to, and so forth. While those of inferior rank were expected to be courteous, (anything less could be construed as *lese majeste*) the superior classes could, if they so wished, indulge in moments of *noblesse oblige* (Elias 1978: 91–2; see also, Bryson 1998). As courtesy demanded asymmetric behaviour it left no space, quite obviously, for inter–subjectivity to function.

The lack of inter-subjectivity in pre-modern societies can also be understood in the manner in which either the conception of the public and the private are non-existent, or when the two, as in the pre-industrial city, are strictly confined to different compartments. In the first case the matter is easier to dispose of. When the superior authority has complete access to the life and liberty of an individual there the conception of the private-public distinction makes no sense. This is true even if contracts are arrived at between two parties who belong to different classes. Sample, for instance, the following medieval oath:

> By the Lord before whom this holy thing is holy, I will to N. be faithful and true, loving all that he loves, and shunning all that he shuns, according to the law of God and the custom of the world, and never by will or by force, in word or in deed, will I do anything that is hateful to him; on condition that he will hold me as I deserve and furnish all that was agreed between us when I bowed myself and submitted to his will: (quoted in Sachse 1967: 11).

Under these conditions the notions of the private and the public are indeed quite meaningless. The most that can be said is that there is still a distinction between inside and the outside, between being secretive and non-secretive, between morality at home and conduct outside it. But as we have discussed earlier, inside and outside are not the same as private and public, for then the terms under discussion would lose all historical significance.

Nor is the modern condition fully served when the all pervasive hold of the church over the individual is sundered. Surely, this is a characteristic of modernity, but by itself this is not enough. Many absolutist rulers undermined the hold of the church and succeeded in undermining the church to the state (see Mannheim 1960), but at best their efforts over time led to a separation of public and private as pure dichotomies. Private lives of people were not significantly affected by public norms—the two could proceed largely independent of each other. Nowhere was the need felt to raise children to be good citizens, as Hegel had insisted. It was more important to be true to one's class and station rather than belong to the egalitarian category of citizen and be leveraged by a concern for the other.

When the public and the private are separated in this fashion the public is not a realm which arouses any commitment in the individual. The public is a world one must necessarily suffer, or craftily prey upon, or dump whatever is not necessary for private lives. Under these circumstances even when people get together, either in village councils or in community groupings, individual idiosyncrasies prevail over common rules and generalized norms which are open to, and can be challenged by others. Malcolm Darling, a legendary I.C.S. officer in Punjab in the 1930s, describes what is often glossed over as a democratic decision making, but in which the idea of public norms is completely missing.

> Four (committee members) were sitting in a shy-looking row on a charpoy...at my side. First one laid his hand on his neighbour's wrist and said—do you agree. He said he did, and making the same gesture asked the same question of his neighbour on the other side, and the third did likewise. And so the loan was sanctioned forthwith. I pulled them up and reminded them that there were a number of questions they must ask first (quoted in Dewey 1993: 190).

The entire transaction of public funds was being done on the basis of private trust at the village level. No institutional norms seemed to exist and nor was there any inclination that there should be such publicly articulated checks and balances.

V

A major difficulty in appreciating that the modern condition does not suffer a pure separation of the public and the private is on account of the fact that individualism is not properly understood. Individualism is generally seen in terms of an unconstrained spirit that can roam and express itself as it pleases. This is not individualism at all—perhaps some variety of indulgence or idiosyncrasy. Individualism is not simply a dissolution of a 'traditional whole'. With individualism comes an awareness of social laws that places 'constraints' upon individual interests (see Wittrock 2000: 42).

Individualism should be appreciated as a phenomenon quite different from that of the individual. Individuals exist in all societies. And, if we were to follow Hegel on this, individuals perhaps have a greater presence, *qua* individuals, in pre-modern settings. Indian tradition recognizes the individual and in fact puts quite a lot of stock in store of those who through great effort and *yogic* meditation are able to achieve higher levels of spiritualism. But it will be readily admitted that in earlier times individuals of this sort were few and far between even if they were admired greatly by the rest of the society.

Take the issue of fashion which is also much misunderstood. Clothes in pre-modern societies clearly demarcate where a person stood and not so much as a means of expression by a person (Sennet 1978: 142–147). In fact, till very recently fashion suppressed individual expression in favour of flamboyance and demonstrative opulence. Sennet informs us that fashion plates in 19th century Lyon and Birmingham show colourful provincial clothes (Ibid.). In a cosmopolitan setting of modern times we see quite the opposite. 'To dress up in a sophisticated way, a cosmopolitan way, meant to tone down one's appearances, to become unremarkable' (Ibid.: 164). If a person's clothes are too loud or obviously very expensive, then that is not quite the regular thing to do. For 'anyone who proclaims himself a gent obviously isn't' (Ibid.: 165). To be a gentleman was signalled in little details as to how a button was fastened, or a cuff turned, or a cravat tied, but nothing more ostentatious than that. Fashion statements in modern times must be made keeping in mind an overall uniformity (remember the 'other'), and within that variations are allowed and indeed valourized.

Individualism is not the preserve of lonely and resolute souls but is a condition that impresses itself on all in modern societies. Individualism functions best when there is a recognition of constraints, and of rules that cannot be transgressed. It is within these rules that the individuals are pressured to exert themselves towards self-realization and even excellence. Standardization is therefore a necessary condition for the expression of individualism. Here Norbert Elias' study of the civilizing process is instructive. Most people read restraint as the critical feature in Elias' work on this subject. Elias too seems to lean rather heavily in this direction. Nevertheless, Elias recognizes that the curve connecting courtesy, to civility, to civilization can be closed only when restraints become *standardized* (Elias 1978: 108–9, 140). To put the matter in a more schematic form one could as well say that individualism requires a clear set of *standardized* rules that unambiguously state *what cannot be done*.

It is only after these rules are standardized that it is possible to internalize them as second nature. Once this is the case then it is not as if individuals need to negotiate at each stage whether or not a particular act is permissible. Social restraints can be observed from now on in a more relaxed form. There is no need to fear at every step how a particular act would be perceived by one's superiors. Thus, while it is clear as to what cannot be done, the field is left wide open as to *what can be done*. This is where individualism comes into its own. Individuals when made to realize themselves under pressure of rules that are unequivocal about what will not be tolerated are forced to be individualistic.

In non-modern societies the emphasis is just the reverse. There is a great degree of pressure in knowing *what must be done* and very little on *what cannot be done*. Thus, one must look after one's elders, be respectful of authority, be protective of one's family, and obey caste norms and rules of etiquette. Rules of etiquette clearly demonstrate this alternate stress on what must be done. Caste etiquette makes clear who one must eat with and there is no quibbling allowed on that. Likewise table manners also dictate how to pierce peas with a fork. There are no two ways of accomplishing this task. In speech too there is clarity as to how a language has to be spoken with no allowances made for dialects and accents that are not quite proper. Consequently, there is little clarity on what cannot be done. This is more so in the case of members of the superior community in non-modern societies. There is hardly anything that could not be done as far as they were concerned. There was very little by way of legal hindrance either to their many whims and fancies.

A modern person therefore is one who functions in a *regime of injunctions*. This should be contrasted with the pre-modern condition when the *regime of imperatives* was the salient feature. In a regime of injunctions a person is obliged to operate in a system of clearly known rules that apply to all equally. This regime of injunctions is a *public* matter. It applies universally with no exception. To understand this more fully perhaps the analogy of sport may be applied. In a sport, like soccer or cricket, what is made very clear in the rule books is what *cannot* be done. In soccer, for example, only the goal keeper is allowed to handle the ball, and in cricket the bowler is not allowed to chuck the ball, and so forth. Once these injunctions are fully internalized only then can players and spectators enjoy the sport, and it is only then that the public becomes truly involved with such events. It is therefore not at all surprising that sport became sport only in the modern period when rules for each discipline were clearly laid out by respective bodies of professionals and they acquired universal adherence and subscription.

In a modern society the presence of the other is therefore paramount. What the regime of injunctions makes clear is that the rules that apply to any one person also apply to others. It is by taking into account the other as a public interlocutor that individuals gain a measure of themselves. This is why Levinas was recalled a little earlier in this paper while discussing the issue of ethics. Ethics is a modern concern because the other is absolutely critical for its realization. Morality does not require the other and it is perfectly content to remain completely privatized. This is why morality abounds in pre-modern settings and there are often clashes over divergent moral standards that brook no mediation. If morality were to be standardized it would not be morality at all!

VI

In this section I should like to summon to my defence a classic work of the 1950s by David Reisman. Engagingly entitled *The Lonely Crowd*, Reisman drove home the point that a modern individual is public oriented—or to put it in his words—'other-directed' (Reisman 1950: 15–18). This other directed individual did not descend fully made in America (recall Trollope's description of the streets of Cincinnati) but gradually evolved over time. This is why the sub-title of the book is '*A Study of the Changing American Character*.'

In Reisman's classification the 'other-directed' type of individual is one for whom the 'peer group' matters most (Ibid.: 15–18). Without doing injustice to Reisman his understanding of 'peer group' can be equated with the public—the world of citizens. This does not violate the basic tenor of Reisman's argument for he believes that the 'inner-directed' people are those who have internalized only the authority of their elders. To continue with Reisman, a tradition directed person 'feels the impact of his culture as a unit, but is nevertheless mediated through the specific, small number of individuals with whom he is in daily contact' (Ibid.: 25). For the tradition directed person all that is worth learning about life has really been learnt within the confines of the home. This is akin to what we argued earlier when we said that in tradition proper an individual has no real conception of the other. For a traditional person socialization is about as deep as family, kin, clan and estate. The undifferentiated and unmarked other does not arise in traditional consciousness.

The 'other-directed' individual, on the other hand, is one for whom the 'family is no longer a closely knit unit to which he belongs but merely a part of a wider social environment...' (Ibid.: 26). This is what allows the other directed person to be 'at home abroad' (Ibid.)—a true cosmopolite, quite at ease with strangers.

The influence of the society through one's peers gets deeply ingrained in the modern person and functions as an internalized social gyroscope. The public is deep within the individual which then prompts the individual to seek self realization in ways that are not outside the ambit of choices that the public makes available, not just to that one individual but to everyone. When Talcott Parsons discussed the dilemmas of orientation, or the motivation-gratification bundle (Parsons 1951) or the normative orientations that confront the actor (Parsons 1964), he was also remarking, in a very pointed fashion, that the choices given to the individual are the ones that the society, the 'other', or the public, does *not* disallow.

Looked at this way it is not as if individuals realize their individualism on their own free will, unconstrained by the public that makes only certain choices acceptable. The private world in a modern society is then that aspect of a person's life that allows a person to choose between different sanctioned alternatives. As long as people choose between alternatives acceptable to society—in other words, as long as they do not break the rules of what is not acceptable—an individual's privacy cannot be transgressed upon. But if individuals are found to break the rules—at home, in the garden, or on the streets—the public will intervene.

Till the advent of modernism the issue of marital rape was practically unthinkable. What a man did to his wife within the house was outside the purview of the public. This was when the public and private were held apart as separate, each spinning on its own independent axis. Today marital rape is a crime in Western societies because the public is within the house, in the recesses of one's bodily space. In India, marital rape is not a crime, at least not yet. This is another indication of how the pubic and private are kept apart in societies where true modernity is still some distance away. Where the public and the private are in synergy they mutually reinforce each other. In such settings it is offensive to the public if one's house does not match up to accepted standards of the peer group with regard to hygiene and cleanliness no matter what a person's family members may think about it. It is illegal also to own rare animals in one's residence or office space. In a truly modern setting it is incorrect to believe that one's house is one's fortress.

The private world is therefore the world of choices. It is a realm of reflection where a person weighs between different alternatives that do not violate the public's understanding of *what cannot be done*. As choice is constrained by rules, and as the sensibilities of the other are so internalized by the person that the effort to do something different and make a mark on one's own is so much harder. This is why an individualist society is infinitely more creative than a traditional society. The standards set are so much higher simply because there is greater headwind against which an individual is forced to exert. This resistance arises simply because the same opportunities are available to all as the 'other', and the peer group is ever present. Whims, idiosyncrasies, wild flings of passionate and unbridled expression occupy a very insignificant space in modern societies. It is only when the public gets domesticated that we can truly realize our private nature.

VII

The public sets out standardized rules of injunctions that have to be observed in the exercise of choice. Choice is a *private* affair when it concerns a few people. Such people are usually bound by ties of friendship and family. The choices that one makes as husband or wife can be called private choices, but in a modern society these choices would have to stay well within the horizon delimited by the regime of injunctions. There is little demonstration of private choice among neighbours in a metropolitan setting. What people living in close proximity do to each other concerns the entire locality, and hence large numbers of people.

Choice therefore cannot be limited to the private sphere alone. There are many other arenas where choice is manifested and these cannot all be called private. People make choices everywhere in the corporate world of business, politics and state-craft, in running institutions like hospitals, universities, and so on. Often all of these are casually subsumed under the term public because that is how the term is popularly understood. But as we have pointed out in the preceding pages, doing things in the open, or outside one's home, or with large numbers of people, does not necessarily mean that the public is active, or that it is a useful term to employ.

The hospital, the university, the government are certainly not in the realm of the private, but that does not mean that in a modern society there are many 'publics'. There is only one public (contra Fraser 1994) regime of injunctions which is observed at a variety of levels. Only one of these levels is properly private. But the regime of standardized injunctions allows for the exercise of choices at other planes as well, such as at the level of political parties, schools and hospitals. But no matter where the choices are made—at home or school, at work or play, in a developed modern society, the public is always there.

To conclude, the private and the public are not contrary principles in modern times but are mutually reinforcing. Moreover, private is one of the many arenas where choices are made but certainly does not exhaust the entire scope for choices. The public, which is empirically available as a regime of injunctions, permeates through the many instances and levels where choices are made and exercised. As long as the fields of choices stay within the regime of injunctions, the public expresses itself in multiple settings without losing itself. This is another reason why it would be incorrect to see the private contrapuntally to the public as is too often the case. If we tend to do this most uncritically in India then it just demonstrates the backwardness of our social condition.

NOTES

1. It is worth recalling in this connection Baudelaire's comment: 'Woe betide the man who goes to antiquity for the study of anything other than ideal art, logic and general method' (Baudelaire 1972: 405).
2. Contrast the modernity of Hegel's position on marriage with that of Immanuel Kant. Kant and Hegel were separated from each other by about a little more than a quarter of a century though it would seem much longer. Kant retained a very traditional attitude towards marriage and towards women as exemplified in his *Anthropology*. According to Kant, 'A harmonious and indissoluble union cannot be achieved through random combination of two persons. One partner must subject himself to the other, and, alternately, one must be superior to the other in something, so that he can dominate and rule' (Kant 1978: 216). There is no trace here of the ethic of freedom that Hegel insisted should characterize marriages.

REFERENCES

Anderson, Perry. 1979. *Lineages of the Absolutist State*. London: Verso.
Baudelaire, Charles. 1972. *Selected Writings on Art and Literature*. New York: Penguin Books.
Bryson, Anne. 1998. *From Courtesy to Civility*. Oxford: The Clarendon Press.
De Certeau, Michel. 1988. *The Practice of Everyday Life, vol. 2, Living and Cooking*. Minneapolis: University of Minnesota Press.
Dewey, Clive. 1993. *Anglo-Indian Attitudes: The Mind of the Indian Civil Service*. London: The Hambledon Press.
Elias, Norbert. 1978. *The Civilizing Process, vol. 1, The History of Manners*. New York: Panthoen.
————. 1983. *The Court Society*. New York: Pantheon.
Fraser, Nancy. 1994. 'Re-thinking the Public Sphere: A Contribution to the Critique of Actually Existing Democracies,' in Henry A. Giroux and Peter McLaren (eds), *Between Border: Pedagogy and the Politics of Cultural Studies*. New York: Routledge.

Hegel, G.W.F. 1945. *Philosophy of Right*. Clarendon: Oxford University Press.

Kant, Immanuel. 1978. *Anthropology: From a Pragmatic Point of View*. Carbondale and Edwardsville: Southern Illinois University Press.

Levinas, Emmanuel. 1998. *Entre-Nous: Thinking-of-the-Other*. New York: Columbia University Press.

Lofland, Lyn H. 1985. *A World of Strangers: Order and Action in Urban Public Space*. Prospect Heights, Illinois: Waveland Press.

Mannheim, Karl. 1960. *Ideology and Utopia: An Introduction to the Sociology of Knowledge*. London: Routledge and Kegan Paul.

Marshall T.H. 1964. *Class, Citizenship and Social Development*. Garden City, New York: Doubleday and Company.

Parsons, Talcott. 1951. *The Social System*. Glencoe: The Free Press.

_____. 1964. *The Structure of Social Action*. New Delhi: Amerind Publication.

Reisman, David. 1950. *The Lonely Crowd: A Study of the Changing American Character*. New Haven: Yale University Press.

Sachse, William L. 1967. *English History in the Making: Readings from the Sources Upto 1689*. Waltham, Massachusetts: Blaisdell Publications.

Sennet, Richard. 1978. *The Fall of Public Man: On the Social Psychology of Capitalism*. New York: Vintage Books (Random House).

Shils, Edward. 1981. *Tradition*. Chicago: University of Chicago Press.

Simmel, Georg. 1978. *The Sociology of Georg Simmel*. Translated and edited by Kurt H. Wolff. Glencoe, Illinois: The Free Press.

Wittrock, Bjorn. 2000. 'Modernity: One, None or Many,' *Daedalus*, vol. 129, no. 1, pp. 31–60.

3

The Middle Classes as Public and Private: Culture, Gender and Modernization in 19th Century Europe

Ute Frevert

All over Central and Western Europe, the 19th century has been called a 'bourgeois' century, that is a period of time heavily shaped by middle-class values and activities. The middle classes not only invented modern industrial capitalism including banking and trading, they also developed a lifestyle and a cultural matrix that distinguished them from any other social group. It focussed on familial intimacy, education, association and a high degree of self-reflection. In addition, they left their mark on the political scenery: either by violently overthrowing the *Ancien Régime*, like in France, or by peacefully transforming absolutist rule into constitutional monarchies with more or less powerful parliamentary systems, like in Great Britain (where this development took place even earlier), Germany, Italy or Austria-Hungary. During the French Revolution, the middle classes as *tiers état*—placed below the nobility and the clergy—staged themselves as the true representatives of the nation claiming political citizenship and sovereignty. In Germany, the middle classes (*Bürgestand*) gradually expanded their influence in the economy and through education before they challenged the noble political elite and demanded their share in political power. In all countries, the middle classes incidentally were defined by their 'middle' social position between the nobility and the peasantry. As the 19th century went on, the peasantry gave way to the emerging working classes confronting the middle classes with another programme of emancipation and participation.

Private/Public

The new economic, cultural and political mapping that took place during the 19th century thus was largely inspired and brought about by a small social group comprising not more than 5 to 10 per cent of the whole population. By giving shape to modern civil society, this group also undertook the task of carving out a new relationship between the private and the public sphere. In this context, the middle classes in 19th-century Europe can be characterized by their very endeavors to find a new definition for both the public and the private sphere. And they placed themselves at the core of this definition: what was called 'public' was identified with middle-class aspirations and conceptions, and so was the private realm.

Compared to the social and political order of the *Ancien Régime*, the public sphere of the 19th century took on a very different shape (Cf. Lucian Hölscher 1993). It not only encompassed the web of 'high politics' governed by the state, i.e., the absolutist prince and his councellors who had long since played politics as a private game. By forcing dynasties to share power, the introduction of parliamentary systems also implied establishing a sphere within which politics had to be legitimized, where they were discussed and criticized by 'public opinion'. When people were no longer satisfied with debating and reflecting, but strove to become equal participants in the political game, the public sphere became wider and wider. This held especially true for the second half of the century, when the gradual expansion of male suffrage led to the development of a political mass market. Structured by parties, unions, the press and all kinds of associations, this market grew even more inclusive. At the same time, the state itself extended its functions and confronted its citizens with its omnipresence. In doing so, it virtually forced society to organize itself, if it did not want to be swallowed by a Leviathan growing ever more powerful.

As mentioned above, the middle classes were at the core of this redefinition and the extension of the public sphere (comprising state and society alike). It was they who were responsible for public opinion—who first demanded participatory rights in the political process, who founded associations, parties and pressure groups aiming to influence (and eventually take over) state politics. The middle classes were, so to speak, the first public force or stratum. Inventing and claiming the title of citizen, they set themselves at the forefront of political progress which, at that time, meant participation and representation of the people within the constitutional order.

The identification of political citizenship and middle-class status became especially apparent in the German case, where language other than in France or Britain, did not even differentiate between a political and a socio-economic *Bürger*. While the French distinguished the *citoyen* from the *bourgeois*, the English talked about *citizens* in contrast to the *middle classes*. In the German linguistical as well as sociopolitical context however, the term *Bürger* originally described the inhabitant of a walled city who as such involved in trade, crafts, and education. It was only during the times of political enlightenment since the late 18th century that this definition was broadened to encompass the political sphere. The political or *Staatsbürger* then emancipated himself from the former subject or *Untertan*. From now on, the *Bürger* strove to be both: an educated, hard-working and thus relatively wealthy urban man as well as a political citizen.

How did this connect with the notions of public and private? A direct answer is given by a German encyclopaedia of 1843 (read mostly by a middle-class audience). It attached several meanings to the word *bürgerlich* which first of all meant as much as did public, i.e., political, or referring to the state and civil society. In a second sense, however, *bürgerlich* was taken as a semantic opposition to public and civic. Here, it implied all those activities in which citizens were involved while leading their 'private lives', i.e., family and property relations, as well as economic and social interests of all kinds. The *Bürger* was thus as much a public being as a private person; he played (or at least attempted to play) a crucial part in society and politics, while maintaining his privacy. (Allgemeine deutsche Real-Encyclopädie 1843).'

Although both spheres were separated on an analytical level, it was clear that in social practice they were closely intertwined. The way a person behaved in his private life, as a family member, among friends, on the labour market or in the pub next door, not only shaped his interests in the public sphere; it also influenced his chances of defending and finding support for those interests. How both spheres worked together can best be exemplified by looking at family relations. As historical research has proven, family was an essential feature of middle-class life. One could even say that the family in its modern 'nuclear' sense, comprising only parents and children, was invented by the middle classes. The separation of outdoor work and indoor life was accompanied by a high moral investment in family values and relations. From this perspective, the family was seen as the realm of privacy, which was separated by a wide distance from anything public. It's functions was to offer individual support and consolation; nurse its male members, fulfill their emotional needs, and teach future citizens all those values and habits that secured their success in public life. As such, it formed a kind of bridge between the individual and society. This in turn demonstrated the family's public function and its ambivalent position as both a private and a public institution. On the one hand, the family should be protected against outside influences, be it social or political. On the other hand however, it formed part of the social performance of the middle classes in that it secured (or at least tried to) their emotional satisfaction, socialized them in the primary and secondary virtues of modern life, and supported them with social and economic ties necessary for public success.

The separation of public and private was thus not very neatly achieved in middle-class social practice. Although it was 'invented' by this very stratum, it stopped short of being realized in absolute terms. To complicate the picture even further, the definition of 'private' and 'public' changed over time. What was called private at the beginning of the 19th century became more and more open to public concern and intervention during the course of the century. As a factory owner, for example, someone was at the same time a private and a public man: he was in charge of private business, but he was under constant observation by the public as soon as the labour movement began to develop and the state began to claim interventionist rights (factory inspection and labour legislation). This ambivalence was reflected in the self—perception of businessmen and entrepreneurs who described their individual and private efforts as serving the public's (i.e., employees' and consumers') needs.

Class/Culture

Although we began with rather general and abstract remarks, at this stage of the discussion an empirical question has to be answered: Who were the *middle classes*? Who were the *bourgeoisie*? Who were the *Bürger*? To call this question empirical does not imply that the middle classes could be defined by simply enumerating a list of such occupations as entrepreneurs, businessmen, engineers, doctors, lawyers, teachers and so on. The professional fragmentation on the contrary poses the question anew: How can the middle classes be defined? Did they have any common features if so, what were they.

Recent research tends to answer these questions by describing the middle classes as a genuine cultural entity, as a social group defined by its very culture. Culture in this sense refers to a set of values, modes and rules of behaviour, life-styles and appearances, and ways of seeing oneself and others. In short, culture means the way of making sense of the world. It is of course highly dependent on material resources, since a given level of affluence is needed to develop special cultural traits and habits. In turn, material prerequisites are themselves shaped by the culture which they help to create.

There were at least two reasons why the middle classes themselves developed a special need for a self-definition which was primarily cultural. First, their status in society was, from the very beginning, precarious and imprecise, and second, their inner structure was highly fragmented and difficult to integrate in economic terms.

The terms—middle classes, middle strata, *les classes moyennes, Mittelschicht* and *Mittelstand*—all these refer to intermediate status. The people belonging to the German *Bürgertum*, to the Italian *borghesia* or the French *bourgeoisie* found themselves in-between, squeezed between the aristocracy and the lower strata of society. Their position was a relative one and thus not easy to define.

This difficulty was already apparent in the late 18th century when the Prussian government issued a new legal code. Trying to stabilize the social pyramid, the codification mentioned the noble and the peasant estate as being characterized by its positive political and/or economic functions. In contrast, the *Bürgerstand* was defined negatively, i.e., by exclusion. Anybody who did not belong either to the nobility or the peasantry was part of the third category, or the *Bürgerstand*. The latter thus presented itself as a clearly intermediate grouping, identifiable not so much by its own traits and rules but by its difference from others (Koselleck 1975: 78ff.).[1]

Although the social order changed rapidly after 1800 the problem of middle–class identity remained, in a structural sense, more or less the same. Being situated in the middle, the *Bürgertum* strove for rigid borderlines and separation from the top and the bottom alike. It feared dissemination and dissolution, if it did not succeed in keeping its distance.

Sharp distinctions were needed to safeguard a separate identity, and avoid being swallowed or invaded by other social groupings.[2]

Proceeding to the second argument, those external distinctions were even more urgent since the inner structure of the middle classes was highly fragmented and differentiated. This had already been felt by the creators of the Prussian legal code in 1794. The code defined the *Bürger* (who was neither a noble nor a peasant) by his place of residence. All those living in a town were called *Bürger*, especially if they enjoyed civic rights. The *Bürgerstand* thus extended to a large range of professions and wealth; it obviously lacked economic or social homogenity.

This was equally true for the *Bürgertum* of the 19th century.[3] It comprised numerous professional groups, which had very little in common. Industrial entrepreneurs, financial and commercial businessmen, lawyers, doctors, university teachers and Protestant clergymen: they were all part of the so-called *Bürgertum*. Later in the century there emerged new groups such as white-collar workers or technicians who also applied for membership. Their material resources ranged from one extreme to the other. While some factory owners, big merchants and bankers accumulated enormous wealth, school teachers and most civil servants found it difficult to make a decent living. Whereas industrialists like Krupp built large villas for their families and employed a squadron of servants, others had to do with just one maid and a cramped flat.

This apparent economic gap however, did not prevent factory owners and school teachers from calling themselves *Bürger* and claiming a *bürgerlich* way of life. What then, did this mean to them? What kind of cohesive matter was attached to the term to include such a variety of people? Let us try different answers.

First: could the cohesive factor possibly be a political one? As was pointed out earlier, from the very beginning the term *Bürger* acquired an explicitly political meaning, in right sense that it referred to citizenship and political participation. As such, it was not a social but political category. Nevertheless, this did not rule out that for some time, political and social categories merged—although never completely. Up to the middle of the 19th century those who were allowed to vote and represent public will, were men of the propertied and educated strata of society (plus urban craftsmen and shopkeepers who traditionally held citizen rights but did not belong to the *Bürgertum* as a sociocultural group). With the extension of the vote to all men in the 1860s, this identification of social and political *Bürger* fell apart. Moreover, the social *Bürgertum* never spoke with one political voice. There were liberals, who soon split up into different wings, and there were conservatives. Some *Bürger* even filled the ranks of the Social Democratic Party. Thus politics were not very well suited to unifying the scattered sections of the *Bürgertum*. Not even with regard to their most important opponent, the working classes, could *Bürger* agree on a common stance.

Second: what about religion? Could this be a unifying element? To cut a long story short, it was not. If at all, it did more to strengthen than weaken the existing cleavages. The German *Bürgertum* was divided into three confessional groups that stayed more or less aloof from one another. The great bulk of it was (in contrast to its Austrian, Italian, French neighbours) Protestant. A much smaller faction belonged to the Catholic church. It developed a separate identity as a distinct Catholic *Bürgertum*, whose ties with the general Catholic milieu were often stronger than its affiliation to the *Bürgertum* as a social class. Much more *bourgeois* in shape and identity was the Jewish population, which stood out for its high level of assimilation and secularization. Nevertheless, there remained strong feelings of disdain and suspicion among Christian sections of the *Bürgertum* so that social integration stopped short of total success.

Third, what about culture? Were there common sets of values, discourses and performances that bound together people of different economic standing, political opinion, and confession? If so, how were these patterns produced, constructed and disseminated? As already stressed at the beginning, recent studies on the European middle classes all agree that those classes were defined by their value systems, lifestyles and modes of behaviour. Here, those cohesive features could be found that transformed heterogenous groups into a more or less homogeneous class—a class which was not in the first place rooted in a common market situation but in an overall idea of representing the most important section of society.

The importance of being a member of the middle classes was based on two major values: work and education/training (*Bildung*). Both were held to be central to modern society, which attributed its progressive development to ardent and incessant labouring as well as to profound and ever-growing knowledge. Of course, knowledge did not grow by itself. Rather, it was produced by never-ending study, and by hard work on a person's character and talents. Thus, the general message was that nothing just fell from the sky, everything had to be striven for. Culture came about as the result of constant endeavour and self-cultivation, although it presented itself in an easy, playful and elegant shape. The efforts required to accomplish a certain performance had to be concealed, although they were known to anybody who took part in the game.

Work and self-formation thus stood at the very centre of middle-class culture. They served at least three purposes. First, they secured hegemony in a socio-economic system, which obviously needed middle-class competence to meet international competition. Second, they set the middle classes apart from other classes, such as the nobility, or workers who either lacked work or knowledge/education. The combination of both distinguished the *Bürgertum* from any other group. Third, they forged the middle classes together and gave them a unique and separate identity.

Of course, there were features other than work and knowledge which characterized the rising *Bürgertum*. In one way or another, they all derived from the two basic assets of middle-class or bourgeois consciousness. Let us draw on the issues of social and political activity. Most men of the middle classes were involved in some kind of social and political work, particularly in local government and administration. They performed such work because they felt competent to do so. Both their professional skills and experience enabled them, so they said, to assume responsibility for communal affairs. Moreover, the self-image of being the dynamic, progressive force in history also strengthened their confidence in believing that they could find proper solutions to problems of all kinds.

Let us take another example: family life. The middle classes were convinced that their way of raising a family was the best and the most civilized. This surely had to do with their level of education—the more educated. The people, the better they were able to plan their reproductive life in a 'decent', i.e., rational and planned manner. To control the number of children born, provide them ample emotional and material support (but not too much!), build a home where family members could relax and find comfort—all this implied foresight, discipline, self-control, and a deep sense of responsibility. As such, these traits of character depended on formal education and constant self-education.

Men/Women

It is time to introduce the concept of gender, which seems to be crucial to the notion of bourgeois or middle-class culture. The latter, as it stands, was highly gender-based in that it distinguished men from women at every practical and theoretical level. To be precise, it was such a salient feature of bourgeois culture that it drew strong and unpassable lines of division between the sexes. Middle-class values, life styles and patterns of behaviour were strictly segregated according to gender. No other social class in 19th-century Europe ever took greater care and consequence to separate male and female spheres of action, feeling and thinking.

Beginning with family education and schooling, the separation programme continued throughout every stage of life. While middle-class boys were prepared for a life dedicated to work and public influence, their sisters received an education fitting to their future roles as mothers, home-makers and wives. They went to schools different from those attended by their brothers; they learned different things, and were taught to think differently.

How deeply this code of difference was rooted in people's minds and habits can be traced very neatly in autobiographical sources. Let me quote one of thousands. It is a letter that Werner Siemens, a famous entrepreneur from Berlin, wrote to his daughter Anna in 1875. He criticized 17 year-old Anna—who had completed her education in an expensive Swiss finishing school—for the unwomanly style of her letters. 'Unwomanly' because they lacked signs of family attachment and affection. A man, Siemens wrote, 'can struggle through life on his own and quiet his opponents by his achievements. For a woman, this is different. Only very rarely can she deserve well of humanity on her own merits. Nature ties her down to the power of her personality by which she can impress people. Like a fragrant flower she has to arouse feelings of comfort in everybody who comes close to her. She has to do so, not being coquettish or by intention, but by her inner and open being; by her sense of the ideal, the good and the beautiful; by her compassion for the grief and the joy of others; by mild and indulgent judgement; by a thankful and loving soul. A woman of this kind is truly the crown of creation, and her authority is based on sympathy coupled with respect. For such an ideal, my dear daughter, I would like to see you strive' (quoted in Frevert 1995: 244ff.).

In the bourgeois setting, women were placed at the centre of a culture, which aimed at representation and concealment alike. They had to represent the power of middle-class values by staging the victory of culture over nature. It was their job to stay close to nature by cultivating such 'natural gifts' as beauty, elegance, love, and social commitment. It was important however, that the work of cultivation itself be kept in dark. Women should appear as the pure embodiment of nature, although everybody knew that this appearance was arduously constructed. Women, thus lent a kind of natural touch to bourgeois culture, notwithstanding the fact that their performance was a work of art in itself.

Middle-class men obviously needed this allusion to nature to make up for their emotional inadequacies and shortcomings. Although full of pride for their personal achievements, they often resented the constraints under which those achievements had been gained. So they sought consolation and compensation in women. The German historian Heinrich von Treitschke, for example, in 1857/58 complained that 'a man's world splits up into a thousand one-sided activities'. In contrast, he found women 'always to be purely human, and much more natural than men'. In their presence, he could therefore feel 'as son of Mother Earth'. Here he could forget his worldly status as well as the 'sorrows and doubts' that his education (*Bildung*) laid upon him (Ibid.).

It would be misleading to think that Treitschke found compensation in female company only at home and with his family. Although home and family were, to be sure, the central place for middle-class women, they were not the only one. The ladies played an equally important role in social communication, as mediators of high culture, as Friedrich Schleiermacher puts it, as 'virtuosi of sociability'. Especially in the higher ranks, the functions of the educated salon hostess were crucial to bourgeois culture. Keeping a good and open house, inviting people and creating an atmosphere of gracious solidity was part of the middle-class life-style.

Contrary to older notions of a family-centred bourgeoisie, the latter in fact set a high value of sociability, which not only encompassed close friends and relatives but also the professional milieu and more distant members of one's own class. This female-based sociability constituted a realm in which the different factions of the middle-class met and merged. Those women who, in comparison to men, were partially 'underdetermined', i.e., who were not tied to a special market position and professional spirit, helped to forge the middle classes together by giving them a more homogeneous shape and a consciousness of common beliefs and behaviour.

Modern/Anti-Modern

Modernization here can be translated into a development aimed at a higher degree of personal autonomy, going along with progressive social differentiation and market dependance. At the same time, traditional social networks tear apart, and the formerly strong ties between religious norms and social practice fade away.

In 19th-century Europe, the middle classes were at the centre of this development. They were, strictly speaking, the avant-garde of modernization and were the first to suffer from its unpleasant side-effects. Middle-class culture tended to weaken religion as an authoritative moral force and replace it with secular patterns of orientation. Even if people remained faithful to certain religious beliefs, they moved away from the church and clergy. However, especially in the Catholic milieu, women took a much less critical stance than men. Bonnie Smith, for example, in her study of the bourgeoise of Northern France, described the gender gap in religious practice and its conflicting consequences. In Protestant circles too, women stayed closer to religion (and the clergy). They seemed to be less doubtful, less reflective, maybe also more dependent on religious consolation. In addition, they remained at a greater distance from what historians nowadays call the *Bildungsreligion* (religion of education/formation). Since *Bildung* for women never assumed the heavy and complex meaning it had for men, they were less inclined (and able) to accept it as a substitute for religion.

Nevertheless, the importance of religion and its impact on people's lives were declining throughout the 19th century. Other cultural systems took its place: for example art, music, literature, especially the 'classics'. The middle classes thus crowded theatre and concert halls, art galleries and museums. They founded art associations and bought paintings. They subscribed to novels, poetry and literary journals. They became the first and most ardent admirers of artists, musicians and poets. They constituted the public for avant-garde culture—and soon found themselves harshly criticized (and even despised) by those they paid and honoured. The pejorative picture of the sated, hypocritical bourgeois, the 'philistine' or *Spiessbürger*, was painted not only by the labour and the youth movement, but also by those artists and cultural workers who tried to overcome bourgeois culture while depending on its material support.

There are other areas of bourgeois culture which corresponded closely with modernity and modernization. Let us take the example of family planning, which, as demographers tell us, middle-class (particularly Jewish) couples were the first to adopt. Reducing the number of babies born into a family enhanced the actual standard of living, and improved the chances of survival of the new generation. It was rational and modern in the sense that it supported individualization of parents and children alike. Moreover, it helped to balance girls and boys. Middle-class fathers who had a son and a daughter, tended to provide both children with a solid education. In families with five to seven children, it was generally only the sons who enjoyed the benefits of good schooling and professional training.

Of course this equalizing of opportunities did not follow automatically from smaller family size. Some other factors had to be added: not the least important of these was the rise of a women's movement which stressed the necessity of helping middle-class girls become qualified for the labour market. Its success—the opening of male high schools, universities and academic professions to women from the turn of the century on—pointed both to the modernizing capacities of the bourgeoisie, and its anti-modern barriers.

The middle classes were not in all respect conscious agents of modernization. One crucial pillar of bourgeois culture—the gender gap—simply denied the promise of individualization and personal decision. By depicting men and women as totally different species of humanity, patterns of behaviour were strictly fixed for each sex and could not easily be changed. People had to play certain roles whose scenario was not open to individual debate and modification. Men and women were judged according to their role adjustment. Their worth and honour depended on how willingly and successfully they complied with gender commands and prescriptions. They had no personal choice, and there was no variation. Contrary to the loosening of social constraints, of restrictions set by social origin, the gender system remained intact, and acquired ever more weight throughout the 19th century.

A second example revealing the anti-modern aspects of middle-class culture, is the ever-growing importance of militaristic and belligerent outlooks and behaviour among the male section of the middle classes. This was true especially for Germany, but could also be observed in the French Third Republic. Originally, middle-class culture was conceived of as purely civil, keeping aloof from military styles and habits. A dramatic change then occurred in 19th-century Germany, starting with the introduction of general conscription, and ending with the notorious bourgeois reserve officer of the Wilhelmine era.

This infiltration of military models and values should not be underestimated; it had a great impact both on political culture and on gender relations. In addition, it brought with it a serious backlash in modernization. It strengthened modes of communication which ran contrary to a culture of rational argument and personal achievement. It introduced authoritarian thinking and behaviour and thereby tended to supress a culture of debate and mutual critique. It favoured conflict and violence at the cost of peaceful arrangement and compromise, and overestimated the male-heroic protector at the cost of the allegedly weak and helpless woman.

Conclusion

First, culture was central to the social identity of the middle-classes in the 19th century. It served both as an element of distinction and as a factor of homogenity.

Second, bourgeois or middle-class culture was deeply gender-based. It allowed men and women to play different parts. While middle-class values such as work, achievement and education were embodied by men; women reigned in the realms of aesthetics, family, and sociability.

Third, where the process of modernization was concerned, middle-class culture presented two faces of itself: a modern and an anti-modern one. On the one hand, the middle classes defined themselves as a political, economic, social and cultural avant-garde. On the other hand, they invented and adopted traditions which contradicted, hindered and postponed modernization. In this respect, however, the European scene was by no means united and uniform, but produced sharp differences with far reaching social and political consequences.

Fourth, in the process of modernization, public and private spheres took on different shapes and meanings. While the public sphere was greatly extended, thereby engendering more and more fields of action formerly restricted to a tiny political elite, the private sphere was carved out ever more neatly and defined largely in opposition to the public and the political. Both developments were more or less headed by the middle classes. They took great interest in public and private matters alike, without, however, being able to separate their private and public lives in practice as sharply as in theory.

NOTES

1. For a comparative analysis of the historical semantics of Bürger, bürgeoisie and middle classes, see Koselleck et al. (1991: 14–58).

2. This need for sharp distinctions is stressed for the English case by Davidoff and Hall (1987) and (1991: 225–47).
3. To obtain an idea of the vast research which has been conducted on 19th-century German *Bürgertum* during the last ten years, see the review article by Halten (1993).

REFERENCES

Allgemeine deutsche Real-Encyklopädie für die gebildeten Stände. 1843. Lexikon, 9th ed., vol. 3, pp. 46ff. Leipzig.
Davidoff, Leonore and Catherine Hall. 1991. 'Family Fortunes neu betrachtet: Geschlecht und Klasse im frühen 19. Jahrhundert,' in Logie Barrow et al. (eds), *Nichts als Unterdrückung? Geschlecht und Klasse in der englischen Sozialgeschichte.* Münster.
————. 1987. *Family Fortunes: Men and Women of the English Middle Class, 1780–1850.* London: Hutchinson.
Frevert, Ute. 1995. *Mann und Weib und Weib und Mann: Geschlechter-Differenzen in der Moderne.* München: C.H. Beck.
Haltern, Utz. 1993. 'Die Gesellschaft der Bürger,' *Geschichte und Gesellschaft,* vol. 19, pp. 100–34.
Koselleck, R. 1991. 'Drei bürgerliche Welten? Zur vergleichenden Semantik der bürgerlichen Gesellschaft in Deutschland, England und Frankreich,' in Hans-Jürgen Puhle (ed.), *Bürger in der Gesellschaft der Neuzeit.* Göttingen: Vandenhoeck Ruprecht.
————. 1975. *Preußen zwischen Reform und Revolution, 2nd ed.* Stuttgart: Klett-Cota.

4

Of the Social Categories 'Private' and 'Public': Considerations of Cultural Context*

T.N. Madan

> You can translate a word by a word, but behind the word is an idea, the thing which the word denotes, and this idea you cannot translate, if it does not exist among the people in whose language you are translating.
>
> Bankimchandra Chattopadhyay (1969)

Private *a.* & *n.* 1. (Of person) not holding public office or official position. 2. kept or removed from public knowledge or observation. 3. not open to public. 4. one's own. 5. confidential. 6. (Of place) retired, secluded.

Public *a.* & *n.* 1. *a.* of or concerning people as a whole. 2. done by or for, representing, the people. 3. open to or shared by all the people. 4. open to general observation, done or existing in public. 5. of or engaged in the affairs or service of the people. 6. *n.* the community in general.

The Concise Oxford Dictionary

Words and Ideas

The social categories of the 'private' and the 'public' are by definition culture specific. In Western society they represent not only social institutions (for example the family and the state), or entities (for example the individual and the crowd), but may also denote a relationship of mutual implication as binary opposites. In other words, each category *usually* acquires its full significance in contradistinction to the other, and does not exist by itself or make sense on its own. Needless to emphasize that contradistinction is a kind of relationship, not its absence. A comparative perspective reveals that these or similar social categories may or may not be present in non-Western societies and, if they are, their mutual relationship may be of a different kind than that characteristic of Western society. It follows that the manner in which they are seen to operate in particular arenas, such as politics, or contexts, such as democratic citizenship, varies from case to case.

As a first and simplistic illustration of difference of connotation, we may consider dictionary meanings. The *Chambers English-Hindi Dictionary* (Awasthi and Awasthi 1985) renders 'private' as *ashaskiya* (nongovernmental), *asarvajanika* (non-collective), *niji* (personal), *vyaktigata* (individual), *gopniya* (secret), and so on. In contrast, 'public' connotes *shaskiya* (governmental), *samuhika* (collective), *prakata* (explicit), etc. Some of these terms (such as *niji* or *prakata*) appear to be original words in Hindi but others (notably *ashaskiya* or *asarvajanika*) may well be lexical fabrications in the setting of cultural and linguistic contact. Examination of Hindi literary texts suggests that the English terms have significations—in Trilling's words 'a culture's hum and buzz of implication' (1951: 206)—that literal translation fails to capture. This obviously is the reason why many Hindi littérateurs reproduce phonetically the original English words 'private' and 'public' in their compositions: thereby they represent sensibilities that are a product of interlinguistic communication and cultural hybridization.

Let me illustrate the foregoing point. In an insightful address on the novel in comparative perspective, the distinguished Hindi prose writer Nirmal Varma (2000) observes that it was inside a 19th century preserved house in Bergen (Norway) that he had the inspiration (*ilham*, 'revelation') to conclude that it must have been within the walls of such homes that the European novel had its birth. Contrasting the openness and wholeness of the epic poem to the enclosed and fragmentary character of the novel, he dwells upon 'privacy'—the English word is used in Nagri script—and its correlate, the individual, in their interrelatedness—*'vyakti ki praivasy'*, the individual's privacy (Ibid.: 60)—as the critical conditions for the genesis of the novel. He conceptually links the epic to relatively open spaces and collectivities, such as audience halls, battlefields and domestic compounds, and employs *sarvajanik* as the generic Hindi term for them, but apparently does not feel the need to use the English word 'public'.

More to the point is the fact that Varma denies the contradistinction of the private and individual, on the one hand, and the open and collective, on the other, in the context of the novel in the Third World. In it, the private and the collective are not 'separate', but 'mirror images' of each other. The novel here is said to acquire its form in the space between the mythological epic and the European novel. He writes that it is not itself an epic or a replica of the original novel, but is inspired by *collective* mythic rituals and constructed from *inter-individual* relationships (Ibid.: 61). Varma's elaboration of the foregoing argument does not concern me here. The point I wanted to make about the significance of cultural difference in the use of words like 'private' and 'public' is, I trust, clear enough.

Discontinuities and Continuities

Let me turn to ethnography for further elaboration. In the course of fieldwork in a cluster of villages in south-eastern Kashmir in the 1950s and 1960s (see Madan 1989), I heard both the terms 'private' and 'public' in everyday Kashmiri speech, but with denotations quite different from those in a standard English dictionary. Of the two terms, 'private' (pronounced *'pray-vut, 'vut'* as in 'but') was not generally used, but when employed it referred to matters of household concern rather than those of individual interest. Privacy lay in the rooms that a household occupied inside a house that often was lived in by another household or other (never more than three, see Ibid.) households. Houses of agnatically related kin were usually located around a commonly owned compound, which was a kind of public (as opposed to private) space, but the term 'public' was not used to refer to it. Nor was it used to refer to more widely shared and utilized intra-religious (Hindu or Muslim) or inter-religious (Hindu-Muslim) spaces such as Hindu cremation grounds, Muslim graveyards, or pasture lands (available to everybody). In fact, religious and village gatherings, marked by highly valued and enduring common interests and emotional bonds, were not even remotely regarded as 'public', nor deemed to have dimensions that could be legitimately called public by the villagers. Collective (*ralith-milith,* 'mixed together') and focused activities of various kinds inside the village were, however, contrasted with the 'goings on' in the nearby town of Anantnag and the remoter city of Srinagar, which the villagers visited from time to time to meet relatives, make purchases, attend school, or seek medical treatment.

Since the 1930s a new and important element had entered into the lives of Kashmiris, namely agitational politics. They aimed at securing economic and political rights from the autocratic government of the Maharaja and the feudal families associated with or created by the ruling family from 1846 onwards, when it came into the possession of the territories jointly designated as the State of Jammu and Kashmir (see Bamzai 1962). The people of the State were formally identified as the 'subjects' of the Maharaja. They had no citizenship rights as such and the only thing they could pray and hope for were kingly favours. These were arbitrary and discriminatory. It was against this state of affairs that the community-based political organizations Muslim Conference and Sanatan Dharma Yuvak Sabha, and the secular National Conference, came into existence in the Kashmir Valley. Given the high incidence of illiteracy, particularly among the Muslims, the most viable modes of political education and mobilization of the masses were public meetings (*jalsa*) in which leaders gave speeches (*takrir*), and processions (*julus*). By the time of the initial period of my fieldwork (1957–58), radical political changes had occurred—the Maharaja's government had been replaced by a (so-called) people's government, formed by the National Conference, which had introduced sweeping land reforms (see Madan 1966). Political mobilization had been put into high gear— political meetings and the processions were still the principal vehicles of securing people's support, although radio broadcasting too had become a major force. It was to such gatherings that the villagers applied the term 'public' (pronounced as in standard English speech). In other words, the 'public' was constituted by political discourse.

Participation in political meetings and processions were voluntary and intentional for some, externally induced for others, and fortuitous for still others. For the villagers it was mostly fortuitous—one listened to the speakers, or watched the processionists, if one happened to be in the town. The public gatherings were considered unstable and occasional: they formed, dissolved, and reformed with never exactly the same people participating on successive occasions. They had important consequences gradually arousing interest in the people's citizenship rights, but many villagers did not take them seriously, and considered them mere spectacles (*tamasha*). Occasionally they were even characterized

as nuisances because of traffic jams, pressure on transport (people trav-
elled mostly by tongas but motor buses also connected some villages to the
towns), disturbance of normal market activities, and other inconveniences.

In sum, the notions of the 'private' and 'public' had entered the
Kashmiri villagers' consciousness and speech, but they were contextu-
ally unrelated and carried different loads of signification. They and the
phenomena they referred to existed independent of each other. They
could not be meaningfully said to be opposites of each other.

Ethnographic and historical evidence from non-Western societies
indicates that even when the 'private' and the 'public' are present as
comparable social categories, their relationship and significance may
not be similarly comparable to what these primarily are in the West.
Thus, in traditional Japanese society, the public is continuous with,
rather than in contradistinction to the private. This holds good in a
variety of contexts. A good illustration is the manner in which the
concept or ideology of the household, *ie*, which is a private, corporate,
residential group, 'penetrates every nook and corner of the society'
(Nakane 1972: 4). A variety of traditional and modern groups are modelled on and legitimized by the ethic of the *ie*. This is as true of the
traditional word for one's work place (*uchi-no*) as of the medieval
ichizoku-roto (a family group and its retainers), or the modern usage of
kokutetsu-ikka (literally 'one railway family') to designate the Japanese
National Railways.

What is noteworthy in this context is that, although the *ie* as an
institution is said to be weakening, the ethic associated with it survives
in extra-familial, public, settings, such as factories or offices. Like the *ie*
these are vertically structured on the lines of the parent (*oya*)–child (*ko*)
relationship. One's employer, superior, or boss is said to enjoy the status
of a parent: he is the caring *oyabun*. Reciprocally, filial obedience is
expected from the *kobun* (one in a position comparable to that of the child).

The continuity of the domestic and extra-domestic domains may
well be a source of both strength and weakness in Japanese society.
While the harmony that is obtained in the work place may have been a
major factor in the rapid post-World War II recovery of a shattered
economy, it has also been asserted that there is 'a serious dearth of the
type of public spirit that transcends both individual and group' (Doi
1977: 42) and is characteristic of Western society. Indeed, what I have
described as the continuity of the private and the public has been characterized as 'confusion' or 'conflation' of the two social categories, resulting in such aberrations as the private use of public property (Ibid.: 43).

The concern for the evolution of an appropriately conceptualized public spirit characteristic of democratic citizenship in the West is paradoxically expressed through the use of the term *oyake*, which stands for the notion of the 'public' and its extensions such as the 'public sector'. The paradox arises from the fact that, traditionally, *oyake* referred to the Japanese imperial family and as such, had a very restricted or private connotation. A positive consequence of this conflation has been the characteristic behaviour of disgruntled factory workers who will resort to over-production to cause losses of profit to the owners but never damage the plant. The flexibility of the social categories under discussion—the fuzziness of their boundaries—may not be in consonance with explicit distinctions made in other contexts, such as that between the notions of the 'inner' and the 'outer', which is regarded as relevant mainly to the individual. But in this context also, discrepancies and stresses are glossed over. In short, the Japanese do not seemingly subscribe to the logic of binary oppositions in the manner of the Western or even Indian mentalities (Nakane 1978).

Contradistinctions, Overlaps, Mergers

In the context of the ethnography of rural Kashmir, I have tried to show that the connotations of the borrowed words 'private' and 'public' were discontinuous—not only were the corresponding domains different, there was no relation whatsoever between them, not even that of contradistinction. Instances of the presence of such a relationship are of course available in India too, emphasizing the bounded character of the two categories and defining the limits of their transgression. The case that I will now present is marked by the confrontation of traditional Hindu custom and modern Western law, and illustrates the reaching out of the domestic (private) sphere into the jural (extra-domestic) for succour. The situation could also be looked upon as an intrusion of the public domain (law courts, newspapers) into the privacy of the home.

Rukhmabai, an eleven year old school girl was married in 1873 by her parents (mother and stepfather) to a young man about eight years older than her. She was not, however, sent to live with him pending the attainment of her puberty and also the acquisition by her husband of sufficient education to enable him to earn a living and assume the responsibilities of a householder. Early marriage and the postponement of its consummation were common occurrences in contemporary

Hindu society. The husband turned out to be not only sickly, but also an indolent person of bad habits. He was averse to being educated and remained a dependent member of his maternal uncle's household. He eventually hoped to live on his wife's patrimonial inheritance. Although Rukhmabai was withdrawn from school, her informal education continued at her parental home.

Eleven years after her marriage, Rukhmabai was still with her parents, and her husband decided to initiate legal proceedings for the 'restitution of conjugal rights' under Anglo-Hindu law. Soon thereafter she herself resorted to another public forum, namely the press, by writing letters under a pseudonym to a newspaper (*The Times of India*) about the low social status of Hindu women and the inequities of child marriage and enforced widowhood. Her views were endorsed by the newspaper's editorial and by persons of socially progressive views, but criticized by the defenders of orthodoxy. The debate in the press (involving English language and vernacular newspapers in such far flung cities as Bombay, Lahore, Allahabad, and Calcutta) bearing upon a wide range of issues concerning Hindu women's duties and rights (or lack thereof) raged throughout 1885 and the following years.

Meanwhile, Rukhmabai's husband's plea for judicial intervention for the restitution of his conjugal rights was heard by a single judge of the Bombay High Court. He decided against the husband even without hearing Rukhmabai's defence, saying that she could not be forced to cohabit with her husband against her wishes. He recognized that accumulated case law would favour the husband, but since conjugal relations had not been instituted in this case, the notion of restitution was inapplicable. His judgement was more in consonance with Western notions of privacy, and the rights and dignity of the individual rather than Hindu notions of wifely duties and family solidarity.

The case was heard again (in 1886) by a two-member appellate bench of the same court on the husband's prayer. The judges reversed the earlier judgment, holding the view that a wife's proper place was in her husband's home. The distinction between the notions of institution and restitution of conjugal rights was, they held, not good in law. The case came up for trial once again, this time before a single judge who decreed (in 1887) that Rukhmabai should go to live with her husband. There was another appeal for review, this time by Rukhmabai herself. The matter, however, came to an anti-climactic end (in 1888) through a compromise decree issued by the court, the elements of which were worked out by the two parties. While Rukhmabai agreed to pay her husband a monetary compensation for the expenses incurred by him in seeking legal remedy, he in return agreed not to demand cohabitation from her.

The Rukhmabai case may be viewed in terms of the contrasting as well as overlapping orders of the private and the public and an evolving notion of citizenship rights. Sudhir Chandra, on whose monograph I have depended for the basic facts, notes that the antagonists in the case partook of both the private world of domesticity, centred round marriage and the family, and the public world comprising the relations between the rulers and the ruled. 'Ironically, those most vocal in opposing the extension of colonial authority into their socio-religious affairs were the keenest ... to utilize the colonial legal system and its alien practices' (1998: 2).

The private domain was the locus of tradition, and Rukhmabai wanted it overturned—because it was discriminatory against women—by public debate and eventually by legislative intervention. In other words, she invited the intrusion of public institutions into the privacy of a Hindu home. Her husband also appealed to a major public institution, the law court, to uphold that same world of tradition, as perceived at that time by some sections of public opinion. As for the judges, the one who favoured Rukhmabai did so in terms of Western notions of individual choice and dignity, confronting one conception of the private, namely the Hindu home, by another, namely the Western individual, through the medium of the public court of law established by the state. The judges who favoured Rukhmabai's husband also confirmed the legitimacy of the law court sitting in judgment over disputed positions within the domestic domain, but in the name of Hindu tradition. In deciding that the wife was obliged to live with her husband, they refrained from defining cohabitation in terms of both coresidence and engagement in a sexual relationship, leaving the latter component to the privacy of the bedroom, a kind of an inner sanctum within the private world.

The issues comprising the Rukhmabai case did not end in the Bombay High Court. They were ultimately selectively debated in the Imperial Legislative Council, which decided to freeze the intervention of the organs of the state in the private domain of conjugal relations at the limits already attained by it. Needless to emphasize that within a colonial setting the unavailability of citizenship rights to the ruled subjects, except within a very limited compass, flowed from the character of the state: it was a restrictive rather than expansive relationship.

The foregoing discussion underscores the point that the private and the public are best understood not in substantive terms (as insulated entities) but interactionally (as open, relatively complex bundles of relations).

The interpenetration or merging of the private and the public, it should be pointed out, is not confined to non-Western cultural settings, although it is these on which the foregoing observations have been based. Even in Western society itself, while the opposition of the categories, and the underlying dualistic logic of classification, are firmly established, there are occasions and situations when social reality becomes fully comprehensible only through their complementarity. Albert Hirschman (1998) has pointed out that one of the basic distinctions in economic analysis is between private and public goods. The former are most simply and accurately represented by the loaf of bread and the latter by public (that is, state sponsored) health and education. The consumption of private goods, which are limited in normal circumstances, is marked by the clash of individual interests. The number of loaves of bread available to each individual depends upon the total number of loaves and of consumers: if someone gets a loaf more than the others, then someone else must get a loaf less. Such a limitation obviously does not affect the consumption of public goods. A further dimension of this distinction is that while the provision of private goods may be left to the market, the production of public goods must be concurrently provided by the state in discharge of its obligations to the citizens. In such dichotomization, Hirschman observes, 'Little attention was paid to goods that would somehow be intermediate between the private and the public category [sic] or would belong to both' (Ibid.: 17).

To illustrate the melding of the two categories, Hirschman cites an insightful essay by the sociologist Georg Simmel on the sociology of the meal (*Mahlzeit*). Anticipating the later distinction by economists noted above, Simmel argued that eating (and drinking) are 'most self-centred', since 'what is eaten by a single person can under no circumstances be eaten by anyone else'. People however normally eat together: 'thus arises the sociological construct of the meal—it turns the exclusive self-seeking of eating into the frequent experience of being together and into the habit of joining in a common purpose' (quoted in Hirschman ibid.: 18).

In an interesting extension of the argument, Hirschman points out that in classical Greece (5th century), the ancient institution of the banquet (which was by definition collective and public) emerged redefined as an obligatory act on the part of the citizens who represented the city of Athens after the democratic reforms of Kleisthenes: it became 'institutionalized as a symbol of the permanence of political power in a democracy'. In the post-classical (Hellenistic) period, banquets fostered and reinforced 'social and citizen relationships': they occupied 'a key position connecting ... the religious, the public and the private spheres': they became 'the preeminent expression of what we like to call today 'civil society'. Hirschman feels persuaded to suggest the plausibility of 'a direct link ... between the banquet and the emergence of Athenian democracy' (Ibid.: 22–23). Examples of commensality linked to socially disruptive activities also are however noted by him (see Ibid.: 25–28). Hirschman concludes: 'From the purely biological point of view, there is no doubt that eating has a straightforward relationship to individual welfare. But once they are done in *common*, eating and drinking normally go hand in hand with a remarkably diverse set of public or collective activities' for good or for bad (Ibid.: 28–29).

To reiterate the importance of the oppositional conceptualization of the categories of the private and the public in Western culture, and the possible relevance of the same to other (non-Western) cultural settings, I would like to draw attention to the notion of privatization of religion. As is well known, the idea had two sources, one religious (the Reformation) and the other secular (the Enlightenment). Among the many strands that comprised the religious reform movements of the 16th century, which are collectively referred to as the Protestant Reformation, mention may here be made of lay piety and practice, scholarly debate about the true character and import of the teachings of Jesus Christ, and an abiding concern with the redemption of the individual sinner and an erring humanity. In all these expressions the Reformation set itself against any mediatory role for the Church and its priesthood between the believer, whose sole justification was said to lie in faith, and God.

The Christian faith, it was asserted, required of the believer acknowledgement of the sovereignty of God and the supremacy of scripture. No other guidance was necessary. Martin Luther and other reformers were accused by their critics of providing unrestricted scope for individual or private interpretations of the scripture (see Bainton 1956). For the present purpose, an examination of the merits of the new formulations and of their critiques is not relevant. The main point is to draw attention to the arrival of the this-worldly individual in the midst of Christian society and the privatization of the religious endeavour (see Dumont 1986). This does not of course mean that the Reformation did not have social and cultural consequences, or that it was unrelated to public activity, such as the establishment of schools, for the promotion of particular versions of it. Moreover, Luther maintained that the Christian as citizen must submit to secular authority.

By repudiating the claims of the Church to speak for all of a Christian's concerns, the Reformation opened the way for secularization and the legitimization of the rights of both the political community and the individual citizen. This process of differentiation—of the carving out of secular areas of activity from a holistic design of living—was reinforced by the rise of the Age of Reason and the Enlightenment (17th and 18th centuries). By its very nature, the Enlightenment in its own various versions included a critique of religion as a worldview centred in the idea of God and as an institutional structure. It called upon human beings to 'dare to know' (Kant's admonition *sapere aude!*) whatever there is to be known through observation and the exercise of reason. Religion was admissible but only 'within the limits of reason' (see Cassirer 1968: 163). Human intelligence was deemed adequate for achieving the goal of the perfection of social institutions. The notion of the reasons of the state (originally formulated by Machiavelli), rather than private religious values, were to be the means of and the justification for an ordered political domain.

In short, religion as faith was relegated to the innermost recesses of private life. In Max Weber's well-known words, a result of secularization ('rationalization and intellectualization') has been not only the ending of magic, miracles and mysteries ('disenchantment'), but also the 'retreat' of 'the ultimate and most sublime values' from 'public life either into the transcendental realm of the mystic life or into the brotherliness of direct and personal human relations' (1948: 155). This is as clear a statement of the antinomy of the private and the public as any other that is possible.

The opposition of the two categories has further implications in Weber's sociology that are of interest here. To mention but one of these, there is his typological distinction between patrimonialism (and feudalism), on the one hand, and the institutions of the modern state, on the other. This could also be represented as the contrast between the private and the public. Patrimonial rule (domination) rests on the *personal* loyalty that the ruler receives from his household, entourage, administrative corps and military force. The modern state is centrally governed, and its economy is regulated by an *impersonally recruited* and *rationally oriented* bureaucracy. It is in the social space that can only be called public that the modern ideas of rational law, legal domination, legislative regulation, legitimate force, citizenship rights, etc. can possibly arise (see Weber 1947, 1948). The antinomy of the categories remains a central strand of Weber's thinking. And yet, on occasion, he drops it, in nostalgia as it were, as when he said:

> Surely, politics is made with the head, but it is certainly not made with the head alone .... Insofar as this is true, an ethic of ultimate ends and an ethic of responsibility are not absolute contrasts but rather supplements, which only in unison constitute a genuine man—a man who can have the 'calling for politics' (1948: 127).

Concluding Remarks

I have been concerned here mainly with conceptual clarification and have suggested that the social categories of the private and the public may be empirically found to be interrelated in different ways in a variety of socio-cultural settings. Analytically too, attentiveness to their interaction may be as productive of understandings of aspects of social reality as a focus on their contradistinction. Thus, a novelist may well consider privacy, or withdrawal from a surfeit of social interaction, an essential condition of his creativity—some have actually gone into hiding—but ultimately he writes for the reading public. The book is published, that is made public, often ceremonially, sold in bookstores, and reviewed in journals. In short, the private merges in the public.

Similarly, a villager who has only known subjecthood under an autocratic-feudal regime, may well consider public political gatherings unfamiliar, impermanent, amorphous and even inconvenient phenomena. But eventually, he finds his individuality redefined, even without his co-operation by such events; he is made aware of his citizenship rights under democratic governance. Such rights not only promote and protect his civil rights, and entail political (public) participation in various forms as a duty, they may also embrace aspects of family (private) life. The relationship of the private and public domains, as evident from the Rukhmabai case, is an evolving (expanding, contracting) one.

Private life in any form should not be, however, regarded as something passive, a field for arbitrary public intervention or imposition from the outside. As the brief reference to some Japanese conceptualizations of the relationship of the two categories shows, public life may in fact be sustained by values that have their origin in private life and are therefore legitimized by it. These values are not static but might occasionally change in significant ways without a total rupture of roots as a result of broad politico-economic and social changes.

There are situations in which the separation of the private and the public may be deemed politically expedient and socially beneficial. A good and familiar example is the identification of certain areas of economic activity (the social sector) that may not be left to the caprices of the market (private sector), but must be controlled directly or indirectly by the state (public sector), so that the interests of the under-privileged sections of the population, and thereby of the society at large, may be served. Similarly, privatization of religion (secularization) may be defended on the ground that public or state religions could threaten significant individual rights such as the freedom of conscience (to choose and profess a religion of one's choice or to opt for agnosticism). But the public sector has been known to be inefficient and corrupt with a tendency to invade areas where private enterprise serves the community better. On the contrary, the last quarter of the 20th century has provided ample evidence from Latin America, East Europe and elsewhere of the positive role of public religion (the Catholic Church) in the promotion of citizenship rights against dictatorial regimes (see Casanova 1994).

In short, experience and deeper reflection reveal that policies of mutual exclusion of domains defined as private and public may produce public (political, economic, social) gains, but they could also have public costs. The interests of the community in general rather than rigid ideological positions would seem to be the obvious guide to collective action, but this is more easily said than done. Moreover, the melding of the private and the public may not always follow from consciously pursued policies, it may be an unintended consequence of indirectly related decisions or fortuitous developments.

Finally, apart from contradistinction or overlapping and merging, the private represented by the family, and the public, by the state, frame a middle ground, a social space for citizen initiatives and action that is designated as civil society. Needless to emphasize, this too is a public sphere and like the political community, may be viewed as a structure of mediation between the state and the society at large. Here the citizens may assert their rights as individuals or corporations against one another or against the state. Civil society is in the foregoing perspective an arena *par excellence* for the dialectic of the private and the public.

NOTE

* Presented here in somewhat expanded form are a few of the observations that I made in the course of the discussions at the seminar. Many points call for elaboration. I regret that other commitments have not allowed me to undertake such an exercise within the available time.

  I am grateful to Gurpreet Mahajan and Helmut Reifeld for their encouragement without which I would not have put pen to paper. I also thank Margrit Pernau for her interest. Sudhir Chandra has put me in his debt by reading the first draft. None of them is of course responsible for my formulations or the manner of their presentation.

REFERENCES

Awasthi, Suresh and Induja Awasthi. 1985. *Chambers English-Hindi Dictionary*. New Delhi: Allied Publishers.

Bainton, Roland H. 1956. *The Reformation of the Sixteenth Century*. Boston: Beacon Press.

Bamzai, P.N.K. 1962. *A History of Kashmir*. Delhi: Metropolitan.

Casanova, Jose. 1994. *Public Religions in the Modern World*. Chicago: The University of Chicago Press.

Chandra, Sudhir. 1998. *Enslaved Daughters: Colonialism, Law and Women's Rights*. New Delhi: Oxford University Press.

Cassirer, Ernst. 1968. *The Philosophy of the Enlightenment*. Princeton, N.J.: The University of Princeton Press.

Chattopadhyay, Bankimchandra. 1969. *Bankim Racanabali (English Works)*. Edited by Jogesh Chandra Bagal. Calcutta: Sahitya Samsad.

Doi, Takeo. 1977. *The Anatomy of Dependence*. Tokyo: Kodansha.

Dumont, Louis. 1986. *Essays on Individualism*. Chicago: The University of Chicago Press.

Hirschman, Albert. 1998. *Crossing Boundaries: Selected Writings*. New York: Zed Books.

Madan, T.N. 1966. 'Politico-economic change and organizational adjustment in a Kashmiri village,' *The Journal of Karnatak University (Social Sciences)* vol. 2, pp. 20–34.

————. 1989. *Family and Kinship. A Study of the Pandits of Rural Kashmir*. Second Enlarged Edition. Delhi: Oxford University Press.

Nakane, Chie. 1972. *Japanese Society*. Berkeley: The University of California Press.

————. 1978. Personal communication.

Trilling, Lionel. 1951. *The Liberal Imagination*. London: Secker and Warburg.

Varma, Nirmal. 2000. 'Upanyas ki parti parikatha (in Hindi),' *Bahuvachan*, vol. 2, no. 2, pp. 60–67. New Delhi: Mahatma Gandhi International University.

Weber, Max. 1947. *The Theory of Economic and Social Organization.* New York: Oxford University Press.

_____. 1948. *From Max Weber: Essays in Sociology.* Edited by H.H. Gerth and C.W. Mills. London: Routledge and Kegan Paul.

5

From a 'Private' Public to a 'Public' Private Sphere: Old Delhi and the North Indian Muslims in Comparative Perspective*

Margrit Pernau

Both in India and Germany, the division between the public and the private has been discussed in connection mainly with the emergence of public opinion as a precondition for the development of 'democratic citizenship'. Owing to the central influence of Jürgen Habermas (1965), the assumption seems to have been taken for granted that this public opinion is necessarily created within the public sphere by a bourgeoisie claiming full-fledged citizenship; that it is dealing with public issues and is constituted in opposition to the ruling powers—be they the state or the church.

If we were to take these definitions, culled as they are from the European historical development, as the starting point for a comparative look at the Indian tradition, the results would probably be disappointing, yielding not more than the (foreseeable) insight that Indian development was different. Rather than end the discussion with an apodictic statement that there was no public opinion in India, the approach chosen here will be an attempt to transcend the European categories: not to start from exclusive definitions but to look for different manifestations of 'the public', de-linking the issues of public opinion and citizenship and including also those areas of the public which have no obvious connection to the process of democratization. This type of comparison may not yet provide a new and all-encompassing theory—as a historian I gladly leave this task to the sociologists and political scientists— but it may enlarge our perception of the spectrum of possible developments, of alternatives to the European way, seen as the norm for far too long.[1] Ina-Maria Greverus, director of the Institute for Cultural Anthropology and European Ethnology in Frankfurt, advocated the adoption of the surrealist technique of the collage by the social sciences: the juxtaposition of apparently unrelated realities yields the 'spark of poetry' (Max Ernst), which illuminates both of them, and permits us to re-view, to see them in a new light.[2]

In the European context, 'public' is taken to be at the same time the contrary of secret: in the sense, for instance, of a public debate or a public trial; the contrary of private, of an area to which access is restricted: in the sense, for instance, of a public place or street; the contrary of particular: in the sense of the public good; the contrary of personal: in the sense of a public opinion. However, there is no necessity, why these strands of meaning should go together at all times and places.

This article, in its first part, looks at Delhi in the first half of the 19th century, and tries to locate the emergence of public opinion in the period of transition between the late Mughal Empire and the early colonial rule and between a communication system characterized by the central place of the oral transmission and manuscript culture, and a system based on mass print culture. Under these circumstances, the argument runs, public opinion took shape in semi-private gatherings. Central to it were not political, but religious and poetic discussions; while it might be divided on a variety of issues, these dividing lines did not follow the boundaries of the religious communities.

The second part will focus on Muslim public opinion in north India in the last quarter of the 19th century—public opinion having at this stage outgrown its local roots to the extent that a limitation to a single town no longer makes sense. While it now made use of all the paraphernalia of the modern public sphere—associations, newspapers, printed books—its concern shifted to the private and personal: the regeneration of the community through the exemplary life of the individual Muslim and above all of his wife and daughter.

Public Opinion in the Private Sphere

The State

Public opinion is interrelated with the structure of the state: on the one hand, it is the state, the embodiment of public power, which sets the framework within which public opinion can be formed and can articulate itself; on the other hand each state, be it democratic or not, is dependent on the belief of at least a section of the public, defined as central, in its legitimacy. In a first step, therefore, it would be necessary to investigate the character of the later Mughal state: its location in the public or the private, its concepts of sovereignty and the monopoly of force, and its transformation through the colonial power. It goes without saying that here the aim cannot be an in-depth study, but rather the highlighting of some comparative aspects. Even at the risk of being qualified as elitist, the present attempt will be limited to the relations between the court, the nobility and the nascent middle classes and will leave out what Habermas calls the 'plebeian public', the representation of the state in public for the people and the possibilities of communication between the state and the people, for instance, through the medium of festivals and processions.[3]

If we look at the Indo-Persian tradition, the terms which could—as a first approximation—correspond to the division between the public and the private would be '*am* and *khas*, as we find it, for instance, in the translation of the *divan-e 'am* and the *divan-e khas* as the public and private audience hall. However, in their original meaning, '*am* and *khas* encompass not so much the notion of public and private, but of the common, the lowly, the vulgar even and the elite, the nobility and the ruler. Hence, the *Encyclopaedia of Islam* can translate *khas* both as 'personal, private', as well as 'pertaining to the state or ruler' (Orhonlu 1960). Far from being exposed to the public, a person gained in *khas*-ness, in nobility but also in power, the more he could distance himself from the common crowd and locate himself in the interior, which was also perceived as the centre.[4] The focal point of the state, if one could locate it geographically, thus would not be in the public audience hall, but rather in the private. This, however, does no more than provide us with a starting point for further questions. We need further research in order to know who were the people, who qualified as *khas* and hence had access to this inner circle of statehood; what was the interrelationship between the rights conferred by birth and the status acquired through royal patronage, and how these could be transformed into each other: birth giving a claim to patronage, and patronage generating a new genealogy; who was allowed to voice his opinion—in advice or in protest— and on what occasions; who could cross the boundaries between the *khas* and the *'am*, permitting communication between the two spheres and linking them together. To what extent and in which directions did changes in this respect occur with the loss of effective power of the court in the 18th century and then again with the advent of the British?

On the other hand, this 'privateness' of the state would correspond to what Max Weber saw as the central element of the patrimonial state, the attempt to rule the extrapatrimonial territory as if it were an extension of the royal household.[5] This patrimonial state was by no means limited to India, but on the contrary, in its estate-feudal (*ständefeudalistisch*) variety, constituted the distinctive structure of the European middle ages and early modern period. The distinction between *'am* and *khas* finds its correspondence in the German *gemein* (common) and *sonderlich* (special, separated) (Hölscher 1972: 413–67), with the same implication of dominion being located in the separated sphere (Habermas 1965: 16). Two differences, however, might be pointed out: the normative power that Roman history held throughout the middle ages, enhanced once again since the Renaissance, provided a framework of reference conflicting with the estate-feudal system of government. *Publicus*, in its Roman use—which remained present through the familiarity with the classics—was standing for everything that happened outside, in the street, as opposed to the house. At the same time, the notion encompassed whatever pertained to the people in their entirety. The *res publica* was public in both these meanings: it took place in public, and it was considered the concern of the people, even if most of them were debarred from shaping its destiny in any concrete form. If Roman history provided an alternative notion and valuation of the public, the institutions which had evolved in the north Italian cities and the German *freie Reichsstädte* (free cities) since the 12th century supplied contemporary models of civil communities administering their own affairs free from any form of feudal domination and subject only to the Emperor. Central to this administration were the city councils, which in turn served as the blueprint for the political ideas of philosophers like Marsilius of Padua (Quillet 1970).

The religious wars of the 16th and 17th centuries brought about a fundamental shift of meaning, both in the notion of the State and of the public. With Thomas Hobbes, the division between public and private now came to indicate the dividing line between the sovereign state and the subjects, between the lawgiver and those subjected to the law (Hölscher 1972: 423). The absolutist state aimed at the destruction of the intermediary powers. In the effort to limit the power and influence of the church and religious authorities, it had taken over fields like public morality and, at a slightly later stage, public education. The goal, though not always as yet the result, was the centralizing of the state power, but also the enhancement of its effectivity and its power of penetration, deep into the everyday professional and private life of its subject. The boundary between the public and the private, which could no longer be transcended from the private side, still proved very permeable for the public power (Habermas 1965: 21, Hölscher 1972: 424–26). Both the evolution of a public opinion, aiming at the control of the state, and the demand for fundamental rights, seen primarily as safeguards against the public power, can be understood as an answer to this drive at increasing the power of the state.

Neither this drive towards the establishment of the state as the sole incumbent of legitimate power and towards an equal submission of all subjects to the law, nor the attempt of an in-depth penetration of stately power, found a correspondence in the later Mughal and early colonial history of north India. The dominion of the Mughal Emperor was restricted to the palace, he still held symbolic authority, but had little power to enforce his decrees even in Shahjahanabad. On the other hand, the British still considered his symbolic authority an asset at an all-India level, and therefore held back with the establishment of their own public institutions, and intervened only when their supremacy was directly challenged, or in case of areas central for the symbolic foundation of their government. At the same time, it was this very reluctance of the colonial power to intervene that led to a situation, where areas were perceived as 'private' by the British—in the sense that freedom from state control rendered an area private—which were still seen as holding immense public and political potential by the inhabitants of Delhi. It is to these fields that we now turn.

Religious Debates

In Germany, the creation of a public sphere in the 18th century was closely linked not only to the philosophy of enlightenment, but also to the fact that it was philosophy—and, to a lesser extent political theory,

Staatswissenschaft—which became the leading discipline for public discourse. Secularization in this context meant not primarily the substitution of reason for faith, but the reduction of religion from the central integrative element of society to a social subsystem among others, the distinction of the individual's role as a believer from his roles as citizen or economic actor. This both permitted the 'privatization' of religion—only a religion divested from its social function could be left to the individual's choice—as well as enhanced it.[6]

At least for the rising middle classes, who constituted the decisive social substratum for this development, the result was less a de-christianization than a de-institutionalization of faith: individual choice rather than submission to authority, the private or familial practice rather than community oriented behaviour became the hallmark of bourgeois identity, certainly for Protestants, but to a large extent also for Catholics.[7]

How far did a comparable privatization of religion occur in Delhi in the first half of the 19th century? Was the division between the political and religious the result of British policy alone, or did it stem from the colonial state's attempts to preserve its neutrality in the religious sphere? Did 'mutual encounters' between the British and Indian notions of religion and private sphere take place (Malik 2000)?

In a thought-provoking essay, Faisal Fatehali Devji equates the mystic discourse of Sufism with a religion perceived as private and in opposition to the legal and state-centred discourse of the *ulama*: 'In denying the controlled character of the public, Sufism saw in the relatively unregulated private a vision of freedom.'[8] Apart from the fact that in Delhi the Chishtis were the only Sufis, who built their shrines at the periphery (Devji 1994: 28), in Nizamuddin and in Mehrauli, whereas the Naqshbandis, both the school of Shah Waliullah and his successors and the shrine of Mirza Jan-e Janan were located centrally, in the Jama Masjid area, and although it might always be difficult to draw a clear line between the Sufis and the *ulama*, it might be necessary to further differentiate within the Sufi traditions. At least for those groups who, like the Naqshbandis, chose not simply to ignore the state, but to actively criticize and thus influence it, it can be argued that in spite of their inner distance to the 'world', they certainly took part in the political discourse of their time. Their shrines were 'private' inasmuch as their heads did not hold office in the state administration, and they were not dependent on the state for their financial needs—nevertheless the same shrines were centres for the formation of a 'public' opinion, a position the rulers, even the British, recognized and strove to use for their own ends.[9]

For the 19th century, two different developments regarding the shifting boundaries between the public and the private in the domain of religion have to be distinguished. The first strand of re-shifting between the public and the private refers to what was discussed earlier under the notion of secularization as the differentiation of the social system and the reduction of religion to a subsystem. Our information on the religious specialists in the first half of the 19th century is at best sketchy. Therefore, the following remarks pretend to no higher status than that of an informed guess; they might however indicate some interesting paths for future research.

As is well known, Islam does not possess a centrally organized church. Religious specialists qualify either through their charismatic holiness, or through their knowledge; however, it is only in ghazals that the division between the Sufi and the sheikh can be pointed out with precision: the poetic images point to two different approaches to the divine, not to two distinct social groups. Nearly every member of the *ulama* was also initiated into one or several of the mystic orders (Malik 1997: 135); Sufis could be soldiers as well as administrators (Ibid.: 29).

Further, traditionally the *ulama* were no separate group within the *ashraf*, the well-born, which comprised the nobility as well as the upper rungs of the middle-classes. Whereas the term *ulama* holds a religious connotation, its singular, *alim*, would better be translated as scholar: an *alim* is a person who has acquired *ilm*, knowledge, and this knowledge encompassed not only theology and philosophy, but also grammar, syntax and rhetoric, law, mathematics, astronomy and medicine (Ibid.: 522–23). This knowledge was in no way monopolized by the religious leaders, but rather it was considered an indispensable part of the education of a well-born Muslim to acquire at least a basic knowledge in these sciences. Those members of the *ulama* who had to rely on their knowledge for their daily bread could become teachers, imams or muftis, or take up some assignment in the administration. The foundation of the great medieval university of Lucknow, the Firangi Mahal and again of the first university of Hyderabad in the middle of the 19th century, the Dar ul Ulum, did not aim at training purely religious specialists, but scholars who would ultimately serve the state. Both categories of scholars were no more sharply divided than the concepts of worldly and religious knowledge.

It seems as if this changed in the 19th century, and the process of social differentiation resulted in the *ulama* reconstituting itself as a separate group undergoing a process of professionalization. To this would correspond the observation that the same curriculum of Firangi Mahal, the Dars-e Nizamia, was taught in the later half of the 19th century in Deoband, but now with the express aim of educating religious leaders for the community (Metcalf 1982: 100). Whereas the influence of the colonial state on this process cannot be denied—one might perhaps even argue, that the privatization of the *ulama* was, at least partly, a result of their being pushed out of the public realm by the British—it would be worthwhile investigating the *ulama's* own perceptions of this development. In his fatwas on whether colonial rule had transformed India into a *dar ul harb*, an abode of war, for the Muslims, Shah Abdul Aziz seemed to take an unequivocal stand on the consequences implied in the government by non-Muslims, even if they were, through lack of power or through indifference not willing to interfere with Islamic ordinances (Aziz 1926: 27–30, Rizvi 1982: 26). Nevertheless, in a later fatwa, he further differentiated between a *dar ul harb* from which migration was obligatory, and a *dar ul harb* of apparently lesser evil, in which Muslims could not only remain resident, but also take up work in the administration (Rizvi 1982: 230–36). The conditions qualifying this second stage—the possibility to preach Islam, to observe fast and prayers and to perform the Friday prayers—could well be constructed as a division between a public and a private religious practice.

The second shift in boundaries between the public and the private concerns the trend towards the relocation of religious debates in the public spaces rather than in the private.[10] Traditionally, as Avril Powell has shown, disputations between the leaders of different religions or sects had their place either at the royal court—Akbar's *ibadat khana* being the most prominent example—or at the house of some noble patron, and were structured by formal rules. They aimed at establishing the respective truth of the positions by the exchange of learned arguments, if conversion would at all be attempted, it would be the individual conversion of a high-ranking personality. The years immediately preceding the Revolt saw both the social widening of the audience and, linked to this, the descending of the preachers to the *bazars* or at least to 'public debates'—accessible to every person—in mosques or shrines (Powell 1993).[11] Unfortunately, we have no indication of changes in the number of people, who took part in the bi-weekly public sermons at the madrasa of Abdul Aziz and the shrine of Mirza Jan-e Janan, but it would fit into the general trend if the regular participation of hundreds of persons, which occasionally might increase to over a thousand, were a contrast to the more restricted, 'private' discussions at religious sites in the 17th and 18th centuries.[12] This development was in turn enhanced by the development of print, which permitted the diffusion of letters, sayings of the spiritual guide (*malfuzat*) and pamphlets to a larger audience.[13]

It remains to be seen how important it was for the character of the emerging public that this forum of discussion was not even in theory one of equals. Instead it was a hierarchical universe where 'truth' was not to be reached through independent exertion of reason open to every human being, but through initiation by a master. This was true even of those schools which had proceeded farthest on the path of the rationalization of theological sciences. If we look for equality, it probably would not be equality among individuals, but the openness of the debate introduced by the very number of shrines and schools, in which this debate took place.[14] It would further be worthwhile to investigate how this diversity was viewed theologically, whether participation in debate among the schools was viewed only as an exercise in 'showing the way to the erring', or whether it was perceived as having a theological and epistemological value.

The Literary Public

This debate, which retained an ambivalent status in theology, however, formed the central feature for the constitution of a literary public, often seen as the precursor of the civil and political public (Habermas 1965: 40). Both in Germany and in north India, these audiences were constituted within a semi-private sphere, but nevertheless had a great influence on the public sphere.

Since some years, an intense discussion is taking place among German historians, as to the constitutive elements of the *Bürgertum*,[15] as obviously this group was linked neither by a common status nor by a common economic background: it was neither estate nor class. What united it in its own self-perception was a common culture and lifestyle (Bausinger 1987: 121–43, Kocka 1995: 9–85), and in this culture, literature and language held a dominant place. Familiarity with the classics, a gift for reciting poetry and the aptitude for a well-placed quotation, but also acquaintance with the different nuances of addressing people and talking to them and the ability for a clear pronunciation, untainted by dialect and slang, were central status indicators. They not only determined whether an individual could claim to be a *Bürger*, but also marked the respectability of the social group as a whole (Linke 1991: 250–81).

The place for this cultural self-celebration of the bourgeoisie was the salon, which had seen its heyday at the end of the 18th and the beginning of the 19th centuries, but continued as a social institution until the end of the empire, and in some rare instances even beyond (Frevert 1994: 96–104).[16] In its initial phase, the salon had endeavoured to embody the utopian ideal of the bourgeoisie of a society of equals, in which persons could met for a literary, philosophical and at times even political discourse, irrespective of their gender, profession and economic status. But even if the arts formed a central topic, the host of the salon was rarely if ever an artist himself. The salon was a profoundly bourgeois institution; the bourgeois relation to the arts, however, was supposed to draw a line at connoisseurship, at the ability to appreciate a work of art and to recite literary works or to play a musical composition. The creator of works of art remained outside the pale of the bourgeoisie—the genius was the counter-image that the bourgeoisie painted of itself, adored, but also feared (Frevert 1999: 292–324).

It fell upon women to bridge this gulf between the bourgeoisie and the arts—first on the individual level, as every salon lived through the personality of its hostess, through her ability to knit together the different composing elements; but second also on the social level: the dichotomy of the images of gender, which ascribed male characteristics to business, endowed women with a special sense for beauty, and hence also for the arts. If this emphasis on the female heart, its spontaneity and its potential transcending of rules, on the one hand, made the women less bourgeois than their husbands, on the other hand, it was in their artistic competence that the central contribution of women to the process of the formation of the bourgeoisie as a cultural community can be seen. Thus, the contribution of the private to the public is once again reproduced on the level of the genders (Frevert 1995a: 133–66).

At a first glance, the *mushairah*, the poetic gathering, seems to constitute the north Indian equivalent to the salon.[17] Unlike in the salon, however, here the artists held the central place. *Mushairahs* were contests among poets, at which they recited their latest works to an audience of peers. Whoever participated—and this held true even for the king and the nobles—did so in his capacity as poet (Naim 1989: 167–73). At least in formal *mushairahs*, women did not take part; however, gatherings in the houses of the courtesans usually also included the recitation of poetry. Though she certainly was not less cultured than the hostess of the salon, the courtesan remained outside the sphere of respectability: hers was not a staging of the *sharif* men's private for the sake of the public, but a world constructed in opposition to the female apartments, which were so private that they could not even be talked about.[18]

Mushairahs could take place at regular events—we know of some held every fortnight at the same place for several years—or as spontaneous gatherings. They could be held at the royal court or at the house of a noble, but also at the houses of the poets themselves or at shrines. Participation was usually by invitation, but every poet felt free to bring along his pupils, and a poet of rank could be sure to be welcomed at local *mushairahs* in whatever city he went.[19]

The ability to appreciate and to compose poetry was a mark of *sharafat* in the double sense of the word: of the inborn nobility of the poet's soul, which endowed him with delicate feelings as well as of his appurtenance to the class of the well-born (Metcalf 1984). But the particular character of the *ghazals* recited on these occasions made them to an even larger extent demarcations of cultural capital: the central feature of the *ghazal* was not so much the expression of the poets' own experience and feelings, but a dialogue with tradition, the taking up and transforming of earlier images and turns of phrases, an answering to and surpassing of a line of the earlier poet (Pritchett 1979: 60–77). It was held that to really appreciate a *ghazal*, not to speak of composing one, one had to master at least 10,000 verses of the classical and 10,000 verses of the modern poets (Naim 1992: 269). It becomes clear that this reduced active participation in *mushairahs* to a relatively small circle of the leisured class. *Mushairahs* thus were events situated in the private sphere, in which social status of the participants, their noble character and hence their legitimacy to rule—eminently public categories—were constituted. This may also explain the eagerness of the British to gain access to these forms of interaction, at least in the first decades of their rule.

If the *mushairah* can be qualified as a literary public, in the sense Habermas uses the term, was it also a public of equals, submitted to a common—if only poetic—law, thus presaging civil society of a kind? The poetic law was certainly the same for all poets, and whereas a poet could expect to gain social status at a *mushairah*, he also faced the risk of being covered by ridicule at the use of a faulty metre or phrase or a metaphor not sanctioned by classical use.[20]

The order of presentation was strictly according to the excellence of the poets, the most senior one reciting last. In theory, the nobility was expected to conform to these rules. When Nawab Amin ud Daula—probably not the ruler of Lucknow, but a minor noble of the same name—once refused due honour to the poets by asking them to sit on the carpet while he sat on the throne, they collectively threatened to boycott his *mushairahs*. The warning was not lost, and from that day, the nobleman and the poets sat on one level (Zaidi 1989: 78). However, poetic excellency never completely succeeded in erasing social differences. Not only the Emperor, himself renowned as a poet, but also the princes and sometimes the nobles were made to stand outside the rang-order by merit of the verses. They recited either before all others, or at some late stage, the possibility of their providing patronage for the poets outweighing the consideration for an equal application of poetic laws.

An interesting occurrence in this context is the figure of the illiterate poet, the *ghazal*-writing water-carrier or rickshaw driver, who figures in many descriptions of *mushairahs*, both in Delhi and in Lucknow in the 19th century.[21] While this can partly be explained by the rivalry for cultural excellency between the two towns, and partly by 20th century nostalgia for a more cultured past, it seems probable that already the second half of the 18th century saw a social mobility manifesting itself in new groups pushing into this cultured universe. Disgusted by the intrusion of these newcomers—of whom we unfortunately have no precise sociological information—the poet Mir exclaims: 'In finer days, this respectable art was cultivated by those whose nature was subtle. They were just and distinguishing, and kept this area free of rubbish. The lower classes (*ajlaf*) had no say in this art, it was taught only to the respectable (translated in Naim 1999: 180).' He continues with the edifying example of the Persian poet Hilali, who had imagined it possible to write poetry without the training by a master of the art. Only after he was beaten up by the Wazir for his bad poetry, he repented, went in search of an *ustad* and finally reached excellence (Mir Taqi Mir 1972: 142–45).

In the 1840s, the influx of newcomers into poetry seems to have reached such an extent that the guild-like teaching from master to pupil was no longer able to cope with it. In Agra, an entire journal could thrive by catering to the needs of those who did not have access to regular *mushairahs* and who struggled with the rules of poetics without being able to find a teacher who would guide them.[22] The printed word, thus, had taken over the function of the oral culture. It is to this aspect that we now turn.

The Beginning of Print Culture

The first Indian newspapers have for a long time been regarded as the outcome of the British influence and example. Certainly, European patronage was an important aspect for the early vernacular newspapers (Sabri: 24). The *Jam-e Jahan Numa*, one of the first Persian newspapers and probably the first carrying an Urdu supplement, published from Calcutta since 1822, bore the crest of the East India Company on its front-page, and had a large share of Europeans among its subscribers. Delhi newspapers, notably those published from the Delhi College, could rely on British support, financial and otherwise.[23] Nevertheless, the recent research by C.A. Bayly and Michael Fisher has pointed out the links of these newspapers to the traditional forms of communication (Bayly 1993, Fisher 1993: 45–82, Khurshid 1988). Since the time of Emperor Akbar, a system of manuscript newsletters had evolved, which permitted communication between the imperial court and the nobles through news-writers. In contrast to the gathering of information through spies, these news-writers were the central institution of a system guaranteeing an open flow of information between the imperial court and the periphery. A system, one might say with only apparent contradiction, which led to the constitution of a public consisting of the *khas*. The letters from the imperial envoys at the nobles' courts as well as the record of the emperor's proceedings were compiled into a daily account and read out to an audience. Here, the envoys of the nobles took notes and in turn informed their patrons. In the early phase of colonial government, and in some cases up to 1857, the British used this method of news-gathering for their own requirements. News-writers were employed at the most important courts, and much of the source material on the court of the later Mughals are these daily reports in Persian by scribes trained in the traditional way, but now working for the British.

While these manuscript newspapers by their geographical distribution transcended a 'local' public and contributed to the creation of an audience encompassing at least the bigger north Indian cities, it is more difficult to judge the social composition of their public in the early decades of the 19th century. When Macaulay estimated the number of these handwritten gazettes despatched daily at 120 only for the city of Delhi (Khurshid 1988: 86), it seems probable that the patronage for the news-writers had begun to transcend the nobility and now included a slightly lower strata of literati, perhaps even of long-distance traders and bankers who were acting at a supra-regional level and hence in need of constantly updated information. The newspapers were not only handed around, at times they even seem to have been read out to a more general public by enterprising journalists themselves (Ibid.: 87). Thus, even before the advent of the printing press, the location of the

public opinion very slowly began to shift from the *diwan-e khas* to a
more generally open public. Almost until the Revolt of 1857, the formation of public opinion was to a great extent through these private
manuscript journals, in which, according to the Governor General
Lord Auckland, 'the most absurd reports and mischievous misrepresentations were made to agitate men's minds, and to produce evil which
might have prevented or guarded against if the circulation had been
effected by printed papers (Khurshid 1988: 86).' Unfortunately, none of
these manuscript papers seem to have been located yet, so that their
contents and the role they played in times of crisis can only be guessed.

Since 1841, the royal diary was printed on a weekly basis in the Red
Fort. The *Siraj ul Akhbar* was written in Persian targetting both the
inhabitants of the Fort and the British. The topics covered as well as the
number of persons involved seem not to have differed from the earlier
handwritten versions (Khan 1991: 117–19, Siddiqi 1957: 257–59).
However, the king himself seems to have realized the importance of the
budding public opinion—both English and vernacular—as he regularly had the printed newspapers read out to him and took care to
correct misrepresentations by means of the *Siraj ul Akhbar* (Siddiqi
1957: 259).

Change through print came only very gradually. We know that Ghalib
brought back the passion for newspaper reading from his travel to
Calcutta and used to read the *Jam-e Jahan Numa* until he found a more
reliable alternative to its notoriously erratic information in the *Aina-e
Sikander*, published by his friend Siraj ud Din, whom he in turn supplied with first-hand news from Delhi (Russell and Islam 1994: 60–62).

While the *Jam-e Jahan Numa* had for some years carried an Urdu
supplement, the first full-fledged Urdu newspaper was started from
Delhi in 1837 under the name *Delhi Akhbar* (Faruqi 1972); drawing
heavily from the traditional models. Neither in the topics discussed—
supplemented by a kind of 'court-diary' of the new rulers, the Governor
General and the Resident in Delhi—in the number of copies circulated,
which varied between 30 and 100, according to the newspaper, in the
persons involved in the editing and publishing, nor probably in the
audience, did any marked departure occur before the mid-century (Bayly
1993: 78–88).

The newspapers maintained close contact with each other throughout north India, not only by exchanging copies—between one-tenth
and one-quarter of the printed issues were reserved for these exchanges
(Sabri: 100–101)—but also by reprinting, commenting and correcting

each other's articles. By 1840, the *Delhi Akhbar* already had a regular column for readers' comments, permitting not only a discussion with the editor, but also among the readers themselves. Both as far as the editorship and also the readership is concerned, religion does not seem to have played a major role. Several newspapers had both Muslim and Hindu editors; with the possible exception of the *Banaras Gazette*, no paper at this stage catered exclusively to the needs of one religious community.[24] The social divisions which influenced the newspapers were the factions within the city: the editor of the *Delhi Akhbar* was a pupil of the poet Zauq, Ghalib's rival for the patronage of the court. Consequently, in 1847 it published the news of Ghalib's imprisonment on the charge of gambling with great relish. Ghalib, on his part, preferred to subscribe to newspapers from Calcutta or Agra, and only borrowed the *Delhi Akhbar* from friends, if it contained some exclusive piece of news (Siddiqi 1957: 273–75).

Although controlled by a British Press Law right from the beginning, the newspapers upheld their claim not only to inform, but also to discuss and criticize. The well-known line of Hafiz, 'Politics are best know to the Emperors' in this context turned out to be no more than a poetic acknowledgement of tradition (Lal 1950: 23). It precluded neither the criticism of the extravagance of an Indian noble, as in the case of the Begum of Samru, who was attacked for her lavish expenses during a period of famine (Qureshi 1943: 282–97), nor of the Crown Prince, whose father's exhortations to careful fund management were quoted in full (Ibid.: 284). However, it might also turn against the British administration, notably against its economic policy, which was believed to be aimed at forcing people either to accept Christianity or to leave the country (Ibid.: 294). The doctrine of lapse is critically discussed in several issues of the *Delhi Akhbar*, the taxation of hitherto rent-free land disapproved as being contrary to the public good (*rifah-e 'am*).[25]

Whereas in north India, the newspapers and pamphlet literature preceded the printing of books on a large scale, in a manner paving their way, in Germany it was the other way round. Even before the age of the press, books had found a distribution, which was no longer limited to the scholars of the upper classes. They certainly included both literature and non-fictional works, but the largest share was taken up by religious books, devotional literature, calendars and almanacs. The first decades of the 19th century brought about what has been called a 'revolution of reading'. The tremendous increase in the number of readers, and also a profound change in the reading habits, which shifted from the intensive and repeated reading of few books to an extensive perusal of a large number of new books (Nipperdey 1983: 587). Before newspapers rose to prominence, reading was already a habit—not only of the middle classes, but, to the great concern of state and church, also of the lower orders (Ibid.: 589, Martino and Prüsner 1980: 45–57, Schenda 1970).

According to Habermas, the press is the central means through which a bourgeois public sphere is organized and the economic category of bourgeois is transformed into the political one of citizen, of a person not only allowed to discuss public affairs, but also through discussion take part in their shaping (Habermas 1965: 53, 72ff.). While in Britain the press had obtained this freedom of commenting on political events at an early stage, both in Germany and India this development towards citizenship was hampered by an autocratic state, aimed at controlling the press (Nipperdey 1983: 590–92, Schmidt 1980: 74–93). It was only under the impact of the French revolution, and definitely after the March-revolution of 1848 in Germany and 1857 in India that printed newspapers gathered enough momentum to be able to influence groups formerly outside the reach of written public discussion and evolve a new style of communication, based on the interaction with an anonymous audience, to which both the newspaper owner and editor were linked primarily by a commercial relation. Only in the second half of the century, we might thus argue, did the public opinion leave the private sphere and become 'public'.

The Private Sphere as the Central Topic of Public Opinion

The original meaning of secularization referred either to the reversion of persons belonging to the clergy back into the laity, or to the transfer of goods or estates of the Church into the possession of the state (Zabel et al. 1972: 789–829). It was used in this sense for the first time during the French Revolution and in the restructuring of the German Reich which followed the upheaval of the Napoleonic War. By implication this same term came to mean the general loss of power of the Church, the reduction of its influence on the public sphere and hence its limitation of the private. Both strands of meaning—secularization as a loss of power, and secularization as a functional differentiation, as discussed earlier—were interwoven and influenced each other, both on the level of historical facts and academic discussion.

For the Catholic Church in Germany, the beginning of the 19th century brought the loss of those territories in which it exercised not only spiritual, but also supreme temporal power—'public' power, so to speak. These were mainly the domains of the three Episcopal electorates, but also numerous prince bishops and monasteries. In 1871, the foundation of the German Empire under Prussian domination and without the Austrian territories for the first time left the Catholics in a minority position. The *kulturkampf* further reduced the Church's influence in the public sphere: on politics, by prohibiting the clergy to introduce political subjects in their sermons; on education by abolishing her supervisory powers over the primary schools and in turn introducing a state control on the training of the clergy; on the family by making civil marriage obligatory.

For Indian Muslims, the traumatic experience of 1857 and its aftermath marked the culmination of the loss of political power in north India, an experience seen to reflect a world-wide trend (Robinson 2000b: 138–56). The loss of power may well have been much less in reality than in perception, specially for those who obtained recognition as the spokesmen of the community in the second half of the century. Unfortunately, we know very little about the process of class formation among the north Indian Muslims. What seems to have taken place was a major redistribution of influence between the old nawabi upper class, grounded in a cosmopolitan Persianized culture, committed to conspicuous consumption, patrons of poetry and music, and the rising bourgeoisie of the *shurafa*, from whom reformist Islam constituted not only a means of gaining respectability, but also of ascertaining the leadership of the community (Minault 1998: 4–6ff.).

However, the formal end of the Mughal Empire meant that the 'Muslimness' of the community could no longer be guaranteed through reference to a Muslim ruler and the 'enjoining of good and prohibiting of evil' he ensured—through public action, so to speak—but had to be brought forth from within the community itself. The 'Muslimness' of the individuals became decisive for the very constitution of the community, the private now constituted the touchstone on which the fate of Islam would be decided. This development was certainly influenced by the British perception of religion both as 'private' and as central for group-formation in India, but could also draw on the traditional discourse of personal salvation in a hostile environment. We have seen earlier that even for the Naqshbandis—who among the leading schools could certainly be counted as being more involved with the ruling power than many others—the state held a deeply ambivalent position, at the same time guaranteeing and endangering the true faith (Fusfeld 1981: 81–105).

The reaction of the Catholic Church to its loss of social and public power were threefold. It worked first towards a strengthening of its internal organization—bureaucratization and ultramontanization (Ebertz 1980: 89–111, 1993: 62–85); second, towards intensification of social interaction within the Catholic community and the reduction of points of contacts between the believers and other people—the creation of a Catholic milieu; and third towards the intensification of personal piety, notably of the women.[26] This feminization of piety can be understood from developments from within the Church: the loosening grip on the male religiosity, notably within the middle classes, which made pastoral care of the women imperative, if the Church did not want to renounce all influence on the families and notably on the socialization of the next generation; the change in the social bases from the middle classes towards artisans and peasants, and to some extent also workers; the shifting of the central theological tendencies from Catholic enlightenment towards an Ultramontanism, favouring a faith no longer based exclusively on reason, but also on emotions and the senses, and reserving a central place in worship for the Virgin Mary.

At the same time, these developments have to be seen in the larger context of an enhanced dichotomy between the public and the private.[27] This dichotomy can be seen on the one hand—in the public sphere so to speak—in the philosophy of law: both the idea of fundamental rights as well as the struggle for a constitution can be seen as endeavours to limit the absolutist state and its possibilities to intervene in the sphere of society in extent and scope. On the other hand, this dichotomy shows—in the private sphere—in the opposition between world and home, an opposition which at the same time became increasingly gendered. In both cases, the private was to be protected from the public, from a public simultaneously seen as masculine ('our state is of masculine gender' [Frevert 1995b: 61–133]). However, this dichotomization not only prevented the intrusion of the public into the private sphere, but also the eruption of women into the public, reserved for men.

Yet, if these boundaries seem very clear-cut at first, at a second sight the dichotomy gives way to a complex intertwining: private was the house, public the street; private the quarter, in which the woman went shopping, paid her visits and went to church, public the town. Private were the charitable activities, public the politics; private the church and public the state. Consumption was private and production public; art was private and economics public, however, it became private, if opposed to the public state.

This same identification between the private and the feminine, can also be found—for the first time—in the Muslim discourse in north India since the 1870s.[28] The female quarters of a house were traditionally regarded as the most private, the women as the domain, which was not only protected from the view of strangers, but also from his polite inquiries: women, at least respectable women, were no topic for public discussion—the very fact that a space was perceived as being inhabited by women and hence as female, rendered it private.[29] By shifting the centre of community identity from the public to the private, however, female behaviour gained a new importance. It was the women's comportment, their conforming the tenets of Islam, which was increasingly perceived as the one essential factor which decided between the salvation or the destruction of the community. However, where Catholic feminization of piety had brought about an enhancement of the agency of women through their pivotal position between the Church and their secularized husbands, this new significance of Muslim women was matched by a tightening of male control over their lives. Explanation for this may sought both in the different role of religion under the colonial state, and in the fact, that unlike in Germany, economically rising groups did not distance themselves from organized religion, but on the contrary endeavoured to enhance their social respectability by conforming more strictly to the rules of reformist Islam, or at least by making their women conform to them (Pernau 2003). Reformed women were enjoined to resist the temptation to leave the house on the pretext of social gathering like weddings and similar celebrations. These gatherings were not only occasions characterized by superfluous and wasteful customs, but they also were seen as an infringement of the strict rules of purdah. Likewise, in the religious sphere, women had to renounce the female congregational prayers in Ramzan as well as the Majalis in Muharram. Though none of these occasions involved a contact with unrelated men, they constituted an opening of the private sphere of the female quarters of the house to a female semi-public world, consisting of the extended family and the neighbourhood. Pointedly, one might say that the price for the appearance of women in the public discourse was their vanishing from the public sphere: the more they were talked about, the more they were expected to remain silent (see, for instance, Minault 1998: 138).

Whether a topic qualified as public or a private thus depended to a large extent on gender. Hali was probably one of the authors who gave the greatest importance to women in the upbringing of a pious and educated Muslim. But even he does not go beyond endowing them with the responsibility of preparing a child, so that 'he will be like a lamp in which oil and wick are ready, and it remains only to be lighted' (Minault 1986: 42). The actual lightening can only be done by a male professional teacher, either traditionally in the context of the home, or increasingly outside the family, in a school, madrasah or college. While many of these educational ventures may qualify as 'private' by the fact that they were not subsidized and controlled by the state, however, the great campaigns for the foundation of the Aligarh and Deoband colleges, for the establishment of female education and the discussions which preceded and accompanied them, were certainly 'public'. The same organized educational activities of the Muslim community were private, because defined as religious, when regarded in opposition to the colonial state; they were public, when looked at from the female angle, insofar as they took place outside the sphere accessible to women.

This brief glance at 19th century Delhi has shown that the evolution of public opinion is not necessarily linked to the idea of democratic citizenship. It can develop within a private sphere, as shown with reference to the *mushairahs* and *mehfils*. It need not even deal with public issues, as pointed out in the discourse on female behaviour. A walk through old Delhi takes us through intertwining spheres: when viewed from the *bazar*, the side-lane is private, however, it becomes public when seen from the *kucha*, the residential quarter, which can be closed off by a gate. This *kucha* in turn becomes public, when seen from the house. Within the house, the public sitting-room for the men can be distinguished from the private inner courtyard, which in turn becomes public, once the women retire behind the screens of the upper galleries.[30] The dividing line between the public and the private consequently loses whatever definiteness it once seemed to have. It varies not only according to space and time, but also at any given moment within the same cultural setting, according to the point of view.

NOTES

* I would like to thank T.N. Madan, Frances Pritchett, Narayani Gupta, Gurpreet Mahajan, Ute Frevert, Jamal Malik, and Christina Oesterheld

for the unfailing generosity in sharing their knowledge and ideas on this topic and working hard to improve my article.

1. As in the meantime it is as politically incorrect to look for similarity—which qualifies the cultural imperialist—as for differences—which marks the orientalist—I prefer to leave the question of my own brand of political incorrectness unanswered. Of course, the article intends to imply no normative statement for present-day politics.

2. Of course, this process always involves the risk, as Professor T.N. Madan rightly pointed out in the discussion of the paper, that the spark of poetry fails to materialize, or that it is perceived differently by different persons. As, however, it is not my ambition to evolve a new theory of the public and perhaps not even to provide new answers, but to de-familiarize known facts and thus to provoke new questions, I feel the risk is worth taking.

3. For this aspect see the studies of Nita Kumar (1988) and Sandria B. Freitag (1989, 1990, 1991) and the other articles in that volume. However, the emphasis of all these works tends to be on the late 19th and the 20th centuries—a study of the popular use of the public sphere and popular perception of the state for the early colonial period in north India would be urgently needed.

4. For further elaboration of this concept of nobility see Margrit Pernau (2000).

5. (Weber 1968: 1013). For the application of Weber's typology to the Mughal Empire see Stephan Blake (1991).

6. Hahn (1997: 17–32); Greschat (1997: 76–86). For the concept of secularization as functional differentiation see Niklas Luhmann (1977: 225–72).

7. For the culture of the Protestant bourgeoisie see the case study of Ann-Charlott Trepp (1996); for the Catholic counterpart see the work of Thomas Mergel (1994).

8. Devji (1994: 28). Similar in the approach of equating the sufistic discourse with dissent also Mukhia (1999: 861–81).

9. Fusfeld (1981); Bayly (1996: 165) refers to the contacts between the Resident and Shah Abdul Aziz in order to avert Muslim-Jain clashes in 1806.

10. Since the 1830s the Delhi College would certainly be one of the most important centres for these discussions. The results of Gail Minault's research-in-progress are therefore eagerly awaited.

11. We have no precise information as to the social standing of the persons taking part or at least listening to these debates, but in view of their number, it seems very probable that they transcended the group of the *ulama* properly speaking and included at least those from the lower strata who were able to follow the arguments.

12. For Abdul Aziz see Rizvi (1982: 93, 196); for the 18th century, Fusfeld (1981: 74).

13. See Robinson (2000a: 66–105). However, it would need further investigation, whether—and within which time—print did influence both the distribution and the structure and content of the texts.
14. To get an impression of this density of religious institutions in 1850 see the map by Malik (1993: 46).
15. For lack of a better alternative, in the following the terms of bourgeois and bourgeoisie are used as the translation of *Bürger* and *Bürgertum*. *Bürgertum* in German, however, encompasses both the notion of bourgeoisie and citizenship—it does not carry the usual negative connotations of the modern use of bourgeoisie.
16. Ute Frevert, 'Der Salon', in: Heinz-Gerhard Haupt (ed.), *Orte des Alltags. Miniaturen aus der europäischen Kulturgeschichte*, München 1994, pp. 96–104.
17. For this opinion, with many good arguments, see Malik (1997: 181–82).
18. See the masterly depiction of the courtesans' world in Mirza Ruswa, *Umrao Jan Ada*.
19. For the background of the *mushairahs* see Pritchett (1994). For a description which, however, should be read critically, as it dates from almost 100 years after the event and the author tends to supply missing sources by imagination, see Beg (1979).
20. A good example of these poetic criticisms can be found in Ghalib's *masnavi Bad-e mukhalif*, the poem in which he recounts his experience with Calcutta's poets and *mushairahs*: *Kulliyat-Ghalib (Farsi)*, edited by Amir Hasan Nurani, Lucknow 1968.
21. For Delhi, Farhat Ullah Beg (1979) mentions the poets Ashiq, 'an ordinary manual workman' (p. 75) and Ghulam Ahmad Tasvir, who 'earns his livelihood by doing ornamental work on huqqah cords'. (p. 77). For Lucknow see Sharar (1994: 81, 93, 100).
22. The *Mayar ush Shora* was published since 1848 by Ghalib's friend Aran, poet and Persian teacher at the Agra Madrasa. See Imdad Sabri, *Urdu ke akhbar navis*, p. 56; Siddiqi (1957: 287–88).
23. Nadir Ali Khan (1991: 28–30) (for the *Jam-e Jahan Numa*); Imdad Sabri, p. 25 (for the *Fawaid ul Nazirin* and *Mohibb-e Hind*); Siddiqi (1957: 268) (for the *Delhi Urdu Akhbar*).
24. Ibid., table giving the number of subscribers of the main pre-1857 newspapers according to their religion.
25. Faruqi (1972: issue of 2 February 1840).
26. For more detail see Pernau (2003).
27. I am grateful to Ute Frevert for drawing my attention to this point.
28. For the comparable Hindi and Bengali literature see Sangari (1999), Walsh (1997: 641–77).
29. The opening up of new spaces to women thus resulted not so much in women penetrating into the public sphere, than in these spaces becoming private.
30. For this image of intertwining see also Schiffauer (58).

REFERENCES

Aziz, Shah Abdul. 1926. *Fatawa-e Azizi* (Urdu translation), Vol. 1.

Bayly, C.A. 1996. *Empire and Information: Intelligence Gathering and Social Communication in India, 1780–1870.* Cambridge: Cambridge University Press.

Blake, Stephan. 1991. *Shahjahanabad: The Sovereign City in Mughal India 1639–1739.* Cambridge: Cambridge University Press.

Bausinger, Hermann. 1987. 'Bürgerlichkeit und Kultur,' in Jürgen Kocka (ed.), *Bürger und Bürgerlichkeit im 19. Jahrhundert.* Göttingen: Vandenhoeck Ruprecht.

Beg, Farhat Ullah. 1979. *Akhri Shama.* Translated as *The Last Musha'irah of Delhi* by Akhtar Qambar. Delhi.

Devji, Faisal Fatehali. 1994. 'Gender and the Politics of Space: The Movement for Women's Reform, 1857–1900,' in Zoya Hasan (ed.), *Forging Identities: Gender, Communities and the State.* Delhi: Kali for Women.

Ebertz, Michael N. 1980. 'Herrschaft in der Kirche: Hierarchie, Tradition und Charisma im 19. Jahrhundert,' in Karl Gabriel and Franz-Xaver Kaufmann (eds), *Zur Soziologie des Katholizismus.* Mainz: Matthias Grünewald Verlag.

_____. 1993. 'Ein Haus voll Glorie schauet ....' Modernisierungsprozesse der römisch-katholischen Kirche im 19. Jahrhundert,' in Wolfgang Schieder (ed.), *Religion und Gesellschaft im 19. Jahrhundert.* Stuttgart: Klett-Cotta.

Faruqi, Khwaja Ahmad (ed.). 1972. *Delhi Urdu Akhbar [January–September 1840].* Delhi: Urdu department, Delhi University.

Fisher, Michael. 1993. 'The Office of Akhbar Nawis: The Transition from Mughal to British Forms,' *MAS 1993.*

Freitag, Sandria B. 1990. *Collective Action and Community: Public Arenas and the Emergence of Communalism in North India,* Delhi.

_____. (ed.). 1989. *Culture and Power in Banaras: Community, Performance and Environment, 1800–1980.* Berkeley: Oxford University Press.

_____. 1991. 'Introduction' to *South Asia, Special Number 1991,* pp. 1–13.

Frevert, Ute. 1999. 'Der Künstler,' in Ute Frevert and Heinz Gerhard Haupt (eds), *Der Mensch des 19. Jahrhunderts.* Frankfurt: C.H. Beck.

_____. 1995a. 'Kulturfrauen und Geschäftsmänner: Soziale Identitäten im deutschen Bürgertum des 19. Jahrhunderts,' in Ute Frevert (ed.), *Mann und Weib und Weib und Mann: Geschlechter-Differenzen in der Moderne.* München: C.H. Beck.

_____. 1995b. 'Unser Staat ist männlichen Geschlechts': Zur politischen Topographie der Geschlechter vom 18. bis frühen 20. Jahrhundert,' in Ute Frevert (ed.), *Mann und Weib und Weib und Mann: Geschlechter-Differenzen in der Moderne.* München: C.H. Beck.

Frevert, Ute. 1994. 'Der Salon,' in Heinz-Gerhard Haupt (ed.), *Orte des Alltags: Miniaturen aus der europäischen Kulturgeschichte*. München: C.H. Beck.

Fusfeld, Warren Edward. 1981. 'The Shaping of Sufi Leadership in Delhi: The Naqshbandiyya Mujaddidiyya, 1750–1920'. Ph.D. dissertation, Pennsylvania.

Greschat, Martin. 1997. 'Rechristianisierung und Säkularisierung: Anmerkungen aus deutscher protestantischer Sicht,' Hartmut Lehmann (ed.), *Säkularisierung, Dechristianisierung, Rechristianisierung im neuzeitlichen Europa*. Göttingen: Vandenhoeck Ruprecht.

Greverus, Ina-Maria. 1995. 'Anthropologische Horizonte zwischen Glückssuche und dem Prinzip Collage. Ist das anthropologische Prinzip Hoffnung verloren?' in Wolfgang Kaschuba (ed.), *Kulturen–Identitäten–Diskurse: Perspektiven Europäischer Ethnologie*. Berlin: Akademie Verlag.

Habermas, Jürgen. 1965. *Strukturwandel der Öffentlichkeit*. Neuwied.

Hahn, Alois. 1997. 'Religion, Säkularisierung und Kultur,' in Hartmut Lehmann (ed.), *Säkularisierung, Dechristianisierung, Rechristianisierung im neuzeitlichen Europa*. Göttingen: Vandenhoeck Ruprecht.

Hölscher, Lucian. 1972. 'Öffentlichkeit,' in Otto Brunner, Werner Conze and Reinhard Koselleck (eds), *Geschichtliche Grundbegriffe*, Vol. 4.

Khan, Nadir Ali. 1991. *A History of Urdu Journalism*. Delhi: Idara-e Adabiyat-e Delhi.

Khurshid, Abdus Salam. 1988. *Newsletters in the Orient: With Special Reference to the Indo-Pakistan Sub-Continent*. Islamabad: National Institute of Historical and Cultural Research.

Kocka, Jürgen. 1995. 'Das europäische Muster und der deutsche Fall,' in Jürgen Kocka (ed.), *Bürgertum im 19. Jahrhundert. I. Einheit und Vielfalt Europas*. Göttingen: Vandenhoeck Ruprecht.

Kumar, Nita. 1988. *The Artisans of Banaras: Popular Culture and Identity, 1880–1986*. Princeton: Princeton University Press.

Lal, K. Sajun. 1950. 'The Delhi Urdu Akhbar and its Importance,' in *Islamic Culture*, pp. 16–44.

Linke, Angelika. 1991. 'Zum Sprachgebrauch des Bürgertums im 19. Jahrhundert: Überlegungen zur kultursemiotischen Funktion des Sprachverhaltens,' in Rainer Wimmer (ed.), *Das 19. Jahrhundert: Sprachgeschichtliche Wurzeln des heutigen Deutsch*. Berlin: Walter de Gruyter.

Luhmann, Niklas. 1977. 'Säkularisierung,' in Niklas Luhmann (ed.) *Funktion der Religion*. Frankfurt.

Malik, Jamal. 2000. *Perspectives of Mutual Encounters in South Asian History, 1760–1860*. Leiden: Brill.

―――――. 1997. *Islamische Gelehrtenkultur in Nordindien: Entwicklungsgeschichte und Tendenzen am Beispiel von Lucknow*. Leiden 1997.

Malik, Jamal. 1993. 'Islamic Institutions and Infrastructure in Shahjahanabad,' in Eckart Ehlers and Thomas Krafft (eds), *Shahjahanabad/Old Delhi: Tradition and Colonial Change*. Stuttgart: Franz Steiner.

Martino, Alberto and Marlies Stützel-Prüsener. 1980. 'Publikumsschichten, Lesegesellschaften und Leihbibliotheken,' in Horst Albert Glaser (ed.), *Deutsche Literatur: Eine Sozialgeschichte, Bd. 5. Zwischen Revolution und Restauration: Klassik und Romantik*. Reinbek.

Mergel, Thomas. 1994. *Zwischen Klasse und Konfession: Katholisches Bürgertum im Rheinland 1794–1914*. Göttingen: Vandenhoeck Ruprecht.

Metcalf, Barbara. 1984. *Moral Conduct and Authority: The Place of Adab in South Asian Islam*. Berkeley.

_____. (ed.). 1982. *Islamic Revival in British India: Deoband, 1860–1900*. Princeton: Princeton University.

Minault, Gail. 1998. *Secluded Scholars: Women's Education and Muslim Social Reform in Colonial India*. Delhi: Oxford University Press.

_____. 1986. *Voices of Silence: Khwaja Altaf Hussain Hali's Majalis un Nissa and Chap ki Dad*. Delhi: Chanakya.

Mir Taqi Mir. 1972. 'Tanbih al Juhhal' and 'Hikayat', in *Kulliyat-e Mir*. Ramnarainlal Prahladdas (ed.), Allahabad: Ram Narayan Lal.

Mukhia, Harbans. 1999. 'The Celebration of Failure as Dissent in Urdu Ghazal,' *MAS* 1999.

Naim, C.M. (trans.). 1999. *Zikr-e Mir: The Autobiography of the 18th Century Mughal Poet: Mir Muhammad Taqi Mir*. Delhi: Oxford University Press.

_____. 1992. 'Mughal and English Patronage of Urdu Poetry: A Comparison,' in Barbara S. Miller (ed.), *The Powers of Art: Patronage in Indian Culture*. Delhi: Oxford University Press.

_____. 1989. 'Poet-audience Interaction at Urdu Musha'iras,' in Christopher Shackle (ed.), *Urdu and Muslim South Asia: Studies in Honour of Ralph Russell*. London.

Nipperdey, Thomas. 1983. *Deutsche Geschichte, 1800–1860: Bürgerwelt und starker Staat*. München: C.H. Beck.

Orhonlu, Cengiz. 1960. 'Khass,' in *Encyclopaedia of Islam*, 2nd edition. Leiden: Brill.

Pernau, Margrit. 2003. 'Motherhood and Female Identity: Religious Advice Literature for Women in German Catholicism and Indian Islam,' in Imtiaz Ahmad, Margrit Pernau and Helmut Reifeld (eds), *Family and Gender: Changing Patterns in Europe and India*. New Delhi: Sage Publications.

_____. 2000. 'Creation of a Royal Personality: The Yadgar-e Silver Jubilee of Mir Osman Ali Khan, Nizam of Hyderabad, 1936,' *Internationales Asienforum/International Asian Quarterly*, vol. 31, no. 3–4, pp. 255–73.

Powell, Avril. 1993. *Muslims and Missionaries in Pre-Mutiny India*. London.

Pritchett, Frances. 1994. *Nets of Awareness: Urdu Poetry and Its Critics*. Berkeley: University of California Press.

Pritchett, Frances. 1979. 'Convention in the Classical Urdu Ghazal: The Case of Mir,' *Journal of South Asian and Middle Eastern Studies*, pp. 60–77.

Quillet, J. 1970. *La philosophie politique de Marsile de Padoue (L'Eglise et l'Etat au Moyen Age 14)*. Paris: Librairie philosophique J. Vrin.

Qureshi, Ishtiaq Husain. 1943. 'A Year in Pre-Mutiny Delhi (1837 AC),' *Islamic Culture*, pp. 282–97.

Rizvi, S.A.A. 1982. *Shah Abdul Aziz: Puritanism, Sectarian Polemics and Jihad*. Canberra: Ma'rifat Publishing House.

Robinson, Francis. 2000a. 'Islam and the Impact of Print in South Asia,' in Francis Robinson (ed.), *Islam and Muslim History in South Asia*. Delhi: Oxford University Press.

―――――. 2000b. 'The Muslims of Upper India and the Shock of the Mutiny,' in Francis Robinson (ed.), *Islam and Muslim History in South Asia*. Delhi: Oxford University Press.

Russell, Ralph and Khurshidul Islam. 1994. *Ghalib: Life and Letters*. Delhi: Oxford University Press.

Sabri, Imdad. *Urdu ke akhbar navis*, p. 56.

Sangari, Kumkum. 1999. *Essays on Gender, History, Narratives, Colonial English*. Delhi: Tulika.

Schenda, Rudolf. 1970. *Volk ohne Buch: Studien zur Sozialgeschichte der populären Lesestoffe 1770–1910*. Frankfurt: Klosterman.

Schiffauer, Werner. 1995. 'Europäische Ängste: Metaphern und Phantasmen im Diskurs der Neuen Rechten in Europa,' in Wolfgang Kaschuba (ed.), *Kulturen–Identitäten–Diskurse: Perspektiven Europäischer Ethnologie*. Berlin: Akademie Verlag.

Schmidt, Peter. 1980. 'Buchmarkt, Verlagswesen und Zeitschriften,' in Horst Albert Glaser (ed.), *Deutsche Literatur: Eine Sozialgeschichte, Bd. 5. Zwischen Revolution und Restauration: Klassik und Romantik*. Reinbek.

Sharar, Abdul Halim. 1994. *Lucknow: The Last Phase of an Oriental Culture*. Translated and edited by E.S. Harcourt and Fakhir Hussain. Delhi: Oxford University Press.

Siddiqi, Muhammad Atiq. 1957. *Hindustani Akhbar Navisi*. Aligarh: Anjuman-e taraqqi-e Urdu.

Trepp, Ann-Charlott. 1996. *Sanfte Männlichkeit und selbständige Weiblichkeit: Frauen und Männer im Hamburger Bürgertum zwischen 1770 und 1840*. Göttingen: Vandenhoeck Ruprecht.

Walsh, Judith. 1997. 'What Women Learned When Men Gave Them Advice: Rewriting Patriarchy in Late 19th Century Bengal,' *JAS*, vol. 56, no. 4, pp. 641–77.

Weber, Max. 1968. *Economy and Society: An Outline of Interpretative Sociology*. Edited by Guenther Roth and Claus Wittich. Berkeley.

Zabel, Hermann, Werner Conze and Hans-Wolfgang Strätz. 1972. 'Säkularisation, Säkularisierung,' in Otto Brunner, Werner Conze (eds),

Geschichtliche Grundbegriffe: Historisches Lexikon der politisch-sozialen Sprache in Deutschland, Bd. 5. Stuttgart: Ernst Klett.

Zaidi, Ali Jawad. 1989. *Tarikh-e mushairah*. Delhi: the author.

6

The Struggle for Social Justice and the Expansion of the Public Sphere

Gail Omvedt

Introduction: Defining 'Public'

Most of the theoretical discussions of the meaning and significance of the public sphere have taken place in reference to European history. However, Partha Chatterjee (1993), among others, has insisted that qualitatively different processes have taken place in the third world. He points to the role of imperialism and national resistance as the main factor behind this. This paper, while keeping in mind the national contradiction and the relationship of 'public' and 'nation,' will examine the question of the public sphere in the context of the traditional social system of India or caste, and look at its emergence as related to the anti-caste movement for correcting historical injustices.

What do we mean by 'public' as opposed to 'private'—and why is it important? The definition given in *Webster's New Collegiate Dictionary* begins with the following: 'of, relating to, or affecting all the people or the whole area of a nation or state...of, or relating to, business or community interests as opposed to private affairs;...accessible to or shared by all members of the community.' Key words here are *all, whole, community,* and *nation*—reminding us that while the 'public' as a term, is an abstraction representing the whole, it is linked to the more emotive concepts of 'community' and 'nation'.

Jotirao Phule, in his posthumously published *Sarvajanik Satya Dharma Pustak* (1891) gives his implicit definition of 'public' (or sarvajanik) when in a critique of the organizations founded by the Brahman elite, which he sees as public in form but are in fact the expression of their private interest:

> Govindrao: From the pure name of the Sarvajanik Sabha it would seem that Kunbis, Malis, Dhangars, Kolis, Bhils and other farmers must be its members, doesn't it?
>
> Jotirao: I think that there is no likelihood that Kunbis and others are its members.
>
> Govindrao: Then those Gujars, Marwaris and other shopkeepers who do business and the Salis, Koshtis, Khatris and others who sell cloth and other goods must be members, don't you think?
>
> Jotirao: The Gujars, Marwaris and other shopkeepers and the Salis, Koshtis, Khatris and others are not even nominal members, as I have heard.
>
> Govindrao: Well, then, at least the Lohars, Sutars, Chambhars, Kumbhars, Nhavis, Parits and others of the twelve balutedars and the Mangs, Bhats, Joshis and other alutedars should be members of the sabha?
>
> Jotirao: In that sabha! Don't even mention the name of the twelve balutes, but among the others, the Brahman Joshis, bhats are the only ones there....
>
> Govindrao: What, of all the 20 crores of population in this Balisthan only two crores are Arya Brahmans. If the Arya brahmans of Pune have included only five or 20 people of other castes in the sabha, then how can anyone call this a Sarvajanik Sabha? (Phule, 1991: 492–93).

Phule goes on to argue that merely formal openness is not enough, pointing out that if the government agreed to recruit Mahars and Mangs who had knowledge of English and Persian for clerical posts, none would qualify. Openness has to be achieved as a deliberate, conscious act, in a hierarchical society it cannot just be assumed to happen automatically. By his criterion then, 'public' requires the true representation, access and membership, of all the sections of a society. When this does not happen, it only becomes a means of masking private interests.

Phule here is bringing to bear upon the general and abstract notion of public, the question of concrete, partial identities. Whether a space or organization is truly public, truly universal, whether the whole people are involved or not, can only be ascertained by asking questions about such identities. They are specific to specific societies; one would not ask about caste identities in the U.S. or whether members are 'Black' or 'white' or 'Hispanic' in India. The public emerges in a concrete historical situation under specific historical conditions of different societies and it cannot truly become a public unless these are taken into account.

Taking Phule's perspective, I would like to argue that the anti-caste movement in India, dating from the 19th century, can be interpreted as a movement that sought to establish, enlarge and make increasingly effective a public sphere. The existence of a 'public' sphere—both in the sense of the state coming to represent all people ('democratic citizenship') and of a healthy non-state public that takes up issues of the general good and represents them to the state and attempts to pressurize the state—is one of the crucial signs of modernity. But modernity has not historically come in a vacuum. The crucial fact of modernity (industrialization, democracy, efforts to establish equality and liberty) in India is that it came to being in a society, first characterized by the solidification of the caste system from nearly a millennium, and second, in a society under colonial rule. Thus the anti-caste movement, or rather the movement for establishing equality of culture and power, emerged at a time and to a large degree in conflict with, a national movement led by the elites of traditional society aiming at independence from the British. Thus I will also argue in contrast to the anti-caste movement, the elite-led national movement, from Tilak to Gandhi, had a tendency to argue for a narrowly defined public sphere.

The Public Sphere and Elite Nationalism

In *The Nation and Its Fragments*, Partha Chatterjee takes up the question of the nation and the public as they concretely emerged in India in relation to colonialism. The public, he notes, unites or links the civil society and the state, in contrast to the family and private life. Following Hegel, he sees civil society as the realm of contract, bourgeois individualism and market, constituted by families coming together under the leadership of their patriarchal heads. This though, occurs under the domination of capital which destroys the pre-capitalist community and makes labour 'universal' while subordinating it to the market and factory production: 'This so-called primitive accumulation is nothing else but the destruction of precapitalist community which, in various forms, had regulated the social unity of laborers with their means of production' (1993: 235). However, since the subordinated worker in the factory is also an equal 'citizen' in the political sphere, in the modern nation-state the 'community' is resurrected or reconstructed at the level of the state when the love and innate belongingness of community/family are 'read into' or 'imagined' in the nation. Thus, the development of the nation and public sphere in the industrialized, imperialist countries takes place with a public sphere constituting the (bourgeois) equality of citizens and the nation serving as the (bourgeois) reconciliation of community with the state. On the whole, though, the nation and the public are seen by Chatterjee as relatively unproblematic in the developed world, and no specific exclusions exist except for the complex exclusions of class, operating in the economic sphere.

In the colonized world, however, Chatterjee argues, there is a different process, precisely because there is no equality, not even bourgeois equality, in the political sphere. For this reason the nation is not, and cannot be, simply created on the basis of the political and the public. Rather, it is created in a very different way, appealing to older forms of community, forms which can in some way be maintained outside the challenge of European power:

> The crucial break in the history of anticolonial nationalism comes when the colonized refuse to accept membership of this civil society of subjects. They construct their national identities within a different narrative, that of the community. They do not have the option of doing this within the domain of bourgeois civil-society institutions. They create, consequently, a very different domain—a cultural domain—marked by the distinctions of the material and the spiritual, the outer and the inner. This inner domain of culture is declared the sovereign territory of the nation, where the colonial state is not allowed entry, even as the outer domain remains surrendered to the colonial power. The rhetoric here (Gandhi is a particularly good example) is of love, kinship, austerity, sacrifice. The rhetoric is in fact antimodernist, antiindividualist, even anticapitalist. The attempt is, if I may stay with Gandhi for a while, to find, against the grand narrative of history itself, the cultural resources to negotiate the terms through which people, living in different, contextually defined, communities, can coexist peacefully, productively, and creatively within large political units. (Chatterjee, 1993: 237–38).

Thus, while the elite strove to extend the powers of Indians within the political sphere, in the nationalist movement against colonial rule, they simultaneously constructed a realm of national identity imagined in terms of spirituality, deriving from the ancient Indian cultural traditions, utilizing a reconstructed 'Hindu' identity based on the Vedic period and the Aryans, and maintained primarily in the sphere of the home and the inner world. Thus the 'nation' in a very major sense was seen as existing outside the state, and constructed in reference to the 'private' sphere of the inner life and the home.

But, while Chatterjee weaves his essay around the issue of the nation in the colonial world, he ignores the issue of the concrete way in which the private, the traditional and the spiritual were constructed within India, the issue of the caste nature of the historically defined 'community'. (Though he has a chapter on caste in his book, this is never related to the elite's construction of the nation). Overlooked here, is also the fact that in the construction of the public sphere and the nation in the European industrialized societies (a different view might have been taken if the U.S. had been the subject of discussion), an already existing linguistic community as the foundation of the nation was assumed. India, in contrast, was fragmented in terms of religion, language and caste. It was, according to Phule and the later nonBrahman intellectuals, primarily caste that served to prevent a true nation from coming into being in India. As he put it,

> Due to the false self-interested religion of the Aryans, the cunning Arya Bhat-Brahmans consider the ignorant Shudras to be inferior; the ignorant Shudras consider the ignorant Mahars to be inferior; and the ignorant Mahars consider the ignorant Mangs to be inferior. As a result not only do the ultra-pure Arya Bhat-Brahmans consider the Ati-Shudras inferior, but since marriage and social relations are forbidden among them, naturally their various customs, eating habits, and rituals don't match each other. How can such a conglomerate of 18 grains be united to become a 'nation' of integrated people. (Phule, 1991: 494)

'Nation' requires belongingness, and a sense of common existence. To bring this into being, it is not enough to assert a spiritual and abstract equality, rather equality and a sense of belongingness have to have a material base in social life.

In pointing to the existence of caste hierarchy, Phule was raising a factor of material life that was as important as, though different from, the material world of labour. For anyone committed to the traditional

'Hindu' way of life, there were large realms of living—notably having to do with kinship relations and eating together—that were inexorably interwoven with caste hierarchy and separateness. Thus in defining the nation as 'Hindu', the elite was ready to accept a modified and reformist version of traditional caste exclusiveness, but not to abandon this in principle. The elite could see unity in cultural and spiritual terms, but the tendency would be to keep the realms of intermarriage and interdining and all the social relationships implied in these outside the public national sphere. This also included education, hostel living, all the areas where young people might meet—since meeting of youth inevitably would lead to social relations and intermarriage.

In this sense, not only did the shadow of colonialism hang over the construction of the nation in India; the shadow of the past did also. This was not only true of India, of course. The shadow of the past, notably in the form of African American slavery, hung heavily over the construction of that most modern of nations, the United States—not until well into the last half of the 20th century did African Americans receive genuine voting rights, for example. (As we shall see, this meant that the 'civil rights' movement of U.S. Blacks paralleled, in many ways, the efforts of Dalits in India to extend the public sphere). In India, it was not only in relation to the colonizers' control of the political sphere that the 'nation' was constructed in peculiarly spiritual terms; the 'spiritual' construction also arose in relation to, and as a way of allowing the maintainence of, the pervasive realm of caste-defined hierarchies and family relations. Defining unity as spiritual and related to the 'inner life', did not simply ignore the continuation of the relations of caste and gender hierarchy; it actively functioned to maintain them because the nature of the spiritual that was being valued included references to all the sacred Brahmanic texts that justified caste. To allow 'sacred' relations to go on operating in the private sphere, a whole level of material reality had to be excluded from the equality of the public sphere, with equality being seen in vague, amorphous and spiritual forms, rather than in concrete form.

Thus, we can understand that throughout the colonial period, the tendency of elite nationalism was to keep the public sphere narrow. Both the 'capitalist' interest in excluding labour from full rights and the caste interest in maintaining a system that justified superiority and excluding social relations of kinship and other kinds of interaction were operative here. One of the defining moments of the national movement was perhaps in 1895 when it took a decision to exclude 'social reform' from its agenda, forbidding the Social Conference from hold-ing meetings in the same premises. Resistance to such legislative re-forms as the Age of Marriage Act showed that any attempt to allow the 'public sphere' to intrude on the private through regulating social mat-ters was to be resisted.

While this resistance climaxed at the end of the 19th century and later gave way to the reformism of Gandhi, this Hindu reformism also resisted the expansion of the public sphere. As the movements of Dalits and non-Brahmans grew, Gandhi took lead of the project of redefining the 'Hindu nation' to remove untouchability and to meet some of the demands of the movements. However, he was against doing this by legislative effort, rather preferring 'change of heart'; he was not enthusi-astic about intermarriage; and he resisted demands of leaders like Ambedkar that the Harijan Sevak Sangh should be under control of Dalits themselves. He insisted to the end on the notion of 'swadharma' or doing one's caste duty; he was never happy about intermarriage; temple entry, though it was to be half-heartedly endorsed and was pro-moted by some Gandhian activists, was never a heavily pursued goal. The Harijan Sevak Sangh devoted itself to campaigns of cleanliness and Sanskritization, urging untouchables to give up meat-eating and alcohol, providing an outlet for the patronizing activities of upper-caste social reformers. The spiritual orientation of Gandhi also meant an avoidance of important material issues of marriage, dining and social relationships. Both the Gandhians and the Nehruvites in the Congress resisted the demands for reservation, or the entry of non-Brahmans and Dalits into public service.

Thus, a major dynamic during the period of colonialism and the national movement was the conflict between an elite concerned to keep the public sphere small, and a growing anti-caste movement fo-cusing on enlarging it.

Constituting the Public Sphere

Colonial rule, even the imposition of capitalism, looked very different from a Dalit and non-Brahman perspective. For instance, the destruc-tion of the community and its social regulation of labour meant that the low castes were freed from caste-defined duties in the villages and some even gained, entry to factory work. For instance, Mahars gained access to the textile mills of cities like Nagpur and Bombay. This was a clear step forward for those who had jobs, and it was in such cities that they developed their communities and the new culture that laid the basis for revolt (see for instance, the description in the autobiography of Moon). Of course there was not full formal equality here either, Dalits were discriminated against at the time of hiring. Mills in Bombay kept them out of the weaving department because workers had to take the thread in their mouths to hold it when it broke. Thus, Dalits had to fight for equal entry to factory employment.

What was true in regard to factory employment was true of all areas of social life. More than anything else, the anti-caste movements fought for access to 'public' spaces of work, consumption and citizen's life. In fact, the anti-caste movement can be defined partly as a fight to expand or constitute the public sphere as one genuinely representing the entire society. This meant dealing with very concrete material issues—water, food, the use of roads and public transport. Of course, the issues of national identity and debates about it went on—as radical Dalits and non-Brahmans contested the 'Hindu' identity of the nation and the caste hierarchies associated with it—but beyond this, concrete struggles emerged over very specific causes.

The first major mass mobilization of Dalits in Maharashtra, which took place under Ambedkar's leadership, illustrates this. The issue was access to the most basic means of life—water. This was of course, the Mahad satyagraha, organized in 1927 in the Konkan town of Mahad, where a resolution had been passed in the municipality under the leadership of progressive caste Hindus that the town tank should be open to Untouchables. A meeting was convened under Ambedkar's leadership to press for its implementation, and at its conclusion people rose with near spontaneity to go to the tank and drink the water. Near riots, and a purification of the tank by Brahmans ensued and the first mass attempt to make a public facility truly 'universal' ended in seeming failure.

Water, of course, was not a new issue. Ambedkar's choice of water for his first major step into mass action, was in many ways as symbolic and topical an issue to all Dalits, as was Gandhi's choice of salt for a nationalist satyagraha. In villages and towns throughout India it was a major symbol of the caste hierarchy—Untouchables could not use the common village well nor could they use the other common facilities of the towns. Phule, in the 19th century, had taken the then-revolutionary step of throwing open the well providing water to his own house in Pune to the Untouchables of the locality. Under the leadership of the non-Brahman Party, which had a strong position in the Bombay Legislative

Council in the 1920s, the issue was taken up, and S.K. Bole, one of their representatives, had got a bill passed in the Council. Thus, the uproar caused by the first attempt at direct action was then used by Ambedkar to rally wider support; he began his first major weekly, *Bahishkrut Bharat*, and declared that the satyagraha would go on. So much tension existed at the second major conference—which drew thousands, much beyond the hundreds who had gathered at the first conference and surprised the orthodox by their action—that the District Collector issued an injunction against any action. Ambedkar chose to respect it, but he responded by an equally defiant act, a public burning of the *Manusmriti* on December 25, 1927 (Omvedt 1994). Water, the means of life, access to public space and cultural-religious identity thus together in a new way, and the day was declared and celebrated for many years after as Untouchable Liberation Day. This was the first major struggle over water, it was not to be the last, in every village the issue of the simple right to use the village well remained a constant issue.

Temple entry was another major issue, though not one that Ambedkar took up personally. Again, it posed tremendous problems for the 'nation'. Were temples public spaces or private? In one sense, religion is the most private and personal aspect of identity, and in the Hindu-Brahmanic tradition, they were never congregational meeting places like churches in any case. If caste Hindu wells excluded Dalits, the more so for the famous temples; and the bhakti movements are replete with stories of Dalit saints like Nandanar in Tamil Nadu, Chokamela in Maharashtra, who were prevented from access to the deity. However, the huge temples of medieval times symbolized more than anything else the Brahmanic Hindu community. Thus, from the beginning of the Dalit movement, the issue emerged; in countless cases where Untouchable conferences were held, the great temples in the town were often closed as a preventive measure to avoid any 'incidents'. By the 1920s several major temple satyagrahas were held—the Parvati and Kalaram temple satyagrahas in Maharashtra and the Vaikom temple satyagraha in Kerala which made Periyar famous. They marked a new challenge by the Dalits—religion was 'public' and what was public must be universal.

In fact, the issue at Vaikom was not really opening the temple as such, but allowing Dalits access to the road in front of it. This represented another aspect of struggle for access—that to public spaces, roads, transport, in villages and towns. The question of access to public roads, in fact, had been the first struggle waged by the Pulayas of Kerala and it was only in 1900 that they had won the right to use most of the public roads in Travancore itself (Sardamoni 1980: 147–48). In Tamil Nadu, the right of access to public transportation was an important early issue taken up (Geeta and Rajadurai). These issues existed everywhere. The fight for access to the simple right to walk openly on roads went on continuously, often in small unrecorded struggles. Dalits sought rights to walk down the main streets of villages; to hold their funeral processions and wedding processions within the villages; to use roads simply for their convenience—rather than having to 'sneak around' out of sight and out of mind of the haughty elite. Similarly, Kerala Dalits had to fight a ban against entering public markets, defying traders of only slightly higher castes, engaging in physical confrontations and building confidence (Ibid.: 149).

In many ways, though, it was the fight for education that was central to the struggle for access to the public sphere. Education is fundamental to equal citizenship because it is what primarily creates the capacities to be equal citizens; what is taught—commonly to all the citizens of a nation—is what defines the 'imagined nation'. Again, historically in India, education was unequal and hierarchicized. The denial of access to the Vedas by Shudras and the general monopoly of knowledge by Brahmans was symbolized in the Marathi saying, 'in the house of the Brahmans there is knowledge, in the Kunbi's house grain, in the Mahar's house song'. Along with this, technical knowledge was fragmented according to caste occupation. Thus, monopolization of knowledge was central to the caste hierarchy. These put their stamp on the colonial period. Not only were non-Brahmans as a whole (including those of aristocratic background) slower to take up the education offered, but Dalits were actively excluded. Throughout most of the colonial period, they were excluded from education, or forced to sit outside the schoolroom so as not to pollute upper-caste students.

Education thus became an important area of struggle. In fact it can be noted that the first strike of agricultural labourers was recorded in Kerala when Pulaya labourers, organized by Ayyanakali, fought for their children's right to schools (Ibid.: 149). Phule had begun his career as a social worker by founding schools for girls and Untouchables, and had been the first to raise the demand for universal compulsory primary education—with teachers trained from among the Shudra and Ati-Shudra farmers. Both in Maharashtra and Tamil Nadu, the non-Brahman movements fairly consistently raised this issue. There was also concern expressed for technical education and not just a 'literary' focus.

Formal and legal openness was not enough, the inherited disabilities of caste required positive action. Both Dalits and non-Brahmans demanded, from the very beginning, representation in government services and in education that would be institutionalized through legal quotas, or reserved seats. This was looked on not simply as a matter of historical justice for the former 'low' castes, but also as a question of governance. Phule, for example, had seen the question of Brahman dominance in the bureaucracy as a central feature of its exploitative nature: the 'indolent, luxury-loving white government bureaucrats' and the 'cunning Arya-Bhat black bureaucrats' were said to be hand-in-hand in this exploitation and in grabbing huge pay and pensions for themselves. The nature of government service, including education, thus depended on who had access to this pubic space. And to gain such access, positive measures were needed: a fixed quota system which would give preference in hiring. This meant that conscious account had to be taken of the nature of traditional society, and that specific 'counting' procedures and 'naming' procedures had to be followed to ensure that access was genuinely open. If we recall Phule's question about the Sarvajanak Sabha, this meant a careful look at the actual occupants of the 'public' spaces: Were they truly representative?

This raised uncomfortable questions about the caste hierarchy of the traditional society, which all members of the elite, progressive or conservative, would have preferred to avoid. The elite used the argument of 'merit' in opposition to these demands for reserved positions. This ignored all the questions of the influence of birth and social conditions upon performance, whether in allowing those of more privileged backgrounds to monopolize positions (the question of access) or in conditioning their actions while in public occupations (the question of governance).

Reservations however, were a demand from very early in the anti-caste movement. The proposal was first raised, apparently, in a 1882 book by Jotirao Phule, *Shetkaryaca Asud*, where he argued, 'In reality, until the children of peasants become capable of taking charge of the government administration, Brahmans should not be given governmental positions beyond the proportion of their caste, and the remaining governmental posts should be given to Muslims or British people in India' (Phule 1982: 320). They were first implemented by the anti-Brahman Maharaja of Kolhapur state in Maharashtra, in a 1902 government order reserving 50 per cent of all posts for non-Brahmans. After the Montagu-Chelmsford reforms of 1917, they were demanded by non Brahman and Dalit repesentatives everywhere, and began to be implemented when non-Brahman parties came to power in Madras and Bombay Presidencies, and in south Indian states such as Mysore. Though it took until 1980 for the demand for 'OBC' (in non-Brahman) reservation to come to implementation, since Independence reservation for 'Scheduled Castes' and 'Scheduled Tribes' has become an accepted way of the political order to deal with the disabilities of caste. This represents a triumph for the movement which had always argued that only by recognizing the reality of existing inequalities, not by ignoring them in the name of an abstract 'universality' of merit, could actual equality be achieved and actual merit recognized.

Imagining the Public Sphere

Thus the issues of water, roads, education, employment—all aspects of public life—became central areas of struggle for the anti-caste movement. These struggles served in crucial ways to define the public sphere itself. With these we become aware that the question of the public sphere is not an abstract one of 'realms' but a very concrete one—both in terms of physical space and social relations.

The public sphere can for instance, be defined in geographical-physical terms: in regard to the meeting spaces where people gather to talk and interact: city squares, 'rally' centres, meeting halls, open coffee houses, even cinema theaters. (In a sense these can be contrasted with the ubiquitous wedding halls or *'mangalkaryalay'* which served for the private, caste-defined and regulated large social gatherings or weddings).

The public sphere also needs to be defined in terms of concrete social intercourse; the issue is not simply formal presence or debate between strangers, but discussions among equals. Here the 'public' required to be created in terms of building up new human groupings, through redefined and widened bonds of social intercourse, which involve the sharing of water and food. These aspects of human interaction were precisely what was regulated, hierarchicized and made exclusive within the traditional caste society. In taking up these issues, in struggling for access to such things as water and food, the anti-caste movement was declaring that the new India would be something very different from the feudal caste society. At points it went beyond simple access to issues that involved widening the public sphere: for instance, when in 1936 Ambedkar wrote in 'Annihilation of Caste' that only intermarriage would be able to actually break down the caste system (and linked this with a full-scale attack on traditional Hinduism), this was, in a sense, to insist that such issues as interdining and the right to marry across caste lines were very much areas of public concern. This was of course related to nation-building: whereas the elite, as Chatterjee has noted, tended to define the 'nation' in terms of a spiritual, inner essence, the anti-caste movement radicals were in the process of constituting a very materially defined nation.

At the same time, the symbols of the 'nation' and the public sphere have become important. In fact, the question of 'names'—of roads, buildings, parks—comes up everywhere in regard to public spaces. While public spaces are universal, they are by no means anonymous, and this lack of anonymity, the naming that exists, has very specific implications. Thus the identification of the public, as well as access to the public sphere, has everywhere been a matter of struggle. It sometimes seems as if India has perhaps more statues per square mile than any other country. In every town, men and sometimes women are memorialized in concrete. Streets, roads, public buildings, universities are named after individuals—and the fight over exactly which individuals they should be named after has gone on constantly, linked to the deep sense of identity of the various castes and communities that make up the country.

The process of naming of public spaces has been one of constant struggle. It has been criticized as 'the politics of flags and statues'. Yet there is a reason why this happens. The question is how the public should be identified, what deep emotions and identities among the people it should be linked to. Those use public spaces—buses, universities etc., feel a sense of identity with the nation because they can find in it links to their own historically constituted collective selves. Particularly in a society in which many of these identities have been downgraded, denigrated and discarded, the effort to stamp them upon the public sphere becomes a way for communities hitherto considered 'low' to regain a sense of humanity and dignity.

The 'public sphere' thus does not simply become an abstract collection of rights or an arena of formal equality of members of a society as citizens. It is a real arena that provides for the equality that the modern era demands. It has emotional implications, that embody many of the symbols that represent an emerging 'nation'.

In this sense, the defining and constituting of a 'nation', appeals to 'private' and often fragmented histories, bringing them together in concrete terms by—that is, in Phule's terms, a 'united people'—for the anti-caste is something that takes place in the public sphere.

Constituting the Nation

If we compare the anti-caste movement, especially the Dalit movement with the equally crucial Black movement in the U.S., we can see crucial similarities. Both the Civil Rights and the Black movements can be said to constitute the public sphere as a truly universal one. 'Desegregation' in all areas of social life meant entry for those formerly degraded as slaves and 'niggers', it meant the end of the centuries-long monopoly by those of white skin. In the first 'sit-in,' when Black college students in Greensboro, North Carolina, refused to leave a restaurant because they were not served coffee, they were making a demand similar to those Dalits who organized movements for access to water. The first major mass campaign occurred in 1959 over access to equal spaces on public transport—the Montgomery bus strike. Just as education proved a central issue for Dalits, so it did for Blacks as well, since they put up their hardest fight against the movement to desegregate schools. Blacks fought for housing rights moving into "white-only" neighbourhoods and defied social pressures and violence in the process. Dalits themselves did not make much of a challenge in the villages, though today the "samanthapurams" (villages in which castes are mixed throughout) in Tamil Nadu bear testimony to the effort to desegregate.

These similarities between the Dalit and Black movements have important general implications. They show, for one thing, that democratic citizenship and the formation of a truly universal public is an ongoing process; it may have its roots in the French revolution and 19th century ideals of the 'rights of man', but it can only be realized when these are fought for on the ground of those who have been deprived for ages. Modernity—with all its faith in progress, rationality, universal human rights—was first an abstraction, a dangerous abstraction since large segments of the human population—women, slaves, etc. to take the most obvious examples at the time of the French and American Revolutions—were excluded from the definition. Making abstract modernity concrete, making the rights concrete, means making this public, this citizen truly universal, precisely by taking into account the concrete nature of the exclusions, the way in which historical subordination and hierarchies have interacted with the initial 'modern' to provide a veil for continuing exercise of power. This has required struggle, as these excluded segments have striven for 'entry' and for their own role in defining the public sphere. And this fight has involved what are often called 'identity' issues. What this signifies is that in fact what is sometimes called 'identity politics' is not politics of the past or of 'primordial' identities; it arises out of the effort to make the modern, abstract, universal public truly material and concrete. The achievement of universality requires asking, as Phule did, the kind of question about 'who is a member'—naming those likely to be excluded, turning attention to the names and social identities of the past in order to create the future. The 'crisis of modernity' occurs when this does not happen, when the processes of exclusion continue.

The same consideration applies, of course, to the nation. For the elite, the 'nation' tended to exist at the level of romanticization; from the 19th century this was associated with a spiritual being, originating in a Sanskritic, Vedic, Aryan, 'Hindu' past. This was made concrete with Rama taken as the foundation for a new nationalist mythology, embodying family as well as caste and gender superiority. Anti-caste activists, of course, contested these symbolic identifications—but more important, the nation for them had to be created at a more material, more concrete level, one in which material social relationships—including inter-dining, access to resources such as jobs and land, educational equalities—had to provide the basis for a real sense of unity. This meant creating a public sphere which was truly accessible to all and which embodied the symbols of identity meaningful to all, thus fostering a 'national community' with a sense of real unity.

REFERENCES

Ambedkar, B.R. 1979. *Dr. Babasaheb Ambedkar Writings and Speeches*. Bombay: Government of Maharashtra.

Chatterjee, Partha. 1993. *The Nation and Its Fragments: Colonial and Postcolonial Histories*. New Delhi: Oxford University Press.

Geetha, V. and S.V. Rajadurai. 1998. *Towards a Non-Brahmin Millennium: From Iyothee Thass to Periyar*. Calcutta: Samya.

Moon, Vasant. 2000. *Growing Up Untouchable in India: A Dalit Autobiography*, translated by Gail Omvedt. Boston: Rowman and Littlefield.

Omvedt, Gail. 1976. *Cultural Revolt in a Colonial Society: The Non-Brahman Movement in Western India*. Poona: Scientific Socialist Education Trust.

———. 1994. *Dalits and the Democratic Revolution*. New Delhi: Sage Publications.

Phule, Jotirao. 1982. 'Mahatma Phule Samagra Vannray (Marathi),' in Dnananjay Keer and S.G. Malshe. Trans. by Gail Omvedt. Mumbai: Maharashtra Rajya Sahitya ani Sanskriti Mandal.
————. 1991. *Mahatma Phule Samagra Wangmay* (Marathi). Mumbai: Government of Maharasthra.
Sardamoni, K. 1980. *Emergence of a Slave Caste: Pulayas of Kerala.* New Delhi: Peoples' Publishing House.

PART II

RETRIEVING THE PRIVATE

7

Law's Magic and Empire Revisited: Public Spaces and Private Lives— The Domain of the Law

Rajeev Dhavan

Law's Magic, Claims and Empire

Law is full of magic. It conjures a world of its own and seeks to capture the 'real' world in its own image. Purporting to be a comprehensive statement on the relationship between persons, things, places and events, 'law' orchestrates its mastery over its empire by a mixture of ideology, ideas, rules, procedures, institutions and sanctions. The *ideology* of law portrays the majesty of the 'rule of law' to prevent the chaos of *matsya nyaya* (the law of fish) and emphasizes law's link with justice. The *ideas* of law take shape as 'legal concepts'. Before we know it, our lives are taken over by concepts like ownership, possession, enforceable promises (contracts), obligations rights, wrongs, duties, trust and persons. Such concepts have both an alluring common sense quality, as well as congeal technical meanings. We are rightly reminded that legal concepts—indeed, all legal words—are moulded by law and can be understood only through, and in the context of the legal system (Hart 1954). Such concepts are resilient and can be made to mean anything (Ross 1956). Corporations and idols can be persons. Animals can be punished, but have few, if any, rights (Keeton 1949: 149–50). A teenager may discover that for many purposes he is not a complete person in the eyes of the law. A person may be an owner of property but not have the ownership rights to own, hold or dispose what he owns. Each concept is carefully sculpted to meet an exigent situation—even though it is sometimes claimed that basic legal concepts are universal to all societies—primitive and modern (Gluckman 1970). The *rules of law* · represent the entire gamut of substantive prescriptions which define obligations (*primary rules*), and work in tandem with *secondary rules* which determine the manner in which primary rules are recognized, applied, adjudicated and perforce, changed (Hart 1961). However, some anthropologists recognize that day-to-day practises (which, too, are perceived as obligatory and, therefore, 'law') are enforced as, and by, a series of social pressures (Malinowski 1926) whilst others take the view that some form of secondary determination of obligations by a third party adjudicator (see Gulliver 1973) or someone authorized to impose sanctions is necessary to distinguish 'law' from a mere social rule (Hoebbel 1954). This esoteric controversy has now become arid and cannot explain or encompass the richness of observed and enforced social practice (Abel 1973). The *institutions, procedures and sanctions* of law grow out of the secondary formations of the legal system and disguise the subtle interplay of social and political power and the manner in which it is institutionalized and encrusted in the legal system. In this sense—despite the Supreme Court's protestations—the law is 'class biased' (cf. Justice Hidayatullah in the *Contempt Case* [1970]). In order to keep up appearances, law is necessarily both 'Janus faced' (see Washbrook 1981) and, perhaps, a 'mixed blessing' capable of providing to the very people who it seeks to exploit or control (E. P. Thompson 1975). There is always some play in the joints to do 'justice'. To that extent, law is the potential site of struggle (Dhavan 1981, 1994a). But, this, too, is as much part of the illusion of law as its reality.

But, where exactly does the 'law' come from? Apart from the theological claims which profess that the 'law' is of divine origin but which subtly avoid God being fully responsible for human laws (e.g., Aquinas 1947), social versions of the law construe it to be no more than a social practice re-institutionalized through a range of apparatti which vary from simple to complex societies (Felstiner 1974). Faced with an array of social regimes, 'modern law', backed by the full 'magic' driven concept of sovereignty claimed by the 'State', ruthlessly—and often destructively and with a penchant for assimilating everything in its fold—demanded that all non-State social and legal systems, customs, 'common' or other social laws be subordinated to, if not taken over, by the modern legal system. For the votaries of the 'modern State', such a subordination was absolutely necessary to clear the cobwebs of the past that stood in the way of creating a new political order [Dhavan 1993a]. The first coherent statement of this approach is associated with the writings of Jeremy Bentham who influenced 19th century transitions to the 'modern' legal system mightily. India became a laboratory for this Benthamite dream (e.g., Stokes 1959). The traditional 'old social system of law' was displaced by the new 'modern law' (Galanter 1989: 15–53). The dharmasastra of the Hindu was given legal recognition, but courts were used to subtly re-define and transform its meaning (Dhavan 1994c).

But, despite all this, 'modern law' has not proved to be a self fulfilling prophecy. Its underbelly is hopelessly exposed and its strength greatly undermined whenever a revolution occurs to overthrow the existing legal system. This has happened in various Commonwealth countries and elsewhere. If the law is so majestic and also claims to be committed to justice, why does it crumble so easily in the hands of the usurper—no less the judges and the legal system as everything else? The juristic explanation that the 'law' survives, but the foundation norm (*grundnorm*) on which the legal system rests keeps shifting is hardly convincing and enables the creation of a pro-'usurper' jurisprudence (Cf Harris 1971). Mystery and mystique surrounds where this grundnorm comes from (Stone 1963). This disconcertingly ingenious explanation is traceable to the views of a Viennese philosopher (Kelsen 1949), and provides an apology for revolution. It is not surprising that judges in Pakistan, Rhodhesia, Nigeria, Ghana and elsewhere pounced on this 'grundnorm' doctrine to provide legality for usurpers (Cf. Harris 1971, see Newburg 1995).

However, the underbelly of the 'modern legal system' is not just exposed at times of revolution *but everyday*. The promises of law falter and stumble because it is breached by millions of mutinies, by millions of people in millions of situations. Each breach may not be serious. Some may be. But, the totality of breaches suggests that something else, other than the strictly legal, is constantly taking place—both in addition to and in derogation of the law and legal system. The answer to explain these breaches is not to draw a distinction between the '*validity*' of the system and its '*efficacy*' or simply push for better enforcement of the 'law'. A more discerning examination would reveal that 'modern law' has simply failed to take over or subordinate the various private law systems which continue—often in full force and more strongly—alongside, and in preference to, the modern legal machinery of the State. The persistent and stubborn continuance of 'private' orderings'—sometimes intruding into, the working of the 'modern law system' and sometimes operating not just outside, but in contradistinction and contrary to it— persuades us to look at the multiple legal systems that inhabit modern regimes in an entirely new light. The list of these 'private orderings' is as varied as it is endless. Apart from the family, school and place of work which develop legal systems of their own, group life manifests itself in an array of control systems. These contain enforceable norms of behaviour through a variety of methods. All this cannot just be reductionistically called 'custom' and subordinated to law. These social orderings are the 'living law' (Ehrlich 1936) by which our day to day lives are defined and controlled. The 'mafia' has its own legal system. Such social systems develop amongst 'castes', communities and groups. No less, people seek 'justice in many rooms' (Galanter 1981). Nor are such social orderings purely 'private' in nature. Some of them are massive in their size and dimension—as in labour relations negotiated outside the legal system. Some of them—like the social system described in Mario Puzo's novel, *The Godfather*—enter into the public domain without remorse; and claim to provide protection and revenge on the basis of 'mafiosi' principles. The Naxalites of Andhra Pradesh provide an alternative method for evicting rural landlords and urban tenants for a 'fee' in a manner contrary to—and in substitution of—the state legal system. Society is full of 'lawful' and 'unlawful' arrangements not just to determine disputes, but in order to discipline the lives of people and the inter-active functioning of persons, actions, places and things *inter se*. It is impossible to create a unified and coherent basis on which the various social 'legal systems' interact and collide with each other or explain how they find their relatively autonomous niches and existences.

So far we have looked to the 'sovereign' claims of law and their discontents, without examining what has been called 'Law's Empire'. Is law just an arrangement for determining and applying rights and duties? Although the initial impetus and continued sustenance that prompted the rise of the modern 'sovereignty based' system of law was the political desire to triumph over all competitor legal and political systems, this systemic quest for power was not just concerned with staking a naked usurpation over governance, but making the usurpation look good as an exercise in social justice. Bentham's 'sovereign' (by which he meant 'parliament') was omnicompetent, but politically charged to strive for the utilitarian goal of the 'greatest good' for the greatest number'. (Bentham 1970). Sovereignty and social justice stood hand in hand to bolster the claims of modern law. This grand union created the basis for an interventionist welfare State and its variations. In this reformist mould, the concept of the 'public interest' was prominently used to bolster the demand that all species of 'private' interests or concerns yield to the 'public interest'. Thus, in the Soviet Union, the official legal theorists of the State totally destroyed even theoretical attempts to suggest that there was no need for 'law' in a self governing classless society (Fuller 1948). America's New Deal and its Kennedy-Johnson era exuded a new confidence in the use of law for social purposes. American jurists (or busy bodies, as the case may be) developed export models of 'law and development' (see Seidman 1978) which was later greatly criticized by the American exporters of the models themselves (Trubek and Galanter 1974) and others (Dhavan 1994a).

Nehru's theory and approach to law—on which India's post-independence legal system was built, was greatly influenced by these English, American and Russian perspectives (see Dhavan 1992a, 1992b). But this model has generally failed—not because, as Nehru ruefully observed that 'lawyers had purloined the Constitution', but because social forces (including greed and corruption) caught up with simple versions of the model and destroyed its viability and credibility. India's public interest law movement is partly an attempt to reinforce Nehru's model of law and social change by monitoring the enforcement of rules, programmes and policies. But, in more radical versions of this movement, the direction of change must come from the 'people', with the State as an ally and not the other way round.

But, if law—especially its modern incarnation—is a sophisticated institutionalized expression of powerful forces in society, what are its links with justice? In the sovereignty based political model of law exemplified by utilitarianism and its many 'left' and 'right' descendants, the impetus for social reform and change depends solely on whether the political masters responsible for creating law ensure the creation of good laws. More often that not, this does not happen. There are scores of studies which reveal the multiple purposes for which law is created and the compromises entered into at the time of its creation both for India (see Dhavan (1978b, 1979, 1982, 1990, 1991, 1992c) and abroad (Roshier and Teff (1977: 19–77). Entire regimes—such as Hitler's Nazi Germany or Idi Amin's Uganda—may be wholly tyrannical and yet produce valid 'laws' (Dhavan 1976a). In these circumstances, it is not satisfactory to essay the words of an English philosopher that in any legal system the sheep might enter into the slaughter house, but the system under which this happens would still be a valid legal system.

(Hart 1961: 114). Judges may not be able to stem the tide of such tyranny and may even *validate* the new tyrannical system on the basis of spurious doctrine. The 'political justice' model of law, which leaves issues of justice wholly to the sovereign 'law creator', freaks the moral senses and undermines confidence in the law. Assuming that the norms of justice are determinate (which is contested), the 'modern law' system desperately needs to ground its 'justice' concerns on firmer terrain than the discretion of the legislator. This remains one of the dilemmas of, and a challenge to, modern law. If 'the law is the law' and that is all there is to it without intimations of justice, it would simply be an expression of power—to be obeyed as an act of compulsive social or political necessity and denuded of *social legitimacy*. The working concepts of *legal validity, social legitimacy, obligation to obey the law* and the *imperatives of justice* do not always coalsce—often with disastrous results and incongruities. If 'Laws Empire' were confined to what the legislature says is devoid of justice, its epistemological foundations would crack and it would die a thousand deaths in its struggle for legitimate survival.

The 'rule-discretion' model of law tries to unsuccessfully surmount this problem by claiming that 'justice' concerns enter into the domain of law not just at the stage of the creation of laws but, more significantly, in its administration. No doubt, when laws are created massive compromises are entered into to suit the needs of powerful competing interests. But, it is argued, there is a moral plimsoll line below which the law cannot go. Equally, the administration of law (whether through courts or bureaucracy) is done in the shadow of moral concepts of due process and substantive (including social) justice. But, the 'rule-discretion' model builds justice into the system of law rather than makes justice the foundation of the law. Jurists and judges find hermeneutic answers by evolving 'just' principles of interpretation and applying them to the facts of a case (Cf. Dworkin 1977). But, the bottom line of the rule-discretion approach, which prioritizes rule over discretion, does not resolve the moral indictment arising from the modern law's positivist separation of law from morals. (Cf. Hart 1958). The criticism of the positivist model varies. In one version, the law can never transgress a minimal morality necessary to the law achieving its own purposes (Fuller 1958). In other versions, 'Law's Empire' is vast and can contain multitudes precisely because it is based on egalitarian notions of justice (Dworkin 1986). Invariably, judges faced with uncomfortable laws switch the responsibility back to parliament. In turn, 'parliament' defends its sovereign (and, latterly, democratic) right to determine issues and priorities of social justice. Nehru's principal complaint about the law was that judges stood in the way of achieving the social transformation decreed by parliament.

All this is relevant to our understanding of the relationship between 'law', public spaces and private lives. (*i*) The law uses a large number of magical invocations to claim its mastery of the entire universe—including every part of it. (*ii*) In particular, faced with an array of competing claims, 'modern law' invokes the magical doctrine of sovereignty and its variations to stake a comprehensive claim over all existing and future legal orders (including those in the private domain) which have to be subordinated and yield to modern law. (*iii*) In its reformist incarnation, 'modern law' goes further to evolve a theory of public interest to ensure that every aspect of social life legitimately falls within the domain of modern law. (*iv*) In fact, modern law has been unsuccessful in its quest for a total and comprehensive monopoly to create and enforce appropriate social and legal norms for everyone and every situation in society. (*v*) To the extent to which numerous social legal orders not only exist but have good reasons to do so, these 'private orderings' have their own place in society; and, often, deserve protection as part of the plural bio-diversity of social life. (*vi*) By its own very logic, both the system of modern law, and any law enacted by it, would remain valid— even if divorced from justice. Many crimes are committed in the name of justice. Tyrannical regimes are created. Public space is invented to destroy private choices of the good life. (*vii*) The internal capacity of law to strive for justice at the stage of law-creation and enforcement is not a sufficient guarantee to let an all encompassing modern 'law' and legal system loose on an unsuspecting society which values 'private life' as much as it values intimations of the 'public interest'. (*viii*) The pluralism of society demands a more sophisticated answer to queries over the extent of 'laws empire' which can otherwise stretch as far and as wide as any usurper, benevolent despot, tyrant or crank might want to stretch it. When that happens the domain of law becomes as wide as our political rulers want it to be. Such a situation is unsatisfactory.

The Redefinition of Law and the Public/Private Distinction

The domain of the law depends on both the *design* and the *ambitions* of the 'law'. We have already seen that both the design and ambitions of 'modern law' were driven by ruthless and uncompromising political forces which sought to ensure that all 'politics', 'power', and 'law', would be exclusively brought into the domain of the modern legal and constitutional system to the subordination and, if need be, suppression of all social or other competitors. Law, politics and power were thus nationalized and made the monopoly of the state. The *design* of this *'political'* appropriation of 'law' was that the law created by the sovereign was theoretically all encompassing. Thus, it was left to the *ambition* of the sovereign—be it king, dictator or parliament—to stretch the domain of the law to the maximal or minimal limits, depending on the political flavour and fashion of the day. In contradistinction, in the *dharmic* version of the 'law', the 'law' claims an existence prior to the political rule-making sovereign whose empowerment and actions are themselves controlled by the 'law' or *dharma*. Since our discussion construes ideal types for the purposes of heuristic explanation, it is not necessary to go into the colonial debate in India as to whether the king's political power could triumph over *dharma*. The better view is that it could not. (Derrett 1968: 75–96). It is in line with this *dharmic* version that Antigone told King Creon that he, too, was a creature of and subject to the eternal laws which did not draw their strength from the enactments of today and yesterday but times immemorial. Between the 'political' and *'dharmic'* versions of the law lies a shadow. The struggle for the mastery of this area of shadow is imbricated in the rise, fall and—at present—continued rise of constitutionalism as a new faith which has taken root in some countries but not in others. It is in this sense, that the 'constitution' has been described as the 'civic faith' of America (Levinson 1988).

The resistance to absolutist claims by the sovereign took many forms. In *dharmic* versions, the king simply has to follow *dharma*—giving people the Mahabharata version to kill him like a mad dog if he did not do so (Spellman 1964: 4–8, 20–21). A less complicated arrangment was simply that the king could not violate custom or the common law. This found expression in the hands of a powerful judge like Sir Edward Coke in *Bonham's* case (1610) where the famous fourth propostion articulated the view that even Parliament's Laws which violated the common law's injunction in favour of giving people a right to be heard were void. *Bonham's* case has become an academic celebrity (see Dhavan 1976b: 66–100). American constitutionalism seeking roots in the common law often sought recourse to *Bonham* and other cases even though American courts in the colonial era were most wary of such invocations (Agresto 1986: 40–56). It has been argued that the juristic ethnology of

India's famous *Fundamental Rights case* (1973), by which the Supreme Court decided that the basic structure of the constitution was inviolate and outside the role of the plenary power to amend the constitution, can be traced to the misty origins of the resistance of judge-made law to political claims of sovereign imbricated in the common law (Dhavan 1977) even though the judgement does not refer to those origins and was a reaction to the excessive use of the power to amend the constitution by the Pandit Nehru and Mrs Gandhi regimes (See Austin 1999: 171–292). The Indian Supreme Court's basic structure doctrine has been both technically and substantively criticized (Dhavan 1976b, Malik 1973). No constitution can be static. The courts are aware that they must not overplay their use of 'basic structure' to restrain or restrict the 'political sovereign'. By clever juristic interpolations, the basic structure has been interpreted by Indian Courts so as to give a wide berth to need for change whilst using the principle underlying the 'basic structure' doctrine as a principle of reasoning for bolstering a more elaborate justification for a more entrenched and far flung theory of constitutional limitations.

The logic underlying constitutional limitations is to limit both the expanse and exercise of 'public' power—including the legislative power to make laws. Although the theory of constitutional limitations has been soundly criticized by 'socialists' as taking away the democratic power of a sovereign parliament and handing them to a bunch of judges (Griffiths 1979), it has generally come to stay. In terms of real politic, both the 'sovereign power' as well as the 'constitutional limitations' approach to law are moulded by powerful social and economic forces. The 'sovereign power' approach was needed by commercial and industrial interests to assert their institutionalized will through the sovereignty backed system of 'modern law'—not only to create more public and private space for themselves but to design a system which would permit these forces to monopolize the 'political' and 'legal' power generated by the system. Ironically, the very same 'sovereign power' doctrine was used by 'socialists' in England, democrats in America and Nehruvites in India to seek empowerment for the welfare state. Likewise, the 'constitutional limitations' theory did not have a neutral sociopolitical pedigree. In America, it was used by the States to resist an expansion of federal power. No less significantly, the 'life liberty and due process' provisions were also a vehicle to sustain an economic *laissez-faire* and exclude state intervention in the areas of business, trade, labour laws and social reform (Beard 1913, Miller 1968). The result of this embarrassing misadventure turned out to be fantastic. At one point, every piece of social legislation concerning health, contracts, the working hours of children, and even the power to levy income tax, was declared unconstitutional in favour of the business classes (Agresto 1986: 26–31). So extensive was this 'abuse' of the Bill of Rights provisions to prevent schemes of social reform and distributive justice that the dissenting Justice Holmes was forced to declare that the American constitution did not enact Spencer's social statics (Justice Holmes in *Lochner Case* 1905). Indeed, Nehru's criticism of the judiciary in India and the left wing attack on the judiciary in England articulate the critique that the 'law' has been used to bolster and in-build class bias in the law (Griffiths 1979, Jacob 1992). The double edge of the law produces ironies. The very same provisions of 'life, liberty and due process' which had been used by the courts in India and America to protect the landed and business interests were later used to create rights for disadvantaged races, groups, castes and blacks, support programmes for the poor and design an elaborate due process to defend the rights and liberties of all citizens, especially the oppressed. But whatever the 'uses' and 'abuses' of any system of constitutional limitations and the partisan social biases underlying their application, there is little doubt that any imposition of constitutional limitations affects the re–definition of the 'public' empire claimed by the law and, perforce, the 'private' domain which it should not—but invariably seeks to—transgress.

Constitutional limitations can broadly concern themselves with those concerned with (*a*) the *political* and (*b*) *justice* texts of the constitution respectively. The *political texts* deal with the division of power between the union, constituent states and local government (federalism), the allocation of governance between law makers, executive government and the judges (separation of powers, the parliamentary and presidential system, the civil service) and various other sundry matters (including constitutional amendments). The *justice* texts are concerned with the broad substantive goals of the constitution (as stated in the Preamble or Directive Principles of State Policy in India) including the fundamental rights of the people. Although the responsibility arising out of the 'justice' texts rests on all aspects of governance, the custodianship of the 'justice' texts vests with the judiciary after a long historic and histrionic struggle for judicial supremacy. Nehru's quarrels with the Supreme Court were part of this struggle. Mrs Gandhi's animadversions against the judiciary were less dignified and lacked integrity.

It is not really possible to separate the constitutional limitations contained in the 'justice' and 'political' texts of the constitution. Both impinge on the 'public' space to be occupied by each branch of governance. Both in England and in America, vast battles took place on the limitations imposed by the judiciary on the executive and legislature; and vice-versa. At first, the 'New Deal' controversies in America were over the empowerment of the regulatory and welfare state. After the Second World War, the American Supreme Court created fresh controversies by itself decreeing a new affirmative action, anti rascist, pro civil rights and pro welfare jurisprudence as part of a new procedural and substantive due process. No sooner was this done, the American Supreme Court was criticized for their non-neutral jurisprudence (Weschler 1959). A mighty academic controversy has followed. Indictments have been made of 'government by judiciary' (Berger 1977). In India, judges and others defend judicial activism whilst others opposed it. (Agarwala 1985, Ahmadi 1996a and 1996b, Cf. Andhyarujina 1992, Bhagwati: 1985, D.C. Jain 1986) Most of the controversy revolves around reposing vast powers in the hands of undemocratically selected judges who use a skewed non-participatory process in coming to their decisions to the exclusion of their true role. These are new variations on the old disputes over whether politicians or judges are the true custodians of the constitution. One ingenious suggestion is that the entire Bill of Rights must be read to do no more than strengthen the democratic components of the political process and not concern itself with substantive issues, affirmative action, socio–economic matters or distributive justice which should remain the preserve of political democracy (Ely 1980, Cf. Dhavan 1980). This is old political wine in new juristic bottles. These debates will no doubt continue as a part of the excitement of governance itself.

Disputes over the constitutional limitations imposed by the 'political' and 'justice' texts go to the root of governance and are determinative of the distribution of 'public' power to various constitutional functionaries and the persons and social forces that use, manipulate or control the nature and quality of 'public' intrusions into 'private' space. Adjudication on federalism determines the power of the union and the states. The American Civil War is traceable, in part, to the *Dred Scott* decision (Cases: Dred Scott v. Sandford (1857) on whether 'slaves' were free in only some of the territories of the United States. The Indian Constitution simultaneously gives exclusive powers to the Union and States on many issues and affords 'space' to both on many others. Sometimes—as in India—a residuary power is given to the Union on all the areas of empowerment not specifically enumerated by the constitution. This is not without importance to the quality of democratic governance and accountability. Parliamentarians claim both resources and powers to interact with each other and the citizenry. A legislator has the right to say what he likes about anyone on the floor of the 'house'—with total immunity from prosecution or even proceedings in defamation. Private lives can be indiscriminately exposed in political debates in the legislatures following an exercise of political free speech. Complex relationships emerge out of governance. Powerful private interests control governance—both directly or indirectly or through a systemic use of the process of governance. The demand for transparency in government brings to the surface revelations which expose how social 'influences' pressurize or take over 'public' governance. The more we know about the real working of government the more we realize how tenuous the distinction between the 'private' and 'public' domain is in real life. The Vohra Committee Report (Government of India 1995) revealed the vast nexus between hoodlums and governance in India. If 'public' power is suborned to, and exercised solely for 'private' purposes, the very basis for 'governance' disappears to become a cruel farce. Implicit in modern 'governance' is the assumption that there is a distinct species of empowerment called 'public power' which is more than the sum total of private powers and influences in civil society. The distinction between 'civil' society (the private sphere) and 'political' society (public governance) is founded on this principle. Although clumsy, and not always tenable, it provides a systemic opportunity for the advantaged in a society to institutionalize and usurp 'public' power. Constitutional limitations attached to the political texts of governance, constitute political society and provide it with an indomitable space. Once created, its cup brimeths over. The entire exercise of creating written or unwritten constitutional texts is to create a distinct space in the form of political society and institutionalize its working so as to control access to governance through rule bound institutions. These 'access to governance' mechanisms are complex, imposing, impregnable to some and malleable in the hands of others. As is often remarked, 'you have to play the game according to the rules. But if you can't win, and don't destroy the institution, change the rules'. The creation of an exclusive 'public space' for governance is both neat and problematic. In our times, there is a great resistance to accepting the supposed existence of a '*noumenal*' area of public governance operating with relative autonomy in its own sphere. A demand has been made that more and more of civil society should be *directly* involved in public governance. Many ideas have been generated to give affect to this 'demand', which seeks to weaken if not collapse the distinction between 'civil' and 'political' society. Geographically, this has led to a strengthening of local government—as in the 'panchayat' amendments to the Indian constitution which entrench and empower a three-tier federal structure with the 'third' local layer closer to the people. *Processually,* new procedures have been devised as part of governance to ensure greater participation by ordinary people to be consulted and be made part of decision making. New concepts of due process and natural justice require that all persons be given an unbiased hearing in all matters that directly affect them. The new 'public interest law' increases participation in judicial and administrative process. This benefits some more than the others. The 'advantaged' take over. Non-governmental organizations seek and acquire space—both to advance their perceptions of the public interest, as well as for the career advancement of their members. But, even after boiling all our intimations in cynical acid, the net result of these new developments does not only result in a consolidation of power by the advantaged of the complex avenues of public space. Much rather, there is a strategic opening up of public space which—to borrow a phrase—'taken at its ebb could lead to (democratic) fortune'. Both the nature and quality of space in political society and governance are being opened up especially in post-modern societies in which the state is forced to interact with a much wider catchment of people than ever before.

Constitutional limitations contained in the *justice texts* of governance deal with an increasingly progressive variety of issues. At first, the only such limitations were those connected with life, liberty and property and various rights dealing with criminal due process. The history of American civil liberties till the 1950's demonstrate how these provisions consolidated powerful economic interests and impeded poverty alleviating welfare schemes. The New Deal of the 1930's (as a consequence of which President Roosevelt entered into a conflict with the Supreme Court and threatened to 'pack' the bench) was more concerned with empowering the emerging regulatory and welfare state than with civil liberties. It was only in the latter half of the 20th century that a richer and more humane egalitarian interpretation was given to civil liberties. The Indian Constitution re-defined constitutional goals beyond the confines of civil liberties and religious freedom to include some socio-economic rights dealing with affirmative action, untouchability and exploitation in the enforceable fundamental rights chapter of the Constitution; and, generally articulated constitutional objectives in the form of Directive Principles of State Policy which though not enforceable were, nevertheless, fundamental in the governance of the nation. These were half way measures. Civil and political rights (CPR) could be enforced but economic and social rights (ESR) which were unclearly inseparable and necessary to enjoy CPR depended for their enforcement on the availability of resources. This dichotomy has troubled the quest for justice. It is artificial and status-quoist, lacking in vitality and courage. Successive constitutional arrangements have enlarged the scope of ESR. But the distinctions between CPR and ESR remain. An interesting decision from South Africa gives enforceable substance to housing rights (*South African Housing Cases* 2000). All this affects both the circumference and quality of protected 'private' space. It is a moot question whether such rights can be claimed only against the state or also against other 'private persons'. Issues concerning racial, gender, caste or associational discrimination arise in 'public' as well as 'private' settings—as, indeed, do matters concerning the environment. Whether a person should 'smoke' tobacco is as much a private choice as well as a public concern. 'Private' concerns and choices are often portrayed by legislation or judicial interpretation as public wrongs. This dilutes legal distinctions between 'public' and 'private' aspects of the law.

Private rights can be classified into various kinds which define the nature and dimension of the private domain of the right holder. Thus, a distinction has been made between 'rights', 'liberties', 'powers' and 'immunities' (Hohfeld 1923). The design of a right determines the kind of private space afforded by the constitutional limitations in the 'justice' texts of governance to the person claiming the right. Certain *rights* clearly demarcate *'non-invasive'* spaces prohibiting others from either (*a*) entering the protected space (e.g. the privacy of a home, or the body the reputation and confidential information of a person or group) or (*b*) preventing the protected person of the right to self expression and choice (such as free speech and freedom of ideas, religious beliefs, social practice or worship). Alongside run *'invasive'* regimes which permit society or the state to enter into the lives of individuals ostensibly to (*a*) protect society or the individual himself or (*b*) ensure that other individuals are not discriminated against or maltreated. Thus, 'discrimination law' has been circumspect about interfering with the domestic lives of people or violating the working privacy of small firms or clubs but increasingly does so. Where there is domestic violence, the 'privacy' of the home may be invaded to prevent the maltreatment of its incumbents. Matrimonial law not only invades the 'private' sphere of the family but restructures the personal relationship between husband and wife, determines who shall have the custody of the children and divides the family property and resources irrespective of who owns it. Television is a matter of watching programmes in the privacy of the home, but regulatory provisions determine what can be watched by whom and when. In virtually every area of life, various public policies and laws seek to ensure equity, fairness and equality of treatment in both 'public' and 'private' arenas of life on an ever expanding scale. Employees cannot be appointed or sacked without due process. But the state and individuals are expected to be fair in their dealings—with a greater responsibility vesting in the state. But apart from 'non-invasive' rights, both state and society exude a responsibility to provide what may be called *quality of life* enhancing rights. Many of these were originally mainly the responsibility of the individual, family or group. But, the 'public interest' dispensation of our times introduces positive welfare obligations in both civil society and the state to provide food, housing, education and health as well as promote the right to clean air, water and environment for all. It is on the progressive achievement of these 'quality of life' enhancing rights that the viability of a person to be a human being depends. What is interesting—and, perhaps, ironic—in this swing of the pendulum, from the State's claims to empowerment to benefit the people to a comprehensive 'rights based' approach, is that both precipitate highly intrusive agendas into the 'private domain', the 'personal spaces' of individuals and the day-to-day lives of people. The discretion of people to order their own lives grows smaller and smaller because in this new dispensation they are expected to be 'fair', 'just' and 'egalitarian' in every aspect of their lives in relation to friends, children, well wishers, detractors, enemies, employers, employees, the work place, home and hearth. This omnibus projection of the possible consequences of the 'public duty' of 'private fairness' is more than slightly overwritten. But, it remains a directional trajectory which inevitably flows from the new social justice and due process priorities of our times. The results could be startling. Our lives could be jettisoned from every quarter. In the name of freedom for all, we could lose all our freedom.

The 'law' continues to manifest a technical and processal fidelity to the 'public/private' distinction. Consistent with this distinction, 'public law' relates to (*a*) the power of the state and state controlled agencies and (*b*) the restraints which attach to their working whether arising out of due process, human rights, social justice concerns or otherwise. The circumference of 'public law' has been greatly enhanced by an increase in the functions, powers and responsibilities of the state which in turn, has come to include not just the formal institutions of state but also agencies owned or controlled by them or over whom they exercise a pervasive influence. (See M.P. Jain 1986: 461–65). 'Public law' breaks up into many components—constitutional governance, administrative law, laws relating to police power, regulatory law and, of course, the law relating to human rights. What is of further significance and importance is that in many countries special and exclusive procedures and institutions have been devised to deal with 'public law' issues. Apart from special regulatory procedures and new institutions, some of these special procedures relate to governance by the state and the enforcement of fundamental rights. France's *droit administatif* deals specifically with the administration. The English system of judicial review has built up a body of judicial review of administrative action and reposed this power and responsibility exclusively in the higher judiciary. India has copied the English system; and, further constituted the High Court and Supreme Court as special, and, arguably exclusive, arenas to enforce constitutionally guaranteed fundamental rights. This is both a technical as well as a political arrangement so that senior and skilled judges dealt with matters of State. But, the consequences of all this is to ensure the distinctiveness of 'public law' as a species of law. Those in charge of governance find it easier to keep control of matters concerning the state within a tight circle of arrangements. Radical ambitions within the law find resistance from within the legal system when they try and collapse the 'public/private' distinctions to break this tight circle of arrangements. Thus, in India, I have argued that relief in 'fundamental rights' cases should be available from local district civil courts and not exclusively from the High Courts and the Supreme Court who, presently, exercize a monopoly over this dispensation. There is a constant endeavour to open up the public law system to make it more flexible. This does not always succeed. Cosy arrangements of this nature are not without functional value to those who aspire to control the system of governance. But they pose a danger to 'Law's Empire' by breaking it into distinct technical parts.

The strategy of the modern law system is to pose a distinction between 'political' and 'civil' society, subordinate the latter to the former, and contain 'political' society into a distinct and unique system governed by its own rules of checks and balances. This process has transited through the many stages of 'conquest', 'expansion', 'consolidation' and 'retreat'. The conquest ensured the supremacy of the system as a whole. Expansion enabled more and more to be brought into the public domain. The process of consolidation tightened the grip over the system and enabled its systemic use and exploitation. Retreat flows from the radical onslaught by 'democratic' forces to get their piece of the action. But while conquest, expansion and consolidation were legitimated on utilitarian principles to empower the state, the retreat is founded on an egalitarian liberal principles demanding 'justice' for all in all arenas of our lives—both public and private. This will inevitably affect the balance of freedom available to individuals and groups to organize their lives as they choose.

Reformist Agendas, Civil Liberties, Privacy and Group Life

Reformist agendas—whether emanating from the State or directly from civil society—infringe civil liberties in the name, and for the protection of a higher order of liberties for all within the framework of a 'just' society. In its original 'modern' incarnation, the state simply sought an overall self-empowerment to preserve public order, its own institutional viability and to advance the cause of justice. The script of state empowerment has been increasingly and invariably vastly re-written over the years so that its functionaries both actually and potentially intrude into the lives, relationships, work and business of people. Justifications for this over-empowerment of the State are made on various bases. *First*, it is argued that the state alone has the status and capacity to take over powerful forces in civil society and discipline them into a just framework. No doubt, the 'state' is not *sui generis* and is often partly controlled by the very forces it seeks to discipline. But, it claims both a relative operational autonomy as well as a sensitivity to democratic values—an assumption which is less credible in some societies than others. *Second*, it is asserted that the State has a duty to provide welfare and social justice for all and equitably re-distribute resources through a variety of complex methods in order to achieve this goal. *Third*, it is suggested that the State has no other choice but to protect civil liberties from chaos. This entails creating schemes of due process to discipline both the State and society to ensure that they operate on the basis of principles of fairness. Reformist agendas impose *fairness not just in relation to the state's own operations or in the corporate or business world but also to ensure egalitarian fairness in areas of private life.* Thus, the 'law' has stepped into ensure fairness in family life, regulate divorces and custody, prevent domestic violence and, *inter alia*, ensure fair schemes of maintenance and common property on the basis of principles of gender justice. Absolutist theories of freedom of contract are no longer available to business which are subject to corporate regulation and anti trust laws as well as laws relating to labour. Group life is not a law unto itself. There are limits to what groups can do in relation to their own members and objectives. The personal laws of communities are often found wanting—and especially gender unjust. In the aftermath of *Shah Bano's* case (1985), which applied the 'secular' law of maintenance in favour of Muslim women, the government ducked the formidable question of reforming 'personal' laws which were unfair to women. Individuals are often to defend and promote the public interest or social justice. A difficult example is that of 'hate speech'. Freedom of speech and expression is cherished both as part of the individual's expression and for democracy. But, vast areas of speech—as for example communal, racist or sexist expressions—are often punished and banned. These demands are supported by powerful—often politicized—forces in civil society. Salman Rushdie's *Satanic Verses* suffered a 'customs' ban to assuage Muslim sentiments. Hussain's paintings were destroyed by Hindu fundamentalists who also opposed celebrating St. Valentine's day in the year 2001 because it was portrayed as something foreign and undesirable even if ordinary people wanted to celebrate the romance in their lives on that date. The quest for social and regulatory control and massive interventions in our day to day's lives do not just come due to the 'private' agenda's of tyrannical rulers, bureaucracy or police. In fact, most of the dilemmas over corrective interventions which intrude into the privacy and civil liberties of people come from reformist agendas devised by the State or civil society—often as part of the political fashion of the day. This is not to suggest that all such reformist agendas are intrinsically suspect. Some are. But many of these agendas are inherently problematic and pose real dilemmas in the quest for finding a balance between governance, social justice and individual and group freedom.

Looked at from the managerial point of view of governance, various demands and interests that contend for recognition (including those relating to human rights and responsibilities) need to be 'managed', reconciled supported or suppressed. But a distinction needs to be drawn between the *compulsions* of governance and its *purposes*. The compulsions of governance proceed from real, imagined and contrived necessities created or fuelled by powerful or populist interests. The *purpose* of governance is to secure the good life for all in a fair and equitable manner by enabling all persons and groups to have the capacity, will and empowerment to script their own choices about their individual social and environmental future under conditions of equal opportunity, including equity between generations. In an often-overlooked passage in *Capital* Marx distinguishes between human and non-human endeavours:

Labour is, in the first place, a process in which both man and Nature participate, and in which man of his own accord starts, regulates, and controls the material re-actions between himself and Nature. He opposes himself to Nature as one of her own forces, setting in motion arms and legs, head and hands, the natural forces of his body, in order to appropriate Nature's productions in a form adapted to his own wants. By thus acting on the external world and changing it, he at the same time changes his own nature. He develops his slumbering powers and compels them to act in obedience to his sway. We are not now dealing with those primitive instinctive forms of labour that remind us of the mere animal. An immeasurable interval of time separates the state of things in which a man brings his labour-power to market for sale as a commodity, from that state in which human labour was still in its first instinctive stage. We pre-suppose labour in a form that stamps it as exclusively human. A spider conducts operations that resemble those of a weaver, and a bee puts to shame many an architect in the construction of her cells. But what distinguishes the worst architect from the best of bees is this, that the architect raises his structure in imagination before he erects it in reality. At the end of every labour-process, we get a result that already existed in the imagination of the labourer at its commencement. He not only effects a change of form in the material on which he works, but he also realises a purpose of his own that gives the law to his modus operandi, and to which he must subordinate his will. And this subordination is no mere momentary act (Marx 1974: I, 173–4).

The purpose of governance cannot be subordinated to its compulsions. Its priorities have to be reworked accordingly.

The distribution of individuals and groups in a society invariably depend on prioritizing some part of a bundle of rights over others. This is often done on the basis of questionable criteria. The Indian Constitution's separation of 'enforceable' fundamental rights and 'unenforceable' directive principles is based on the 'dustbin' logic that whatever was not agreed upon was relegated to the chapter on the unenforceable Directive Principles of State Policy. Likewise, Economic and Social Rights (ESR) were internationally covenanted into a separated convention because they were politically problematic and raised questions of finding resources to give effect to them. The priority status accorded to 'civil liberties' assumes that all persons will have similar and equal opportunities to enjoy them—an assumption not vouchsafed to three—quarters of the world's population. Yet, it is possible to separate certain rights and treat them as subject to a more rigorous threshold of non-negotiability even when confronted with reformist agendas. These are broadly the 'private' rights of a person which relate to protecting the body, home, thoughts, belief, personal information and relationships from unwanted non-consensual invasive intrusions. These 'private' rights which protect the mind, body and home from invasion are not just negative in nature but defend and enhance 'freedom' of thought, belief and expression and the right to define one's own persona and personal and other relationships in pursuit of a person's own view of the good life. Such rights are not just enjoyed by individuals but also groups. The 'good' life is also defined in terms of, and by, the various traditions, practices cultures and belief systems that bring people together. If the bio-diversity of individuals adds to the colour and variety of human life, a multi-cultural society protects this diversity with passion. Both the private rights of an individual as well as providing due protection to the multi-cultural diversity of group life deserve priority attention. Neither are *sui generis*. Individuals cannot claim absolute support for everything they may wish to do. Nor are all 'groups' just and fair in their dealings. But together, the private rights of individuals and 'groups' mark out a 'private domain' that invites special protection. This is not to ignore the importance of various other rights that makes these rights possible, but simply to state an emphasis.

The law has been reluctant to recognize 'privacy' as a distinct right. Way back in a landmark article on 'privacy' in 1890, a case was made out for the recognition of 'privacy' whilst accepting that there was no composite legal right to 'privacy' which encompassed a series of rights which, if brought together, provided that protection (Warren and Brandies 1890). In this configuration, the law protected the body and mind of a person from assault and battery, protected the *home* from trespass, the reputation from defamation and various other aspects of life from other intrusions. Over the years, these classifications have been made more sophisticated. But for many years, 'privacy' was not recognized as a distinct actionable wrong. People could not go to court and claim that their right to privacy was invaded. Instead, 'privacy' in law continued to be seen as a collection of distinct rights which protected the body, person, persona, reputation and confidential relations of an individual. 'Confidentiality' was recoganised as a distinct interest worthy of protection much later. The extent of this protection remains blurred even in the newer dispensations dealing with freedom of information. It has, thus, been legitimately argued that 'privacy' is not a composite right but merely an 'idea'—an alluring exercise in 'persuasive definition' eclipsing the fuzzy realities of the law (Dhavan and Kennedy 1979). However, the cause of 'privacy' to be recognized as a distinct right received a boost in constitutional cases in America which read 'privacy' as a component of the right to life and liberty to protect individuals from invasive intrusions such as electronic and other eavesdropping, compulsive medical treatment and so on. In India, a basis for including 'privacy' as a constitutionally guaranteed fundamental right arose in 1964 in a case of nocturnal police surveillance; and, more specifically in 1995 (*Privacy Case* 1964, ibid 1975, ibid 1994). Since then at least one politician has successfully got injunctive relief against journalist writers in a case founded on both 'privacy' and 'defamation'. (see *Maneka Gandhi Case* 1997). Those not involved in the technicalities of the law may find these squabbles as to whether 'privacy' is a separate cause of action protecting a distinct right too sophisticated by half. To some extent, they would be right; but not entirely. Open textured rights like 'life', 'liberty', 'privacy' and the like have to be re-defined and deconstructed into material particulars to define the exact contours of what they actually protect. We are back where we started. 'Privacy' is a bundle of rights contained in an emotionally alluring imaginative idea (Dhavan and Kennedy 1979). But, in its present incarnation, 'privacy' as defined in 'common law' systems is a *passive* rather than an active right. It protects the person, home, reputation, confidentiality and related areas of a person's life from intrusions by others. But the *active* components of a person's life are the freedom to *do* what he wants, *go* where he wants, *say* what he want, *'believe' and 'practice'* whatever faith he wants and *relate* to whoever he wants. This right, to 'do', 'go', 'say', 'think', 'believe and practice' and 'relate to' what and whom he wants, do not fall within the distinct areas of the right to 'privacy' but are a part of the wider canvass of 'freedom' contained in the rights relating to liberty (to *do* what one wants), free speech (to *say* what one wants) religious freedom (to *think, believe* and *practice* what one wants) and freedom of association, business and personal relations (to relate to whom and what one wants). The right to property which was used by the rich as a vehicle to protect their economic interests, was abolished as a guaranteed fundamental right in India in 1979. This was a political over-reaction. It was a symbolic waving of the flag of social justice which over looked the fact the poor also need to defend the property rights they possess. In fact, it has been suggested that the right to welfare should be recognized as a property right (deFriend 1979). But, it is unlikely that a modified right to property will be re-introduced in the Indian Constitution. The controversial history of the right to property haunts its future. Privacy is an insufficient vehicle to protect the entire gamut of rights that protect the viability of individual persons and human endeavour. But 'privacy' read with the other freedoms constitutes the 'private domain' of a person or group which needs protection from both the 'public' intrusions of the state and by civil society.

The area of group life which constitutes a part of the 'private' domain has received insufficient attention in both 'public' and 'private' law. This is not surprising. The architect of India's Constitution, B.R. Ambedkar, had no qualms about declaring that the 'individual' and not the 'group' was the basic unit on which the Constitution was based (see Dhavan and Nariman 2000). As an 'untouchable', Ambedkar had suffered greatly at the hands of the 'group'. But, at the same time, the Constitution that he helped to create not only celebrates 'group life' as part of the diversity of India but also caters to the interests of endemically disadvantaged groups through a wide species of affirmative action provisions. The 'group' represents a significant area of 'private' life and simultaneously commands a 'public' presence. Groups abound, ranging from religious associations, caste and tribal formations, gender based bonding, non-governmental organizations, new and old 'societies', trusts, labour unions, voluntary associations and many others. These 'groups' vary in status, social power and prestige. Some 'groups' are very powerful not just in their own 'private' sphere, but more generally in the public domain to exercise a pervasive direct and indirect influence on governance. Due recognition needs to be given to the multicultural variations of group life that emanate from society. Group life is as valuable a right and social interest deserving of recognition and protection as individual freedom (Dhavan and Nariman 2000, Kymlicka 1989 and 1995).

However, no group is *sui generis*. Ambedkar's life and concerns show how various groups and communities can be invidious in their dealings with their own members and others. Many questions arise. Can groups be permitted to be a law unto themselves without any regulation? Should such regulation be limited to clothing the group with a legal personality even if that? Can a scheme of administrative or financial accountability, be imposed on a 'society', trust or religious endowment? Can the 'state' go further and take over the management of temples permanently—as has been done for so many temples in India (See generally Dhavan 1978a, Dhavan and Nariman 2000). Deeper issues can be raised. If groups are not treated as *sui generis*, what happens with groups which amass arbitrary powers to themselves and their institutions and behave in a discriminatory unfair or tyrannical manner? Can 'private' groups indulge in caste, gender or racist or communal discrimination? If so, to what extent? Should a religious group have unlimited power to excommunicate its members? Should some due process be attached to this process of excommunication? Can groups be gender unjust in their private dealings and controlled only if they enter the public domain? Can certain associations—like the Ku Klux Klan or others—be banned altogether? And, if we go one step further, what is the human rights, legal or constitutional status of 'personal laws', including Hindu, Islamic, and other laws? Are they part of the 'private domain' of these faiths or are they in the 'public domain'? Faced with these dilemmas, the Supreme Court of India brushed the issues arising in respect of personal laws under a constitutional carpet. Accordingly rights arising out of religion based 'personal laws' can be enforced in ordinary courts of law, but invidious practices congealed in uncodified personal laws cannot be declared invalid and contrary to the 'equality mandate' of the Constitution because the very same 'laws' which are enforceable in a court of law are not treated as 'laws' which attract the 'fundamental rights' chapter of the Constitution! (*Personal Law Case 1997*). Such a decision is both clever as well as skewed if not juristically dishonest. The truth is that Parliament does not want to risk reforming 'personal laws' because it fears a social back lash. So, the problem is passed on to the judiciary. In turn, the judiciary passes the buck back to parliament. We are still left with the basic issue of finding a balance between protecting the integrity of group life and ensuring that groups are not corrupt, arbitrary, unfair or unjust in their dealings with others as well as their own constituent members or adherents. Assuming it was desirable, a Mustapha Kemal may have possessed the power to 'cleanse' traditional life and modernise it in Turkey. Nehru both respected group life and was fearful of its invidiousness (see Dhavan 1992a). The Indian Supreme Court's score card on group rights has been confused—wavering *from* an assimilative passion for over regulation in the name of 'modernity' *to* finding a sensitive balance between group rights, individual freedom and the need for state regulation (see Dhavan and Nariman 2000). This is equally true of the unresolved dilemmas raised by the antimonies of group life in other parts of the world.

A great deal of care and caution is required in resolving the priorities of the 'private domain' against the 'public interest'. At one extreme, individuals and groups are treated as *sui generis* and, therefore, relatively untouchable. At the other extreme, demands of the 'public interest' intimate the need for the control, regulation and invasion of the private domain of both individuals and groups. In between, lie a massive array of arguments and bargaining positions. Reformist agendas are both suspect and bonafide. In some agendas, all 'traditional' associations are required to be assimilated into a 'modern' society. Some reformist agendas—like those of Hindu fundamentalists in India—have simply been evolved to have a 'go' at other communities. Some agendas concentrate on preserving the rich diversity of individual and group life; but seek to cleanse society from injustice—especially gender injustice. Priorities have to be re-worked. If people and groups are not *sui generis*, neither are reform agendas. But a balance needs to be worked through so that individuals and groups do not acculturate arbitrary and unjust powers which can be discriminatingly malexercized against others. This is not easy. But, in a post modern society, we need to recover a great deal of lost ground to reverse the undue and hasty passion with which 'modernity' claimed the world in its own image for its own sake.

Revisiting Law's Empire

The empire of modern law knows no limits. It expects all things, great and small, to yield to its self declared pre-eminence. But, living people, driven by their own compulsions are much too stubborn to yield to the imperial claims of the law. They resist—to set up their own version of the 'good', and ever so often, 'bad' life. The law strikes back—with brute force as well as subtlety. When claims of divinity fail, the law claims to come from a 'sovereign'. When the 'sovereign' is found to be a front for the powerful in society, the law claims to represent a wider 'public policy' in the 'public interest'. When these invocations are discerned as vague and dangerous, the 'law' is linked to 'justice'. When justice is found to favour the advantaged, the script of 'law' is re-written to proclaim a wider 'equality', and 'social justice' for all. There is no end to the inventive genius of the 'law' which further reinforces its empowerment through a web of legal ideas and concepts. The career of law in the 20th century has been to demand more and more power to effect its elusive purposes. This thirst for power—albeit in the name of social justice—precipitates an on-going confrontation between the 'law' and the various 'private' orderings that define peoples' lives.

In fact, there is not just one but many kinds of laws in society. The rise of the modern nation State was predicated on a distinction between 'civil' society and 'political' society and giving 'sovereign' control to the latter over the former. The modern 'legal' and 'political' system was created in the form of a 'State' which sought to subordinate, control and assimilate all other social and legal systems in society and create ground rules on how the institutionalized power of the legal and political system of the State could be accessed. These ground rules favoured the advantaged, but—with increasing democratization—could not remain insensitive to the demands and aspirations of the disadvantaged. But the triumph of 'political society'—including its grand legal system— over social resistance was not a foregone conclusion. The various plural orders in society continued to mark out their own 'private' domain even if the 'law' did not permit it. In turn, 'modern law' had no other choice to respond to the infinite resistances of civil society. Concessions were wreaked out from the modern legal and constitutional system to protect 'private' domains. At first, the 'private domains' that obtained protection were mostly business, landowners and the advantaged. But, the system was not unyielding to demands from others—if for no other reason than the cynical perception that the entire system of governance would suffer a 'legitimation crisis', exhibit contradictions and become unmanageable if such concessions were not made (Habermas 1976, Unger 1976).

Theoretically, modern law continues to claim suzerainty over every aspect of our lives. In practice, this claim suffers diminution—both within and without the law. Externally, the law's writ has no meaning over what it cannot possibly control or even regulate. Internally the law has had no choice but to recognize the existence of areas of relative autonomy within society and accomodate their demands. 'Customary practices'—including religion based personal laws—were recognized but re-defined and controlled through the judicial process. Bills of Rights, in the form of 'constitutional limitations' on the 'sovereign' power created enclaves of 'protected private space' which were, more often than not, used almost exclusively by the well-off to advance their interests. It was only in the latter part of the 20th century that the 'new' constitutions—such as those of India and South Africa—increased and consolidated this 'protected space' to specifically include for recognition the 'social justice' concerns of the poor and disadvantaged. But, the willingness of the 'law' to expand its social concerns inevitably led to an expansion of both the capacity and the empowerment of the law to enable social justice. With this massive empowerment in place, the 'State' virtually became a law unto itself to unleash its arbitrariness over society whose betterment it had mandatorily sworn to protect. With technological advances, both the power of the 'State' and powerful forces in society grew further. For the menace was not just the power of the 'state', but also that of others—including corporates and mutinationals. The dilemmas increased. If it was left to the 'state' to control the powerful, the power of the 'sate' itself would increase. And, if the social justice concerns to create a fair and unjust society were to extend into the 'private' dominions of hearth, home and group life, little would be left of peoples' 'private' lives when pitted against the extraordinary powers ranged against them. Yet, at the same time, no social justice programme worth its salt could ignore violence within the family or racism or casteism in the work place. Faced with this new 'Leviathan', the doctrine of 'privacy' was invented to create an 'inner protected area' within an expanded Bill of Rights which was more inviolate than the rest. In fact, the resurrection of the notion of 'privacy' to defend the 'inner space' of individual life does not provide a concrete protection. The 'inner space' is not really inviolate. It is impossible to argue that even within this 'inner protected space' people were free to inflict injury, humiliation and unjustice to each other. All that will happen is that the judiciary would extend a stricter scrutiny and surveillance over violations of this inner space. This, in turn, would depend on the mood of the judicial system and the judges who give effect to it. Such an arragement is weak and vacillating; and, hardly inspiring.

In this, we cannot be guided by the *compulsions* of governance but its *purposes*. If the purposes of governance are to protect the right of all persons and groups to define their version of the group life, two agendas emerge. The broad 'private domain' agenda seeks to protect the diversity of individual and group endeavour. The 'reformist agenda'—whether emanating from 'civil society', political tumult or government—seeks to ensure that the 'private domain' does not become an unjust law unto itself. These 'agendas' interact and conflict with each other. Their interactive equities need to be fundamentally re-examined. Nothing will be left of the private domain of our personal lives, choices and creativity if these are easily surrendered to the public domain. Nor can the public domain remain an exclusive cosy arrangement for those who will pave away their lives to exercise power over others. 'Public' governance cannot ignore egregious private injustices No less, the 'private domain' of individuals and groups cannot become a vehicle for powerful individuals and groups to develop their personal fiefdoms or empires. While seeking to influence and control the exercise of power in the public domain. However, in our quest for social justice the very purpose of governance would be lost if the freedom to be what we are and want to be is lost to some higher purpose which seeks to protect all of us for its own sake.

The juxtaposition of a responsible 'public domain' committed to social justice against unjust 'private enclaves' of social life takes a topsy turvy view of ground realities and issues of principle. It reinforces Hobbesian assumptions that people are not fit to rule themselves. A hierarchy is created between the 'public domain' and 'private life'—according a lesser priority and significance to the latter. In the 20th century, the 'state' imposed itself on society albeit, supposedly, for the common good—with electoral democracy adding musical chairs to peoples' choices. In the incoming 21st century, a more real peoples' centred democracy must move towards viewing 'law' and 'state institutions' with less veneration to enable more and more self governance for both people and group life. In the new, and hopefully emerging configuration, the artificial distinction between 'civil' and 'political' society—and, perforce, the 'public/private' distinction which flows from it—would diminish. The 'state' and 'law' would be just another domain—working alongside, and not in supercession of, other social domains. This will enable a fundamental re-examination of democratic governance itself as well as the place of law within it. To carry the baggage of modern law—as, indeed, the awesome concept of the 'public domain' on which so much of its working rests—into the incoming century would eclipse our vision from the endless possibilities of democratic self governance. A new and fresh look at the possibilities of social democracy will not blunt the fight for social justice, but enhance it by firmly reposing it with people other than governments, bureaucrats and judges.

What is at issue here is not the entitlement of all peoples to social justice, but the system of governance by which it is to be achieved. In its imperial reincarnation as modern law, the law demands a near total surrender to its often whimsical and exaggerated claims. The terms of this surrender are onerous. Taken to its limits, the 'law' usurps even our own struggle to fight for social justice and define our version of the good life. (This is not to suggest a premium does not attach to prioritise the struggle for social justice for all.) Nor is it the case that 'law' cannot be actively suborned to this struggle. But, people at the receiving end of the law need to be wary about it. It is not a gift from Olympus but a creation of society—enmeshed with all the contradictions that society itself is heir to. The law has been as much an enemy of the badly-off as it claims to be their friend. Its track record has been uneven, often dismal. Its 'empire' needs to be dismantled. Its claims need to be cut down to size. Looked at from below, the law is best a site for struggle. This is equally true of any 'public domain' marked out by the law in the public interest. This can only happen if it is designed to be vulnerable to appropriation for the just claims of all, especially the badly-off. As soon as we recognize that 'law' is a social creation which has to be forced and disciplined to work with other 'legal' orders in society, the grandness of its omnicompetence is cut down to size. This necessitates the need for a larger rejection of the very basis on which modern law claims and extends its dominium. Electoral political democracy as we know it cannot vouchsafe either democracy or justice. The quest for both must lie in the multiplicity of people's social orderings which compose society with all its discontents. An important step in the right direction is to unmask the law and keep its public interest dominion under strict surveillance. As we transit into the next century, we need to view the law for what it is. Not what it most artfully claims to be.

REFERENCES

Abel, R. 1973. 'A Comparative Theory of Dispute Settlement Institutions in Society,' *Law and Society Review*, vol. 7, p. 217.

Agarwala, S.K. 1985. *Public Interest Litigation in India*. Bombay: N.M. Tripathi.

Agresto, J. 1986. *The Supreme Court and Constitutional Democracy*. New Delhi: Prentice Hall.

Ahmadi, A.M. 1996a. 'Zakir Hussain Memorial Lecture,' 2 *SCC* (Jul), pp. 1–15.
_____. 1996b. 'Speech on Justice Process,' 4 *SCC* (Jul), pp. 1–10.

Andhyarujina, Tehmtan R. 1992. *Judicial Activism and Constitutional Democracy*. Bombay: N.M. Tripathi.

Aquinas, St. Thomas. 1977. *Summa Theologica*. New York: Benzinger Bros. Inc.

Austin, G. 1966. *The Indian Constitution: Cornerstone of a Nation*. Oxford: Oxford University Press.
_____. 1999. *Working a Democratic Constitution: The Indian Experience*. New Delhi: Oxford University Press.

Beard, C. 1913. *An Economic Interpretation of the Constitution of the United States*. New York: Macmillan.

Bentham, J. 1970. *An Introduction to the Principles of Morals and Legislation*. London: Athlone Press.

Berger, R. 1977. *Government by Judiciary: The Transformation of the Fourteenth Amendments*. Cambridge: Harvard University Press., Mass.

Bhagwati, P.N. 1985. 'Judicial Activism and Public Interest Litigation,' *Columbia Journal of Transnational Law*, vol. 23, pp. 561–77.

deFriend, R. 1979. 'Welfare Law, Legal Theory and Legal Education,' in M. Partington and J. Jowell (eds), *Welfare Law and Policy*. London,: Frances Pinter.

Derrett, J.D.M. 1968. *Religion, Law and the State in India*. London: Faber and Faber.

Dhavan. R. 2000. 'Judges and Indian Democracy: The Lesser Evil?' in Francine Frankel (ed.), *Transforming India: Social and Political Dynamics of Democracy*. New Delhi: Oxford University Press.
_____. 1999. 'Kill Them for their Bad Verses: On Criminal Law and Punishment in India,' in Rani D. Shankardass (ed.) *Punishment and the Prison: Indian and International Perspectives*. New Delhi: Sage Publications.
_____. 1994a. 'Law as Concern: Reflecting as Law and Development' in Yash Vyas and K. Kibwana (eds), *Law and Development in the Third World*. Nairobi: Faculty of Law, University of Nairobi.
_____. 1994b. 'Law as Struggle: Public Interest Law in India,' *Journal of the Indian Law Institute*, vol. 36, pp. 302–38.
_____. 1994c. 'Dharmasastra and Modern Indian Society: A Preliminary Exploration,' *Journal of the Indian Law Institute*, vol. 34, pp. 515–40.
_____. 1993a. 'Law, State and Sovereignity'. Mimeo.
_____. 1992a. 'Introduction', in R. Dhavan (ed.), *Nehru and the Constitution*. Bombay: N.M. Tripathi.
_____. 1992b. 'If I Contradict Myself, Well, Then I Contradict Myself ….
Nehru, Law and Social Change,' in R. Dhavan (ed.), *Nehru and the Constitution*. Bombay: N.M. Tripathi.

Dhavan. R. 1992c. 'Mining Policy in India: Patronage or Control' *Journal of the Indian Law Institute*, vol. 34, pp. 218–46.

_____. 1991. 'Power without Responsibility: On Aspect of India's Patent's Legislation' *Journal of the Indian Law Institute*, vol. 33, pp. 1–75.

_____. 1990. '"Whose Interest": India's Patent Law and Policy' *Journal of the Indian Law Institute*, vol. 32, pp. 429–77.

_____. 1987. *Only the Good News: On the Law of the Press in India*. New Delhi: Manohar.

_____. 1982. *Contempt of Court and the Press*. Bombay: N.M. Tripathi.

_____. 1981. 'Managing Legal Activism: Reflections on India's Legal Aid Programme,' *Anglo American Law Review*, pp. 281–309.

_____. 1980. Book Review of *Democracy and Distrust: A Theory of Judicial Review, Anglo-American Law Review*, pp. 193–99.

_____. 1979. *Amending the Amendments*. Allahabad: A.H. Wheeler and Co.

_____. 1978a. 'The Supreme Court and Religious Endowments: 1950–75,' *Journal of the Indian Law Institute*, vol. 20, pp. 51–102.

_____. 1978b. *The Amendment: Conspiracy or Revolution*. Allahabad: A.H. Wheeler and Co.

_____. 1977. 'Juristic Ethnology of Kesavananda's Case,' *Journal of the Indian Law Institute*, vol. 19, pp. 489–97.

_____. 1976a. 'Nazi Decrees and their Validity: An English Decision,' *Banaras Law Journal*, vol. 12, pp. 151–61.

_____. 1976b. *The Supreme Court and Parliamentary Sovereignty*. New Delhi: Sterling.

Dhavan R. and B. Kennedy. 1979. 'Privacy: Adventures of a Concept,' *Indian Journal of Comparative Law*, pp. 19–48.

Dhavan R. and F.S. Nariman. 2000. 'The Supreme Court and Group Life: Religious Freedom, Minority Groups and Disadvantaged Communities,' in B.N. Kirpal et.al (eds.) *Supreme but not Infallible: Essays in Honour of the Supreme Court of India*. New Delhi: Oxford University Press.

Dworkin, R. 1977. *Taking Rights Seriously*. London: Duckworth.

_____. 1986. *Law's Empire*. Cambridge Mass. Belknop Press of Harvard University.

Ehrlich, E. 1936. *Fundamental Principles of the Sociology of Law*. Cambridge, Mass: Harvard University Press.

Ely, J. 1980. *Democracy and Distrust: A Theory of Judicial Review*. Cambridge, Mass: Harvard University Press.

Fitzpatrick, P. 1992. *The Mythology of Modern Law*. London: Routledge and Kegan Paul.

Felstiner, W. 1974. 'Influences of Social Organization on Dispute Processing,' *Law and Society Review*, vol. 9, p. 63.

Fuller, L. 1948. Pashukanis and Vyshinsky. 'A Study in the Development of Marxist Legal Thinking' *Michigan Law Review*, vol. 47, p. 1157.

Fuller, L. 1958. 'Positivism and the Fidelity of Law to Morals: Reply to Professor Hart' in *Harvard Law Review*, vol. 71, p. 630.

Galanter, M. 1989. *Law and Society in Modern India*. New Delhi: Oxford University Press.

——. 1981. 'Justice in Many Rooms: Courts, Private Ordering and Indigenous Law', *Journal of Legal Pluralism*, vol. 19, pp. 1–47.

Griffiths, J.A.G. 1979. *The Politics of the Judiciary*. London: Fontana.

Government of India 1995. *Vohra Committee Report*. Mimeo.

Gulliver, P. 1973. 'Negotiations as a Norm of Dispute Settlement: Towards a General Model', *Law and Society Review*, vol. 7, p. 667.

Gluckman, M. 1970. *Ideas in Barotse Jurisprudence*. Manchester: Manchester University Press.

Habermas, J. 1976. *Legitimation Crisis*. London: Heinemann.

Hart, H.L.A. 1954. 'Definition and Theory in Jurisprudence', *Law Quarterly Review*, vol. 70, p. 37.

——. 1961. *The Concept of Law*. Oxford: Clarendon Press.

——. 1958. 'Positivism and the Separation of Law from Morals', *Harvard Law Review*, vol. 71, p. 593.

Harris, J.W. 1971. 'When and Why does the Grundnorm Change', *Cambridge Law Journal*, p. 103.

Hoebbel, E.A. 1954. *The Law of Primitive Man*. Cambridge, Mass: Harvard University Press.

Hohfeld, F.W. 1923. *Fundamental Legal Conceptions as Applied in Judicial Reasoning*. London: Yale University Press.

Jain, D.C. 1986. 'The Phantom of Public Interest', *SCC* (Jul), vol. 3, pp. 30–37.

Jain, M.P. 1986. *Indian Constitutional Law*. Bombay: N.M. Tripathi.

Jacob, A. 1992. 'Nehru and the Judiciary', in R. Dhavan (ed.), *Nehru and the Constitution*. Bombay: N.M. Tripathi, 63–76.

Keeton, G.W. 1949. *Elementary Principles of Jurisprudence*. London: Pitman & Sons.

Kelsen, H. 1949. *General Theory of Law and the State*. Cambridge, Mass: Harvard University Press.

Kymlicka, W. 1995. *Multicultural Citizenship: A Liberal Theory of Minority Rights*. Oxford: Oxford University Press.

Kymlicka, W. 1989. *Liberalism, Community and Culture*. Oxford: Oxford University Press.

Levinson, S. 1988. *Constitutional Faith*. Princeton: Princeton University Press.

Malik, S. (ed.) 1973. *The Fundamental Right Case: The Critics Speak*. Lucknow: Eastern Book Company.

Malinowski, B. 1926. *Crime and Custom in a Savage Society*. London: Routledge and Kegan Paul.

Marx, K. 1974. *Capital*, Vol. I. London: Lawrence and Wishart Ltd.

Miller, A.S. 1968. *The Supreme Court and American Capitalism*. New York: Free Press.

Newburg, Paula. 1995. *Judging the State: Courts and Constitutional Politics in Pakistan*. Cambridge: Cambridge University Press.

Roshier, B. and H. Teff 1977. *Laws and Society in England*. London: Tavistock Publication.

Ross, A. 1956. 'Tu-Tu,' *Harvard Law Review*, vol. 70, p. 812.

Seidman, R.B. 1978. *The State Law and Development*. London: Croom Helm.

Spellman, J. W. 1964. *Political Theory in Ancient India*. Oxford: Clarendon, 4–8, 20–21.

Stokes, E. 1959. *The English Utilitarians and India*. Oxford: Oxford University Press.

Stone, J. 1963. 'Mystery and Mystique of the Basic Norm,' *Modern Law Review*, vol. 26, p. 34.

Thompson, E.P. 1975. *Whigs and Hunters*. New York: Pantheon Press.

Trubek, D.M. and M. Gallanter 1974. 'Scholars in Self-Estrangement: Some Reflections on the Crisis in 'Law and Development' Studies in the United States,' *Wisconsin Law Review*, p. 1062.

Unger, R. 1976. *Law in Modern Society: Towards a Criticism of Social Theory*. New York: Free Press.

Warren, S.D. and L. Brandies 1890. 'The Right of Privacy,' *Harvard Law Review*, vol. 4, p. 193.

Washbrook, D. 1981. 'Law, State and Agrarian Society in Colonial India,' *Modern Asian Studies*, vol. 15, pp. 649–72.

Weschler, H. 1959. 'Towards Neutral Principles of Constitutional Law' *Harvard Law Review*, vol. 73, p. 1.

Cases

Bonham's Case. 1610. *Co. Rep*, 114.

Contempt Case. 1970. *E.M.S. Namboodripad's* v. *T.N. Nambiar*, AIR 1970 SC 2015.

Dred Scott v. *Sandford*. 1857. 19 *How*, 393.

Fundamental Rights Case. 1973. *Kesavananda* v. *State of Kerala*, 4 *SCC*, 225.

Maneka Gandhi v. *Khushwant Singh*. 1997. unreported.

Personal Law Case. 1997. *Ahmedabad Women's Action Group* v. *Union of India, SCC*, 573.

Privacy Case. 1964. *Kharak Singh* v. *State of U.P.*, 1 *SCR*, 332.

Privacy Case. 1975. *Gobind* v. *State of Madhya Pradesh*, 2 *SCC*, 148.

Privacy Case. 1994. *R. Rajagopal* v. *State of Tamil Nadu*, 6 *SCC*, 632.

Lochner's Case. 1905. *Lochner* v. *New York*, 198 *US*, 45.

Shah Bano's Case. 1985. *Mohd. Ahmed Khan* v. *Shah Bano*, 3 *SCR*, 844.

South Africa Housing Case. 2000. *Grootbroom* v. *Ostenbury and Others*, 3 *BCLR*, 1977 (Cape Town High Court); 11 *BCLR*, 169 (Constitutional Court).

8

Transcending Categories: The Private, the Public, and the Search for Home

Neera Chandhoke

If the carving out of collective life into discrete and perhaps mutually exclusive categories is peculiar to social science in the modern mode, it is not surprising that modern political scientists tend to subdivide collective life into plural and perhaps incompatible, categories in thought. They then proceed to add up all the parts they themselves have crafted with some dexterity, in order to construct a whole. Even as collective life is partitioned into autonomous categories in order to analyse the human condition, the domestic/home/the private + the market + civil society/public sphere + the state add up to generate a picture of how human beings live out their individual and collective lives.

On the face of it, there is nothing wrong with this method of approaching the human condition; of thinking of the different ways in which people make their own histories, howsoever badly they may make them. The problem arises when we realize that for additive political theory, not only is collective life separated into mutually exclusive categories, each category is granted a distinct logic that demarcates this sphere from others. Consider that whereas the home for political theorists is marked by a particular logic: that of unreflective affection, emotions, imagination, subjectivity, and interiority, the market is characterized by instrumental self-serving action. Whether civil society or the public sphere[1] is stamped by the Marxist logic of exploitation or by the Tocquevillean logic of co-operation, it is distinctive compared to the state, which functions according to a different set of dynamics altogether.

The modern individual seems to spend his or her time in remarkably exhausting activity: shedding one set of roles and assuming another set, even as s/he exits one sphere and enters another—a nice problem for social psychologists here.

Howsoever neat and rigorous such mental activity may appear to be in theory; it carries its own set of problems. For an additive picture of collective life may distort understanding to a remarkable extent. Copernicus had once written about the astronomers of his day thus: 'With them it is as though an artist were to gather the hands, feet, head, and other members for his images from diverse models, each part excellently drawn, but not related to a single body, and since they in no way match each other, the result would be a monster rather than man' (Kuhn 1962: 83). Something of the same kind mars modern political science. For when we add up mutually exclusive categories to generate a picture of collective life, we discover that no one category influences, let alone constitutes the other, no category is central to human life, and no category determines how we understand other activity. But—and this is the question—do not categories of collective existence constitute each other? Does *not* the logic of one sphere tend to spill over to another sphere? Or does not the logic of one sphere become a *prerequisite* for the other?

Feminist theory was quick to catch and focus on this precise problem when it challenged the *raison d'être* and the foundation of modern political theory: that is the division of individual and collective life into the public and the private as the *fundamental* ordering categories of modern political thought (Pateman 1993: 281–306). For long, it was assumed by (male) theorists that since the two spheres in which human beings make their lives together were marked by distinctive, different, and perhaps incommensurable logics, the private or domestic life was protected from either power or competition by the domestic gaze. In the family, the German philosopher Hegel was to write, particular interests are transcended in a natural and unreflective unity, because love and concern guide transactions between members. Civil society by contrast is the domain of particularity and of the self-seeking individual concerned with the fulfilment of his private needs. Such arguments—when pushed to their logical conclusion—were to naturally locate the household outside the sphere of not only the public but that of the political.

Feminists subverting this supremely male centred reasoning were to tell us that the household is a supremely political institution, replicating and condensing the logic of the public. As a producer of labour power

for the capitalist market it is an integral part of the structures of production. Equally as an institution that consumes commodities, it is an
integral part of the market. As an institution that codifies patriarchal
power, the home mirrors the power equations of civil society,[2] and as an
institution that codifies patriarchal violence, it happens to be the one
founding moment of the state as a structure of violence. Households,
Fraser was to write, are 'sites of egocentric, strategic, and instrumental
calculation as well as sites of usually exploitative exchanges of services,
labour, cash and sex, not to mention sites frequently of coercion and
violence' (Fraser 1987: 37).

By politicizing the domestic, and portraying it as the site for patriarchal
domination, as the site of production, and as the site of consumption,
feminists have told us that what is thought of as private is a *microcosm* of
the public. Or that the logic of the public *constitutes* the home or the
private. They argue that the relegation of the household to the private
sphere has depoliticized gender discrimination and disempowered
women by removing it from the circle of political intervention. Not
only did feminists reveal the complicity of political theory with the
legitimization of patriarchy; they inverted the fundamental ordering
categories of modern political theory. Political theory is not only built
on the systematic exclusion of women, it reflects the way men imbricated in structures of patriarchy imagine the world to be. The way
women may imagine this world is completely blocked out and political
theory becomes in the process one-dimensional.

Feminists have expended much theoretical energy on overturning
the way the activity called politics has been theorized, but this is not the
focus of this essay. The focus is on the unexpected consequences that
flow from the feminist critique. For when we look at this *genre* of theory
closely, we are compelled to conclude somewhat sadly, that in this
world of violence and competition, power, and conflict that permeates
both the public as well as the private, the modern individual has no *home*
in the sense of belonging.[3] For what has been thought of as home is but
part of the wider world that we ironically wish to escape when we come
home. Our modern individual is fated to homelessness in this world.

In this essay I suggest that significant strains of political theory were
to recognize precisely this conundrum. Theorists—and I am thinking
primarily of the 18th century work of Adam Smith on moral sentiments here—were to recognize the *differentia specifica* of modern life—
homelessness. And they were to strive to create a home for the modern
individual in civil society, or in the spheres of everyday interaction.

(Theorists continue to do so. Consider for instance the rush of theorization on social capital and trust in today's world.) We might not find such theories persuasive, we may well consider them deeply flawed—as apologetics for capitalism for instance. What is important for our argument is the manner in which such theorists have subverted neat distinctions reified by political theory between the public and the private. What is important for this argument is the way in which theorists have sought to negotiate the peculiarly modern problem of homelessness.

Admittedly, the search for home in the sense of belonging is a self-defeating one. We can as suggested above, hardly find a home or a domestic world that is insured against precisely those logics that characterize other spheres of human interaction—power, terror, subjugation, and loss of agency and self–hood. A battered woman who experiences repeated violence at the hands of male members of the family can hardly be faulted if she thinks of the household not as home in the sense of belonging, but purely as a site of oppression. For her there is little distinction between the repeated, insistently dehumanizing brutality she experiences as a woman, and the exploitation of bonded labour in the mines or the factories of the economy, or the torture that a political prisoner experiences in the detention chambers of the coercive state apparatus.

On the other hand, it is conceivable that she may find a home in the sense of belonging in the webs of solidarity that feminists create in the public sphere of civil society. Ironically, the *public may provide a refuge for her battered body, bruised mind, and damaged psyche*. But even this may be partial and temporary, for movements decay even as they come to be invested with power and domination. They fragment, they subdivide, they proliferate, and the homelessness of our woman is reiterated and reinscribed.

Conversely, by the logic of this argument, we can only construct a home or cultivate deep feelings of belonging in the domestic sphere, when the outside world is characterized by sympathy, affection, and sentiments of belonging. For the household is constituted by the wider world—by society, by politics, by the economy. They relentlessly intrude into the inner world; they hammer it and fashion it in their mode. The reverse may not be equally true. It is *after all the public world of the market, the state, and civil society that moulds the domestic sphere, not the other way round*. This is the nature of modern society deeply imbricated as it is in the deeper structures of capitalist accumulation—accumulation that dehumanizes, accumulation that emerges out of a blood spattered history to alienate our individual from everything that she may have considered once to be her own.

Therefore, conceivably, the search of various theorists who sought to provide a home for the modern alienated individual in the anonymous, potentially terrifying public spaces of civil society, may be as self-defeating as the search for a home in the private world amidst widespread and pervasive fear. But what *is* interesting is the way in which theorists recognize the predicament of the modern human being; the way in which they negotiate the phenomena of homelessness in the modern world. And it is this aspect of modern political theory that I wish to explore in this essay.

II

We are all familiar with the phenomena of homelessness: it happens to be one of the major consequences of capitalist modernity that separates the producer from the product and the individual from her or his dwelling. Recollect the massive migrations that occurred when people left their homes as the site of memories and affections, as the site of the familiar and as the site of repeated encounters that make it a dwelling, to chase a somewhat elusive commodity called capital. From the 18th century onwards, people were to migrate in large numbers to the urban areas or the colonies—Prussian peasants going to Berlin, Russian peasants moving to St. Petersburg and Irish peasants to New York. Or they were coerced into migrating to the new centres of capitalist accumulation that colonialism had built up through the migration of indentured labour from South India and Bihar to the sugar, tobacco, and cotton plantations from Trinidad to Mauritius, from South Africa to Fiji. In the process they were to leave behind their sense of place and rootedness.

The individual leaving behind her home and her sense of belonging was to step into a free, but also an unknown, unbound, and conceivably frightening future. In the 'free', predominantly urban world marked by impersonality, anonymity, and squalor, people may build new homes with their existing families. Or they may search for new domestic worlds, particularly if they happened to be male migrants who had left their original families behind in the villages. But build a home they must because they sensed somewhat urgently that it was only home that would give them refuge from the transitory, fugitive, and contingent quality of modern life that Marshall Berman has captured so magnificently in his work on modernity as experience.

Witness for instance the manner in which Heidegger, distressed with what he called the 'object-character of technological domination', was to seek refuge in dwelling. He was to write evocatively how '[i]n self-assertive production, the humanness of man and the thingness of things dissolve into the calculated market value of a market which not only spans the whole earth as a world market, but also, as the will to will, trades in the nature of Being, and thus subjects all beings to the trade of a calculation that dominates most tenaciously in those areas where there is no need of numbers'. Heidegger's response to the domination of technology was to withdraw from the world market and seek ways to uncover the truth of human existence through meditation by dwelling in a Black Forest farmhouse. His description of dwelling evocatively codifies the sense of longing for shelter amidst the destructive and self-destroying properties of capitalism:

> Here the self-sufficiency of the power to let earth and heaven, divinities and mortals enter in simple oneness into things, ordered the house. It places the farm on the wind-sheltered mountain slope looking south, among the meadows close to the spring. It gave it the wide overhanging shingle roof whose proper slope bears up under the burden of snow, and which, reaching deep down, shields the chambers against the storms of the long winter nights. It did not forget the altar corner behind the community table; it made room in its chamber for the hallowed places of childbed and the 'tree of the dead' for that is what they call a coffin there; the Totenbaum—and in this way it designed for the different generations under one roof the character of their journey through time. A craft which, itself sprung from dwelling, still uses its tools and frames as things, built the farmhouse (Harvey 1993: 10–11).

For Heidegger, remarks Harvey, dwelling is the capacity to achieve a spiritual union between humans and things. 'Although there is a narrow sense of homelessness which can perhaps be alleviated simply by building shelter, there is a much deeper crisis of homelessness to be found in the modern world; many people have lost their roots, their connection to the homeland' (Ibid.: 11).

However, even as the household as dwelling or as the domain of the private is increasingly seen as a refuge from the exigencies of modern life marked by ephemeral, haphazard, chancy, and above all instrumental social action, ironically, it can no longer provide the fulcrum of human existence. For the household in capitalist society becomes a residual category. Let me elaborate on this. In the pre-capitalist period, the family provides the locus of attention and energies simply because it is the site of production for subsistence. Production is in turn dependent on norms of paternalistic authority, nurturing of children, and familial division of labour. The economic in short, is embedded in non-economic institutions governed by laws that are peculiar to the family or the household.

Capitalist modernity, however, separates economic production from the household and locates it in a new institution called the economy. Economic production falls into the hands of legally independent private producers, the social stock is converted into private property, and labour is converted into a commodity owned by the labourer and sold in exchange for money (Polanyi 1944). Consequently, though the family remains the source of paternal authority, it becomes both subordinate to and residual to the income seeker, whether male or female.

It becomes subordinate to the capitalist economy, for as the theorists of the Frankfurt School such as Adorno and Marcuse tellingly argued, the technical rationality of capitalist societies exerts a repressive effect on personality leading to passivity, conformity, and suppressed subjectivity. Human personality cannot flower in the home, simply because the home like other areas of human interaction, is hammered into shape by capitalism. Sennett for instance was to perceive gross compression and one–dimensionality of the inner realm even as the public world intrudes relentlessly on the private world (Sennet 1986 [1974]). The home is no longer a home because it is *controlled* by the logic of the outer world. Much later Foucault was to inform us that the most private parts of experiences, inner passions, and impulses, are governed by the public world of knowledge as power. The inner, or the domestic world, incorporates the public, even as forms of desire are customized by social power. *The home becomes a chimera even as the ordinary, rootless, homeless individual is consumed by the passion for home.*

There is a second aspect to this—home as a residual entity. The paradox of modern life is that people may long for home or dwelling but they can no longer stay at home. For increased division of labour and expanded specialization brings people till then unknown to each other together in intricate linkages of dependence and interdependence. It becomes impossible in this world of want, creation and satisfaction—a world that the classical political economists termed civil society—to live or work alone. The home as suggested above is constituted by the same logic that controls the production, distribution, and exchange of goods—that of accumulation. And accumulation sweeping up everything into its own trajectory, succeeds in fashioning a world in its own image.

It was Adam Smith, who first recognized this particular characteristic of the modern world in his conceptualization of civil society as the centre of modern existence. And in the process he was to perform a spectacular inversion in political theory. Aristotle had told us that it is politics that is natural to man, for man is by nature the *zoon politikon*. Man's nature unfolds in all its fullness through and in the activity that the Greeks called politics. It was in the political community or in the *koinonia politika* that the individual would discover a sense of belonging. Adam Smith writing in the period of transition from mercantile to industrial capitalism reversed this dictum and theorized the modern man as essentially *homo economicus*. It is not politics but economics that happens to be the natural habitat of man. In fact, full time involvement in politics is neither feasible nor even desirable once men find their true essence as economic beings. It is not feasible, for the early modern state has become a specialized unit simply unavailable to the ordinary man once the city-state has given way to more complex society. It is not desirable, because it is economics that men respond to from the deepest core of their beings, it comes naturally to them through activities that require the creative application of labour, even as human beings appropriate their world through labour.

Hegel writing a few years later than Smith was to term civil society the 'theatre of history'. We see a profound turning in the way history is conceptualized here. It is not the quirks of kings or of the feudal lords, which is the stuff history is made of: ordinary people pursuing a living in the sphere of civil society make history. But our relationships with others do not give us a sense of belonging, for they are fashioned by the cold, hard, and harsh calculus of the contract, which as Hobbes theorized is the prime metaphor of market society. Such is the experience of modern life. Therefore, although the home may be a refuge in and for imagination; it is also the proverbial fantasy we seek constantly and which perhaps like all fantasies is never really realized.

It is this longing, this spectre of homelessness that permeates the works of several modern theorists. They, acutely sensitive to the homelessness of modern life, to the incivility of civil society, strived to give the individual a sense of home, a sense of belonging. It is to such theorizations that I now turn to.

III

Philosophers of modernity—and I have in mind particularly Adam Smith and Hegel—could analyze with remarkable clarity the dangers that modernity holds for the individual psyche. Modern society is freed from the stifling rules and ascriptive privileges of pre-modern societies, and it offers avenues, which were not hitherto available for the expression of the self. But modern society is restless, self-seeking, and self-serving, searching endlessly for individual gratification, for all those benefits that can compensate for the loss of belonging. Human beings emancipated from all normative constraints on thought and behaviour, from all that constituted what Hegel was to call *sittlichkeit*, become competitive, indulgent, and egocentric. There are no limits upon desires and hence no guarantees of belonging.

Modernity in other words is not simply a question of undergoing a joyful experience of freedom, because relinquishing the familiar can lead to alienation and doubt, homelessness and fear, all those consequences that theorists such as Karl Marx, Georg Simmel, and Freud, were to chronicle in such evocative detail. Ironically for Hegel, civil society as the site of everyday social interaction, carries all the dangers that the state of nature did for Hobbes. For in civil society the ethos of the family, i.e. natural love and altruism, disintegrate. It 'affords the spectacle of extravagance and want as well as of the physical and ethical degeneration common to both' (Hegel 1942). Civil society in the Hegelian vision is remarkably uncivil.

But civil society is also one of the founding moments of ethical life—the other two being the household and the state. For the ethos of universality emerges in an embryonic form in and through the division of labour. Civil society cannot be left alone warns Hegel, for it is here that the tension between particularity and universality is negotiated. Hegel's answer to the dilemma posed by modern civil society is to organize it into and by the state. Civil society is the theatre of history, but it is the state as the condensate of universality, which provides the complete spirit of belonging to the homeless individual.

Significantly, Hegel begins with civil society as the *precondition* for the state inasmuch as the Hegelian State is what it is because Hegelian civil society is what it is. Ultimately however, it is the state that becomes the precondition of civil society. This is perhaps understandable. For deeply permeated by a sense of loss for the ancient political community of the Greek *polis*, Hegelian theory was primarily concerned with establishing an ethical social and political community in a world where the division of labour provides nothing but an exchange oriented means to social interaction. The modern individual Hegel recognizes is rootless, bereft of the traditional support structures of community life. His project was to provide a home to this rootless individual; a home that can only be provided by an ethical community realized in and by the state.

It is interesting that though Hegel's notion of civil society—as the domain of the intricate division of labour—is deeply influenced by Adam Smith whose writings Hegel seems to have become familiar with in his Jena days—he [Hegel] looks outside civil society, to the state to provide belonging to the rootless individual. On the other hand, Adam Smith, who did much more than any other modern theorist to privilege civil society, was to look for the redemption of this sphere *within* the sphere itself.

Hegel was to conceive of civil society as the site of the battle between particularity and universality, a battle that could only be resolved by the state. Adam Smith, (1723–1790)—man of letters, historian, critic, teacher of rhetoric, political advisor to governments, public speaker, civil servant, and above all, the professor of moral philosophy and political economy in the home of the Scottish Enlightenment at the University of Glasgow—was to perceive civil society as the site for the fashioning of moral sentiments, such as, sympathy, and propriety.

Indeed, for Smith, such sentiments can arise only in civil society, which he conceives as a property of commercial society. They cannot be fashioned in a society where production is organized in and through, the household. Household–based production, based as it is upon the premise of patriarchal authority, simply cannot allow the flowering of autonomy, creativity, and sense of self–worth, which are indispensable for the modern individual. Gentler, softer sentiments such as civility need as a pre–requisite commercial society, because such a society is organized around the concept of freedom. And it is only freedom that allows for the efflorescence of subjectivity.

IV

'Society', wrote Smith, as one of the most distinguished members of the Scottish moralists[4] 'cannot subsist among those who are at all times ready to hurt and injure one another. The moment that injury begins, the moment that mutual resentment and animosity take place, all the bands of it are broke asunder, and the different members of which it consisted are, as it were, dissipated and scattered abroad by the violence and opposition of their discordant affections' (Smith 1871: 124). Two paragraphs earlier, he argues that '[a]ll the members of human society stand in need of each other's assistance, and are likewise exposed to mutual injuries. Where the necessary assistance is reciprocally afforded from love, from gratitude, from friendship, and esteem, the society flourishes and is happy. All the different members of it are bound together by the agreeable bands of love and affection, and are, as it were, thereby drawn to one common centre of mutual good offices' (Ibid.: 127).

Adam Smith is, however, better known and certainly more celebrated for the following observation. 'It is not from the benevolence of the butcher, the brewer, or the baker that we expect our dinner, but from their regard to their own interest. We address ourselves not to their humanity but to their self-love, and never talk to them of our own necessities but of their advantages. Nobody but a beggar chuses [chooses] to depend chiefly upon the benevolence of his fellow citizens. Even a beggar does not depend upon it entirely' (Smith 1952: 7). The Smithian individual in the magnum opus published in 1776: *An Inquiry into the Nature and the Causes of the Wealth of Nations* (hereafter WN) is seemingly driven completely by material incentives. He is motivated purely and solely by self-interest and self-love.

Yet the first sentence of Smith's earlier work published in 1759: *A Theory of Moral Sentiments*[5] (hereafter the TMS) had this to say about men. 'How selfish soever man may be supposed, there are evidently some principles in his nature, which interest him in the fortunes of others, and render their happiness necessary to him, though he derives nothing from it except the pleasure of seeing it' (Ross 1995: 3). At another point, he argues that man has a natural love of society, and that the orderly and flourishing state of society is agreeable to him and he takes delight in contemplating it.

Scholars tend to tear their hair in exasperation every time they are faced with these two inconsistent statements, because they simply do not seem to jell together. If individuals relate to each other only to gratify their own desires, there is no way that they can be interested in the fortunes of others, there is no way that the happiness of others is rendered necessary to men. But if sociability and sympathy motivates them, they cannot by definition engage in self-interested behaviour. It is not surprising that much theoretical energy has been expended on what was termed by the Germans in the 19th century as *Das Problem Adam Smith* inasmuch as he seems to have had one concept of man in one work, and another concept of man in another work[6].

For whereas TMS dwelt upon the phenomena of emotions and emotional bonds in society, the WN dwells upon the phenomena of self-aggrandising economic action. Whereas TMS explores the process of moral judgement that flow from sympathy, WN explores selfish motives. Understandably, some theorists argue that there is nothing common between the WN and TMS, and that Smith had moved away from his central concerns in TMS—whose first edition was published in 1759—when he wrote WN, which was published in 1776. In other words, the sensitive and sympathetic man in TMS, a man whose feelings towards others have been finely tuned through sympathy, the man who provides a sense of belonging to others, simply disappears when he comes into the economic habitat of WN.

We are compelled to wonder whether Smith was speaking of a different man when he wrote his later WN. This speculation seems unlikely. Consider this: TMS was first published in 1759 and was quickly sold out within the first six months. The third and the fourth editions of the TMS were published in 1767 and 1774, at the very time that Smith was preparing his WN that was published in 1776. After the publication of WN two more editions of TMS were brought out in 1778, and the sixth and final edition that was substantially revised without modification of his basic thesis was published in 1790, the year of his death. Therefore, Smith could not have drastically moved away from his earlier work since he continued to be involved with it even as he was preparing his better known WN. In fact, Campbell cites a letter written by Smith to Sir Samuel Romilly that he always considered TMS as a superior work (Campbell: 85). How do we resolve the *Das problem Adam Smith* if we want to make sense of his work as a whole?

It seems to me that the moment we go beyond the two texts that have pre-occupied scholars, and look at the context in which Smith wrote, we might be able to make sense of seeming discrepancies. The context recollect is that of transition from mercantile to industrial capitalism. And if there is one feature that tracks capitalist society, it is the dissolution of all accepted ways in which individuals have hitherto related to each other, as Marx was to tell us in such evocative detail later. In commercial society, people can no longer afford to be isolated, solipsistic beings cut off from others, since they have to plan together all sorts of political, economic, and social projects, that are indispensably a part of the modern imagination. Modern economics and modern society demand co-operation, collective endeavour, and concerted action. But these projects demand more than mere economic transactions, for they demand trust. People have to trust each other, but the paradox is that even as they engage in economic transactions that involve perhaps lifetime investments, they do not really know each other.

In a village economy for instance, people know each other, along with their genealogies, histories, family lines, castes, tastes and habits. People by and large know how to behave with those they consider their own, and with those they do not. They have role models, and they have customs and traditions to help them. In the modern world however, the economic individual is peculiarly clueless. The irony is that even as the worker is thrown upon the mercy of others, he does not know whether mercy will be extended to him.

Of course, there is the quintessential Hobbesian solution to the problem of economic transactions—the contract. But a contract between two anonymous people provides little security for the participants, since one of the partners may facilely renege on his obligations, and the other may be condemned to spend the rest of his life in the law courts. What is to ensure that strangers who enter into the contract can be depended upon to honour their obligations except the reach of the law? However, the law is far too unreliable a guarantee since it may or may not compel everyone to redeem their promises. But transactions in the increasingly intricate sphere of the economy demands that participants be constantly reassured that their partners will not renege on the contract, or decamp with large investments, or not pay salaries, upon which depends the reproduction of the worker's family, or indeed that they will not deliver. Therefore, the project of living and working together demands *social* prerequisites and undertakings—trust, mutual reciprocity, and beneficence so that economic transactions can be secure. The modern economy simply requires the setting into place of a moral order— what can be schematically called the social structures of accumulation.

Adam Smith can conceive of such an order, for his individual possesses the precise properties required for such an order. Rejecting reason as the motivation of social action—for Smith along with his friend David Hume was a member of what was referred to as the society of the Sentimentalists—Smith was to make emotions the motive of human actions. Whereas it is incontrovertible that human beings are selfish, they are motivated by another emotion: that of sympathy. And it is sympathy or rather empathy, which Smith was to make the linchpin of his theory of moral sentiments.

Individuals are basically selfish agrees Smith, but they are also sociable since they have the capacity for sympathy: '[h]ow amiable does he appear to be, whose sympathetic heart seems to re-echo all the sentiments of those with whom he converses, who grieves for their calamities, who resents their injuries, and who rejoices at their good fortune? When we bring home to ourselves the situation of his companions, we enter into their gratitude, and feel what consolation they must derive from the tender sympathy of so affectionate a friend'. Equally, we can understand 'how disagreeable does he appear to be, whose hard and obdurate heart feels for himself only, but is altogether insensible to the happiness or misery of others. We enter, in this case too, into the pain which his presence must give to every mortal with whom he converses, to those especially with whom we are most apt to sympathize, the unfortunate and the injured' (Campbell: 26).

And we can understand the feelings of others, because we as human beings are gifted with imagination. Drawing upon the experience of the torture chamber just as Hume had drawn upon the analogy of the surgical operation, Smith argues that we can form a conception of the torture our brother experiences when he is on the rack through our imagination. Our imagination allows us to feel for others, and to experience their sentiments of pleasure and pain. There is no other way of experiencing what other people experience, or what they feel in response to situations that evoke pleasure and pain, since our own pains and pleasures are purely personal. Our *senses* can never take us beyond our own experiences. But through imaginative projections we have the unique facility of being able to switch roles with the victim and, therefore, form some idea of his pain and suffering.[7] We are thus able to feel pleasure in response to another's pleasure, and pain in someone else's pain. This sentiment Smith terms sympathy.[8]

Sympathy can mean in one sense fellow feeling, but it can also mean more than that. 'He who admires the same poem, or the same picture, and admires them exactly as I do, must surely allow the justness of my admiration. He who laughs at the same joke, and laughs along with me, cannot well deny the propriety of my laughter. On the contrary, the person who, upon these different occasions, either feels no such emotion as that which I feel, or feels none that bears any proportion to mine, cannot avoid disapproving my sentiments on account of their dissonance with his own... To approve or disapprove, therefore, of the opinions of others, is acknowledged, by every body, to mean no more than to observe their agreement or disagreement with our own' (TMS 1759: 14–15).

But admiring the same picture and the same poem is not the same thing as sympathizing with the predicament of others. When two people consider an object, he writes, 'wherever his sentiments correspond with our own, we ascribe to him the qualities of taste and good judgement' (Ibid.: 19). On the other hand, we may be differently affected by the same picture, therefore, we conclude that we have different tastes. This does not mean that we do not admire the other person for his acuteness, or for his superior knowledge. But we have no occasion for sympathy, which belongs to a different genre of sentiments.

> Though your judgement in matters of speculation, through your sentiments in matters of taste, are quite opposite to mine, I can easily overlook this opposition.... *But if you have either no fellow feeling for the misfortunes I have met with, or none that bears any proportion to the grief which distracts me; or if you have either no indignities at the injuries I have suffered, or none that bears any proportion to the resentment which transports me,* we can no longer converse upon these subjects. We become intolerable to one another. I can neither support your company, nor you mine. You are confounded at my violence and passion, and I am enraged at your cold insensibility and want of feeling (Ibid.: 22, emphasis mine).

Sympathy goes beyond fellow feeling because it establishes a link between the self and the other, reducing the gap between self-ness and otherness. If we are able to feel for others and with others, the other person is not a stranger for we share something in common. This establishes bonds of humanity and fellow feelings, it establishes belonging. At this stage, sympathy has no evaluative connotations, it is simply the ability to see a situation from the point of view of another person. There are three aspects to this emotion, the ability to see the context in which another person acts in a particular way, the ability to observe his emotions in response to that context, and the ability to understand these emotions.

Such bonds have their limits of course. For no one can *entirely* know or experience what the other person undergoes. Sympathetic emotions can only be *similar* to that of the other, they are, therefore, far weaker than the original. Never fully knowing what the other person experiences, we can only approximate in a milder form his or her feelings, since we judge from the vantage point of our own feelings. 'Every faculty in one man is the measure by which he judges of the like faculty in another. I judge of our sight by my sight, of your ear by my ear, of your reason by my reason, of your resentment by my resentment, of your love by my love. I neither have, nor can have, any other way of judging about them' (Ibid.: 18). The compassion of the spectator must arise altogether from the consideration of what he himself would feel if he were reduced to the same unhappy situation.

Therefore, our capacity for sympathy is limited by our own capacity to feel pleasure and pain. We cannot ever experience sympathy for say the bodily emotions of others—of hunger or sex for instance. Internal injuries like the 'gout and the toothache [sic] though exquisitely painful, excite very little sympathy'. 'What a tragedy would that be of which the distress consisted in colic', writes Smith amusedly (Ibid.: 36). On the other hand, we can readily sympathize with those passions 'which take their origin from the imagination'. Expanding upon this, he writes thus. 'The frame of my body can be but little affected by the alterations which are brought about upon that of my companion: but my imagination is more ductile, and more readily assumes, if I may so, the shape and configuration of the imaginations of those with whom I am familiar. A disappointment in love, or ambition, will upon this account, call forth more sympathy than the greatest bodily evil' (Ibid.: 35). 'The true cause of the peculiar disgust which we conceive for the appetites of the body when we see them in other men, is, that we cannot enter into them' (Ibid.: 34).

Equally, it is difficult to sympathize with those sentiments that are peculiar to the other individual, the excessive passion that he feels for another person for instance. Unless we ourselves feel passionately for the object of my friend's passion, it will be difficult to enter in to his feelings. 'Love, though it is pardoned in a certain age because we know it is natural, is always laughed at, because we cannot enter into it' (Ibid.: 39). Endearingly, Smith writes of how 'we grow weary of the grave, pedantic, and long-sentenced love of Cowley and Petrarcha who have never done with exaggerating the violence of their attachments, but the gaiety of Ovid and the gallantry of Horace are always agreeable' (Ibid.: 40). Neither can sympathy be extended to those who have been frustrated in their ambition, or to those who are intense about things that are limited to them alone—their profession, their studies, their friends. 'A philosopher is companion to a philosopher only; the member of a club, to his own little knot of companions' (Ibid.: 100). It is also, confesses Smith, easier to sympathize with joy rather than with sorrow, because joy is a pleasanter emotion.

There is more importantly a flip side to the argument. Two things happen at the stage of extending sympathy. One, the recipient of sympathy is perfectly aware that the observer cannot identify with excesses of sentiment. He will therefore, moderate his reactions and responses. In other words, the extension for sympathy generates moderate behaviour and softens excessive passions and feelings into conformity with propriety. The emotion that motivates people to conform to our expectations is the selfish but universal desire to acquire the approval of others.

Second, the universal tendency to observe others, and to sympathetically understand their point of view naturally brings the awareness that we ourselves are being observed and evaluated. This is what has been called a 'looking glass' conception of the self. Accordingly, we tailor our behaviour in such a way that we can win the approval or the sympathy of others. 'To be observed, to be attended to, to be taken notice of with sympathy, complacency and approbation, are all advantages which we can propose to derive from it'. As our spontaneous tendency to observe others is invariably turned upon ourselves, we learn to observe ourselves from the standpoint of a third person. Therefore, our passions and instincts are arbitrated by a metaphorical figure—neither wholly real nor wholly imaginary—who Smith calls the 'the impartial spectator'. 'We endeavour to examine our conduct as we imagine any other fair and impartial spectator would imagine it. If, upon placing ourselves in his situation, we thoroughly enter into all the passions and motives which influenced it, we approve of it, by sympathy with the approbation of this supposed equitable judge' (Ibid.: 162).

The closest approximation of the 'impartial spectator' is our conscience. 'When I endeavour to examine my own conduct, when I endeavour to pass sentence upon it, and either to approve or to condemn it, it is evident that, in all such cases, I divide myself, as it were, into two persons; and that I, the examiner and judge, represent a different character from that other I, the person whose conduct is examined into and judged of. The first is the spectator, 'whose sentiments with regard to my own conduct I endeavour to enter into by placing myself in his situation, and by considering how it would appeal to me, when seen from that particular point of view. The second is the agent, the person whom I properly call myself, and of whose conduct, under the character of a spectator, I was endeavouring to form some opinion. The first is the judge; the second is the person judged of' (Ibid.: 164–65).

If we were to theorize that individuals are split into two characters: the agent and the spectator of the actions carried through by other agents— the impartial spectator, occupies a distance from both. He simply represents the universal point of view, the point of view of a third person who is distanced from both. We see how propriety and merit make their appearance in a hitherto uncomplicated emotion called sympathy. We sympathize, suggests Smith, with those emotions, which seem to us proper and meritorious. Sympathy is no longer about constraining our emotions for others within the bounds of our imagination; it is about the way we evaluate the behaviour of others on the basis of propriety and merit. Conversely, when we turn this reasoning onto ourselves, we find that we also moderate our passions and instincts in order with what the impartial observer tells us.

The idea of the impartial spectator had been introduced and conceptualized by scholars such as Francis Hutcheson who, concentrating on disinterested judgement of approval, suggested that we admire actions exactly in the same manner as we would a beautiful painting. In Smith's hands, the impartial spectator is initially identified with a disinterested party who expresses a universal point of view. Residing in the breast of all human beings, the impartial spectator allowing us to evaluate situations from the third person's standpoint motivates us to temper our 'mutinous and intemperate passions'. As spectators of our own behaviour and endeavouring to imagine what effect this behaviour produces on others, we constantly scrutinize the propriety of our own actions from the viewpoint of others. Therefore, every individual is led to pre-empt the assessment of others through self-observation and self-assessment. In time these moral judgements create a moral order through law and custom.

What is important for us is that our individual is no longer a stranger amidst a sea of disinterested humanity. He has found himself a home because he has learnt to rise above self-interested instincts and self-oriented desires to feel for others, to extend the gift of sympathy, and to receive sympathy.

V

Smith gives us a highly interactive picture of human beings. Human beings are able to relate to each other, they are able to do so on grounds of virtue or self-control, which in turn is the source of other virtues since it subdues anger, resentment, 'malevolent and unsocial passions'. Civil society thus offsets the homelessness of the modern condition. For civil society has been tamed, and this by itself allows the subordination of harsh selfishness to finer and softer sentiments.

But the taming of civil society has other (unintended) consequences: the construction of a predictable and secure civil society as the context for capitalist accumulation. One, any desire or instinct that is palpably anti or un-social is ruled out by the demands of propriety and the insatiable desire for merit based approval. We need have no fear that someone somewhere will wreck the intricate design of capitalist society or the give and take of market relationships. They would be too mortified to do so.

Second, the desire for approval secures the ends of capitalism since it prompts men to accumulate wealth and fortune. For since wealth and fortune draw maximum approbation from others, men desire to emulate them. Heilbroner argues that moral sentiments socialize the individual of the TMS into the acquisitive individual of the WN (Heilbroner 1994: 122–33). Developing Macfie's argument that the economic man who *is* the active agent of the WN *is* the prudent man of TMS, Heilbroner argues that the task performed by the TMS is compatible with the Hegelian 'cunning of reason'. The TMS, his argument runs, is concerned with the way in which 'primal human nature' is transformed into 'socialized man, the actor who inhabits and activates the moral and economic world with which Smith is concerned' (Ibid.: 123). The socialization of the economic behaviour of man, concludes Heilbroner, is the formation of the accumulating capitalist who is the driving force of the WN.

And it is true that Adam Smith slowly reveals the true purpose of his civil society: we emulate the successful because they are the objects of praise and admiration, because we passionately desire the same approval and admiration that the wealthy draw so readily. Driven by the need for approval Smith's man cultivates to a nicety habits of hard work, economy, industry, discretion, attention and application of thought, he pursues riches and material self-satisfaction in order to gain approval, attention, and approbation. But a man who searches endlessly for approval can hardly provide belonging to and for others. His search is self-indulgent and there is always the danger that self-indulgence can wreck bonds of sympathy. Our individual, who yearns for belonging and home is once again condemned to homelessness.

But there is more: what of those who necessarily become the victims of the ambitions of others? For capitalism invariably produces and reproduces its victims as much as it produces its survivors. But Smith shows extreme callousness towards the victims of capitalism. The poor man is ashamed of his poverty, for no one takes notice of him and he is both unheeded, and obscure. People turn their eyes away from his misery, and if they are forced to look at him they spurn so disagreeable an object.

The message is clear: the internalization of the impartial spectator within our breast hammers us into conformity with the demands of capitalism, even as we learn to emulate the rich and the powerful and avoid poverty like the proverbial disease. These pressures or the super-ego argues Heilbroner, shape the virtues of man in society and give rise to that epitome of socialized humanity, the prudent individual (Ibid.: 123–24).

The persuasiveness of Smith's solution to the problem of homelessness stops short precisely here. It stops short the moment we ask a rather obvious question: can sympathy be enough to serve as a regulator of moral social interactions in an increasingly complex society. 'Though it might so instinctively bind a flock of sheep, it could hardly create the wealth of concrete social activities and institutions which for us constitute societies' suggests Campbell (Macfie 1971: 87–104). For in a given civil society, we may witness sympathy, but we also witness a lack of sympathy, alienation and belonging, a sense of home and homelessness, friendship, enmity, and indifference, exploitation and profit making. Not all these transactions are covered by sympathy. In fact some of them may well fetch the opposite of sympathy—aversion to misfortune for instance as Smith himself suggests.

But if this is so, then where does civil society relegate those who suffer from misfortune? To the margins? For whereas we sympathize with others who suffer from non-economic misfortune we shun the economically deprived. The mere want of fortune argues Adam Smith excites little compassion but evokes contempt. We despise a beggar; and even though his importunities may extort alms from us, he is scarce ever the object of any serious commiseration.

Smith's theory of moral sentiments thus does not intend to challenge either the ranking of society, or the fact that civil society produces its own victims. It accepts both these consequences. The better off integrate into the ranks of society without challenging the ordering of society into ranks. The poor are left on the margins condemned not only to their material poverty but to humiliation and insults from those who either do not see them or subject them to contempt. If this is so, then how can civil society lay claim to sympathy, morality, and the finer sentiments that provide a home to the rootless individual? Is civil society fated to be civil only to people who are privileged? But since the realm of privilege is historically narrow, historically exclusive, and historically closed off, the regime of sympathy in Adam Smiths theory can only regulate a truncated sphere, impervious as it is to the demands of the disprivileged.

Therefore I find it difficult to believe that Smith's theory of moral sentiments can resolve the question of homelessness. The very fact that the poor and the wretched find no place within the domain renders the consensus on moral sentiments frail and easily breakable. Such exclusion carries the implication that the poor are outside moral experiences, and if this is so, then morality itself is exclusive and narrowly defined. Smith's civil society cannot give us any answer to our problem of homelessness because it is far too narrow.

Conclusion

I have suggested here that the division of spheres of collective life into the private and the public rests on a fundamental assumption—that the two or more spheres are characterized by different logics. But if we look at social life in totality, it becomes clear that the private is moulded and hammered into shape by the public. Conversely, one genre of theory has recognized that the public also needs to be transformed from the alien and the alienated into a warm and sympathetic habitat where our individual can feel at home. I turned to the theory of Adam Smith as a possible resolution of the problem, but the theory as we have seen is sadly deficient because it refuses to recognize that civil society is peopled by human beings who are condemned to the peripheries of social existence. And to ignore them is hardly to resolve the problems of homeless civil societies. Adam Smith's theory of moral sentiments remains as a historically limited answer to the problems of homelessness.

Notes

1. Some theorists differentiate between civil society and the public sphere as for instance Craig Calhoun (1993: 269), who suggests that the two are not equivalent. 'We should not follow the example of many recent analysts who have jumped onto the bandwagon of enthusiasm for the two concepts, casually assuming that "civil society" and "public sphere" are more or less synonymous'. My argument as put forth in an earlier work (Chandhoke 1995) suggests that if we refer to civil society as social per se, then there is little reason to call it 'civil society'. We may well collapse civil society into society. When society organizes itself politically and socially through the articulation of a set of discourses marked by publicity and accessibility, we call the site of that mode of activity, civil society.
2. I am—in contrast to the picture we get of civil society in contemporary theory—assuming that the sphere is not the site of harmony but as that of contestation.

3. Contrast this to the notion of the home as a discrete bounded off entity. Of course, the home is the domain of the private and not of the public inasmuch as it is not accessible to all, and it is not marked by publicity or publicness. But the idea of home, it seems to me, is that of *belonging* as contrasted to the idea of alienation in the public sphere.

4. Among the most notable of Scottish Moralists were Frances Hutcheson, John Millar, High Blair, Adam Ferguson and Adam Smith.

5. The origins of TMS that deals with human sensibility lie in the lectures in ethics that Smith delivered as professor of moral philosophy 1752–1764, after a short stint as professor of logic and rhetoric. These lectures were recast as a scholarly work to bring out the nature of what he called virtue. The placement of the work is clear when we see that the last section of the book contains a historical survey of moral philosophy up to the times of Frances Hutcheson, Smith's own teacher at the university and his main inspiration for the TMS. Hutcheson refuting Mandeville's *Fable of the Bees*, develops the idea that the creator implants a sixth sense or a moral sense in human beings. This moral sense, which allows man to take pleasure in benevolence, provides the psychological basis of virtuous behaviour. Challenging egoistic philosophy, Hutcheson argued for disinterested judgement and disinterested motives. Our moral sense leads us to approve disinterestedly of disinterested actions that further benevolence, and to disapprove of those motives and actions that lead to the contrary, exactly in the same way as we approve of a beautiful object. But Smith thought otherwise. 'Smith', argues his biographer Ian Simpson Ross, 'had surely been impressed with Hutcheson's teaching, following on from that of Carmichael, that the principle of our approval of moral acts is not based on self-love, and that 'it could not arise from any operation of reason' (Ross 1995: 159). However, he jibes at Hutcheson's solution to the problem of the source of moral approval and disapproval through the theory of a special 'moral sense'. Rather, Smith builds on the new insights of his friend Hume, developed in the *Treatise* and the subsequent *Enquiry Concerning the Principles of Morals* (1751), and certain suggestions of his patron Kames in *Essays on the Principles of Morality and Natural Religion* (1751).

6. In 1853, Karl Knies insisted on the incompatibility of Adam Smith's moral philosophy and economics, and in 1878, Witold von Skanzynski formulated an argument on the contrast between the two works. For a full treatment of this see D.D. Raphael and A.L. Macfie (1871).

7. We can trace the influence of David Hume's philosophy here, particularly, his theory of the imagination, as active mental power that shapes a specifically human world within nature. Imagination allows us to create connections between the perceived elements of the physical as well as the moral world, from particular events to the cosmos and humanity.

The search of the imagination is a spontaneous search for coherence and order in the world.

8. Hume had argued in the *Treatise* that men are similar in their feelings and operations and if one is aroused emotionally, others in some degree are subjected to the same emotion. Exactly in the same manner as the movement of one string in a tautened set spreads to other strings, emotions spreads to other human beings who through the liveliness of their minds are able to not only grasp but experience the emotion experienced by someone else. The law of nature thus transforms moral sense into pure sympathy. Moral sentiments of approval arise from sympathy with the pleasure or pain of the person affected by particular actions. Virtue is whatever mental action or quality gives to the spectator the pleasing sentiment of approbation and vie the contrary. Kames in his Essays on Morality and Natural Religion published in the same year extended the argument to the principle that compassion is the great cement of human society. Since 'as no state is exempt from misfortune, mutual sympathy must greatly promote the security and happiness of mankind'. We, he argued, are filled with peculiar feelings when actions directed against others hurt or prejudice their persons, their fame, or their goods. We are able to feel that such actions should not be done, that they are simply unfit.

REFERENCES

Calhoun C. 1993. 'Civil Society and the Public Sphere,' *Public Culture*, no. 5, pp. 267–80.
Campbell, T.D. 1971. *Adam Smith's Science of Morals*. London: George Allen and Unwin.
Chandhoke, Neera. 1995. *State and Civil Society: Explorations in Political Theory*. Delhi: Sage Publications.
Fraser, Nancy. 1987. 'What's Critical About Critical Theory? The Case of Habermas and Gender,' in S. Benhabib and D. Cornell (eds), *Feminism as Critique*. Cambridge: Polity.
Harvey, David. 1993. 'From Space to Place and Back Again: Reflections on the Condition of Postmodernity,' in Jon Bird, Barry Curtis, Tim Putnam, George Robertson and Lisa Tickner (eds), *Mapping the Futures: Local Cultures*, Global Change. London: Routledge.
Hegel, G.W.F. 1942. *The Philosophy of Right*. Translated by T.M. Knox. Oxford: Oxford University Press.
Heilbroner, R.L. 1994. 'The Socialization of the Individual in Adam Smith,' in John Cunningham Wood (ed.), *Adam Smith: Critical Assessments*, Second Series, Vol. 5. London Routledge. pp. 122–133.
Kuhn, Thomas. 1962. *The Structure of Scientific Revolutions*. Chicago: University of Chicago Press.

Macfie, A.L. 'Adam Smith's Moral Sentiments as Foundation for His Wealth of Nations,' in J.C. Wood (ed.), *Adam Smith: Critical Assessments*, Vol. 2. London: Croom Helm.

Pateman, Carole. 1993. 'Feminist Critiques of the Public/Private Dichotomy,' in S.I. Benn and G.F. Gauss (eds), *Public and Private in Social Life*. London. Croom Helm.

Polanyi Karl. 1944. *The Great Transformation*. Boston: Beacon Press.

Raphael, D.D. and A.L. Macfie. 1871. 'Introduction,' in Adam Smith (ed.) *A Theory of Moral Sentiments*. Oxford: Clarendon.

Ross, Ian Simpson. 1995. *The Life of Adam Smith*. Oxford: Clarendon.

Sennet R. 1986 [1974]. *The Fall of Public Man*. London: Faber.

Smith, Adam. 1871. *The Theory of Moral Sentiments:* With a Biographical and Critical Memoir of the Author by Dugald Stewart. London: Bell and Dadly.

————. 1952. *An Inquiry into the Nature and Causes of the Wealth of Nations in Great Books of the Western World*. Chicago: William Benton.

9

Feminism and the Public-Private Distinction

Patricia Uberoi

I Prologue

I put it to a friend of mine, a well-known feminist author: 'Supposing *you* were asked to write on the public-private distinction in feminism, where would you begin?'

'But I thought we'd finished with *all that* long ago', was her spontaneous reply.

Of course, she had to be wrong. A distinction so intrinsic to modern conceptualizations of citizenship and governance, freedom and accountability, justice and the limits of state power, cannot be simply 'finished with': it will surely take on new names and new guises. But her reaction was interesting all the same as a confirmation of the built-in obsolescence of academic fashions, whereby yesterday's ideas are cheerfully discarded like last year's wardrobe. Indeed, 'Second Wave' feminism was not even two decades deep when Dale Spender remarked:

> Unless we take preventive measures, feminist ideas which no longer have the appeal of 'novelty' but which are nonetheless essential to our understanding and a vital part of our traditions will drift—as they have in the past—to the brink of oblivion. Unless we keep reminding ourselves of our heritage we endanger it; we risk losing it as we contribute to our own amnesia (Spender 1985).

Perhaps another reason for collective amnesia, beside academic fashion-consciousness, is the fact that ideas which had once seemed simple and straightforward tend to get elaborated, refined, contested and subject to so many qualifications that they soon become impossible to hold on to. The Sex-Gender distinction is one such concept that was essential to the articulation of the basics of contemporary feminism, yet almost instantly challenged. Another is the famous slogan: 'The personal is political.'[1]

At one level, 'The personal is political' may simply imply that the feminist ought to live her life by certain standards of political correctness: her personal or private life should be in line with her principles, and above reproach. Thus, even Simone de Beauvoir, who argued so powerfully for the proposition that one is not born, but *made*, a woman (1953), was all too womanly in her private-personal relations with Jean-Paul Sartre to pass muster as a blue-blooded feminist. And generations of would-be (Western) feminists have fretted that their hetero-sexual proclivities might impugn their feminist credentials.

However, 'The personal is political' has a more serious side to it. Beyond its limited but strategic goal of 'consciousness-raising', it suggests (*i*) that the so-called private and public spheres defined by liberal political theory are governed by the same patriarchal principles; (*ii*) that the identification of women/women's interests with the private sphere is one of the major mechanisms of women's historical and continuing subordination; and (*iii*) that demystifying and challenging the distinction is the first step in women's liberation.

Of course, nothing is so simple, in theory or in practice. Ultimately, there are as many feminist 'takes' on the private-public distinction as there are versions of feminism—minimally, the established (if no longer very helpful) Liberal, Marxist, Socialist and Radical types. And a lot depends on the sort of issue at stake—for instance, whether one is talking about a woman's right to abortion, or the right of women to feel secure in public space. Besides, as is often pointed out, the notion of the 'private' has several different connotations in common language and political philosophy,[2] each of which may have different implications for feminist theorizing. There is 'private' in the sense of 'personal', referring to the sphere of the autonomous individual (as in 'pro-choice' arguments over the woman's right over her own body [cf. Menon 1995]), or in discussions of a woman's individual citizen's right in the context of universal or constitutional rights). There is 'private' in the sense of 'sexual' (the 'private' of 'private life', nobody's business but one's own).

And there is 'private' in the sense of 'the family' or 'household', which, according to one line of thinking, is governed by a code of conduct that is (and must necessarily be) distinct from that of the public domain, and which should be subject to outside intervention only under extraordinary circumstances. As the connotations of the private vary, so too does understanding of the nature and function of the public domain, which may be identified with the extra-household domain of the state *and* civil society, or with the state alone, *contra* civil society and the family (see Okin 1998: 117). It is all rather confusing.

In this essay, I will not attempt a comprehensive survey of feminist positions on the public-private distinction (but see, e.g., Nicholson 1992, Okin 1998, Pateman 1987). Given the complexities just mentioned, that would be far too vast a canvas. Instead, I will delimit my focus in two ways. First, I will concentrate on those issues that interest me particularly as a sociologist/anthropologist of the family, that is, a set of issues where feminists have sought to interrogate the exclusiveness of 'the family' vis-à-vis the public sphere. Such an interrogation is implicated in the foundational concept of 'patriarchy', used to refer to the principle of male dominance in the family and society at large (Tuttle 1987: 242–43), though one might add here that 'patriarchy' is a concept with which many feminist anthropologists feel somewhat uncomfortable (Uberoi 1995).

I will further delimit my focus by considering the issues mainly from an Indian standpoint, that is, how the ideas referred to have been accepted, critiqued, elaborated, or indeed ignored, in the Indian context. As is well-known, there are significant discrepancies between the positions of Western and Indian (or other non-Western) feminists on some of these issues which bear thinking about (see Bulbeck 1998, John 1996). Also, I will need to skirt around a particular tricky issue, namely that a number of so-called Indian 'feminists' and stalwarts of the Indian Women's Movement resist the label 'feminist'—for tactical reasons, and also because they cannot accept *in toto* the agenda and priorities of Western feminism (see, e.g., Kishwar 1999). Different attitudes to sexuality and the family, as well as resentment over asymmetries in the production of feminist knowledge, may be at the base of this resistance (see Uberoi 1993a). There is also a degree of tension, manifested in many interactive situations, between *academic* feminism (Women's Studies) and Women's Movement activism. Many activists would prefer to think of theory *as emerging from* political practice and engagement with 'the issues at stake' (see Gandhi and Shah 1992, Kumar

1993)—the 'theory of the practice', as it were—rather than the other way round.

My coverage of issues here will also be very uneven. In fact, I will focus primarily on two strands of recent feminist theorizing that have sought, in different ways, to challenge the liberal public-private distinction in respect to gender relations within the family: the 'bargaining' approach, and the 'contract' approach. The former has been applied, and indeed refined, in the context of India. In fact, it is one of the few areas in which South Asian scholars can be said to have contributed substantially to contemporary feminist theorizing.[3] The latter has had few 'takers' among Indian feminists and, as far as I know, has aroused little interest. Before narrowing my focus to these two strands of thought, however, I will set out, albeit skeletally, the wider range of issues on which the public-private distinction is challenged in respect of the family. My reason for not addressing these questions more fully in this paper is quite simple. Each theme has produced a voluminous and robust literature and meta-discourse. Already in the best of hands, so to speak, my own input would be largely redundant.

II Pegging the Ground

Communitarian Personal Law

The Indian context provides a peculiar (though by no means unique) challenge to thinking about the public-private dichotomy in respect to the family, in so far as 'personal' or family law (on marriage, divorce, inheritance and adoption) varies by religious community, though the state offers civil alternatives as well. Since the legal constitution of the family is identified with religion, the debate on the desirability (or otherwise) of a Uniform Civil Code applicable equally to all citizens is one in which the universal claims of human rights and gender justice are pitted against the principles of the religious exclusivity of the family and the protection of community identity (see, e.g., Hasan 1994). Though Prime Minister Nehru and other Congress leaders were committed to the eventual institution of a Uniform Civil Code, the passions aroused in the course of drafting the Hindu Code Bill persuaded them to compromise. The Uniform Civil Code thus remains one of the Directive Principles of the Constitution, but its practical realization is subject to indefinite deferral (see, e.g., Parashar 1992: esp. Ch. 5, Som 1992).

From the start, it seems, the Indian Women's Movement was divided on this issue (see Chaudhuri 1995). However, the general opinion of both activists and academics from the 1970s reflected a strong commitment to the ideal of the Uniform Civil Code, both to remove discrepancies *between* communities, and to ensure a greater degree of gender justice overall (GOI 1974: Ch. 4). Many feminist scholars and Women's Movement activists would still hold to this position, but the earlier certainty has been eroded over recent years as feminists find themselves uncomfortable bedfellows on the issue of the UCC with the so-called 'Hindu Right' who aspire to impress a Hindu majoritarian hegemony over the 'minority' rights of other communities (Hasan 1999, Kapur and Cossman 1996: Ch. 4, Sangari 1995, 2000).

Domestic Labour and Women's Workforce Participation

The second issue on which feminists in India (as elsewhere) have sought to challenge the privacy of the family is that of women's work both inside and outside the home. The 1974 *Towards Equality* Report (GOI 1974: Ch. 5) played a major role in figuring the rate of women's workforce participation as a measure (supposedly) of their emancipation from patriarchal control. It also confirmed the gender-based horizontal and vertical segmentation of the labour market; the historical downturn in women's paid work in certain important sectors of the economy; the geographically uneven rates of women's workforce participation through South Asia, correlating with other indices of women's backwardness and deprivation; the under-enumeration and under-valuation of women's work; and women's preponderance in the informal or unorganized sector of the economy, where their work is underpaid, unregulated, and largely 'invisible' (GOI 1988, Mukherjee 1999). Feminist scholars have also contributed substantially to making this invisible work more visible, both at the level of national accounting, and in the context of the household economy. Numerous studies of women's home-based production over the last two decades or more have shown how this work adds crucially to household income even as it incorporates these women workers on highly exploitative terms into a late-capitalist world system of production (Mies 1982, Menefee-Singh and Kelles-Vitanen 1987). Feminist studies have also carefully documented women's critical role in ensuring household subsistence, as well as keeping a vigilant eye on changing employment patterns at the state and national levels, especially in the light of the potential impact of recent structural adjustment programmes. In all this, there has been relatively little theoretical or empirical consideration of the nature of women's 'housework' *per se*, or of the role of the housewife in the modern bourgeois sense, a major preoccupation of Western feminist writings (e.g. Delphy 1984, Oakley 1976, Pateman 1999: Ch. 5), though Hannah Papanek has usefully speculated on the middle-class housewife's important role in 'family status production work' (Papanek 1989, also Sangari 1993). This blind-spot in respect to the middle-class is clearly a hiatus, though the compulsion to concentrate attention on the most exploited and vulnerable of women workers needs no justification.

The question of the work women do inside and outside the home, the rewards they receive for their work, and its economic valuation and social recognition, are closely connected to the question to be taken up here shortly, namely, the strength of women's 'bargaining' position in the context of intra-household relations of the sexes (see Section III). It also connects up with the question of the terms of the marriage 'contract', which creates 'housewives' out of wives (see Section IV).

Domestic Violence

Feminist scholars have also taken the lead in foregrounding the issue of domestic violence, demanding that the law should reach into the home to prevent or punish interpersonal violence, including wife-battery, child-abuse and incest, neglect of the aged or of the girl child, marital rape, etc. This has been a fundamental thrust of feminist legal research and of social activism (Gandhi and Shah 1992: Ch. 2, Karlekar 1999, Rao 1996), resulting in amendments to the law and new rules of evidence and procedure, along with the creation of new institutional mechanisms for dealing with complaints of domestic violence. Of course there remains a long way to go to 'break the silence' around domestic violence, and to ensure that the family home is a safe haven for all its members.

As noted, issues of religion-specific personal law, women's domestic and extra-domestic work, and domestic violence, are questions that have received considerable attention from feminist scholars and women's movement activists, both internationally and in the Indian context. We now turn to consider two other types of challenges to the public/private dichotomy of liberal political theory: the 'bargaining' approach to intra-household gender relations, and the 'contract' approach to marriage. The former will command the greater attention for the reason that it has been elaborated in special reference to the South

Asian context. The neglect of the latter by feminists in this region is something on which we will have cause to speculate.

III The 'Bargaining' Approach

In a crude way, one could characterize the bargaining approach as an attempt to interpret gender (and other) relations in the family according to secular principles operating in the 'market'. This approach has developed fairly recently (from the 1980s) as an extension of game theory, to address distributional inequalities within the household that have adverse effects on certain categories of household members—especially women, but also children and the aged. These effects are measured in the differential access of family members to food, clothing, healthcare and education, resulting—at the starkest—in differential mortality and levels of morbidity.

A foundational text in the formulation of the bargaining approach is a paper by Amartya Sen, 'Economics of the Family', published in the *Asian Development Review* in 1983 (see Sen 1993, similarly, Sen 1990). The approach has since been elaborated by a number of other economists using game–theoretic approaches (see Agarwal 1994: 54–60, 1997: 3–5), and more recently in reference to the Indian context by Bina Agarwal in her justly acclaimed *A Field of One's Own* (1994), as well as in a comprehensive lead article in the *Feminist Economist*, published in 1997 (see also Agarwal 1999). For the non-economist, much of this literature is truly daunting and, when the chips are down, economists seem to have a disconcerting way of hiding behind the arcane mysteries of their discipline. But it is important, I believe, that these issues be opened up to interdisciplinary engagement.

As a first step in probing the 'economics of the family',[4] Sen begins with an examination (in effect, a caricature) of the 'assumptions' that economists are wont to make about the family in relation to the individuals who constitute it. These fictions are of several different, and contrastive kinds, each of them in its own way ridiculous or counter-commonsensical. There is, first, the notion of the 'glued-together family', where the family acts as an individual writ large: 'There are ... no individual decisions, individual utility, etc., but only family decisions, family welfare, etc.' (1993: 453). But 'the family does not think', Sen therefore goes on to remark in criticism: 'the members of the family do.... Living and dying, illness and health, and joys and sufferings happen to persons, and welfare economics can scarcely ignore these personal conditions' (Ibid.).

There is a second sense in which the family is treated as a single economic unit, acting like an individual. Sen characterizes this as the 'despotic family' image, whereby the family head acts as a benevolent dictator exercising choice, supposedly 'altruistically', on behalf of all family members and allocating resources for their individual and the family's collective good. But, can one assume the head's disinterested benevolence? Definitely not, many feminists would say, judging by the grim evidence of differential male/female life-chances throughout the region. The assumption of the family head as sole decision-maker is itself an indication of the 'patriarchal' constitution of society, through the collusion of the state, the community, and the patrilineal family system against the material interests of women as a class. Regrettably, it is an assumption that is very firmly embedded in public policy (see Agarwal 1999).

Against these so-called 'unitary' theories of the family is the notion that Sen attributes to the prolific economic theorist, Gary Becker: the concept of the 'super-trader family'. In this model, 'individuals are assumed to be relentlessly pursuing their individual utilities, and in doing this, they enter into trades at implicit prices resulting in marriages and the working of the family' (Sen 1993: 453). Here, relations within the family are seen as quasi-market relations. 'Market transactions take place within the family in an imagined way at imagined prices and imagined wages...', with marriage being like a two-person firm in which each party 'hires' the other (Ibid.: 454). Though this perspective has the merit of venturing into the 'black box' of the family, Sen notes (albeit in a footnote) that 'such maximizing behaviour without constraints of norms and duty, and other influences, may not be a sensible assumption even outside the family, but it is hardly credible inside it' (Ibid.: 454n).

Having roundly dismissed the various fictions regarding the family that other economists live by, Sen proposes a mediating position to account for *both* the unity of the family, *and* the diversity of individual interests and outcomes within it. The family, he suggests, should be conceived as a site of 'co-operative conflict'. That is, while individual members have different and conflicting interests, it is in their interests to stick together as a family because cooperation has economically calculable benefits over non-cooperation (Ibid.: 456). In this model, resource allocation within the family is seen as the outcome of implicit or explicit 'bargaining' between members, some of whom are in a better bargaining position compared to others, either because they already command superior resources in the family or have better exogenous support, or because their 'fall-back' position is better should they ever decide or need to quit. The result is that some family members, or *categories* of family members, succeed in cornering a relatively greater share of family resources compared to others. In poor countries, or under extreme conditions, this can mean the difference between death and survival.

Bina Agarwal's feminist revision of the 'bargaining *approach*' (as she calls it, to distinguish it from the narrower 'bargaining *model*') seeks to make the bargaining model more comprehensive by greatly enlarging the range of factors that may moderate women's bargaining power within the family, and the fallback position outside (1997: 6–7). Focusing on the South Asian context, she seeks (*i*) to go considerably beyond Sen and add to the usual quantitatively measurable factors the *qualitative* aspects of social norms and value perceptions; (*ii*) to determine their hypothetical order of ranking and relative weight; and (*iii*) to give due recognition to the linkages between an individual's intra-household bargaining position and extra-household forces and structures. This formulation is the background for her privileging of *land* as the most important asset to which South Asian women do not generally have title, and ownership/possession of which would critically enhance their bargaining and fallback positions (esp. 1994: Ch. 1, 1997: 12–14). Needless to say, the focus on women's rights in land has been a major contribution of Agarwal's work, making Sen's preoccupation with women's literacy and education seem trifling in comparison, like a vestige of 19th century social reformism.

From the perspective of a sociology of the family, however, Agarwal's elaboration of the bargaining approach is not without its problems. Ironically, she seems to go both *too far*, that is, by taking on board too many factors of a non-quantifiable kind, and—to the contrary—*not far enough*, by evading the challenge of 'altruism' to a perspective which still, despite Agarwal's more nuanced rendition, presumes individual self-interest as the fundamental motivation of human conduct in the family and society. Let me try and explain this apparent paradox.

First, the assessment of the factors that may contribute positively to enhancing women's bargaining power and fallback position in the family comes over with greater clarity when there are *fewer* variables to be considered, and when these variables are easily amenable to quantification and empirical testing. A good example is the calculation of women's economic contribution to household subsistence in terms of time spent and product generated, a calculation which can provide a telling answer to the assumption of women as 'dependents' and non-contributors to family income. Or measurement of women's food intake and blood haemoglobin levels may reveal that they have not received adequate nutrition compared to the men in the family. But assessment of the role of many other, essentially non-quantifiable factors like values, attitudes, norms and customary expectations, is infinitely more difficult. Sen had himself sought to go beyond his fellow economists to reflect on the role of some of these factors in determining women's bargaining position in the family or their fallback position outside, and in establishing the social legitimacy of women's claims to more equal treatment in the family—for instance, *social perceptions* of the value of women's work, or women's *own perceptions* of their self-interest and social role (see Sen 1990, also Agarwal 1997: 10–12). But Agarwal seeks to extend (and to some extent modify) these insights by further expanding the range of endogenous and exogenous factors that might enhance or diminish a woman's bargaining position in the family. For instance, a woman's claim to inherit family land may be affected by existing inheritance laws; by the community's concept of legitimacy; by her educational status and legal literacy; by her access to economic and social resources for survival; by her economic and physical access to legal machinery, etc. (Agarwal 1997: 14), *as well as* by the general norms, values and customary expectations of her community. These norms and values define, for instance: the rules of marriage; the gender division of labour inside and outside the home; rules of modesty and deportment and notions of gendered space; modes of decision-making; and understandings of entitlements (Ibid.: 15). They set limits on what can be bargained about, determine and constrain bargaining power, affect the style of bargaining ('overt' or 'covert', for instance), or are themselves subject to negotiation in individual and collective struggles for greater entitlements (Ibid.: 15).

Agarwal's observations are all well-taken, and endorsed by ethnographic accounts. The problem for the bargaining perspective is simply that the factors involved are mostly unquantifiable, and belong to a different order of empirical reality when compared to, say, the monetary 'value' that can be placed on women's work or economic contribution to household subsistence, etc., in the narrower version of the bargaining model. Adducing such social attitudes, values, norms and customs affecting intra-household gender relations to the bargaining approach ultimately means treating qualitative data *as if* it were quantitative. Or else the analysis is obliged to resort to sociological/anthropological *description*, often enough in the decontextualized style that anthropologist Max Gluckman has disparagingly termed 'apt illustration'. To put it differently, consideration of the social values and norms that impinge on a woman's bargaining and fallback positions is something which can probably be done better in other presentational styles (narrative, biographical, thick description, case method), rather than by appropriating them to a quasi-economic model of familial interactions. Needless to add, one does not really need the elaborate conceptual apparatus of the 'bargaining' model in order to describe the complex 'give-and-take' of intra-family relations.

A second, and really tricky question for the bargaining approach, is the role of 'altruism', as against individual self-interest, in determining the allocation of household resources.[5] In his 1983 article, Sen had acknowledged, and then dismissed, altruistic action in one breath:

> The acceptance of the bargaining perspective in the fixing of household arrangements (i.e., who does what work and gets what goods and services) does not, of course, deny that feelings, such as love, affection and concern, may also play important parts in the choice of arrangements. The parameters of the bargaining problem can include many complex ones (Sen 1993: 456).

But, he insists that these motivations 'should be seen in terms of an 'as–if' market with implicit prices', and *not* as non-market issues (Ibid.: 456). Ultimately, there is no accounting for altruism, Sen seems to say, though he is quick to add that the economist's recognition of the market-driven, self-interested realities of intra-family power relations should not be taken to imply their '*normative* acceptance' (1993: 457).

Similarly, Agarwal adds a footnote rider to her discussion of the many factors that affect a woman's bargaining power and fallback options, including the perceived legitimacy of claims: 'My emphasis on these factors is *not to deny* that feelings of love and concern are also important in shaping family relations and economic outcomes' (1994: 55n, emphasis added). Once again, that is, altruistic motivations are not completely discounted. (Apart from anything else, as Agarwal points out, a woman's short-term altruism might be in her long-term material self-interest [1997: 25–28].) Nor are they dismissed as 'false consciousness', which is the most convenient way of dealing with inconvenient paradoxes. But there can be no real accounting for them, even in the 'less restrictive' version of the bargaining approach that she seeks to propose. As she concludes her discussion of the thorny issues of women's self-perceptions, altruism and self-interest:

> ...the idea of women's false-perceptions [of their own worth and entitlements] appears to have been overstated,[6] as also the arguments concerning the gender-specificity of altruism. At the same time, it cannot be assumed (as most bargaining models do) that women are solely motivated by self-interest. To the extent that women as well as men might be motivated by *both* altruism and self-interest (as appears realistic to assume), but in degrees that cannot be specified *a priori*, it would be difficult to predict outcomes.... (Agarwal 1997: 28).

For a sociologist of the family, such arguments are both familiar in other guises (the 'conflict' versus 'consensus' models and their mediation, a standard tutorial topic in political sociology), and rather weird. Sociologists and anthropologists (and many others) have debated endlessly on whether the family or marriage or the incest taboo are (or are not) 'universal' institutions of human society and, if they are, what universal social functions these institutions perform. But the idea that families exist because individuals—despite their conflicts of interest—find cooperation in this frame to be more beneficial than non-cooperation, certainly appears to be a rather crude 'take' on the question.

Of course it is no doubt true that quitting is an option that some individuals, more than others, have the wherewithal to exercise, and that some family members continue to be exploited within the family set-up on that account. We can readily observe, for instance, that many Indian women hesitate to walk out of abusive marriages and exploitative family situations, even risking their lives, because they have nowhere to go and precious little to fall back on, and we can surely concede that seeking the reasons for this state of affairs and remedies for it should be an important plank in feminist scholarship and activist intervention programmes. All the same, we must recognize that there is another issue at stake here, too.

As elsewhere, 'the family' in India is perceived as a value *in itself*, over and against the material interests of the individuals who constitute it. Indeed, this value is considered to be an important *civilizational* achievement, *especially* in the age of globalization. Several authors have remarked on the fact that Indian social reformers have hesitated to attack the institution of the family, even while seeking to ameliorate the position of women within the family and society (see Béteille 1993, also Chatterjee 1993). It is notable, too, that Indian feminists have on the whole been cautious in their critiques of the family, though they realize that family 'values' (so-called) often provide the legitimization for gender inequalities, persuading women to accept less than they deserve, and to condone their own oppression and exploitation. The reason is, perhaps, that the family is recognized to be the archetypal human institution, where members may act *altruistically*, out of love for others, and against their own self-interest and all rational explanation, though they may also no doubt act self-interestedly. It is also true that women are often expected to be, *naturally*, more altruistic than men, and that their self-denial is often to their serious material disadvantage. All the same, this 'femininized' virtue of 'sacrifice' on behalf of others, and without expectation of immediate reward, is regarded as the ideal for all in the context of family life, for men *and* for women, to preserve an institution which commands great social value (see, e.g., Das 1993, Uberoi 2001).

The question then remains: Is the principle of altruism to be only a paradoxical footnote to the narrative of material self-interest, a residual factor in the understanding of household dynamics? Can there be a model of intra-family relations which is *not* based on the individualistic model? Might we expand the currently fashionable social science concept of the 'moral economy' to provide an understanding of the dynamics of household relations beyond the market, without at the same time condoning an ideology of women's oppression? In other words, how can one recognize the undoubted role of love and altruism in intra-family relations (*contra Realpolitik* and the morality of the market), without returning defeated to our starting point, that is, the need to critically interrogate the liberal public-private distinction from a feminist standpoint?

Perhaps one can merely say, in answer to these questions, that the problem cannot be solved by treating family relations as 'as-if' market relations, any more than it can be solved by discounting the exercise of power, and the implicit and explicit bargaining that constitutes the bedrock of family dynamics.[7]

IV The 'Contract' Approach

We now come to consider an approach which, in various forms, has had a long history in liberal theory, and which has been quite influential in

Western feminist appraisals of the political constitution of the family as the foundational site of women's oppression. Brilliantly (though to my mind inconclusively) reviewed by Carole Pateman in *The Sexual Contract* (1988), this 'contractarian' feminist position asserts that the 'Social Contract' (that is, the association of free and equal individuals on which civil society is founded) extends only imperfectly into the 'private' sphere of the family. The historical progress 'from Status to Contract', to follow Sir Henry Maine's famous usage, is incomplete, because the institution of marriage retains vestiges of an unfree past. Or, as Pateman argues here, the other side of the 'Social Contract', and its hidden complementary opposite, is the 'Sexual Contract' between unequals, based on the sex (male or female) of the contracting parties. The 'Sexual Contract' operates mainly in the 'private' domain of the family—it *sustains* the family as we know it—though it may also be discerned in the public domain, in prostitution and surrogacy contracts, for instance (Ibid.: Ch. 7).

Thus, on the one hand, marriage creates the category of 'housewife', which automatically, and seemingly naturally, puts the wife's (unpaid) labour at the disposal of her husband and family. Since the 19th century in Europe, Pateman writes,

> [t]he domestic relations of master-slave and master-servant, relations between unequals, have given way to the relation between capitalist and worker. Production moved from the family to capitalist enterprises, and male domestic labourers became workers. This wage labourer now stands as a civil equal with his employer in the public realm and the capitalist market (Pateman 1988: 117).

To the contrary, however,

> A (house) wife now performs the tasks once distributed between servants of different rank or undertaken by the maid of all work. Her 'core' jobs are cleaning, shopping, cooking, washing-up, laundering and ironing. She also looks after her children, frequently cares for aged parents or other relatives, and is sometimes incorporated to a greater or lesser degree in her husband's work. ...[Yet] the problem is not that wives perform valuable tasks for which they are not paid (which has led some feminists to argue for state payment or wages for housework). Rather, what being a woman (wife) *means* is to

provide certain services for and at the command of a man (husband). In short, the marriage contract and a wife's subordination as a (kind of) labourer cannot be understood in the absence of the sexual contract and the patriarchal construction of 'men' and 'women' and the 'private' and 'public' spheres (Ibid.: 128, original emphasis).

Here the focus is on the terms under which women, in consequence of marriage, contribute their labour as housewives in the domestic sphere, as against the employment contracts that govern the work that both men and women do in the public domain of the market. The issue is closely connected, of course, with the question of the *economic* valuation of women's domestic and non-domestic work, discussed in Section II.

The second issue is the nature of the marriage 'contract' *per se*. According to the 19th century legalist, Sir W. Blackstone, English law 'considers marriage in no other light than as a civil contract' (Ibid.: 154). As a number of feminist authors have pointed out, however, echoing the earlier critiques of William Thompson and J.S. Mill, the marriage contract is in a number of respects quite unlike most other civil contracts. For instance, it is not a written document, but simply the law of the land governing marriage and family life. Its 'essential' aspects ('the husband's duty to support his wife, and the wife's duty to obey her husband' [Weitzman 1981: 338]) are not decided upon, and cannot be wilfully changed by, the parties to the agreement. Marriage is presumed to be a life-long arrangement (you can not contract to marry for just three years, or five years!), and is terminable only on grounds approved by the state, which are defined more strictly than for the termination of other forms of contract. Odder still, a marital contract becomes valid by virtue of two 'acts': a *performative* act in a civil or religious ceremony approved by the state ('I do'); and a *sex* act, the consummation of the marriage, without which the marriage is deemed void (Pateman 1988: 156–63). Marriage thus implies that the parties must be of the opposite sex (I leave aside the complicating issue of legalized homosexual 'marriage'), and that the wife's body will be at the sexual disposal of the husband (notwithstanding the recent recognition in some countries of marital rape). In this way, the principle of 'status'—that is, *sexual* status—subverts the supposedly 'contractual' basis of the marital relation.

A number of feminist authors have argued that the solution to these anomalies is to make marriage fully and properly a contractual relation between equals. As Pateman summarises this position:

The completion of the movement from status to contract, entails that status and sexual difference should disappear along with 'status' in its other senses.... In contract, the fact of being a man or a woman is irrelevant. In a proper marriage contract, two 'individuals' would agree on whatever terms were advantageous to them both. The parties to such a contract would not be a 'man' and a 'woman' but two owners of property in their persons who have come to an agreement about this property to their mutual advantage (Ibid.: 167).

The trouble is, as Pateman argues, that the radical 'contractarian' solution can lead only to an 'incongruous' situation, whereby the main burden of the contract is to set the conditions for later divorce (as some celebrities currently seek to do, amidst worldwide publicity), or to encourage exit from the marriage: the most advantageous arrangement for the individual, she says, would be 'an endless series of very short-term contracts to use another's body as and when required' (Ibid.: 184). Unfortunately, Pateman herself seems to have no better solution to offer, considering it sufficient to bring to the forefront of feminist political consciousness the intrinsic link between the overt Social Contract and the hidden Sexual Contract in a patriarchally constituted society (Ibid.: 233–34).

The 'contractarian' perspective on the public-private distinction has not, as far as I know, found favour with Indian feminist writers. Nor has it made much sense to activists, except possibly at the point of overlap with the issue of women's domestic labour.[8] One reason may be the overall inhospitality of the Indian context to constructions of marriage as a 'contractual', rather than a sacred/sacramental, relationship.

As critics observe, this dilemma of understanding is manifested in the legal system itself. Contemporary Indian law, as is well known, is based in English law, and shares with that system the perspective that legal 'progress' will be expressed in a move 'from Status to Contract'. In the case of Indian family ('personal') law, this ecumenical ideal is already compromised by the existence of *community*-specific family law, implying that the institution of marriage is defined and constrained by religious belief and soteriological considerations. Though the 'contractual' aspect is quite prominent in Muslim marriage,[9] judgements and judges' *obiter dicta* under Hindu law on issues concerning nullity and divorce are ambivalent, sometimes affirming marriage as a sacramental union, sometimes as a contractual agreement, and sometimes both at once (see Uberoi 1996).[10] A key issue here is the nature of 'consent'. For instance, a Hindu marriage is voidable (though still valid) if it can be proved that consent was obtained fraudulently or by force, but it is inevitably emphasized that the concept of 'fraud' (in reference to marriage) should differ from that specified in the Indian Contract Act, because marriage is a sacred bond and an important social institution that should not be lightly voided. Again, unsoundness of mind renders the marriage voidable, but not void *ab initio*. Similarly, the prevalence of child and arranged marriage in India has required that the notion of consent be broadened so that the 'consent' of the bride and the groom is merely their consent to allow marriage negotiations to go ahead on their behalf. These modifications of the principles of contract in the context of marriage suggest that statute law, based in English law, is seriously at odds with the wider 'culture' of Hindu kinship and marriage. Specifically, Hindu marriage is conceived as an alliance between two families through the 'gift' of a woman, rather than as a contract between two consenting adults. Arguably too, the ideology of the 'joint family' implies that it is the father-son bond, rather than the conjugal bond, which is the core support of the family, a fact which rather complicates the notion of 'patriarchy' in patrilineal kinship contexts.[11]

Indian feminist authors are well aware of the pathologies of the Hindu kinship system, which are brutally evident in cases of domestic violence and dowry murder, but they are scarcely enthusiastic to follow the Western family system, either. As noted earlier, their critique of the marital contract tends to be cautious, and addressed to remedying specific problems and pathologies, rather than an attack on the Indian family system *per se*.

V Conclusion

We began this essay by attempting to restrict the range of issues on which feminists in India and abroad have sought to challenge the public-private distinction, focusing on the role of the family in the wider political economy of gender relations. Nonetheless, we found ourselves confronted with quite a broad range of issues on which, in the compass of a single paper, we could provide only a rather breathless Cook's Tour. All the same, it is both important and instructive to undertake such excursions in order to recuperate the coherence that underlies a wide range of writings on women and the family. The reason is that the feminist critique of the public-private distinction is often left inexplicit and unexamined, as Indian feminist authors and Women's Movement activists proceed with the everyday tasks of describing and document- ing the inequities of women's domestic and extra-domestic work, intra- family violence, the working of communitarian personal law, etc.

In fact, we have seen that the work on the gender politics of the family that is expressly theorized may be effected more through the disciplinary resources of different academic disciplines, than by recourse to a distinc- tively 'feminist' theoretical apparatus such as the Sex-Gender distinc- tion, or the Public-Private distinction, regarded as fundamental planks of the feminist enterprise. This bears on the much-debated question of whether feminism is a discipline in itself, with a theory, method, prac- tice and curriculum of its own; whether it is a perspective that should eventually transform the orientation and practice of *all* disciplines; or whether it is simply an interdisciplinary enterprise whose focus is the study of women (Women's Studies in the narrower sense).

Observers discern an overall consensus on the second of these three alternatives in the Indian context (see John 2001), setting one to won- der how different disciplines are doing, comparatively speaking, both in the international context and in India. In the course of this essay, we examined two specific instances of theorizing about the family which, explicitly or inexplicitly, could be said to be implementing a feminist 'take' on the public-private distinction. We had first of all the 'bargain- ing approach', based in economics, and then the 'contract approach', based in political philosophy, the former being fine-tuned in reference to Indian data, the latter as yet undomesticated. Admittedly, there are other related approaches we might have considered, too: for instance, the so- called 'capabilities approach', derived from a different strand in Amartya Sen's writing and again developed with special reference to India by philosopher Martha Nussbaum (Nussbaum 2000).

From the viewpoint of a sociology of the family, both the bargaining and the contract approaches would seem to leave unanswered ques- tions and problems which are of great interest to the sociologist of the family. The former evades consideration of altruistic behaviour (except as the expectation of the family head in the 'despotic family' model). The contract approach proffers a strong critique of the 'sexual' side of the social contract, yet fails to provide a convincing solution. It also assumes that it is the conjugal couple which comprises the basic unit of the family, and the originary site of the sexual contract, but this is not altogether a helpful observation when one is confronting the realities of a patrilineal kinship system, whose organizing principles and under- lying kinship ideology are quite different.

But what of the role of the sociologist or anthropologist?[12] What have these disciplines had to offer in this discursive realm? Sociology and anthropology, along with psychology, are in fact disciplines in which the study of the family has been a central preoccupation, both as an empirical object of study, and as the focus of theorizing about social structure and social institutions, about nature and culture, about particulars and universals. Feminist studies have drawn extensively on the insights of comparative anthropology, and the work of feminist anthropologists has been an important input into feminist debates on the gender implications of the public-private distinction since the 1970s (see e.g. Moore 1988).

Elsewhere in the world, feminist anthropologists and sociologists complain, nonetheless, that feminism has made insufficient impact on their disciplines, and that just 'adding women' to everything is a token gesture that does not entail a feminist perspective, though it might be a first step in the right direction (Uberoi 1995). Be that as it may, a number of critics are of the opinion that the feminist perspective is, and remains, on the sociological margins in the Indian context (see John 2001, Rege 2000). Moreover, while Indian feminist writers in general (notably, economists and historians), have regarded 'the family' as the key institution of Indian 'patriarchy', and have focussed extensively on aspects of familial production and reproduction, and on the linkages between family, community and state, the *sociology* of the family in India has remained relatively immune to this considerable volume of work. In fact, as far as general teaching and research goes, the main 'problem' of the Indian family, sociologically speaking, is still conceived as the transformation of the joint family to the nuclear family form as postulated by the 'modernization' model; anthropology, on a somewhat different trajectory, continues to see its focus as the recording of the varieties of family types and kinship practices in a multicultural environment. There are exceptions, of course, but one might think of them as the exceptions that prove the rule; for instance, a number of papers included in my own reader on Indian family and kinship (Uberoi 1993b)[13]; recent publications by Rajni Palriwala (1994) and Leela Dube (1997); papers in the 'Women and Household in Asia' series from the mid-1980s; as well as quite a number of anthropological monographs (for citations, see Uberoi 2000). Indeed, these works remind us that Indian data may be productive in highlighting the unthinking ethnocentrism of Western feminism, or in reinvigorating the truly comparativist dimension which the self-centred and self-assured Western sociology of the family continues to lack.

But meanwhile, it is surely challenging to look again at familiar data from an expressly feminist perspective, and to wonder, perhaps, if that critical perspective itself needs rethinking in a different, non-Western light.

NOTES

1. The slogan was apparently first used in the US in the late 1960s, but first appeared in print in 1970 as the title of an article by Carol Hanisch arguing for the importance of 'consciousness-raising' groups in feminist practice. See Code (2000: 412); also Okin (1998: 122–25), Tuttle (1987: 245–46).
2. See in brief Williams (1976: 133–36), 'individual'; and pp. 203–4, 'private'.
3. In an earlier article (Uberoi 1993a), I had suggested a number of themes on which Indian feminist writings had potential to contribute to the further development of feminist theory. These were: (*i*) Eco-feminism or feminist environmentalism; (*ii*) the concept of female 'power'; (*iii*) the ideal of androgyny, for which there is a religious model in the concept of Ardhnarishwara; and (*iv*) the exploration of cultural pluralism.
4. Note that Sen uses the term 'family' to refer to the unit that many sociologists prefer to call 'household'—that is, a coresidential, commensal unit, usually comprised of related persons. Sociologists like to distinguish this grouping from the 'family', defined by kinship relations of descent, filiation and affinity, but making no presumption of coresidence, commensality, etc. (see Shah 1998: Ch. 2 for clarifications).
5. My discussion here is somewhat complicated by the fact that the idea of 'altruism' has apparently been specialized in much of this literature to refer to the conduct of the benevolent family head.
6. Agarwal's discussion on this point makes interesting reading. She argues that just because women appear to agree to their own oppression in the family 'system', does not mean that they suffer from 'false consciousness'. They may just be being prudent; or they cannot see other options; or they resist in 'covert' rather than 'overt' ways. See also Agarwal (1994: Ch. 9).
7. I am reminded here of a reading I had done some time ago of the revolutionary writings of the Chinese 'May Fourth Movement' (c. 1915 to 1922). In an initial phase, the institution of the family was denounced as the instrument of individual oppression (of youth by age, of women by men), and as the model and origin of inequality in society at large: the traditional family system had to be abolished before a democratic republican society could be established. A few years later, some of the same writers—disillusioned by warlord politics at home and by the

betrayal of Chinese interests at the Versailles Peace Conference—propounded the view that the family is the human institution in which one sees in operation the altruistic values that are part of humankind's natural inheritance, and that social and political reform should seek to generalise familial selflessness to the wider public domain (Uberoi 1984).

8. Even here, there is a difference, as noted earlier. While Western feminist authors have focussed especially on the creation of the 'housewife' category, Indian authors have focussed in addition on the political economy of home-based production, that is, women's participation in the informal market economy.

9. The question of the 'meaning' of Muslim marriage is still hampered by inadequate research, notwithstanding the enormous publicity that surrounded the Shah Bano case.

10. The civil marriage law (the Special Marriage Act, 1954), modelled on the English Matrimonial Causes Act, 1950, also falls short of the ultimate contractarian ideal, in the respects noted by Pateman.

11. On the 'joint family' as ideology and family form, see Uberoi (2000).

12. There is a slight confusion here regarding disciplinary identities: sociology in India is *mostly*, but not entirely, aligned with anthropology elsewhere in the world, though it innovates in so far as the Indian sociologist usually studies his own, not other, societies.

13. For a critique of this volume's treatment of gender issues in family and kinship studies in the context of the overall engagement of sociology and women's studies, see John (2001).

REFERENCES

Agarwal, Bina. 1999. *'The Family' in Public Policy: Fallacious Assumptions and Gender Implications*. New Delhi: National Council for Applied Economic Research.

_____. 1997. '"Bargaining" and Gender: Relations Within and Beyond the Household', *Feminist Economics*, 3, 1: 1–51.

_____. 1994. *A Field of One's Own: Gender and Land Rights in South Asia*. Cambridge: Cambridge University Press.

Beauvoir, Simone de. 1953. *The Second Sex*. London: Jonathan Cape.

Béteille, André. 1993. 'The Family and the Reproduction of Inequality,' in Patricia Uberoi (ed.), *Family, Kinship and Marriage in India*, pp. 435–51. New Delhi: Oxford University Press.

Bulbeck, Chilla. 1998. *Re-orienting Western Feminisms: Women's Diversity in a Postcolonial World*. Cambridge: Cambridge University Press.

Code, Lorraine (ed.). 2000. *Encyclopaedia of Feminist Theory*. London and New York: Routledge.

Chatterjee, Partha. 1993. *The Nation and its Fragments: Colonial and Postcolonial Histories*. Princeton: Princeton University Press.

Chaudhuri, Maitrayee. 1995. 'Citizens, Workers and Emblems of Culture: An Analysis of the First Plan Document on Women', *Contributions to Indian Sociology*, vol. 29, nos 1 and 2, pp. 211–35.

Das, Veena. 1993 [1976]. 'Masks and Faces: An Essay on Punjabi Kinship,' in Patricia Uberoi (ed.), *Family, Kinship and Marriage in India*, pp. 198–222. New Delhi: Oxford University Press.

Delphy, C. 1984. *Close to Home: A Materialist Analysis of Women's Oppression*. Amherst: University of Massachusetts Press.

Dube, Leela. 1997. *Women and Kinship: Comparative Perspectives on Gender in South and South-East Asia*. Tokyo: United Nations University Press/ New Delhi: Vistaar.

Gandhi, Nandita and Nandita Shah. 1992. *The Issues at Stake: Theory and Practice in the Contemporary Women's Movement*. New Delhi: Kali for Women.

Government of India (GOI). 1988. *Shram Shakti: Report of the National Commission on Self-employed Women and Women in the Informal Sector*. New Delhi: Government of India Press.

_____. 1974. *Towards Equality: Report of the Committee on the Status of Women in India*. New Delhi: Department of Social Welfare. Government of India Press.

Hasan, Zoya. 1999. 'Gender Politics, Legal Reform and the Muslim Community in India,' in Patricia Jeffery and Amrita Basu (eds), *Resisting the Sacred and the Secular: Women's Activism and Politicised Religion in South Asia*, pp. 71–88. New Delhi: Kali for Women.

_____. (ed.). 1994. *Forging Identities: Gender, Communities and the State*. New Delhi: Kali for Women.

John, Mary. 2001. 'The Encounter of Sociology and Women's Studies: Questions from the Borders,' *Contributions to Indian Sociology*, vol. 35, no. 2, pp. 237–58.

_____. 1996. *Discrepant Locations: Feminism, Theory and Postcolonial Histories*. New Delhi: Oxford University Press.

Kapur, Ratna and Brenda Cossman. 1996. *Subversive Sites: Feminist Engagements with the Law in India*. New Delhi: Sage Publications.

Karlekar, Malavika. 1999. 'Breaking the Silence and Choosing to Hear: Perceptions of Violence,' in Fanny M. Cheung, et al. (eds), *Breaking the Silence: Violence Against Women in Asia*, pp. 59–81. Hong Kong: UNESCO and Equal Opportunities Commission.

Kishwar, Madhu. 1999. 'A Horror of "isms": Why I Do Not Call Myself a Feminist,' in *Off the Beaten Track: Rethinking Gender Justice for Indian Women*, pp. 268–90. New Delhi: Oxford University Press.

Kumar, Radha. 1993. *The History of Doing: An Illustrated Account of Movements for Women's Rights and Feminism in India, 1800–1990*. New Delhi: Kali for Women.

Menefee-Singh, Andrea and Anita Kelles-Viitanen (eds). 1987. *Invisible Hands: Women in Home Based Production*. New Delhi: Sage Publications.

Menon, Nivedita. 1995. 'The Impossibility of "Justice": Female Foeticide and Feminist Discourse on Abortion,' *Contributions to Indian Sociology*, vol. 29, nos 1 and 2: 372–92.

Mukherjee, Mukul. 1999. 'Women and Work in India: A Collage from Five Decades of Independence,' in Bharati Ray and Aparna Basu (eds), *From Independence Towards Freedom: Indian Women Since 1947*, pp. 56–79. New Delhi: Oxford University Press.

Mies, Maria. 1982. *The Lace–Makers of Narsapur: Indian Housewives Produce for a World Market*. London: Zed Books.

Moore, Henrietta. 1988. *Feminism and Anthropology*. Minneapolis: University of Minnesota Press.

Nicholson, Linda J. 1992. 'Feminist Theory: The Public and the Private,' in Linda McDowell and Rosemary Pringle (eds), *Defining Women: Social Institutions and Gender Divisions*, pp. 36–43. Cambridge: Polity Press.

Nussbaum, Martha C. 2000. *Women and Human Development: The Capabilities Approach*. New Delhi: Kali for Women.

Oakley, Ann. 1976. *Housewife*. Harmondsworth: Penguin Books.

Okin, Susan Moller. 1998. 'Gender, the Public and the Private,' in A. Phillips (ed.), *Feminism and Politics*, pp. 116–41. Oxford: Oxford University Press.

Palriwala, Rajni. 1994. *Changing Kinship, Family and Gender Relations in South Asia: Processes, Trends and Issues*. Leiden: Women and Autonomy Centre.

Papanek, Hannah. 1990. 'To Each Less Than She Needs, for Each More Than She Can Do: Allocations, Entitlements and Value,' in Irene Tinker (ed.), *Persistent Inequalities*, pp. 162–81. New York: Oxford University Press.

————. 1989. 'Family Status–Production Work: Women's Contribution to Social Mobility and Class Differentiation,' in Maitreyi Krishnaraj and Karuna Chanana (eds.), *Gender and the Household Domain: Social and Cultural Dimensions*, pp. 97–116. New Delhi: Sage Publications.

Parashar, Archana. 1992. *Women and Family Law Reform in India: Uniform Civil Code and Gender Equality*. New Delhi: Sage Publications.

Pateman, Carole. 1988. *The Sexual Contract*. Cambridge: Polity Press.

————. 1987. 'Feminist Critiques of the Public/Private Distinction,' in A. Phillips (ed.), *Feminism and Equality*, pp. 103–26. Oxford: Basil Blackwell.

Rao, Arati. 1996. 'Right in the Home. Feminist Theoretical Perspectives on International Human Rights,' in Ratna Kapur (ed.), *Feminist Terrains in Legal Domains: Interdisciplinary Essays on Women and Law in India*, pp. 100–21. New Delhi: Kali for Women.

Rege, Sharmila. 2000. 'Histories from the Borderlands,' *Seminar*, no. 495, *Situating Sociology*, November, pp. 55–61.

Sangari, Kumkum. 2000. 'Gender lines: Personal Laws, Uniform laws, Conversions,' in Imtiaz Ahmed, Partha S. Ghosh, and Helmut Reifeld (eds),

Pluralism and Equality: Values in Indian Society and Politics, pp. 271–319. New Delhi: Sage Publications.

_____. 1995. 'Politics of Diversity: Religious Communities and Multiple Patriarchies,' *Economic and Political Weekly*, vol. 30, no. 51, pp. 3287–3310.

_____. 1993. 'The Amenities of Domestic Life: Questions on Labour,' *Social Scientist*, vol. 21, nos 9–11, pp. 3–46.

Sen, Amartya. 1993 [1983]. 'Economics and the Family,' in Patricia Uberoi, (ed), *Family, Kinship and Marriage in India*, pp. 452–63. New Delhi: Oxford University Press.

_____. 1990. 'Gender and Cooperative Conflicts,' in Irene Tinker (ed.), *Persistent Inequalities: Women and World Development*, pp. 123–49. New York: Oxford University Press.

Som, Reba. 1992. 'Jawaharlal Nehru and the Hindu Code: A Victory of Symbol Over Substance?' Occasional Paper No. 30. New Delhi: Nehru Memorial Museum and Library.

Spender, Dale. 1985. *For the Record: The Making and Meaning of Feminist Knowledge*. London: The Women's Press.

Tuttle, Lisa. 1987. *Encyclopedia of Feminism*. London: Arrow Books.

Uberoi, Patricia. 2001. 'Imagining the Family: An Ethnography of Viewing *Hum aapke hain koun...*!', in Rachel Dwyer and Christopher Pinney (eds.), *Pleasure and the Nation: The History, Politics and Consumption of Popular Culture in India*. New Delhi: Oxford University Press.

_____. 2000. 'The Family in India: Beyond the Nuclear versus Joint Debate.' Institute of Economic Growth, Occasional Papers in Sociology No. 2.

_____. 1996. 'When is a Marriage not a Marriage? Sex, Sacrament and Contract in Hindu Marriage,' in Patricia Uberoi (ed.), *Social Reform, Sexuality and the State*, pp. 319–45. New Delhi: Sage Publications.

_____. 1995. 'Problems with Patriarchy: Conceptual Issues in the Engagement of Anthropology and Feminism,' *Sociological Bulletin*, vol. 44, no. 2, pp. 195–221.

_____. 1993a. 'Reciprocity in Social Science: Gender Issues,' *The Indian Journal of Social Science*, vol. 16, no. 3, pp. 243–58.

_____. 1993b. *Family, Kinship and Marriage in India*. New Delhi: Oxford University Press.

_____. 1984. 'Suicide, Incest and Cannibalism: An Anthropological Exegesis of a Modern Chinese Short Story,' *Social Analysis*, vol. 16; pp. 60–78.

Weitzman, Lenore. 1981. *The Marriage Contract: Spouses, Lovers, and the Law*. New York: The Free Press.

Williams, Raymond. 1976. *Keywords: A Vocabulary of Culture and Society*. London: Fontana-Collins.

10

Protecting Individual Rights as Safeguards of the Private Sphere: The German Setting from the Legal Point of View

Clauspeter Hill

From the legal point of view the distinction between the Public and the Private is mainly related to the question of protection of the private sphere against state (public) infringement by basic rights guarantees. However, one has to first define the keywords in this very context since their interpretation can vary.

There are also historical aspects to highlight in order to fully understand the development of basic rights both in German practice and today's implementation.

Definition

The so-called private sphere normally means a state of being away from others, alone and undisturbed. It has the notion of secrecy within the family and house (*Advanced Learner's Dictionary of Current English*, S.V. 'private sphere'). It describes an area for self-fulfilment and activities which are only determined by the individual will without influence of any authority.

Unfolding one's personality however, as the nucleus of private sphere does also include being in public. Marriages for instance are celebrated publicly in most cases. Doing business, even as private enterprises is impossible in secrecy. There are social contacts and activities which need publicity to a certain extent.

Thus, we must widen the definition of the private sphere for our purposes when we look at the public-private distinction from the legal point of view. It is the closed comfort of the family and home (*my home is my castle*), as well as the wider field of self-determination within the society. The opposite then should be the public authority which has the power to interfere into the area of private activities when overall interests shall prevail. The public may be described as the instrument of collective interests.

Consequently, if we talk about public-private we should understand it as *individualism* versus *collectivism*.

Historical Aspects

In feudal Europe most people did not have any privacy. They lived and worked in slavery which was reduced gradually but to a limited extent only. There was no participation in decision making and ruling their country. Ordinary people could not even decide their personal fate. The private sphere was actually limited to secrecy only.

The change was initiated in 18th century England by John Locke with his 'Theory of Law and State', the *Bill of Rights* in the United States and with Jean-Jacques Rousseau and the French Revolution.

Germany being split up in dozens of smaller kingdoms, dukedoms or counties did not have any nation-wide movement at that time. However, there were a number of those small states which joined Liberalism in Europe, for instance Prussia which was the most important state in the German empire. In 1794 it promulgated the '*Allgemeines Landrecht für die preußischen Staaten*' (Hattenhauer 1970). But it took until the mid 19th century for national efforts to be made to introduce certain standards to ensure personal liberty.

First of all, the liberalization movement focused on defensive aspects in order to preserve a small and rather limited field for individual determination. Basic rights were written down to protect the private sphere against the interference of the monarch. This enabled citizens to unfold their individuality according to their own will. There was also an increasing demand for equal treatment in all situations regardless of rank, religion and gender.

So we see, the two most important topics of the French Revolution—Liberté et Egalité—were also pointed out in Germany. In 1848/49 a constitutional assembly drafted the first comprehensive constitution for the whole empire. It's deputies gathered in Paul's Cathedral in Frankfurt and worked out a rather modern document with a detailed catalogue of Basic Rights and surprisingly ensured these rights by a kind of constitutional court. It is no wonder that this revolutionary 'Paul's Cathedral Constitution' was never enacted. The monarchs did not agree to these far reaching consequences. It took exactly hundred years before those standards were implemented with our current constitution.

Meanwhile, the constitutions of various kingdoms in Germany laid down the Basic Rights but these were not enforceable and were to the disposition of the king. The first all-German constitution was promulgated in 1871 and was still a document of the Emperor especially of the later Chancellor Otto von Bismarck. Its main purpose was the unification of the split empire without any emphasis on Basic Rights and private sphere protection.

The next attempt in safeguarding the private sphere of citizens was the so-called Weimar Constitution enacted in 1919 after World War I. However, it did not pay much attention to this issue and placed Basic Rights at the end of the legal document. Most importantly, it did not provide any instruments for enforcing civil rights.

The following period was one of dictatorship—by Hitler's national socialists. Both Basic Rights and the private sphere were badly affected. Privacy meant secrecy and secrecy meant undercover opposition. The constitution was practically abolished.

Learning from those experiences, the authors of the West-German constitution established an advanced system of Basic Rights at the very beginning of the document (Articles 1 to 19), as the leading philosophy of the Constitution and State. This *Grundgesetz für die Bundesrepublik Deutschland* GGI—Basic Law for the Federal Republic of Germany came into force on 24 May 1949 and still remains the German constitution. Reflecting on the common values in today's German society the Basic Law and the derived legal provisions pay great attention to protecting individualism.

On the other hand, from mid 19th century until now, the development shows an increasing importance of not only defensive measures but also a demand for participation and social security. This requires a legal system which can balance these opposite interests—that is, both of the individual and the collective.

The Distinction Between Public and Private Sectors

As a general perception unlimited individual liberty is given without the need for further justification. This principle reflects the natural law theory, that man is born free and equipped with a number of fundamental rights (Rousseau 1762). The state as the collective authority may encroach upon this freedom sphere only with strong limitation and on good reasons. The whole legal system in Germany is designed according to this understanding.

From the Basic Law two major fields are derived: the private law and the public law.

Private Law

It regulates relations among individuals or legal entities and follows the principle of private autonomy. Anything which does not violate the rights of others or common values may be done. Private law provides a wide range of facilities for personal affairs based on equality of every individual or entity. These regulations typically are the Civil Code (including Family Law and Inheritance Law), Commercial Code, Company Law etc. They deal with the relations between citizens or entities and set the rules for interacting within the sphere of private autonomy. This includes activities in public, and even in lawsuits, the individual parties are to decide on the content and evidence they bring before the court.

Public Law

This sector includes Administrative Law and Criminal Law and prescribes in detail the conditions under which a public authority may interfere into the private sphere. Regarding the above mentioned principle that unlimited individual liberty is given, the state can take action against it only when justified. This is usually the case when higher collective interests must have priority. With those legal provisions the position of individuals is strengthened in administrative and criminal procedures. Every kind of measure taken by the state authority is subject to reconsideration or appeal at a higher level.

The public law refers to the relations between citizens (or groups of those) and the state. It is the state that has to present evidence to show the grounds on which it is entitled to restrain the personal liberty of private subjects.

Functions of the Basic Rights

At first we have to look into the principles of the Basic Rights system in the German constitution. As mentioned above the Basic Rights are laid down in the first chapter of the Basic Law in Articles 1 to 19 as the leading philosophy of the German nation. They are not just programmatic guidelines towards a long-range goal but rather directly enforceable laws binding all state powers (Art. 1 Par. 3 GG). That is an important principle when it comes to ensuring the validity of the Basic Rights. They cannot be abrogated by ordinary legislation or undermined by administrative acts. In contrast, all kinds of action by state authorities must obey the standards set out by the Basic Rights. By this the Basic Law provides the major guideline in protecting individual rights since it is the most prominent legal document. The statute as directly enforceable by law causes that anyone who feels his Basic Rights are offended in by state action may seek judicial relief. In fact the Basic Rights in the German constitution are legal foundations for each individual case and thus are capable of being adjudicated.

Each Basic Right is twofold. It comprises of an individual guarantee for everybody with regard to his relation towards state power. At the same time it also expresses an objective principle providing guidelines for any action of the state and its organs regardless of a specific person.

The Individual Guarantee

Primarily, the Basic Rights function as protection of a single citizen's liberty against any encroachment by state power. As elaborated earlier it has been the first and foremost task of those constitutional provisions to ensure a certain area for citizens where they can unfold their personality and strive for self-fulfilment.

In this regard the individual guarantees of Basic Rights have three aspects:

- As **defensive rights** they function as the legal position of individuals in order to prevent the entire state power from any interference into the liberty set out by the specific Basic Rights. They grant a legal claim to citizens for self-determined organization of life, free behaviour and individual self-fulfilment.

This would include the right to fight against any violation of Basic Rights by legislation although it has been passed by parliament in an ordinary procedure. Being of constitutional rank even normal legislative acts are subject to reconsideration when they violate the protected sphere. However, this can only be checked through a complaint with the Federal Constitutional Court which is entitled to declare laws null and void if they encroach upon one of the Basic Rights. That very special kind of instrument will be described in a later section (*Enforceability of Basic Rights*: Chapter 3).

Most important and by far the largest number of cases is related to executive actions or non-actions. Here we find the typical situation of citizens or private entities opposing practices of public organizations namely local or state authorities. All these laws and ordinances regulating the citizen state relationship are derived from the Basic Rights and provide the legal framework for protecting personal liberty. For example, a family wishes to build a house on its own land according to its individual taste. However, but the construction department does not allow this house to be built that way because it does not like it. It is the Basic Right of every individual to use his property as he likes—provided it does not interfere with the rights of others. It is up to one's own discretion to use these rights but the instruments are provided to defend the sphere of private liberty.

Furthermore, those standards are also valid in court procedures—no matter whether civil, criminal or administrative law is in question. A court of law is regarded as a special kind of public authority and thus, its decisions are subject to checking for any encroachment of protected individual rights. In this case judges have to regard Basic Rights when adjudicating. Mistakes can be scrutinized by way of appeal or—in specific cases—through Constitutional Court procedure.

- The **demanding character** means the obligation of the state to provide certain standards for its citizens whom it has granted a legal entitlement as well. However, there are only a few Basic Rights which give a direct legal claim. The wide field of social welfare is generally regarded as the claim of having a minimum to live in human dignity. Nevertheless, this is not brought into a direct legal claim since one has to consider the state's financial capability. It cannot be foreseen whether there are sufficient recourses in future to provide necessary facilities and funds.

The Basic Right to protection of human dignity and personal integrity can possibly lead to the state's obligation to actively protect those values. For instance, in the event of riots and acts of violence from protestors police forces may be obliged to intervene. Another prominent example is the problem of prohibiting abortion. Here is the understanding, that the principle of safeguarding human dignity leads to the obligation to protect the new life although it is not born yet. The state—legislature and executive may allow abortion only in exceptional cases.

Other examples are the right to asylum, to uninfluenced petition, the guarantee for recourse to law and a fair trial. In all these cases the state has to take action and provide necessary institutions and procedures.

- Third, there is a **participatory aspect** of Basic Rights that enables every citizen to take active part in public affairs be it elections (Article 20, Par. 2 and Art. 38 Par. 2 GG), membership to political parties (Art. 9 GG) and equal chance of access to public offices (Art. 33 GG).

  In a broader sense, participation is realised by using certain liberty rights like taking part in demonstrations and assemblies (Art. 8 GG) or expressing one's opinion freely in the media (Art. 5 GG). These rights call for public participation to be successfully exercised. They arise from the protected private sphere and come into full play on a public platform. But they can never serve that purpose if they are not protected strongly.

The Objective Principles

The objective functions of Basic Rights are both institutional guarantees and general principles as the order of values.

A number of Basic Rights not only guarantee personal liberty but at the same time demand certain legal institutions as well. In those cases the state is obliged to support the exercise of Basic Rights and provide necessary organizational structures and legal systems.

For instance, the Basic Right of private autonomy and the liberty to close contracts (Art. 2 Par. 1 GG), the guarantee of private property and right to inheritance (Art. 14 Par. 1 GG) call for Civil Code provisions and of course a corresponding judicial system. The freedom of research and teaching (Art. 5 Par. 3 GG) implies the existence of universities, the right to form associations to safeguard working conditions (Art. 9 Par. 3 GG) needs Trade Unions.

It might sound self-evident but these examples uphold the principle that protection of civil rights is necessary for a public or better collective benefit. Without unfolding these private activities the community cannot be organized and made to function sufficiently.

Beyond this, Basic Rights contain objective determinations of values and general principles for the entire life of the whole nation. These are based on a wide consensus within the society. Article 5, Par. 1 GG for example protects the freedom of speech of every person in order to enable self-fulfilment by free expression of one's opinion. That is the individual aspect. But this very article also determines freedom of speech as a value itself and as the precondition for a liberal democracy. That is the objective principle established through this Basic Right.

Thus, Basic Rights determine the validity, interpretation and application of lower laws in the light of the sphere of liberty they protect. Basic Rights also affect relations among private persons since nobody may violate the freedom of others when using his rights (Art. 2. Par 1 GG).

Safeguarding Basic Rights is made sure through orderly procedures in legislation, executive and jurisdiction. And last but not least, the objective principles set forth by Basic Rights provisions leads to the obligation of the state to actively protect the sphere of freedom of any person in extreme situations.

Enforcement of Basic Rights

Although the Basic Rights are directly applicable laws that are binding on all state powers (Art. 1 Par. 3 GG), the protection of the private sphere can only be successful if there are instruments to enforce these rights. Alleged violations are therefore scrutinized by various institutions assigned by law. Higher levels in the executive branch decided whether applicable laws or ordinances are contradictory to Basic Rights principles. The courts of law do the same with even more emphasis if the case comes to trial.

Additionally, unconstitutional acts—by whomever—are subject to specific reconsideration by the Federal Constitutional Court. This so-called

Constitutional Complaint is guaranteed by Article 93 Par. (1) No. 4a GG, which is considered a Basic Right itself. Practical experiences over the last fifty years have shown that a significant number of people are using these instruments.

One might question that parliament could change the constitution in a formally correct procedure and undermine Basic Rights guarantees. This lesson has been learned after the bad experiences with the national-socialist dictatorship who in the 30's set aside the basic principles of the then constitution in the procedurally correct way. Consequently, there is a provision in the Basic Law that prohibits any amendment to the constitution which might affect federalism and the principles laid down in Articles 1 and 20. Whilst Article 1 guarantees human dignity and other fundamental rights the latter constitutes the free democratic order. Thus, the principles of Basic Rights, as safeguards of personal liberty, are guaranteed forever in Germany.

Despite this, it is not prohibited to amend or change fundamental rights in the context of developments in society. It is the essential content of the Basic Rights that must not be touched—some restrictions in the event that an overwhelming common interest needs to be fulfilled—are still possible. However, the system has proven to possess a very high degree of stability and it can not be abolished overnight.

Conclusion

By ensuring Basic Rights we protect the exercise of personal liberty against the state as a functional structure—irrespective of whether this freedom is practised privating or publicity. The whole legal system in Germany is a check-and-balance between the two interacting areas.

People can enjoy complete privacy. Ensuring privacy and individual autonomy remains the most important function of Basic Rights in the German constitution and law system.

At the same time however, it calls for engagement in the public by using the well-protected personal liberty rights. Internal peace and stability in society can not be balanced properly unless people are assured of a certain area for their activities of self-determination.

Thus, the final conclusion is that both: the public and the private are equally valid and cannot exist without the other.

Appendix

Excerpt from the Basic Law of the Federal Republic of Germany, last amendment dated July 16, 1998.

Article 1 (Human dignity)

1. Human dignity shall be inviolable. To respect and protect it shall be the duty of all state authority.
2. The German people therefore acknowledge inviolable and inalienable human rights as the basis of every community, of peace and of justice in the world.
3. The following Basic Rights shall bind the legislature, the executive and the judiciary as directly applicable law.

Article 2 (Personal freedoms)

1. Every person shall have the right to free development of his personality insofar as he does not violate the rights of others or offend against the constitutional order or the moral law.
2. Every person shall have the right to life and physical integrity. Freedom of the person shall be inviolable. These rights may be interfered with only pursuant to a law.

Article 3 (Equality before the law)

1. All persons shall be equal before the law.
2. Men and women shall have equal rights. The state shall promote the actual implementation of equal rights for women and men and take steps to eliminate disadvantages that now exist.
3. No person shall be favoured or disfavoured because of sex, parentage, race, language, homeland and origin, faith or religious or political opinions. No person shall be disfavoured because of disability.

Article 4 (Freedom of faith, conscience and creed)
Article 5 (Freedom of expression)
Article 6 (Marriage and the family; children born outside of marriage)
Article 7 (School education)
Article 8 (Freedom of assembly)
Article 9 (Freedom of association)
Article 10 (Privacy of correspondence, posts and telecommunications)
Article 11 (Freedom of movement)

Article 12 (Occupational freedom; prohibition of forced labour)
Article 13 (Inviolability of the home)
Article 14 (Property, inheritance, expropriation)
Article 15 (Socialization)
Article 16 (Citizenship, extradition)
Article 16a (Right of asylum)
Article 17 (Right of petition)
Article 17a (Restriction of certain Basic Rights by laws respecting defence and alternative service)
Article 18 (Forfeiture of Basic Rights)
Article 19 (Restriction of Basic Rights)

1. Insofar as, under this Basic Law, a Basic Right may be restricted by of pursuant to a law, such law must apply generally and not merely to a single case. In addition, the law must specify the Basic Right affected and the Article in which it appears.
2. In no case may the essence of a Basic Right be affected.
3. The Basic Rights shall also apply to domestic artificial persons to the extent that the nature of such rights permits.
4. Should any person's rights be violated by public authority, he may have recourse to the courts. If no other jurisdiction has been established, recourse shall be to the ordinary courts. The second sentence of paragraph (2) of Article 10 shall not be affected by this paragraph.

Article 79 (Amendment of the Basic Law)

1. This Basic Law may be amended only by a law expressly amending or supplementing its text. In the case of an international treaty respecting a peace settlement, the preparation of a peace settlement, or the phasing out of an occupation regime or the designed to promote the defence of the Federal Republic it shall be sufficient, for the purpose of making clear that the provisions of this Basic Law do not preclude the conclusion and entry into force of the treaty, to add language to the Basic Law that merely makes this clarification.
2. Any such law shall be carried by two thirds of the Members of the Bundestag and two thirds of the votes of the Bundesrat.
3. Amendments to this Basic Law affecting the division of the Federation into Länder, their participation on principle in the legislative process, or the principles laid down in Article 1 and 20 shall be inadmissible.

Article 93 (Federal Constitutional Court: jurisdiction)

1. The Federal Constitutional Court shall rule:

4a. on constitutional complaints, which may be filed by any person alleging that one of his Basic Rights or one of his rights under paragraph (4) of Article 20 or under Article 33, 38, 101, 103 or 104 has been infringed by public authority.

REFERENCES

(GG) *Basic Law for the Federal Republic of Germany.* From 23 May. 1949.
H. Hattenhauer (ed.). 1970. *The General Country Law for the Prussian States.* Frankfurt: Metzner.
Rousseau, Jean Jacques. 1762. *Le Contract Social.* G.D.H. Cole (trans.). www.constitution.org/jjr/socon.htm.

11

Voluntary Action and Citizenship: Issues of Civil Rights

Aswini K. Ray

The asymmetry in the historical evolution of liberal democracies in Europe's ancien-regimes and India's 'Post-Colonial Democracy'[1] have shaped their respective structural attributes differently; they have also influenced the scope of voluntary action, and issues of civil rights in democratic governance in different ways.

For a start, western liberal democracies evolved from the struggle of individual as citizens to secure their rights against the authoritarian state. The Magna Carta (1215), Petition of Rights (1627) and the Bill of Rights (1688) in England; the Declaration of the Rights of Man and Citizens (1789) in France; and the American Bill of Rights (1787) consisting of the civil and political rights of individual citizens guaranteed their freedom of speech and ensured against arbitrary arrest and/ or custodial violence by the state. The subsequent phase of the evolution of western liberal democracies involved widening the sphere of the citizen's right to encompass the social and economic sphere; and, simultaneously, widening the group of enfranchized citizens leading to universal adult franchise. The new generation of group rights, like that of minorities, indigenous people, victims of developmental distortions, rights of sustainable development against environmental degradation, gender justice etc. became politically legitimate within the democratic discourse in more recent times only after a threshold level of individual rights of citizens had been institutionally opertionalized. The state, and voluntary action within the civil society, have continued to reinforce the political legitimacy of these concerns around citizen's rights, both as individuals and groups, in western liberal democracies.

In sharp contrast to this historical trajectory, political democracy in India emerged from the struggle of the nation as a community to secure the right of self-determination directed against alien colonial rule. The individual and his rights as citizen, which fuelled the evolution of European liberal democracies, was not the central focus within the intellectual and political discourse of India's struggle for national liberation.

Consequently, while the operational attribute of western liberal democracies evolved till the fifties like a charter of rights. Periodic elections based on universal adult franchise and free liberal institutions of governance and accountability were institutionalized within India's Republican constitution in 1950, their operation was constricted by the narrow social base of democratic concern around the individual rights of citizens (Chaubey 1973, Desai 1948, Gupta 1979). This built-in inherited inadequacy in the social base of India's post-colonial democracy has enabled the Indian State, and with massive majority support, parties, to cut corners when faced with the endemic complexities of democratic governance. This has resulted in frequent constitutional amendments more specifically directed at constricting the citizen's Fundamental Rights; recurrent resort to Executive ordinances as a substitute for legislative enactments; increasing repressive legislations and preventive detention; and the proliferation of new coercive instruments of governance, like the police, intelligence apparatus and paramilitary outfits (Desai 1986).

This process of operational de-liberalization of the formal institutions of constitutional democracy of western vintage have been facilitated by some specific historical inheritance of India's post-colonial democracy. For example, in the evolution of European liberal democracies, the struggle of the citizens for their individual rights automatically involved their struggle to delink the church from its alliance with the authoritarian state. Consequently, western democracies emerged simultaneously with the secular state. In sharp contrast, India's post-colonial democracy ushered by its Republican Constitution, emerged in the midst of the most massive onslaught of communal politics within civil society as a result of the partition of the subcontinent. In fact, this historical specificity shaped the primary concern of the post-colonial Indian State. This was to operationalize the secular component of its nation-building agenda within the democratic framework. Paradoxically, this occurred in the midst of increasing assertion of communal politics and myriad ascriptive identities within the civil society including periodic violence. Therefore, unlike in western liberal democracies, political democracy grafted on India's post-colonial political economy has spawned greater social revivalism, creating in the process, new complexities for democratic governance in India's diverse social plurality. They have also brought in new concerns within India's civil rights agenda.

Two other historical specificities of India's post-colonial democracy that have impinged upon the scope of voluntary action and issues of civil rights are worth mentioning: *i*) the inherited duality between the modern state machinery (created by the advanced industrial capitalist state to ensure the colonial process of accumulation) and the traditional society distorted by colonial rule; *ii*) the duality between the relatively developed coercive instrument of the colonial state and the democratic institutions of conflict-resolution. Political democracy, through universal adult franchise, linked these dualities right from the inception of India's post-colonial democracy. This created a concentric series of vicious circles impinging upon democratic governance. Of these, the most significant one, which has raised new issues of civil rights in India, has been of increasing social revivalism which has undermined the professional efficiency of democratic institutions leading to greater social violence and increasing use of the coercive instruments of the state. Cumulatively, these have tended to undermine the political will within the democratic structure to pursue the unfinished secular agenda of nation-building.

The civil rights movement in India, conjuncturally emerged in the mid-seventies when the inherited structural specificities of India's post-colonial democracy were compounded through orchestrated manipulation by the erstwhile populist political leadership. In this sense, the National Emergency of 1975–77 constitutes a watershed in the operational evolutions of India's post-colonial democracy, sharpening its complexities and creating new ones by attempting to short-circuit solutions outside the democratic process.[2] The revocation of the Emergency regime in India by its authors, mercifully after nineteen months, underscored its counterproductive relevance to resolve the manifest complexities of democratic governance in India's social diversities. Though elections have always been a deceptive indicator of political participation in India, the massive verdict against the authors of the Emergency during the elections of 1977 helped to reinforce the structural imperative of India's political economy beyond possible authoritarian options.

This was also the political conjuncture that catalysed the operational convergence of the two divergent ideological strands of Indian politics—the liberals who took the country's post-colonial democratic institutions for granted till the Emergency, and the radical Marxists who dismissed them as 'Bourgeois' facades. Their operational convergence as watchdogs of the rights of citizens as guaranteed in the constitution, and the widening of their ambit to be in conformity with the new generation of human rights, and to ensure the autonomy of democratic institutions as its institutional pre-condition—spawned the civil rights movement after nearly twenty-seven years of the formal operation of political democracy in India.

The historical milieu of its fortuitous origin lay in the political conjuncture of the orchestrated dent of the weak democratic institutions, and the narrow social base of democratic legitimacy of the rights of citizens. These shaped the initial focus of India's fledgling civil rights movement. As a voluntary watchdog of the civil and political rights of the citizens, still under seige from the residual excesses of the Emergency regime, many of them being irreversible—the movement has sought to fill a historic gap within India's democratic political process, with its fractured consensus, partisan and anomie politics, and grappling with its unfinished post-colonial agenda of economic development, social transformation, and nation-building, aborted by the global cold war. Under these circumstances, its attempts to remain politically non-partisan as a defence-mechanism for moral legitimacy, the movement and its activists have elicited the wrath of all mainstream political parties with stakes in governance, inevitably through the misuse and overuse of the coercive instruments of the state and powerful vested interests resisting the democratic bias in favour of the majority of the poor and oppressed in India's segmented social diversities. They have posed new questions about the scope of voluntary action within India's civil rights movement.

Firstly, within India's post-colonial political agenda of secular and democratic nation-building through economic development and social transformation, the role of the state has remained central. There has been considerable historical legitimacy around the state as the hegemonic power in the public domain, which is manifest in the popular legitimacy of the concept of '*Sarkar-mai-Baap*'. The agenda of national liberation had revolved around the control of the state machinery, rather than contesting its overriding dominance of the public sphere. In fact, the conceptual and operational distinction between the domain of the 'public' and 'private' that has characterized the evolution of liberal democracies and welfare states in the western industrial societies has had little salience within the intellectual and political discourse during, and in the aftermath of India's liberation struggle. The post-colonial nation-building agenda provided little space for the domain of the 'private' for the citizens; even their constitutionally enshrined rights were periodically amended whenever they conflicted with the nation-building agenda, as Prime Minister Nehru unambiguously asserted this priority in the parliament while piloting the 4th Constitutional Amendment bill (1951) nationalizing private property for 'public' purposes. Notwithstanding India's religious diversity, its secular agenda has acted as a structural imperative of the post-colonial, revivalistic civil society because even 'religion' as the realm of the 'private' as associative in western liberal democracies, did not have the same operational legitimacy'. In fact, with increasing social revivalism, the Indian State has tended to be more and more involved with the politics of most ascriptive identities, including religious communities; its secular credentials underpinned by being equally linked to most religious groups, than being insulated from them as in the western version of secularism. This operational trend of secular politics in Indian democracy has raised new questions within the civil rights movement, like issues of regionally specific communal politics of minority groups threatening the rights of citizens, and stoking violence.[3] But the hegemony of the Indian State—in the primary agenda of post-colonial nation-building—has remained largely uncontested within the democratic discourse. This has enabled the political consensus around centralized planned development, its enormous public sector controlling key and basic industries, and the central bias in the operation of Indian federalism. The democratic bias of the centralized state in favour of the majority of the poor and the oppressed citizens, provided moral legitimacy to the over-riding dominance of the state, as the representative of the 'public' in pursuing the primary agenda of nation-building.

The Emergency regime dented this political consensus around the legitimacy of the State's sovereignty in the domain of the 'public', and opened the space for the emergence of non-governmental organizations in the sphere of development, and civil rights groups as watchdogs against state repression and violation of citizen's rights by powerful vested interests. In the post-emergency era, this space has continued to widen with increasing manifestation of professional inefficiency, ascriptive bias, and corruption of the state machinery. In fact, the transformation in the popular perception of the post-colonial Indian State from the '*Sarkar-mai-baap*', in the aftermath of national liberation, with its benign underpinnings as the fountain of welfare, to its anomic post-Emergency version of the repressive 'License-permit Raj', underscores in many ways, the moral exhaustion of the domain of the 'public'. Increasingly, the successful Indian citizen is popularly perceived as one who is able to insulate himself from the hazards of an inefficient, corrupt and repressive state. For his welfare needs like education, health, transport, communication, drinking water, electricity, or even physical security and investigations, the citizen chooses to opt out of the state. The state is increasingly left to dispense an inefficient criminal justice system and corrupt tax machinery, for the citizen thereby underscoring its repressive image in the citizen's perceptions.

But while the state is losing its legitimacy as the neutral mediator of private disputes either among individuals or groups, as well as the benign dispenser of public welfare, there is yet to be a democratic consensus around a substitute for the state. The market, as a potential substitute, has historically remained illegitimate in India; and, its present globalized version in the aftermath of economic liberalization, is widely perceived to be potentially 'anti-national'. In the absence of an alternative, the professionally inefficient, corrupt repressive Indian State still remains the central focus of the sphere of the 'public' in a de-liberalizing political democracy that has jettisoned its earlier nation-building agenda and pursuing economic liberalization according to the 'conditionalities' of the external funding agencies and monitored by them. In fact, the global funding agencies are increasingly undermining the legitimacy of the Indian State as the sovereign over the domain of the 'public'.

This has opened new space for civil rights groups to act as watchdogs of the rights of citizens, and for non-governmental voluntary action in the sphere of public goods. This has also spawned newer concerns within the civil rights groups, particularly around group-rights like those of environment, gender justice, child-labour, physically challenged and old age.

As watchdog of the citizen's rights, voluntary action of civil rights groups has now established some moral and political legitimacy within India's anomic political process. It's contribution in ushering the only new right for its citizens in the post-colonial era, in the form of Public Interest Litigation has elicited widespread popular legitimacy, and opened a new instrument of defence against the violation of their rights, and of good governance as well as the pursuit of the right of sustainable development. The post-Cold War global milieu of normative concerns, along with economic globalization, has enabled a wider globalized network in pursuit of these normative concerns also within the domestic politics of the country.

But voluntary action of the NGOs, and civil rights groups, are faced with newer problems. First with international funding, these concerns are increasingly becoming attractive career options for the unscrupulous and the reckless rather than the professionally trained idealist. This replicates in these organizations some of the problems that contributed to the dent in the moral and ideological legitimacy of the state, particularly of the welfare state and the socialist state. Besides, the vested interests, including some within the state machinery, tend to project these groups as another extension of the ubiquitous mystique of 'foreign hand' which has some residual demonized image within India's post-colonial political culture. This problem is particularly prevalent in areas affected by terrorist violence threatening national security. At any rate, the civil rights groups are yet to respond creatively to these new challenges posed to their legitimacy as a result of political terrorism and violence by communal groups and of other ascriptive identities. Their increasing recurrence in contemporary Indian politics exposes the prevailing ideological and operational inadequacy of the civil rights movement as a substitute for the atrophying institutions of democratic governance in the country; but these groups are emerging as a catalytic agent of the civil society to mitigate the threats to the citizen's 'private' domain increasingly under seige by an anomic 'Public' sphere.

To conclude, while the Indian State by its acts of omission and commission has increasingly undermined its own democratic legitimacy as the sovereign authority over the all encompassing domain of the 'public', the market, particularly its increasingly globalized incarnation, is yet to establish its legitimacy as a potential substitute. That has left the space open for voluntary action of non-governmental organizations within the civil society to support democratic governance and sustainable development. The present democratic legitimacy of these groups in this direction is not inconsequential, but still inadequate in the context of the challenges and opportunities.

NOTES

1. This concept has been elaborated in my paper Ray (1989).
2. I have discussed these in some detail in two papers (Ray 2000, 1986).

3. As in Punjab in the 1970s, and Kashmir since the 1980s. Even smaller religious communities like the Bohras, or on the issue of women's rights among the Muslims, these complexities periodically confront the civil right groups.

REFERENCES

Chaubey, S.K. 1973. *Constitutional Assembly of India: Springboard of Revolution*. New Delhi: PUB?

Desai, A.R. 1948. *Social Background of Indian Nationalisms*. Mumbai: Popular.

Desai, A.R. (ed.). 1986. *Violation of Democratic Rights in India*. Mumbai: Sangam Books.

Gupta, S.D. 1979. *Justice and the Political Order in India*. Calcutta: PUB?

Ray. A.K. 1986. 'Civil Rights Movement in India,' in *Economic and Political Weekly*, vol. 21, no. 28, pp. 1202–205.

Ray, A.K. 1989. 'Towards the Concept of Post-Colonial Democracy: A Schematic View,' in Hasan, Jha and Khan (eds), *The State, Political Processes and Identity*. New Delhi: Sage.

Ray, A.K. 2000. Civil Rights Movement in India: A Historical Perspective, Paper presented at a seminar on Fifty Years of India's Independence in Calcutta.

Grassroots. February 2001. Is This a Book? Journal?

12

Public Ethics and Accountability

L.C. Jain

Let us first examine the meaning of 'public', 'ethics' and 'accountability'—to illumine our understanding of the three characters in the title, namely

Public
Ethics
Accountability

The Webster's Dictionary defines these terms as follows:

Public: Of or pertaining to the people; relating to, belonging to, or affecting a nation, state, or community at large—opposed to private. (The *Dictionary* defines Private as belonging to, or concerning, an individual; personal; one's own; not general or common; as private property or opinions.)
Ethics: The science of moral values and duties; the study of ideal character, actions and ends. (The *Dictionary* defines Moral as characterized by excellence in what pertains to practice or conduct; right and proper. Pertaining to character, conduct, intentions, social relations etc, viewed ethically as moral ideas; moral convictions).
Accountability: is synonymous with responsibility, also, moral accountability.

I

Clearly, of these three characters, the kingpin is ethics. We cannot arrive at 'public ethics' without first exploring the fundamentals of ethics. And much depends on how extensive a view we take of ethics and moral code.

Sanatana Dharma (Swarup 2000) provides an illuminating view of moral code:

Different available moral codes have derived from what men have thought of their deity, of themselves and of their neighbour. If divinity and even morality are external to man, then so is his moral code. Sanatana dharma however believes that man is spiritual and moral in his essence; that compassion, truthfulness, disinterestedness reside in his soul, therefore it expresses these luminous and divine qualities in his action too. Man is depraved and sinful by nature, he neither needs nor is he capable of a developed moral action. What does a sinner need morality for?

Similarly, a limited physical-vital view of man does not need much ethics. If a man lives only for himself and the present, he owes little to others and to tomorrow. Only a higher vision of man gives and can sustain a exalted system of ethics.

An ordinary man's moral code is prudent in intention. He refrains from doing many things unto others lest they also do them unto him; he also sometimes does good unto them expecting they would do the same unto him. But Sanatana dharma teaches that one should be good and do good for the sake of goodness itself. One does good because it is part of one's nature.

An ethical code defines a man's behaviour, his duties and obligations towards his neighbour. But who is a neighbour?

Sanatana dharma's definition of a neighbour is very inclusive. It includes all men, if fact, all living beings, and even all elements; it includes Gods and angels; it includes beings who have gone before and those who are yet to come; beings on all planes and in all modes of existence. Man owes duties towards them all, that he is indebted to them. It preaches that he pays his debts to them. Therefore he is asked to make daily 'sacrifices' to them, to offer his daily oblations to Gods, to ancestors, teachers and rishis of old, to men; in fact to all orders of beings including oceans, rivers, mountains and heavenly bodies; that man is capable of higher moral action only when he grows into the qualities and powers of the Spirit: he grows morally when he grows spiritually: therefore it teaches an ethics of personal spiritual growth.

Sanatana dharma regards God as the inner-controller, and moral action as spontaneous and natural. In being moral, a man is being true to himself.

We turn now to Vivekananda (Swami Vivekananda 1998).

Q—How does the Vedanta explain individuality and ethics?
A—The real individual is the Absolute; this personalization is through Maya. It is only apparent; in reality it is always the Absolute. In reality there is one, but in Maya it is appearing as many. In Maya there is this variation. Yet even in this Maya there is always the tendency to get back to the One, as expressed in all ethics and all morality of every nation, because it is the constitutional necessity of the soul. It is finding its oneness; and this struggle to find this oneness is what we call ethics and morality. Therefore we must always practise them.

Q—Is not the greater part of ethics taken up with the relation between individuals?
A—That is all it is.

The rational West is earnestly bent upon seeking out the rationality, the raison d' etre of all its philosophy and its ethics; and ethics cannot be derived from the mere sanction of any personage, however great and divine he may be. Such an explanation of the authority of ethics appeals no more to the greatest of the world's thinkers; they want something more than human sanction for ethical and moral codes to be binding, they want some eternal principle of truth. And where is that eternal sanction to be found except in the only Infinite Reality that exists in you and in me and in all, in the Self, in the Soul? The infinite oneness of the Soul is the eternal sanction of all morality, that you and I are not only brothers—every literature voicing man's struggle towards freedom has already preached that—but that you and I are really one. This is the dictate of Indian philosophy. This oneness is the rationale of all ethics and all spirituality.

In every religion, the manifestation of this struggle towards freedom can be found. It is the groundwork of all morality, of unselfishness, which means getting rid of the idea that men are the same as their body. When we see a man doing good work, helping others, it means that he cannot be confined within the limited circle of 'me and mine'. There is no limit to this getting out of selfishness as the goal.

Karma-Yoga is the attaining through unselfish work of that freedom which is the goal of all human nature. Every selfish action, therefore, retards our reaching the goal, and every unselfish action takes us towards the goal; that is why the only definition that can be given of morality is this: *That which is selfish is immoral, and that which is unselfish is moral.*

II

We may now bring forward the definition of Public: pertaining to the people; relating to, belonging to, or affecting a nation, state or community at large. More importantly that which is 'opposed to private'.

This should help us to recognize that the preceding elucidation of ethics is not an academic exercize. Vivekananda leaves no scope for it to be academic. Ethics is embedded in and is realized through human character, actions and ends. 'What does a sinner need morality for'. Moreover, if the individual human being is private that is 'one's own, not general or common' and worse still is 'selfish', then by definition, the door is shut on public ethics.

For, public ethics means pursuing the good of the community at large—unselfishly. If the individual or the collectivity of which he is a part turn the goal of public good to private gain ethics will not sustain in the public domain. And, the best safeguard recommended, as we saw, is the 'inner-controller' and the reminder that man is capable of higher moral action if and only if, he adheres to 'ethics of personal spiritual growth'.

Early in my public life in the 40's, I recall being told by one of Gandhi's associates that an important leader, once argued before Gandhi, that 'his private life was his private business'. 'It is not', Gandhi is reported to have remarked. 'If you have chosen to be in public life, then you cannot live two lives. Moral in daylight and different in the dark. You have to be an openbook at all hours'.

This was Vivekananda applied.

Gandhi's almost obsessive emphasis on purity of means assimilated the essence of public ethics wholesomely. Unethical means could promote no public good.

In *Mahatma Gandhi—The Last Phase*, Pyarelal (58: 189–90) recalls:

On more than one occasion at a crucial stage in the Cabinet Mission's negotiations two philosophies of action contested the stage—the philosophy of 'ends and means' on which Gandhiji's life was built, and the British philosophy of empiricism which the Cabinet Delegation represented. Gandhi believed that if we keep the means unadulterated, the ends will take care of themselves. The Cabinet Mission proceeded on the principle that one has at times to make compromises even with principle for the sake of expediency and choose 'the lesser evil'. When the Cabinet Mission and all the Indian parties found themselves on the horns of a dilemma, Gandhiji sent Lord Pethick-Lawrence an advance copy of his article in *Harijan* entitled *The Unknown:*

> Some learned men describe Him as Unknowable, some others as Unknown, yet others as 'Not This'....
>
> When yesterday I said a few words to the prayer audience, I could say nothing more than that they should pray for and rely upon the strength and the guidance that this big X could give. There were difficulties to be overcome by all parties in the great Indian drama that was being enacted before them. They were all to rely upon the Unknown who had often confounded man's wisdom and in the twinkling of an eye upset his tin-pot plans. The British party claimed to believe in God the Unknown....
>
> In spite of my irrepressible optimism I am unable to say decisively that, at least in political parlance, the thing is safe. All I can say, therefore, is that if, with the best efforts of all the parties, the unsafe happens, I would invite them to join with me in saying that it was as well and that safety lay in unsafety.

To this Lord Pethick-Lawrence replied:

> 'I, too, have a strong feeling, where I am dependent on forces outside myself, that I must be content to accept the will of Divinity that you call X; and that sometimes in Bjornsen's words a result may be "uber unserer kraft" (beyond the power). But where a decision of my own enters in I have a grave responsibility to all those who will be affected by it, to make it aright.'

Lord Pethick-Lawrence, however, proceeded to show that the attitude he represented did not rule out faith just as Gandhiji's faith did not rule out the exercise of reason:

> Did I ever tell you the following story illustrating the profound human belief in the rightness of things lying behind injustice? A

parson said to a farmer who was worried about something, 'Put your trust in Providence, my man'. 'No', said the farmer, 'I have no trust in Providence. He lost me my pig two years ago. He let my home be burnt last year. He took away my wife last summer. No, I refuse to trust in Providence. But I will tell you what. There is a power above Him who will pull him up if he goes too far!'

The fundamental difference in the two attitudes is, however there for all to see. If faith to be 'the substance of things hoped for, the evidence of things unseen,' belief in the 'rightness of things lying behind injustice' should never lead to a compromise with the dubious in the pursuit of the good. For it is given to mortals control over their actions only, none over the fruit of their actions. Faith has, therefore, to step in where reason fails, to enable us to persevere in the right means and see safety in unsafety, if the 'unsafe' happens inspite of all human foresight and care. One may not substitute the expedient for the right because the latter appears to be 'unsafe'. As Prof. Jacks has put it, it is just where certainty ends that morality begins.

III

Accountability can now sit with ease with public ethics, that is, public ethics of the character we have opted for here.

In public domain, accountability is to the 'community at large' as the dictionary defines it. But as elucidation of ethics points out, ethics rests on an 'inner-controller' inside the human being—individually or as a group, opting to serve the public goal. They have to be moral in themselves—inner-directed.

Thus, the social actors have to be accountable to their own moral self for the means they choose before they can walk through the fire of public scrutiny. Shallow bricks cannot give us a safe wall.

However, ethics and moral accountability are not principles meant merely to adorn the book. Their value lies in informing and governing public conduct. But it is a road full of thorns, and often these were planted way back in history.

It is tragic that in India the virtues of accountability and moral responsibility in the public domain received a mortal blow at the hands of Robert Clive who not only siphoned off public funds to his private account but stoutly justified his depraved behaviour (Pyarelal 1965: 25–26).

At the turn of this century, a brilliant young attorney, yet unknown to fame outside his own country, coined an expression that has since become world famous—'A Century of Wrong'. It was the title of a brochure that Jan Christian Smuts wrote on the eve of the Boer War in South Africa to describe the series of wrongs that his people had suffered at the hands of the British, beginning with the first occupation of the Cape by Britain in 1795 and culminating in the Jameson Raid that led to the Boer War.

In the case of India, her 'Century of Wrong' began with the battle of Plassey, when Clive defeated Bengal forces with the loss of only 22 British killed, making the John Company virtual rulers of 'the richest province of India'. Following upon it a flotilla of more than three hundred boats in a single shipment carried down the river, 'flags flying and music playing' a treasure of eight hundred thousand pound sterling, in coined silver from Murshidabad to Fort William. 'A word of guns' were fired, the Ladies all got 'footsore with dancing'. Clive received as his share of booty, $234,000; altogether the Company and private persons netting three million sterling.

Three years later Clive returned home 'perhaps the King's wealthiest subject'. He purchased two hundred $500 shares of the Company, which he used to set up in the Parliament a caucus of his nominees, who were to vote as he bade; entered the House of Commons, and engaged in 'the tremendous corruption of men's consciences' which became a by-word even in an age known for its sordid politics. Impeached before the Parliament, he defended himself with an air of righteous indignation. 'When I think of the marvellous riches of that country', he said, 'and the comparatively small part which I took away, I am astonished at my own moderation'.

Clive was expected to be an exemplar on the moral accountability side of the fence, but became an exemplar on the wrong side of it (Ibid.):

Clive's successors, following the pattern that he had set, conspired and intrigued, resorted to forgery to gain their ends and were ennobled, while they hanged others for forging documents. They forcibly imposed treaties, then broke them, and deposed and set up rulers as suited their purpose, using every such occasion for the proverbial shaking of the 'Pagoda tree of the East'. In less than a decade following the battle of Plassey they had thrice made and unmade Nawabs. Engineering a revolution became 'the most paying game in the world'.

The Company's servants living in Bengal alone received during this period $2,169,665 as 'presents' from rulers dependent on their guns and favours, in addition to Clive's jagir of $32,000. Further sums claimed and obtained as 'restitution' within this period amounted to $3,7770,8883. 'The English in Bengal', wrote the Directors in their general letter, in 1765, 'have been guilty of violating treaties, of great oppression and a combination to enrich themselves.... An unbounded thirst after riches seems to have possessed the whole body of our servants to a degree that they have lost all sight of justice to the Country Government, and of their duty to the committee'.

Regarding in retrospect the conduct of the Company's servants upon this occasion, James Mill wrote in his *History of British India* that it 'furnishes one of the most remarkable instances upon record of the power of interest to extinguish all sense of justice, and even of shame'.

Thus began the rape of a sub continent by a trading company 'utterly without scruple or principle ... and greedy of gain'. In the words of two British historians of India, G.T. Garratt and Edward Thompson, 'A gold-lust unequalled since the hysteria that took hold of the Spaniards of Cortes' and Pizarro's age filled the English mind'. 'Birds of prey and passage', Burke called them. The company's servants individually and corporately engaged in private inland trade, profiteered and exploited without end, forcibly took away goods and commodities from people for 'a fourth part of their value', and obliged them 'to give five rupees for goods which are (were) worth but on rupee'. They refused to pay the tolls that everybody else was obliged to pay, though that concession belonged to the Company only; and amasses vast fortunes. Back home with their millions, they set themselves up as 'Nabobs of the East', married into the peerage and were themselves ennobled. 'Only a shade less cruel than their prototypes of Peru and Mexico', wrote Herbert Spencer, 'image how black must have been their deeds when even the Directors of the Company obtained by a scene of the most tyrannical and oppressive conduct that was known in any age or country. Conceive the atrocious state of society described by Vansittart who tells us that the English compelled the natives to buy or sell at just what rates they pleased on pain of flogging or confinement'.

The Company paid such fabulous dividends that its stock rose to $6,400 per share. Jobbery became rampant. 'Everybody and everything was on sale'. 'Directors and Directors' relatives, peers, even the Royal Family saw no reason why they should not push a young friend or dependent into a service which within an incredibly brief period would bring him back enormously enriched.' In the words of Edward Thompson, 'English politics and morals became corrupted. English ideas of India became vulgarized, to an extent and permanency which we do not yet realize'.

We started this account of Clive's contribution with Jan Smuts of South Africa. In South Africa another contemporary of Smuts, Mohandas Karam Chand Gandhi was struggling with a dillema of public-private ethics and accountability (M.K. Gandhi 1927: 183–85):

Gifts had been bestowed on me before when I returned to India in 1899, but this time the farewell was overwhelming. The gifts of course included things in gold and silver, but there were articles of costly diamond as well.

What right had I to accept all these gifts? Accepting them, how could I persuade myself that I was serving the community without remuneration? All the gifts, excepting a few from my clients, were purely for my service to the community, and I could make no difference between my clients and co-workers; for the clients also helped me in my public work.

One of the gifts was a good necklace worth fifty guineas, meant for my wife. But even that gift was given because of my public work, and so it could not be separated from the rest.

The evening I was presented with the bulk of these things I had a sleepless night. I walked up and down my room deeply agitated, but could find no solution. It was difficult for me to forego gifts worth hundreds, it was more difficult to keep them.

And even if I could keep them, what about my children? What about my wife? They were being trained to a life of service and to an understanding that service was its own reward.

I had no costly ornaments in the house. We had been fast simplifying our life. How then could we afford to have gold watches? How could we afford to wear gold chains and diamond rings? Even then I was exhorting people to conquer the infatuation for jewellery. What was I now to do with the jewellery that had come upon me?

I decided that I could not keep these things. I drafted a letter, creating a trust of them in favour of the community and appointment Parsi Rustomji and others trustees. In the morning I held a consultation with my wife and children and finally got rid of the heavy incubus.

I knew that I should have some difficulty in persuading my wife, and I was sure that I should have none so far as the children were concerned. So I decided to constitute them my attorneys.

The children readily agreed to my proposal. 'We do not need these costly presents, we must return them to the community, and should we ever need them, we could easily purchase them,' they said.

I was delighted 'Then you will plead with other, won't you?' I asked them.

'Certainly', said they. 'That is our business. She does not need to wear the ornaments. She would want to keep them for us, and if we don't want them, why should she not agree to part with them?'

But it was easier said than done.

'You may not need them', said my wife. 'Your children may not need them. Cajoled, they will dance to your tune. I can understand your not permitting me to wear them. But what about my daughters-in-law? They will be sure to need them. And who knows what will happen tomorrow? I would be the last person to part with gifts so lovingly given.'

And thus the torrent of argument went on, reinforced, in the end, by tears. But the children were adamant. And I was unmoved.

I mildly put in: 'The children have not yet to get married. We do not want to see them married young. When they are grown up, they can take care of themselves. And surely we shall not have, for our sons, brides who are fond of ornaments, I am there. You will ask me then.'

'Ask you? I know you by this time. You deprived me of my ornaments, you would not leave me in peace with them. Fancy you offering to get ornaments for the daughters-in-law! You who are trying to make sadhus of my boys from today! No, the ornaments will not be returned. And pray what right have you to my necklace?'

'But', I rejoined, 'is the necklace given you for your service or for my service?'

'I agree. But service rendered by you is as good as rendered by me. I have toiled and moiled for you day and night. Is that no service? You forced all and sundry on me, making me weep bitter tears, and I slaved for them!'

These were pointed thrusts, and some of them went home. But I was determined to return the ornaments. I somehow succeeded in extorting a consent from her. The gifts received in 1896 and 1901 were all returned. A trust-deed was prepared, and they were deposited with a bank, to be used for the service of the community, according to my wishes or to those of the trustees.

Often, when I was in need of funds for public purposes, and felt that I must draw upon the trust, I have been able to raise the requisite amount, leaving the trust money intact. The fund is still there, being operated upon in times of need, and it has regularly accumulated.

I have never since regretted the step, and as the years have gone by, my wife has also seen its wisdom. It has saved us from many temptations.

I am definitely of opinion that a public worker should accept no costly gifts.

Later, Gandhi was to trace the infirmities in the working of public institutions to their failure to adhere to moral values (Pyarelal 1965: 152–53):

Visva-Bharati (founded by Rabindranath Tagore) will fail to attract the right type of talent and scholarship if it relies on the strength of material resources or the material attractions that it can offer. Its attraction must be moral or ethical. 'From each according to his capacity to each according to his need' is generally speaking a sound maxim, but it should not take you beyond current market values. You belong to Visva-Bharati, not because it finds you creature comforts but because your moral worth increases day by day by working for its ideals I have been connected with many institutions for sixty years and I have come to the conclusion that every difficulty in their working was traceable to a defect in the understanding of moral values.

It is difficult to fathom to what extent Clive's unethical behaviour cast its shadow on morality at high places. But once public morality was scoffed away at the highest level, and unethical behaviour became the 'done thing' it became easy for those below to act likewise without a sense of shame. Even those employed by one of the otherwise best administered princely states—Mysore were found guilty. M.A. Sreenivasan, a Minister in the Mysore Maharaja's cabinet recalls (Sreenivasan 1991) how he caught two such British officers. One was a Major who was stealing black gram meant for the palace horses. Poor physique of the horses at a 'customary review of the lancers and their mount' led to the discovery that 'the horses were fed on cooked muster rolls'. The other was a chief line Inspector, who was caught putting his own thumb impressions on payment of rolls and pocketing away the hard earned wages of labourers laying the electrical transmission lines.

Since Independence in 1947, the Republic of India has played host to the virus of corruption in public offices. Right under his gaze several ministers in Nehru's Cabinet, took liberty with public morality, and some had to be shown the door. The recent past, witnessed siphoning away of massive funds from public banks—a sordid act which has been shielded by the authorities as 'systemic failure'. Worse still, poverty alleviation funds are being pocketed by public officials. Website of the Planning Commission is carrying a severe indictment of public officials across the country (Planning Commission 2000).

The following is the latest publicly acknowledged case from a remote village where the people have begun to expose and combat immoral practices somewhat successfully—which is a hopeful sign (*Grassroots* 2001: 1 and 3.):

On December 18, 1999 Mazdoor Kisan Shakti Sangathan (MKSS, an activist organization working on issues of Right to Information) organised a public hearing. Villagers from Bori village in Jmarwaas panchayat spoke to a crowd of 2,000 about rampant corruption.

Money to be spent on community development had been pocketed by a trio of rich, powerful and politically well connected persons. Nain Singh, Bhanwar Lal Sevak and Laxman Singh had set up Pyarji as the sarpanch. Unable to stand for elections themselves, as the Umarwaas panchayat in 1995 came under reserved category for dalits, Pyarji a Khatik by caste was considered an ideal choice. A thin small built man, he was easily intimidated by six-footer Nain Singh. Pyarji used to sign all documents put before him to release panchayat funds. The money released used to find its way into Nain Singh and his coterie's pockets. Fearful of corruption charges of around a lakh and fear of jail persuaded Pyarji to ask for people's help and the Bori jan sunwai took place.

As for Nain Singh and his cohorts, the jan sunwai exposed their swindling habits. Community pressure forced them to return the money they had usurped. On March 24 and 26 last year, they deposited Rs 3,04,716 at Umarwaas panchyat's account in the State Bank of Bikaner and Jaipur.

IV

These days, we are increasingly relying on Ombudsmen for the states, media, banks, social audit of development programmes, gender equity audit, environmental equity audit, the investigating agencies, election observers, invigilators et al—to ensure that fairness and integrity prevail in pubic administration of all descriptions. But alas, what we are reaping are diminishing returns.

Those who ought to be accountable have a vast armoury that allows them to go scott free. Institutional mechanisms to enforce accountability are indispensable, but not sufficient to uphold public ethics. The 'inner-control' meters are pivotal to safe returns on the accountability front. Such meters are of least-cost and consume no energy to run—but perhaps it is precisely this inherent virtue of theirs that has made them scarce.

Michael M. Cernea offers a choice to those who want to try something different than inner-meter.

He, although not known to be a Vendantist, argues for what he eloquently calls the 'equity compass' (Cernea 2000: 3659–678):

> Redressing the inequities caused by displacement and enabling affected people to share in the benefits of growth is not just possible but imperative, on both economic and moral grounds. Socially responsible resettlement—that is, resettlement genuinely guided by an equity compass—can counteract lasting impoverishment and generate benefits for both the national and local economy. Yet, much too often, those who approve and design projects causing displacement are deprived of an 'equity compass' that can guide them in allocating project resources and preventing (or mitigation) the risks of impoverishment.

The agenda for action therefore is to pray that the meters or compasses for the starters—proliferate in plenty—so that public ethics can flourish for the benefit of all.

REFERENCES

Cernea, M. 2000. 'Risks, Safeguards and Reconstruction—A Model for Population, Displacement and Resettlement,' in *Economic and Political Weekly*, vol. 35, no. 41, pp. 3659–78.

Gandhi, M.K. 1927. *The Story of my Experiments with Truth*. (Reprint, 2001). Ahmedabad: Navjivan Publishing House.

Grassroots. 2001. Vol. 1, No. 3. Press Institute of India. 1–3.

Planning Commission. 2000. *Mid Term Appraisal*.

Pyarelal. 1965. *Mahatma Gandhi: The Early Phase*. Ahmedabad: Navjivan Publishing House.

Pyarelal. 1958. Mahatma Gandhi: The Last Phase, Vol. IX, Book I, Part I.
   Ahmedabad: Navjivan Publishing House.
Swami Vivekananda. 1998. *The Complete Works of Swami Vivekananda.*
   Advaita Ashram: Second Edition.
Swarup, Ram, 2000. *On Hindiusm—Reviews and Reflections.* New Delhi:
   Voice of India.
Sreenivasan, M.A. 1991. *Of the Raj, Maharajas and Me.* New Delhi: Ravi
   Dayal Publishers.

PART III

THE PUBLIC IN THE CONTEXT OF GLOBALIZATION

13

Public Sector in a Market Economy

Arjun Sengupta

Introduction

In this note I would like to discuss certain aspects of the role of the public sector in a market economy. Defining my subject this way, rather than 'Public Sector and the Market Economy' the subject assigned to me, allows me to narrow the focus to a limited field of interaction between these two institutions. The public sector and the market economy are often viewed as mutually exclusive institutions. It is sometimes held that a market economy can organize the behaviour of individual agents much better than the public sector. The logical extreme of that position would be calling for a minimal state. The public sector is then seen not just as a worse performer but also as actually a nuisance or worse, a harmful institution that distorts the functioning of the economy, resulting in inefficiency and avoidable waste. On the other hand, it has also been argued that when judged from the standards of various social objectives, markets fail to organize individual activities to arrive at desirable and optimal outcomes and that the public sector should regulate if not replace the markets when the goal is to manage the economy to achieve a social optimum. Much of the economics literature is devoted to examining these questions, theoretically and empirically, with conflicting views about the nature and the functioning of the markets as well as of the state.[1]

Like most other debates in economics, that debate is still not settled, and it is very tempting to get into it, take sides and express judgements, because ultimately the issues involved are not so much empirical as they are judgmental. There is as much evidence of government failures as of market failures, and one is left making judgements about how the State or the markets are expected to behave or should behave. I want to avoid that debate and concentrate on a narrower field: Assume the economy is a market economy where most of the interactions between individual agents are determined by markets. What role should the State play in that economy? The answer to this question is not unequivocal, although the question itself is unavoidable. However much one may like it, the existence of the State cannot be wished away, even if the economy is completely dominated by the free play of market forces. And if the State exists, it will have powers to influence, intervene, guide or dominate the operation of the markets. One is thus inevitably faced with the question, and an attempt must be made to, at least, trace out the answers.

Market Economy

A market is a mechanism through which individual agents in an economy negotiate and settle the demand and supply of goods and services (Dasgupta 1993: especially Chapters 6 and 7). The essential element of the market is the opportunity to negotiate freely. This implies that whatever the outcome of the negotiation, it is not imposed upon the parties, and that they always have the option of withdrawal. If the cost of withdrawal is destitution, hunger or non-survival, the negotiations cannot be free and markets cannot exist. But if markets exist, and negotiations take place, market outcomes are by definition preferred to non-market situations, because individuals would not negotiate if they did not gain from it.[2]

It is important to understand the link between markets and the freedom to negotiate because many proponents of market mechanisms often fail to see the full implications of that freedom. A proper market cannot exist without the institutions that guarantee that freedom by law, by property rights, by tradition or trust. Such institutions cannot be created suddenly, by dictate, or with a blind eye to history.

The other important characteristic of a market is that all goods and services must have a price, reflecting the rate at which any one of them would exchange for another. Indeed, it is the price of a commodity (or of goods and services) in terms of money or a medium of exchange that forms a basis for carrying out the negotiations. Even if commodities are traded over time, they are mediated by prices quoted today, which means all commodities (available today or in the future) will have a price today and a market today.[3]

Individual agents engaged in the negotiation are either buyers or sellers, consumers or producers, and have self-regarding objective functions by which different configurations of available goods and services can be ordered in terms of utilities or preferences for consumers and profits for producers. If these functions are interdependent, complications arise, and markets often fail to produce stable outcomes to the negotiation. Thus, it is usually assumed that these self-regarding functions are independent of each other. If the individual parties are 'households' or 'firms' where a number of individuals operate together, there has to be some mechanism that reconciles the preference functions of all of them. Each firm is expected to maximize its profits, while each individual supplies a factor of production, whether labour, capital or other asset, so as to derive the maximum benefit according to the self-regarding objective functions. For a household, either a patriarch or a matriarch, or some custom would combine the individuals' preferences into the household's preferences. What is required is a method of ordering the options in a manner that enables the negotiations to take place.

Markets do not need a specific geographical location. They may be missing or malfunctioning and in fact, very few markets are competitive. But when the market mechanism is championed, it is usually the competitive markets to which references are made. Thus, a competitive market is one where there is only one price for each commodity and where each commodity has a market. It is useful to remember that having markets or having an economy where markets determine most individuals' activities or transactions between them—which is how a market economy is defined—does not necessarily mean that those markets are competitive.

The most important characteristic of a competitive economy is the parametric functions of prices where all individuals act as price-takers, and adjust their actions to the prices, which they cannot individually manipulate. If a competitive equilibrium exists, then there will be a set of prices for all commodities at which the quantities demanded would equal the quantities supplied, and all individuals will achieve the maximum of their self-regarding objective functions. If the goal of social activities is to maximize the individual self-regarding objective functions, such a competitive equilibrium will be the optimal state of affairs.

The seminal works of Arrow and Debreu (Arrow and Debreu 1959) helped formally establish the conditions for the existence of such equilibrium only to bring out how improbable it is that they are to be found in any actual economy. The market failure literature initially addressed external economies, increasing returns and public goods, and expanded steadily to many areas and characteristics of a real economy. Eventually it came to the analysis of imperfect information which showed that market failures were not only widespread but almost endemic to a modern economy (Stiglitz 1997). Thus the competitive market paradigm ceased to be even an abstract representation of an actual economy. It was no longer possible to suggest that if state interventions were minimized, and markets left alone, so that individuals could freely bargain and negotiate with each other, the outcome would simulate a competitive economy. The competitive model, which was built up as a part of positive economics (an extension of the Walrasian general equilibrium system), came to be treated more as a model to help make normative prescriptions.[4]

As a result, economic policy prescriptions mostly concentrated on promoting competition and creating conditions that enabled economic agents to behave as if they were operating in a competitive economy. This meant that the State was assigned an explicit role in formulating and implementing policies to make the market economy work by simulating competitive conditions, or to counter and correct the sources of market failures. Initially these policies often took the form of extensive state intervention, so much so that public sector operations came to be seen as an alternative mechanism of resource allocation and contrasted with the market mechanism. The central planning models, whether of the Lange–Lerner variety which mimicked the competitive equilibrium or the Frisch–Tinbergen models that built on optimal investment decisions, not to mention the crude, rule-of-thumb mechanisms of the Soviet Gosplan, all suggested that it was possible to construct an effective alternative to the market economy. But soon the limitations of such extensive government interventions became apparent and the market failure literature was complemented by writings on government failure. The central planning models of resource allocation were thoroughly discredited, not only by the practice in the socialist economies, but also by almost the same issues of imperfect information and the principal–agent problem that undermined the basis of competitive equilibrium.

Nevertheless, the importance of the State playing a role in making markets function in a market economy was generally recognized. State actions came to be increasingly seen as complementing the operation of market forces, facilitating the coordination of private sector activities, dealing with problems of imperfect information, incomplete markets, dynamic externalities and increasing returns, as well as multiple equilibrium. The government need not do what the private sector can do better, provided the government enacts policies removing obstacles and distortions from the market, especially in the direct production of consumer and producer goods. But there are areas where the private sector will have very limited competence, such as providing public goods and supplying merit goods, like health care and education, or creating physical and social infrastructure. The government will have a natural role to play in those areas of a market economy.

This complementary relationship between the State and the market has been described as 'market-enhancing'. In such a situation the government does not try to substitute for the market mechanism or correct market failures but instead attempts to enhance the capabilities of private sector institutions to circumvent such failures (Aoki and Fujiwara 1997). Such a market enhancing role can extend from rule-making and affecting incentives to direct intervention in re-structuring and deepening the markets, regulating excessive competition or restrictive practices.

Markets and Efficiency

The reason for an almost universally renewed appreciation of the market mechanism, freeing market forces and the State's role of market-enhancer, is a better understanding of the relationship between market competition and efficiency. The Arrow–Debreu model demonstrated how a competitive market generates Pareto-efficiency by reaching an equilibrium from where no reallocation of resources can make at least one individual better off without making anyone worse off. This led to the enunciation of the First Fundamental theorem of Welfare Economics that states that competitive equilibrium is Pareto-efficient.

There are two sides to this equilibrium—one is related to production and the other to exchange. On the production side, each unit is profit maximizing. On the exchange side, each individual is maximizing his utility according to his preference function. The grand competitive equilibrium covers both sides. It yields efficient outcomes on the exchange side where no individual's satisfaction of wants can be improved without making at least another worse off. On the production side it yields efficient outcomes when output of no one product can be increased without a reduction in output of at least one other product, and still have all firms maximize their profits.

It may be problematic and unacceptable to interpret the equilibrium of the exchange side as efficient in terms of maximizing the utilities or satisfaction of wants of individuals, which are not comparable, which cannot be aggregated and which do not cover all aspects of social choice and welfare. Indeed, as will be discussed later, this may give the public sector a role far beyond what is assigned under a liberalist-individualist paradigm. But interpreting the competitive equilibrium on the production side as efficient makes sense, since it effectively means that given the land, labour, technology and other resources of an economy, that equilibrium results in the maximum amount of a commodity that can be produced without reducing the production of any other commodity.

In the common-parlance of an economist, this means that the economy will be operating from a point (the equilibrium) on the country's production possibility frontier. That frontier is a locus of all the points of competitive equilibrium in production which represents a combination of maximum outputs of any product, given the levels of production of all other products.[5] Any arrangement of production that results in the economy landing at a point below or inside the production possibility frontier, will be inefficient because it will be wasting resources. It will mean getting stuck in a situation where it would have been possible to have more of one commodity without a fall in the production of any other commodity.

It is therefore plausible to advocate policies that promote competitive equilibrium in production, (to avoid waste and get the maximum out of existing resources) and then move to attain the optimal position in terms of the consumption of these products through exchange and in accordance with social preferences. In practice, the recommendation for promoting competition would be to bring prices of commodities closer to their marginal costs of production—the competitive equilibrium being a situation where prices are equal to marginal costs. Removing the barriers to entry and exit of the firms,[6] eliminating all distortions created by policies or institutions and correcting market failures, may do this. Most of the prescriptions in the mainstream literature for making market competition work would become fully relevant and eminently justified. This is because the closer the economy is to competitive equilibrium, the lower the waste of resources for any economic arrangement that society may choose to secure through policy.

The possibility of separating the exchange economy from the production economy allows us to think of and advocate for efficiency in production through promoting competition among the producers, even if a case is made for intervening in the exchange economy and moving away from the position of equilibrium of exchange which is based on the existing distribution of wealth and assets. This may, however, not always be possible; we may like to intervene in the exchange economy, in order to redistribute the incomes, alter the economic structure, change the property relations or the distribution of assets in such a manner that prices and incentives—the basis of the production economy—are seriously affected. It may not be possible then to reach the position of competitive equilibrium in production without taking into account the developments in the exchange economy. In the neo-classical literature, the costs of such deviations from the competitive equilibrium are referred to as 'deadweight' loss, and should be compared with the gain that is made, appropriately calculated, from the policies that affect the equilibrium of the exchange economy. But these losses and gains are not always comparable, as they affect different people differently. In spite of that, it may be necessary to adopt social policies that attempt to alter the distribution of resources compared to the competitive equilibrium of exchanges. But in doing so, every effort should be made to minimize waste in the production economy and to keep the relationship between the producers as competitive as possible.

The Role of the Public Sector

From the perspective of the operations of an economy, the role of the public sector or the state in the production economy may appear to be very limited. It should be engaged mainly in promoting competition among producing units and individual agents, making the markets free and liberal and correcting market failures. It need not be involved directly in production activities, unless there are areas where private units cannot be motivated to perform. The existence and functioning of public enterprises in producing and supplying goods and services have to be justified by the characteristics of the activities. These should include those which could not be carried out effectively by the private sector or at least on a scale or to an extent that can be regarded as optimal.

Traditionally, the supply of public goods is recognized as a justifiable area for public sector involvement because, even if motivated to perform, the private sector will undersupply those goods. In an underdeveloped economy, there are however many areas which are not public goods proper,[7] where the private sector may not perform in full because of very large sunk costs in fixed capital, long gestation periods and non-appropriability of returns. An effective case can thus be made for public sector operation in those areas, (such as infrastructural industries or supply of merit goods like health care, education and sanitation), at least until institutions that can capture the widely spread out returns and convert them into negotiable assets materialize.

Even then there are two aspects of the functioning of the public sector that should be carefully noted. First, when a public sector unit is operating in the production sector, it should function very much like a private sector unit operating in a competitive framework. Specifically, it should respond to market prices and incentives in a similar manner, maximize profits, or minimize the costs of production that produce equivalent results under competition. The so-called principles of social obligations or distributive justice or favourable labour contracts, which are often required of public enterprises, should be seen as taxes imposed on them. These should be imposed equally on the private sector units, so that they too respond to market costs and prices, adjusted by these taxes, in a similar manner. Alternatively, the public sector units should be fully compensated by the budget for assuming such obligations.

Second, the public sector need not be identified only with the State. The feature that distinguishes the public sector from the private is motivation. In the private sector, consisting of individuals, firms or households, the motivation for any economic activity is private benefit, namely profit or utility. In the public sector, the motivation is decided by the group which supports the public sector, preferably, although not always, by a democratic process of social choice. That motivation can go well beyond the individual or joint private benefit of the members of the group. It may involve the exercise of some rights, some form of affirmative actions, or some notion of equity or distributive justice. While private benefits can be conceived of as a function of market prices and incentives, the social motivations of public sector activities cannot be reduced to dependence on such market variables. In that sense, the public sector is regarded as exogenous to the market economy; it acts autonomously, as its behaviour is not determined by market variables.[8]

When viewed from this angle, the public sector need not be confined only to the State. Any group motivated by objectives decided by social choice, and not by the aggregate of private benefits, can be regarded as belonging to the public sector. It can operate in a market economy in accordance with its motivations, just as the State does for all practical purposes. Under this understanding, cooperatives or even NGOs and civil society organizations could be regarded as public sector organizations. In many areas, such as the provision of health care, education and similar services, they can be much more effective than State organs.

This brings me to my last point regarding the relation between the public sector and the market economy. For analytical purposes, the operations of the production economy may be separated from those of the exchange economy, although in the actual functioning of the market economy, they are interdependent. Both sides must operate together to define the behaviour of the market economy, and it is not possible to identify the market economy with the operations of only one side by abstracting from the other.

Thus, even if we can create and implement a policy framework that allows the production economy to operate efficiently, (so that at any point of time the economy is able to operate from some position on the production possibility frontier), the economy can still operate at a suboptimal level, in terms of the overall social objectives, if the exchange economy cannot be adjusted appropriately. For example, under a competitive equilibrium, a market economy may be operating at its production possibility frontier, avoiding all wastes and inefficiencies. However, it may also be at a point where although all individual preference functions have been maximized, income distribution is extremely unequal, and a large number of people remain poor, illiterate and malnourished or where many basic economic and social rights are violated. It is the exchange economy's equilibrium conditions that determine the position of the production frontier from where the market economy would function under competitive equilibrium. If that economy follows the procedure of constrained maximization of individual utility functions under competition, it will land on a point of that frontier that develops from the initial distribution or endowment of assets and wealth and capabilities, and not according to any consideration of equity or justice.

If the public sector has a different view of equity and justice or distributional preference, it has to operate on the exchange economy to move the equilibrium of the market economy from the point where free market forces would land, to a point that can be regarded as socially optimal. There is no automatic market mechanism that would make this shift. It has to be achieved by policy and public action and cannot be left to market forces to resolve. In my opinion, this is the primary role of the public sector in a market economy.

There are two essential characteristics of that role. First, the social objectives have to be clearly identified and should be adopted by the public sector through, as I mentioned above, a democratic process of social choice. Effectively this means identifying the points or the plane on this commodity space where the economy should aim to operate. Second, a programme of policies has to be designed so that these objectives can be realized at the least possible cost. Every attempt must be made to retain efficiency in production that is to move along the production possibility frontier by promoting a competitive process as found in a liberal market economy. But a cost-less movement on the production possibility frontier may not be possible and the policies may force the economy to sacrifice some resources or potential output by moving inside the frontier for sometime, until the economy re-emerges on the frontier again. It is this loss of output and resources that will be regarded as the cost of such adjustment. And the design of the policy should aim at minimizing that cost.

One cannot say whether the public sector will succeed in performing this role in all economies. But just because the costs appear to be too intractable or the adjustment process too contentious and subject to too much conflict and strife it must not give up trying to play the role.

NOTES

1. These issues have been discussed exhaustively in Malinvaud et.al (1997). The Introductory Overview essay by Arjun Sengupta discusses the major issues relating to objectives of development, market failures, the role of planning, macroeconomic and industrial policies. The article by Amartya Sen talks about the meaning of a development strategy, the one by Joseph Stiglitz discusses the characteristics of market failure and the role of the government, and complements the article by Malinvaud on the role of planning. In their articles, Nicholas Stern, Kotaro Suzumura and Jean-Claude Milleron discuss macroeconomic policy, industrial policy and global aspects.
2. Consider the following statement of Hayami (1997: 199) 'By definition, transactions in the market are voluntary, based upon the free will of buyers and sellers. Any transfer of goods and services against their will (such as stealing or plundering) is not a market transaction. Therefore if information is perfect, all the participants in market transactions gain, since sellers would not sell and buyers would not buy unless they were to gain.'
3. See Partha Dasgupta (1993: Chapter 7), that spells out the resource allocation mechanism in competitive markets and the issues related to efficiency.
4. On the other extreme was the rational expectations theory, according to which the real world was not only competitive with full price-wage

    feasibility, which always cleared the market, but also all the market agents made full and unbiased use of all information, and as a result all policies become ineffective. See, for instance, Begg (1982).

5. The most elegant and exhaustive treatment of these issues was by Koopmans (1957).

6. The importance of the removal of barriers to entry and exit of the firms has been fully brought out in the literature on contestable markets, where even with a limited number of firms, the characteristics of competitive equilibrium can be replicated if the markets are contestable. See Baunol et.al (1982).

7. The definition of pure public goods is one where the consumption is non-rival and non-excludable. The implications of dealing with such goods were explored in Samuelson (1954).

8. In the public choice literature, the state is made endogenous to the market economy, with its behaviour determined by the interaction of interest groups who respond systematically to market prices and incentives. The discussion on government failure in that literature has largely followed the analysis of these motivating factors (Buchanan 1975).

References

Aoki, Kim and Okuno-Fujiwara (eds). 1997. *The Role of Government in East Asian Development*. Oxford: Clarenden Press.

Arrow, K.J. and G. Debreu. 1959. 'Existence of Equilibrium for a Competitive Economy,' in G. Debreu (ed.) *Theory of Value*. New York: John Wiley.

Baunol, W.M., J.C. Panzar and R.D. Willing. 1982. *Contestable Markets and the Theory of Industrial Structure*. New York: Harcourt, Brace, Javanovich.

Begg, D.K.H. 1982. *The Rational Expectations Revolution in Macroeconomics Theories and Evidence*. Oxford: Philip Alston.

Buchanan, J. 1975. The Limits of Liberty: Between Anarchy and Leviathan. Chicago: University of Chicago Press.

Dasgupta, Partha.1993. *An Inquiry into Well-Being and Destitution*. Oxford: Clarendon Press.

Hayami Yujiro.1997. *Development Economics*. Oxford: Clarendon Press.

Koopmans, Tjalling. 1957. *Three Essays on the State of Economic Science*. New York: McGraw Hill.

Malinvaud, Edmond et.al. 1997. *Development Strategy and Management of the Market Economy*, Volume 1. Oxford: Clarendon Press.

Samuelson, Paul. 1954. 'The Pure Theory of Public Expenditure,' *Review of Economics and Statistics*.

Stiglitz, Joseph. 1997. 'Market Failures, Public Goods, and Enternalities,' in Edmund Malinvaud et al. (eds), *Development Strategy and Management of the Market Economy*, Volume 1. Oxford: Clarendon Press.

14

Privatization as Reform: Liberalization and Public Sector Enterprises in India

Kuldeep Mathur

India is currently experiencing a pronounced shift in state form and governing practices. Since 1991, when the economic reforms began to be unfolded, it came to be widely recognized among both its critics and supporters, that the central planning model and the dominant role that the state had played in the economy and society cannot survive the combined onslaught of economic crises and the processes of globalization. Even in western countries, the Keynesian welfare state is under pressure and is giving way to a restructuring of the economic and political system. The New Right is leading the intellectual attack on the state and the public sector primarily through the enunciation of public choice theory. The emphasis on the virtues of the market is highlighting the weaknesses of the public sector and hence the felt need for its privatization. Political leadership promoting economic reforms in India, in which privatization and slimming of the state is the major agenda, has articulated pragmatic reasons for reform. The purpose of this paper is to examine some of the issues raised by the public choice theory in questioning the efficient performance of the public sector and also to explore the question whether reforms in the public sector are possible without dismantling it. The first part of the paper will look at some general theoretical issues, the second part at the characteristics and pattern of public enterprises in India, the third at the efforts of reform and possible reasons for their failure and finally, the last section will conclude with the argument that wholesale privatization is not desirable and is an easy solution to a complex problem.

I

Much of the discussion of the concept of a liberal democratic state is concerned with the questions of the public-private divide. The early liberal theorists took the old feudal order, which was grounded in impositional claims about natural hierarchies and the organic whole, and recast it as a 'world of walls'. (Brodie 1996: 384) The church was separated from the state so that the latter could be shaped and governed according to the principles of liberalism and later liberal democracy. The state was separated from the economy so that the market could develop according to its laws of supply and demand. Such division helped develop rules and practices of state or public terrain that could be distinguished from those of the private. But as Bowles and Gintis (1986: 66) point out, the public-private partition is neither fixed, nor natural or obvious. Historically, the boundaries have been drawn and redrawn. The Keynesian welfare state was one such attempt in post-war years and now another attempt is being made. The Keynesian state asserted the primacy of the public over the 'invisible hand' of the market and engendered expectations that the state was responsible for meeting the basic needs of the citizens. (Brodie 1996: 386) The current attempt tends to reverse this formulation and seeks to rearrange public and private by shrinking the state and expanding the autonomy of the market. The neo-liberal agenda stresses the primacy of the market in generating a new social order.

Central to the concept of privatization is the idea of competition. Competition is accepted as a powerful tool and an essential dimension of economic, political and social life. Competing for the efficient exploitation of natural resources and the generation of new means to satisfy individual and collective needs at lower costs and higher quality is seen to have contributed greatly to the improvement of both material and non-material levels of well being. It is also seen as a driving force behind technological innovation. One might say that competition triggers market growth, cuts costs and drives technological change. Competition and the market go together and it is widely believed that public sector is inefficient because it does not face competition. Today competition has been elevated to an ideology and represents an important reason for privatization. As The Group of Lisbon (1995: xii) point out, 'A new era of competition has emerged in the last twenty years, especially in connection with globalization of economic processes. Competition no longer describes a mode of functioning of a particular market configuration (a competitive market) as distinct from oligopolistic and monopolistic markets. To be competitive has ceased to be an end; competitiveness has acquired the status of a universal credo, an ideology.'

Market and competition go together in the new liberal state, which is then led to perform two important functions: promote the market, and create conditions for free and fair competition to take place. Politics also gets redefined in this framework. The attempt is to depoliticize the economy by arguing that market driven adjustment and regulation provide greatest good to society. Critical governing instruments of a welfare state like public enterprises are seen as ineffective and inefficient delivery systems and should be removed from the realm of political negotiation. Much of this argument for depoliticization is based on an understanding of the way the rulers behave and why they do so. This can be subsumed under the broad rubric of what has come to be known as the theory of predatory rule. It is assumed that rulers play a critical role in determining state policies. Their power rests on coercion and also on raising revenues. Levi (1988: 2) hypothesizes that greater the revenue of the state, the more is the possibility to extend its rule. Revenue enhances the ability of the rulers to elaborate the institutions of the state, to bring more people within the domain of those institutions, and to increase the number and variety of public goods provided through the state. For reasons of self-interest to extend their rule and for state reasons, rulers attempt to extract as much revenue as possible. In the process of extraction, the rulers may line their own pockets and divert funds in their personal direction. The capacity of the rulers to serve their own interests increases with the size of the public sector. As the public sector is reduced, market regulation takes over, limiting the perfidious role of the rulers. Thus, it becomes important to keep politics and economic decision-making separate. A liberal state is a democratic state where competition takes place through elections without its impact being felt in the economic arena, which is governed by the market.

The motivation of rulers is at the heart of the public choice theory that provides the intellectual grist to the privatization mill. And this is what we turn to now. The public choice theorists have attempted to identify explanations of political and organizational behaviour on the basis of motives of actors. Their central assumption is that human beings behave in the political arena in the same way as they do in the economic arena. They are rational maximizers of their self-interest. Their self-interest is defined purely in terms of material income or satisfactions derived from it. The stress in this theory is on mono-motivation in contrast to the generally understood diverse motivations of individual's behaviour. In explaining political behaviour, then, values, culture or history are ignored.

The pursuit of self-interest works for wider social interests when regulated by the market. Thus, there are two important and basic assumptions: first, the market best regulates that individuals work for their material self-interest and the second is that pursuit of self-interest. Advocacy for slimming the government and reducing the public sector follow from this formulation. While recognizing that individual self-interest is a powerful and pervasive motive, it is still open to question whether the market is the best way to regulate it to serve public interest. Institutional discipline could be another method, which can harness self-interest for good purposes.

Emphasis on individual motivation has also led to the exploration of institutions as a source of discipline and re-examination of the bureaucratic design for state activities. Weber had contended that bureaucratic organization was the manifestation of rationality and a powerful mechanism to bring about efficiency. Well laid down formal rules, hierarchy and obedience to rule of law ensured that individual bureaucrats would respond with rational behaviour and work for public interest. According to the public choice theorists, the engine of rationality has lost its sheen. The case of state failure is based on how monopoly rents are created through the imposition of regulation and control over the economy. Political pressures dominate economic policy making and execution leading to misallocation of resources. Corruption and favouritism surround bureaucratic allocations of investment licences, import licenses and the award of government contracts. A consequence of this system is that government machinery is increasingly used to serve personal interests. Government bureaucratic organization has been discredited not only in theory, but also in practice, and therefore there is a search for alternative ways of implementing state activities.

The new institutional approach is based on the previously mentioned assumption that self-interested individuals, who pursue optimizing strategies, will require reference to appropriate sets of decision rules or decision making arrangements in dealing with structures of events if the welfare potential of a community of individuals is to be enhanced. No single form of organization is presumed to be 'good' for all circumstances. (Ostrom 1989: 48) Public goods because of their very nature cannot be delivered through bureaucratic organizations. Gordon Tullock (1965) analyzes the consequences that follow when rational, self-interested individuals pursue maximizing strategies, in very large public bureaucracies. A typical career oriented bureaucrat will act to please his superiors because his advancement depends on their favourable recommendation. Distortion of information will take place because the tendency will be to forward only favourable information. Large-scale bureaucracies will thus become error-prone and cumbersome in adapting to rapidly changing conditions. Efforts to correct the malfunctioning of bureaucracy by tightening control will magnify errors. (Ostrom 1989: 53) Control will engender 'bureaucratic free enterprise' (Tullock, 1965:167) when groups and individuals within the organization set themselves up to formulate their own goals and to create opportunities for side payoffs leading to graft and corruption. Organization goals get distorted and they begin to work in contradiction to the public announcements of their goals and purposes.

Starting from these basic premises, the public sector has been attacked for the failure in its fundamental institutional design. The new public management perspective, shaped by neo-classical economic principles and the public choice theory, questions its size, roles and structures. Asserting that public bureaucracies are unable to manage the production and delivery of goods where exclusion is not possible or difficult, or where monopolistic conditions prevail, private sector is seen as having the managerial capacity, flexibility and competitive drive essential for the efficient and effective provision of many activities previously assumed to be the province of the public sector (see Minogue, Polidano and Hume 1998 for elaboration of this theme). Much of the discussion therefore is in terms of exploring alternative strategies for privatizing the public sector (Osborne and Gaebler 1993, Savas 1982).

This section has attempted to highlight the major contours of the intellectual attack on the public sector. Among its weapons is the economic theory of politics where the fundamental assumption is that a rational man is a maximizer and tends to be so whether he is involved in economic or political activities. Further, this theory suggests that the market is the best way to allocate public goods, manage public enterprises or arrive at collective social decisions, or even to govern democratically. It also suggests that public bureaucracies have to be organized keeping the individual motivations in mind and the nature of goods and services that they seek to provide. Reform movements that have been subsumed under what has come to be known as new public management are inspired by diverse strategies that can privatize different kinds of public sectors.

II

At the time of independence, political leadership identified the future of India with developments in the West. Of particular significance was its perception of the role of science and technology in transforming those societies. Nehru was fascinated with developments in the Soviet Russia and was impressed by the achievements made possible by planning and rational allocation of resources. He saw India quickly attaining the levels of economic development achieved by the Western nations through industrialization and modernization. With the emphasis on rational allocation of resources and industrialization, planning and state intervention became central to the strategy of development initiated through the various Five Year Plans. In this strategy, public enterprises occupied a significant place. The reason was the limitations of the private sector at that time. There were private monopolies and there was little capacity to make large-scale investments. The stepping in of the state in areas of infrastructure development that required heavy investments was something that was welcomed by the private sector. It was only later, as a matter of fact in the 1956 Industrial Policy Resolution that the ideological basis of the public sector was underlined: 'The adoption of the socialist pattern of society as the national objective, as well as the need of planned and rapid development, require that all industries of basic and strategic importance or in the nature of public utility services should be in the public sector' (Industrial Policy Resolution 1956). Thus at this time, the role of the public sector in the economy was defined more in terms of filling in the gaps of the limitations of the private sector even though a philosophy of socialist pattern of society had been enunciated. The Second Five Year Plan was based on the now well known Nehru–Mahalnobis model which recognized that irrespective of the ideological bias, the private sector would not find it attractive to undertake investments of the magnitude required under planning, when the new projects were likely to be more capital intensive, with long gestation periods and with unattractive rates of return.

It was the Indira Gandhi period from 1969 onwards that saw a strengthening of state controls and state entry into the service sector on a larger scale. Public sector played a leading role in the manufacturing sector during the Second and Third Plan period. This was the period when the public sector walked in areas where the private sector was unable or hesitant to tread. Public policy stressed regulation of monopolies and the public sector came to acquire a more ideological role of providing greater equity and justice in society. This led it onto the realm of the service sector too. Even otherwise, the perspectives on the role of the public sector had begun to change. The Seventh Five Year Plan saw the public sector as a 'pace-setter' in high technology industries and an institution to generate sizable resources for new investments. It also talked about the leading role of the public sector in stimulating development of efficient ancillary manufacturing, which in turn will strengthen the sinews of industry. A variety of justifications and objectives of the public sector have been documented (see for a listing in Goyal 1986).

Indeed, there has been no formal government document like a White Paper that clearly lays down the rationale of public sector in India. There have been suggestions from various committees (see Iyer 1991: 9–11). The Administrative Reforms Commission (1967) had recommended that the Government should make a comprehensive and clear statement on the objectives and obligations of the public sector. Several parliamentary committees as also much later, the Economic Administration Reforms Commission headed by L.K. Jha said the same. As a result, the rationale of public investment or roles of public enterprises as perceived by the government have to be inferred from government documents and the kind and range of investments made. As a consequence, the public sector in India has developed with multiple objectives that are quite often contradictory. To assess it on one single criterion would be both unfair and inadequate. This becomes very clear from the listing of objectives given by the Public Enterprises Survey, 1995-96:

- To help in the rapid economic growth and industrialization of the country and create the necessary infrastructure for economic development;
- To earn return on investment and thus generate resources for development;
- To promote redistribution of income and wealth;
- To create employment opportunities;

- To promote balanced regional development;
- To assist the development of small scale and ancillary industries;
- To promote import substitutions, save and earn foreign exchange for the economy.

It is obvious that public sector means everything to policy makers and has become an umbrella concept that ultimately does not specify whether the public sector is a business or a commercial proposition, and the manner in which it needs to be attended to.

Usually public sector refers to all activities funded out of the government's budget. In this paper, we will restrict our attention to public enterprises of a particular kind. Public sector in India refers to all government activities that are run as departmental and non-departmental enterprises. Departmental enterprises form part of the government's financial systems but have separate accounts of income and expenditure. Their surplus or deficit is merged in the accounts of the departments of the government, e.g., telecommunications, the postal department etc. In the case of the railways a separate budget is presented. Highway construction and maintenance, irrigation, housing, health and educational services fall into the departmental enterprises. Non-departmental enterprises refer to activities that are carried out by entities, which are legally separated from the government and are made to maintain a separate account of all their financial transactions and set them out in the form of a profit and loss account. These enterprises are set up under the companies act or under special statutory provisions. Public enterprises can be further classified into central government or state enterprises.

The public sector, then, comprises of three types of organizations: administration by a government department, the joint-stock company governed by company law and controlled by the government as a major shareholder, and autonomous public corporations. Our reference in this paper is to central enterprises, which are either joint stock companies or statutory autonomous corporations. In the 1950s, there were only 21 public sector enterprises with an invested capital of Rs 810 million. This increased to 85 enterprises in 1960s with Rs 39,020 million in the invested capital. The 1970s saw near doubling of enterprises to 169 and the invested capital had grown four times to Rs 155,340 million. The increases accelerated in the 1980s with the number of enterprises growing to 244 and the capital to Rs 993,290 million. (Kalirajan and Shand 1996: 2683) As pointed out earlier, the reason of this expansion was the spread of the public sector in all sectors of the economy.

The size of the public sector can be gauged from another point of view as seen from Table 14.1. The share of public sector in total capital stock was 46 per cent while value added was only 26.8 per cent. Investments in the public sector formed 9.4 per cent of GDP while savings were only of 1.6 per cent leaving a savings-investments gap of -8 per cent. As seen in Table 14.1 savings of both public and private corporate sector are low but those from the public sector are considerably lower than those from the private sector. In other words, public sector works at very low levels of profitability.

The number of Central government non-financial enterprises stood at 236 in 1997–98 (*Indian Economic Survey*, 1999–2000). Some of these units are very large and the largest among them account for around 95 per cent of the total assets. Among these are Indian Oil, ONGC and SAIL. Of the total capital employed, it appears the main share has been claimed by oil, steel, coal and power. A good deal of investment has also gone into medium and light engineering industries. Most of these enterprises are the ones, which like the sick private textile industries had to be taken over as a rescue operation by the government (Goyal 1986).

Even though the profitability of public enterprises has been low, there has been an appreciable improvement in it during the eighties. The ratio of gross profit to capital employed showed a marked improvement from 7.79 per cent in 1980/81 to 11.4 per cent in 1992/93. The net return on investment improved from –1.11 per cent to 4.47 per cent between 1980/81 and 1989/90, although the ratio came down to around 2.4 per cent in the early 1990s (Raghavan 1994: 39). The picture about the profitability of enterprises becomes clearer if we disaggregate the public

Table 14.1
Public Sector in the Indian Economy

Public Sector	Share in Net Capital Stock March 1992 (Per Cent)	Share in Gross Value Added 1990–93 (Average Per Cent)	Saving (Per Cent of GDP)	Investment (Per Cent of GDP)
Administrative Departments	12.6	9.3	–2.2	1.9
Departmental Enterprises	13.6	4.0	0.7	2.0
Non-departmental Enterprises	20.0	13.0	3.1	6.2
Public Sector	46.2	26.8	1.6	9.4
Private Sector	53.8	73.2	18.6	14.2
Total	100.0	100.0	21.8	23.8

Source: Gouri (1996: M64).

enterprises into two categories of profit making and loss making enterprises. As can be seen from Table 14.2, the increase in profits has been accompanied by an increase in losses but the net profit has registered a rise in 1992/93 over 1980/81. Out of the 104 loss making enterprises, 80 were in manufacturing industries and the rest were in the services sector. The public enterprises in the manufacturing sector accounted for 80 per cent of the losses incurred by all loss-making public enterprises and also accounted for nearly 87 per cent of employment in such enterprises. It is this feature of profitability that dominates the larger perception of inefficiency and over employment in the public sector.

Later figures for 1997–98 show considerable rise in profitability of central public enterprises. During this year, out of 235 operating units, 134 earned profits and 100 incurred losses. According to Gupta (2000: 8) public sector units earned a net profit of Rs 132.35 billion during 1998–99 after providing for income tax of Rs 64.99 billion and adjusting a loss of Rs 92.74 billion incurred by 106 enterprises. Out of the 106 loss-making enterprises, 33 were already sick and were taken over by the government from the private sector. The government has acted as 'hospital' for failed enterprises and thus has incurred losses when the turnaround has not been possible.

Together with this question of profitability is the issue of employment, which has gradually acquired the characteristic of what is now commonly known as overstaffing. The trends in employment in the organized sector of the economy show that total employment in the public sector registered a relatively high growth rate of 2.4 per cent per annum between 1976 and 1991 as compared to very low growth rate of 0.8 per cent in the organized private sector during the same period (Raghavan 1994: 18). The share of public sector in the total employment in the organized sector increased from 66 per cent in 1976 to 71 per cent in 1991. The average annual per capita emoluments of public sector employees turns out to be around Rs 105,879 in 1995–96 as mentioned in the Public Enterprises Survey 1995–96.

Over the years a very comprehensive and complex system of relationships has emerged between government and the public enterprises. The government as owner and as an agency accountable to the Parliament has tended to administer, control and monitor the performance of public enterprises very closely. Departmental enterprises were in any case under the government but joint-stock companies and corporations also came to be controlled through administrative ministries

Table 14.2
Trends in Net Profit/Loss of Central Public Enterprises:
1981–93 (Rs million at current prices)

Category	1980/81	1992/93
Profit of Profit Making Enterprises	55.7	734.6
	(94)*	(131)
Loss of Loss Making Enterprises	76.0	395.0
	(74)	(104)
Net Profit/Loss of All Enterprises	−20.3	339.6
	(168)	(235)

Source: Raghavan (1994: 41).
Figures in brackets relate to number of enterprises

where civil servants and not the managers of the enterprises became the decision makers. Issues of autonomy and accountability have dominated the discussion about reforming the public sector. Increasing autonomy and reducing bureaucratic interference was the major recommendation of the Appleby Report that was brought out as far back as 1956 and has been a refrain taken up by parliamentary committees as well as academic writings since then.

Little structural reform has followed, though, in the last decade or so, the idea of regulating the relationship between the government and public enterprise by means of a Memorandum of Understanding (MOU) has led some enterprises to sign contracts with government, which clarify the objectives of the enterprise, identify responsibilities on either side and provide a basis for evaluation of performance. This path of reform has not been easy because the enterprises come in various sizes and forms with different bargaining capacities. As mentioned by Iyer (1991: 60), who was Secretary of the Jha Commission, the role of government qua government tends to seep into that of owner, and it is rather difficult to persuade the government to forget its 'sovereign' aspect and accept a contractual relationship with an enterprise. Second, while the Chief Executive is expected to make firm commitments to the government, the administrative ministry is unable to do so on behalf of the government.

A neglected area of reform has been that of raising productivity of the use of existing resources through upgrading of technology. Kalirajan and Shand (1996: 2683–86) have argued that technical efficiency can contribute substantially to improving the performance of the public sector. What has happened is that budget constraints in public sector enterprises, generally, are unduly soft, and political accountability prevails over performance accountability. Performance accountability requires that resources are not wasted and are used to their full capacity. A necessary condition for this is that the enterprises should not enjoy soft budgets which come in terms of subsidies, favourably administered prices, easily arranged tax reliefs and easy credit availability and repayment. In essence, soft budgets allow enterprises to produce outputs by using inputs liberally and not use them to their full capacity. On the basis of data for 50 manufacturing public enterprises, [Ibid.] show that on average these enterprises realized only 60 per cent of their potential output. From their point of view, this carries the crucial implication that output in public enterprises can be increased without increasing levels of inputs (labour and capital) but just by improving technical and management practices.

Another theme in examining the working of public enterprises in India has been the issue of internal organizational structure and questions of incentives and motivations. While initiating debate on the Second Five Year Plan in the Lok Sabha, Nehru had stated that the way a government functions is not exactly the way that business houses and enterprises normally function. He argued that normal government procedures when applied to a public enterprise would lead to failure of that public enterprise. Therefore, he preferred a system for public enterprises that had adequate checks and protections but had enough freedom to work quickly and without delay. This balancing act led to the designing of various kinds of organization structures and their relationship with the government. But this search for a balanced organization has been an elusive dream. In the initial years, the difference among enterprises were seen only in terms of ownership and therefore, it was argued that any professional manager could manage them. This allowed for movement of managers from private sector to public sector. At this time too, public enterprises were seen as part of the expanding domain of the civil service and thus civil servants also began to seek managerial positions in public sector enterprises. Very soon, the choice became clear and civil servants went on to man public enterprises and mould them according to their own experiences. The autonomy debate was a non-starter with both administrative ministries and public enterprises being headed by the same group of people whose incentives did not lie in the specific organization that they worked in, but in the larger civil service system.

Institutional autonomy without professional strength in the management of an enterprise was difficult to achieve. The debate about professionalizing the management was never resolved. The result was that there was no stop to making public enterprises resemble government departments in work and procedure. In an interesting formulation, DiMaggio and Powell (1993) have put forward a theory of 'institutional isomorphism', which aims at a general explanation of the development of institutional similarities. Isomorphism is defined as 'a constraining process that forces one unit of population to resemble other units that face the same set of environmental conditions' (1983: 148). They argue that professionalization and bureaucratization are not necessarily the product of strategic plans for more rational organizations, but may reflect, or be caused by dependency or closeness to other organizations. They suggest that a general mechanism is at work: 'The greater the dependence of an organization on another organization, the more similar it will become to that organization in structure, climate and behavioural focus' (DiMaggi and Powell 1993: 154). Thus, public enterprises, large or small, began to acquire the characteristics of administrative departments that they were linked to and lost the special character for which they were established. The incentive system like in bureaucracy was not related to performance but ability to fulfil obligations of hierarchy and the command and control system. Exhortations of national service and work in public interest were relied on to encourage good and efficient performance.

Growth of institutional isomorphism led to even greater difficulties in reforming and professionalizing the public sector. For, unless reforms in civil service were affected, reforms would not follow in the public sector. And, repeated efforts to reform the civil service had ended in failure. The last concerted effort at administrative reform was the establishment of the Administrative Reforms Commission, which submitted its reports in 1969. Despite extensive research that involved a large number of academics, civil servants and concerned citizens in producing the recommendations, little change that had an impact on the people took place. Under pressure to downsize government from the international funding agencies, some more attempts at preparing reports for administrative reforms have followed. The Fifth Pay Commission in 1996 included suggestions for reform. The civil service was instrumental in seeing that the recommendations to increase their pay packets were accepted by the government while those that would have led to changes in the structure and working of the government were allowed to languish.

The Government of India presented an Action Plan for Effective and Responsive Government to the Conference of Chief Ministers on 24th May 1997. The wait for reform continues.

There is no dearth of policy recommendations for making the government more effective and efficient and most of them were made even before downsizing was the fashion of the day. Public enterprises have been under focus for a long time. It is just that these recommendations rarely get implemented or when implemented fail to get institutionalized. In many cases the ruling politicians have wrested the authorized initiative from the official hierarchy to stall changes; in other cases bureaucratic hierarchy has acted as a barrier to any political initiative to bring about reform. What has happened over the years is that bureaucrats have emerged as a powerful component of the decision-making process, largely because the political establishment was only too happy to abdicate its responsibility and to concentrate more on matters that were political. But in providing continuity in civil administration, despite political turbulence and change in governments, bureaucracy also proved to be an obstacle in the path of prompt action. 'Red-tapism' is as much a product of the rulebook written by the government as its interpretation and application by bureaucrats. The existence of the book has undoubtedly provided crucial checks and balances required to prevent abuse of power by political authority. But it has led to another consequence. A new breed of politicians who have to do things in a hurry have emerged. This breed finds the rulebook an impediment, would like to bend the rules and make them flexible for its own advantage. Bureaucrats are damned if they accept the assertions of such a group of politicians and also damned if they do not. In such an uncertain situation, they have become apprehensive of their future and have got prone to stick to their traditional ways. Reforms need bold action and this is not forthcoming.

Lack of institutional and procedural reforms in the public enterprises have much to do with what has happened in the governmental sector, particularly because the managers in public enterprises have moved to them after notching up years of experience in traditional government departments and have thus readily accepted the incentive system or the procedures that they have been most familiar with. The difficulties of a private sector executive brought in to manage a public enterprise—Air India—were so indomitable that he had to leave finding little support for reform either among politicians or bureaucrats or among the managers of the enterprise itself!

In concluding this section, it is important to stress at least a few important features of the public enterprises in India. One is that they emerged in order to fill the gaps that could not be met by investment from the private sector. The ideological justifications were added only later. The concerns were more pragmatic and as Nehru declared introducing the Second Plan in Parliament, 'May I say here that while I am for the public sector growing, I do not understand or appreciate the condemnation of the private sector. The whole philosophy underlying this Plan is to take advantage of every possible way of growth and not to do something which suits some doctrinaire theory or imagine we have grown because we have satisfied some textbook maxim of hundred years ago' (Government of India 1958). Second, all enterprises have not performed badly if profit is the only criterion. But it needs to be accepted that they could have done better. Despite the investment of Rs 2,300 billion, the net profit of public enterprises was only Rs 19,473 billion in 1998–99. Third, the need to reform the public sector has been on the political and administrative agenda literally from the time that enterprises were established, but for various reasons, the reform suggestions have not been implemented in a way that created an impact. It was widely accepted that if the enterprises had to function on a commercial basis, they had to be liberated from government and bureaucratic controls. This wide acceptance could not be operationalized. And, finally, the public sector employees have become a political force on their own or as Bardhan (1984) points out, a partner in the ruling coalition. They have stalled any move to reform that does not serve their self-interest.

In face of this situation, the Government of India announced a Statement on Public Sector Policy as part of its industrial policy in the liberalization package of 1991. This policy included recommendations for disinvestments to raise resources and to refer chronically sick public enterprises to the Board of Industrial and Financial Reconstruction for revival or rehabilitation. By 1996, a total of 56 central enterprises had been registered with the Board (Public Enterprises Survey 1995–96: 40–42). Against a target set by the government of Rs 443 billion, the actual amount of receipts from the sale of equity amounted to only Rs 183,93 billion. Other recommendations included professionalization of the Board of Directors and signing of a Memorandum of Understanding.

Three issues emerge from the pace of disinvestments provided by the above data. First, of the 246 public enterprises (CPEs), only 40 CPEs' equity was sold during this period of 1991–96. Second, the quantity of equity that was sold was not significant: in 19 of the CPEs in question, the equity sold added up to less than ten per cent points, in seven, between 10 and 20 per cent points; in six between 30 and 40 per cent points and two between 40 and 50 per cent points. Finally, the controlling ownership of all the 40 CPEs continued to remain with the Government of India. In addition, most of the equity that has been sold so far has been only to public entities in the financial sector like the Unit Trust of India (Gupta 2000: 110). This was done because, as the Finance Minister put in the Parliament, as it was the government's intention to ensure that the benefits accrued to public sector institutions rather than the private entities in the event of the sales taking place at an under priced level (quoted in Gupta, op.cit.). No sick public enterprises have been shut down so far.

III

It is widely believed that public enterprises suffer from what may be called 'theory of public incompetence' (Stretton and Orchard 1994: 80). This incompetence arises from several factors. Centralized planning mechanisms are poor substitutes for people's market demands. Public sector managers lack the personal financial incentives, which profit seekers have. Private employees endanger their jobs if they achieve pay conditions that their employers cannot afford, but there is no such market limit to what organized, hard bargaining public employees can extract from the tax-payers. And inefficient private enterprises are automatically thrown out of the market but governments can and do allow inefficient enterprises to continue. While some of these beliefs may be well founded but the case for privatization rests mostly on the efficient use and allocation of resources. But the efficiency criterion is appears to be understood differently in the public sector with its multiple objectives. Even the private sector is hesitant to pursue efficiency single-mindedly. But, what is important is to realize that there is little empirical evidence to show that one is more efficient that the other. According to a recent study by the Reserve Bank of India as reported in *The Pioneer* (September 20, 2000: 6) the financial performance of selected private sector corporate firms has decelerated in the last few years. The gross profits declined for a second consecutive year in 1998–99 and growth rates in sales and value of production were also lower. Comparisons are difficult and public and private enterprises rarely produce the same goods under same conditions with same purpose.

The quest for efficiency follows a purely economic path, which implies a least cost notion of efficiency. It is achieved when least amount of resources are used to produce specific good or service. It does not say how this 'least amount' is achieved. The argument is based on a crude division between productive economic relations and unproductive social relations. The economic motive is given more weight than social motives. (Gupta 2000: 22) Social equity does not feature in this consideration of efficiency. State owned enterprises all over the world have been burdened with social obligations that the private sector has been generally free from. This is particularly true for the obligations of expanding employment and entering in such sectors or area of economic activity, which carry a social purpose.

In India from the very beginning, the public sector was not seen as profit making efficiency machine. It was visualized to fill in the weakness of the private sector which did not have the capability to make large investments in basic and heavy industries and also of fulfilling social responsibilities of the state of developing backward areas, or entering into social sectors where profit was not the goal. Very often, this objective has been achieved by not allowing prices of their products and services to be raised or to raise capital from the open market to meet the rising costs and inflation.

The second bulwark of privatization is the theory that managers and workers in public enterprises have poorer incentives than their private counterparts. Here again the question of comparison comes up. Incentives in what type of organization? A large enterprise, whether public or private is managed by salaried employees on behalf of the owners of the enterprise. What matters then is the incentives of the owners. Public owners are not profit seeking but the private owners are and they use this criterion to induce salaried managers to work for profit. In the public sector, performance incentives are resisted because they run counter to civil service norms. These norms are founded on the presumption that civil servants work for public interest in a spirit of benevolence. They are a legacy from the early days of independence when the bureaucracy was considered a protector of the people from the avaricious capitalists, imperialist masters and the vagaries of the market. It was never considered that people with the same instincts for self-interest might staff the government. Hence, the institutional design was based on the assumed public interest motivations of individuals and allowed for hierarchy, command and control structure to be dominating concerns in creating organizations. Incentives, too, were not related to performance. Institutions were deliberately designed to constrain and influence individuals within public sector management, the issue of incentives and motivations and designing institutions that can mould them to work in consonance with institutional goals has always been considered the most difficult to handle.

Public sector reforms in this area have been difficult to achieve because the civil service has resisted any link between pay and performance. The resistance stems from the belief that public interest traditions will continue to endure. The issue of motivation is complex and there are frequent examples of public interested bureaucrats, but the point that needs to be accepted, is that the gap between self-interest and public interest as motivators needs to be narrowed. This can be done only through an appropriate organizational design.

IV

It appears that the progress on the privatization front has not been very encouraging in India. The question that keeps coming back is whether privatization is the only answer to public sector reforms. The ideological argument for privatization does not seem to have made an impact on policy makers. The image of the private sector has never been one of benevolence in India. Modern capitalists in India have to contend with prejudices and images that portray them as heartless moneylenders or greedy merchants or powerful social exploiters. Profit is perceived as an ill-gotten gain at the expense of the consumer or the labourer or society and not a source of capital accumulation for investment. The celebration of entrepreneurship and that of creating private wealth is a recent phenomenon mostly associated with the accession of Rajiv Gandhi and the globalization that began with the reform policies of 1991. Till recently, private capital did not have an influential public political voice. It was able to protect and advance its interests through political channels that were not in the public arena. This further created a public image of a scheming and manipulative private sector that thrived on a relationship with politicians and bureaucrats that could not usually be termed as lawful or honest.

In addition, the political forces that have not allowed public sector reform seem to be in the forefront of opposing privatization. The public sector employs more than two million throughout the country. It has provided opportunities of patronage to both the politicians and the civil servants. It is not an uncommon phenomenon for public sector enterprises to offer jobs as rewards or pacifiers to disgruntled members of the ruling elite. The public enterprises serve so many purposes, and efficiency or profit making are not among the prominent ones. When a unit suffers losses, closure is not considered an option and therefore the belief that work performance does not matter has gained in strength. This belief is sought to be justified on the social role of the public sector. It is constantly reiterated in public discourse that public sector has a social function of providing employment, and its performance cannot be measured by profit alone. Even measuring profit in the public sector is a subject of debate and controversy (see Gouri 1996).

There has been poor mobilization of public opinion in favour of privatization. Policies are neither emerging out of ideological convictions or practical performance of the public sector enterprises. There are mixed experiences and this is what adds complexity to the problem of privatization. What has, however, happened as Rudolph and Rudolph (1987: 34) point out, is that the commitment to public sector has diminished for more pragmatic reasons. Declining confidence in the public sector has been fuelled by a growing perception that an over directed and over regulated economy has become an obstacle rather than an agent of economic growth; that the unfavourable capital-output ratio of the public as against the private sector reflects, inefficiency, corruption and poor management; and that the socialist benefits of the public sector have become less apparent and convincing. Public enterprises are being distrusted not because they may prove to be inefficient, but because politicians and bureaucrats can misuse them. Public choice theory embedded in the larger belief in the supremacy of the market has fuelled this expectation.

REFERENCES

Bardhan. 1984. *Political Economy of Development*. New Delhi: Oxford University Press.

Bowles, Samuel and Herbert Gintis. 1986. *Democracy and Capitalism*. London: Routledge and Kegan Paul.

Brodie, Janine. 1996. 'New State Forms, New Political Spaces,' in Robert Boyer and Daniel Drache (eds), *States Against Markets: The Limits of Globalisation*. London: Routledge and Kegan Paul.

DiMaggio, Paul J. and Walter W. Powell. 1983. 'The Iron Cage Revisited: Institutional Isomorphism and Collective Rationality in Organizational Fields,' *American Sociological Review*, vol. 48, April, pp. 147–60.

Gouri, Geeta. 1996. 'Privatisation and Public Sector Enterprises in India Analysis of Impact of non-Policy,' *Economic and Political Weekly*, 30 November, pp. M–63 to M–74.

Government of India. 1958. *Jawaharlal Nehru's Speeches*, vol. 3. New Delhi: Ministry of Information and Broadcasting Publications Division.

Goyal, S.K. 1986. Public Sector in India. New Delhi: Indian Institute of Public Administration. Mimeograph.

The Group of Lisbon. 1995. *Limits to Competition*. Cambridge: MIT Press.

Gupta, Anand. 2000. 'The Political Economy of Privatization in India,' in S. Kahkonen and A. Lanyi (eds). *Institutions, Incentives and Economic Reform in India*. New Delhi: Sage Publications.

Gupta, Asha. 2000. *Beyond Privatization*. London: Macmillan Press.

Gupta, VR. 2000. *The Economic Times*. 31 August, p. 12.

Industrial Policy Resolution. 1956. *In Guidelines for Industries*, 1982. New Delhi: India Investment Centre.

Indian Economic Survey. 1999–2000. Government of India, New Delhi: Aklank Publishers.

Iyer, Ramaswamy R. 1991. *A Grammar of Public Enterprises Exercises in Clarification*. Jaipur: Rawat Publications.

Kalirajan, K.P. and R.T. Shand. 1996. 'Public Sector Enterprises in India Is Privatization the only Answer?' *Economic and Political Weekly*. 28 September, pp. 2683–686.

Levi, Margaret. 1988. *Of Rule and Revenue*. Berkeley: University of California Press.

Minogue, Martin, Charles Polidano and David Hume. 1998. *Beyond the New Public Management: Changing Ideas and Practices in Governance*. Northampton, Mass: Edgar Elgar Publishing Ltd.

Osborne, David and Ted Gaebler. 1992. *Reinventing Government: How the Entrepreneurial Spirit is Transforming the Public Sector*. New Delhi: Prentice Hall.

Ostrom, Vincent. 1989. *The Intellectual Crisis in American Public Administration*. Tuscaloosa University of Alabama Press.

Public Enterprises Survey. 1995–96. Government of India Publications.

Raghavan, S.N. 1994. *Public Sector in India Changing Perspectives*. New Delhi: Asian Institute of Transport Development.

Rudolph L.I. and S.H. Rudolph. 1987. *In Pursuit of Lakshmi: The Political Economy of the India State*. Hyderabad: Orient Longman Ltd.

Savas, E.S. 1982. *Privatizing the Public Sector: How to Shrink the Government*: Chatham, NJ: Chatham House Publishers.

Stretton, Hugh and Lionel Orchard. 1994. *Public Goods, Public Enterprise, Public Choice: Theoretical Foundations of the Contemporary Attack on Government*: London: St. Martin's Press.

Tullock, Gordon. 1965. *The Politics of Bureaucracy*. Washington, D.C.: Public Affairs Press.

15

NGOs in the Era of Globalization: Reworking the State–Citizen Dialectic

Harsh Sethi

These are strange, somewhat troubled times, with words, terms, phrases, concepts, institutions and values acquiring new meanings, often radically dissociated with those enjoying currency even a few decades back. The changing contours of the debate on State and Society or Public and Private seem to be indicating more oppositionism than constructive association—a tendency which, I believe, can have disastrous consequences for fragile institutional democracies and under-governed societies such as ours.

In a significant paper, Pranab Bardhan explores the great divide in the Indian social science discourse on the fundamental issues relating to a strong nation-state and its projects of modernization and industrialization. 'On the one side of this divide are the anarcho-communitarians which include, among others, Gandhian anarchists, anti-industrial 'small is beautiful', 'back to the village' utopians, cultural-relativist anthropologists, intellectuals involved in grassroots movements for preservation of the environment and tribal autonomy, as well as radical historians of 'subalternity' deconstructing nationalist historiography. On the other are the usual positivist economists (neo-classical liberals in the uncomfortable company of state socialists), die-hard Stalinists and left over Fabians, Mandarin administrators and technocrats, ideologues of the military-industrial complex, nationalist anti-imperialist historians as well as right-wing intellectuals espousing a combination of Hindutva and Chanakyian statecraft' (Bardhan 1997).

Between these two poles, the space for a reasoned, pragmatic discussion of strategies and activities that might help people as citizens recover their battered sense of citizenship has been squeezed out. The increasing excitement with NGOs (whatever the favoured nomenclature—private voluntary organizations (PVO), civil society organizations (CSO), non-party political formations (NPPF), non-governmental development organizations (NGDO), to name a few) evident since the last three decades, given the disappointment with both state and market institutions to ensure participative, humane governance, needs to be re-cast in the new era of a globalized economy and society.

For the purposes of this brief note, I propose to comment on only a specific sub-sector of the NGO world—the micro-grassroots organizations/movements that are not, at least self-consciously involved in conventional charity, welfare or development activities, and to interrogate the discourse concerned with their potential to transform Indian politics, and through that both state and society—an avowed goal of these efforts. Many of these entities may not even be formally registered under one or the other of the Acts that govern NGOs in the country.

In addition, I comment on those modern NGOs who claim to be political, albeit in non-party political terms. Most of these are middle-class and professional, located mainly in urban areas, and conduct their activities with the express purpose of linking upto, extending support to, and improving the effectivity of the micro-struggles at the grassroots. Even if partially/substantially involved with development or charity work, their distinguishing feature is not the delivery of services/goods, but through conscientization and mobilization contributing to the organized assertion of the poor and the organizations working for and with them. Often what is perceived today as the radical and transformative edge of voluntary work has emerged from these two different streams and locations of politics.[1]

The Context

Many of these 'movements/organizations' occupy social spaces created by the 'decline' of the conventional, mainstream politics of legislatures, elections, political parties and trade unions. And while, with the exception of the period of the Emergency (1975–77) we have witnessed regular elections at all levels (if anything, given the endemic instability of the electoral process, the frequency has of late increased), most analysts would agree that our formal, representative institutions are in a state of decay. This despite the fact that participation in the electoral process, especially of the more marginalized groups, has in the decade of the nineties seen an upturn. Nevertheless, the continuing popularity of elections has done little to increase the popularity/efficacy of political parties and politicians.

'This has resulted in the retreat of democratic institutions from open, competitive politics where they (political parties) continually sought to establish their claims for legitimation, into the pure politics of power and manoeuvre. In the process, political parties have lost their national character, both in political and geographical terms. Their role in inducting new groups into politics through waging struggles for their legal and political rights has been considerably reduced. As has been their ability to process issues arising in the economy, society and culture' (Sheth 1991).

The emergence of grassroots movements and organizations needs to be located within this context of the larger retreat of institutional politics. The increasing enmeshing of Indian economy and society into a globalization process has further contributed to a feeling of a growing inefficacy of our institutional structures.

The recent years have seen the growth of sporadic short-run movements that address specific concerns like child labour, dowry deaths; long term movements with developed organizational forms like the farmers' movements; the emergence of human rights, ecology and feminist groups; groups seeking to re-define notions of education, health, culture, or issues relating to ethnicity and cultural identity, focusing particularly on the discriminatory and exclusivist traditions in society buttressed by state policies that affect scheduled castes and tribes, minorities and women.

These groups engage with issues of displacement and inadequate compensation and rehabilitation of those affected by large development projects, with the appropriation of common property resources by the state and industry and so on. These stirrings are often linked to para-professional groups, mainly urban and middle class, who use their skills in networking, training, research and documentation, law, media-communication—all to create national (and international) campaigns and public awareness around such issues and sectors.

By taking up issues and constituencies 'abandoned' by political parties and trade unions and ill-served by the bureaucracy, the activist formations have sought to re-formulate the issues and expand their constituencies in a framework that is primarily non-electoral. The organizational form that has emerged is neither that of a political party nor of a pressure group; rather the effort is to evolve a participative and mobilizational form of politics which can sustain struggles on issues articulated by the people themselves and work for their empowerment. In the process, they have sought to expand the meaning of constitutional politics by justifying their struggles in terms of the Directive Principles of State Policy—a section in the Constitution, provisions of which are not justiciable in a court of law.[2]

Before analyzing the impact of these diverse stirrings and thus their potentialities and limitations, we need a clearer appreciation of the environment they operate in, more specifically that of the micro social action groups and movements and the para-professional support NGOs.

Micro-Struggles

In most discussions of Indian democracy and its multitudes of institutions—not just representative but those of the judiciary and press—the disjunction between what is theoretically posited and empirically available is rarely appreciated. Nor is the difference that obtains in different parts of the country.

In the areas and the sections of populace the social-activist formations work with, the congruence between the agencies of the state and local vested interests is near complete. Except at the margin, this leaves little legitimate space for operation. At one level, the very enormity of problems that the grassroots groups/movements have taken upon themselves or are expected to tackle becomes so great that exhaustion and breakdown is inevitable. The inability of the state, the bureaucracy and institutional politics to process these problems meaningfully creates an overwhelming situation such that to expect scattered, localized efforts to act as buffers between the chaos and violence in society and the neglect, if not coercion by the state, appears an exercise foredoomed to failure.

The activists of these movements are constantly on the run, spending their time and energy on fire-fighting which leaves little time for reflection and interaction with others. Even limited success at tackling one local issue creates pressures to enter another. Since both issues and power at the local level are highly concentrated, the activist groups face simultaneously a growing complex of issues and concerted resistance from those whose power is being challenged. And though periodically, some help is forthcoming from the more sensitive and concerned sections of the state apparatus—in terms of legitimacy, funds, sometimes direct support and validation—and success, even if limited, does enthuse, fighting constant coercion and harassment does tend to be wearying.

As important as the brutality encountered in the local environment is the lack of cohesion and coordination amongst these different efforts. While in itself not unexpected, for afterall grassroots stirrings have to be environmentally sensitive and rooted, as issues merge into each other and the need arises for coordination with a wide array of actors, consensus has to be achieved on ideological questions—a process often resented by groups zealous about safeguarding their own autonomy, identity and territory. Not that voluntarist and spontaneous groups are known for their ability to work out a coherent perspective. Bitter quarrels and further fragmentation are thus not unusual.

The need to escape local boundary conditions, of being heard by those who matter, and being able to create an environment more sympathetic to the sets of issues that the social activist formations are working on brings to the fore concerns related to networking—lateral coordination with similar groups, linking up with support groups in urban areas, often both. A quandary arises precisely because while such a move is seen as both desirable and necessary, networking on a weak and divided base often implies that the 'power' and 'ability' to formulate and present issues passes into the hands of the non-grassroots paraprofessional groups and individuals.

This has major implications for the process on the ground. As against a deepening of grassroots mobilization and organization, the focus shifts to efforts at achieving media coverage in a bid to influence the environment and policy processes, a strategic impulse favoured by those removed from the ground. The local groups thus get drawn into organizing and participating in seminars and workshops, preparing audio-visuals and films, using public interest law to intervene via the courts, and so on. Even their research is designed primarily to provide information to others so that a proper case is made on their behalf rather than facilitate the process of enriching their activism (Sethi 1992).

Not that there is any easy way to overcome this quandary. Ever so often the local space is so constrained and tilted against those fighting for the rights of the dispossessed that expanding visibility is seen as the only route to survival, even physical survival. Take for instance, the case of police-firing resulting in the death of three tribal activists who were protesting against alumina mining in the forest lands of Kashipur, Orissa. (*The Hindu*, 16 December 2000). This struggle had been going on for nearly five years. A local NGO—Agragamee—otherwise involved in 'safe' activities such as watershed development, literacy, and helping tribals set up grain banks for food security—was drawn into the struggle. As a result, it faced extreme harassment and repression—ranging from a stoppage of funding to filing of police cases. To restrain the local power structure, it was forced to organize press conferences in the national capital, and to approach the National Human Rights Commission to challenge the unconstitutionality of the takeover of tribal lands, otherwise protected by the Fifth Schedule. All this has led to a major reorientation of its strategy, working style, network of allies and so on, with local activities being downgraded in favour of a national awareness campaign.

The most extreme form of distortion comes via an increasing involvement of these groups into a new 'politics of symbolism'. Thus fighting the deep-rooted social inequity, exemplified for instance in a restricted access of the 'untouchables' to places of worship often gets transformed into well-publicized marches for the liberation of temples; struggles for the improvement in the status of widows, into episodic and media-focussed protests around *sati* or films like *Water*. Little do the votaries of this event-based, episodic, media-centred approach realize that far from highlighting issues or preparing the ground for a more concerted attack on the evils within us, such a politics of symbolism only serves to distort and caricature issues, becoming instead a 'politics of rituals'. Often, such a process only makes the tasks of those trying to work on a more sustained level at the grassroots even more difficult.[3] (The more recent enlargement of engagement from the national to international level provides further examples of this distortion.)

Support NGOs

Quite unlike the social activist formations at the grassroots whose emergence can be traced to the contradiction at the base of society and the inability of the state and political structures to meaningfully respond to the survival and dignity issues of the poor and excluded, the phenomena of support NGOs (middle class and urban) which seek to effect a radical transformation of Indian politics and society is relatively recent. Though they too, like all efforts in our society, claim inspiration from earlier attempts during the anti-colonial struggle for social reform and change, effectively they are the offsprings of the post-Emergency phase.

The realization of the inefficacy of working through official structures in responding to widespread but localized issues of oppression and survival led to a commonalty of approach, both within the country and international organizations. From the formal recognition granted to NGOs in the Seventh Five Year Plan to the shift in the priorities of multilateral, bilateral and private co-financing agencies—the period witnessed a major escalation of both funding and support to NGO formations. For instance, the Ford Foundation, one of the biggest international supporter of the official programmes and institutions in the first 25 years of the Republic, consciously changed its policies in the late '70s to partner private voluntary organizations—PVOs. This was co-terminus with the 'discovery' of NGOs by both the World Bank and the UN System of organizations. Such examples can be multiplied.

Not unexpectedly, this change in environment led to a major explosion in the number of NGOs. While most of this new munificence was channelized towards conventional charity and development organizations, a large residual market was simultaneously created for NGOs working with a 'political' orientation. New groups, whether working directly with the concerned populace in the field, as support organizations mediating between micro-social action groups, or between them and the state—through diverse activities like networking and coordination; social research and documentation; monitoring, evaluation and training; creating pedagogic and media packages to impart information and skills; accessing formal structures; preparing the environment; or lobbying for policy changes—activities which earlier were unknown in the NGO world, acquired a new presence. Through seminars and workshops, theatre and films, newsletters and journals—these new groups with their specialized skills attempted to reach out, both to the grassroots and the policy-makers. Central to this new enterprize were new ideological debates—on human rights, ecology, feminism, identity and the law—efforts at re-structuring the espistemological universe in which meanings are ascribed to political activity.

Some early and noteworthy successes—the reformulation of the rape law, the stalling of the forest bill, the national campaign on housing rights, the success at using the new innovation of public interest litigation, the presenting of a private bill on child labour in the Parliament, to name a few—generated a new excitement. More than the ongoing struggles at the base of society, it was this 'new NGO' effort and its 'success' in reshaping the development and political discourse that caught the attention of both policy-makers and the public.

Without trying to undermine the genuine impulse behind many of these new efforts—networking, coordination and evolving a new ideological crystallization for understanding and representing the new stirrings in society—it does merit mention that unlike the efforts during the anti-colonial struggle, many of the present initiatives depend strongly on an external infusion of funding, often international. This combination of legitimacy, excitement and relatively easy funding has, however, led to a range of unforeseen consequences—the primary amongst them being that internalist criteria of self-assessment seem to have been supplanted by those sensitive to donor concerns. More specifically, the availability of larger amounts of 'easy money', and the shifts in the language of description and analysis have radically redefined the relationship between the new NGOs and the micro-social action groups, and through that, the discourse on politics and social transformation.

The shift towards NGOs as a favoured entity for funding support owed much to their 'brand distinction' from official agencies. In relative terms they were seen as locally rooted and environmentally sensitive, flexible, low cost and honest, and thus 'proper instruments' to reach the people. As criticism grew of top-down, non-participative approaches to development and democracy, greater stress started being placed on processes that helped in the conscientization, mobilization and organization of the poor rediscovering themselves as subjects not objects of social transformation. It was this new, 'radical' impulse that the NGOs were able to successfully capture and tap, bringing to the fore the new activities mentioned earlier.

While many of these changes in the thinking of both the government and the aid establishment were indeed welcome—for it is apparent that the earlier strategies were not working—the massive expansion of the 'grassroots market' invited a 'taking over' of the new issues, vocabulary and sector of concerns by a new breed of actors. Today with everyone, from donor governments and agencies, our own governments, the social commentators and the middle class para professional agencies finding it lucrative to enter the 'grassroots business', what can be discerned in the process is a hegemonizing of the voice of the grassroots, often so mutilating it that it becomes unrecognizable even to the concerned subjects.[4]

At one level this heightened radicalism (of language if not purpose) has led to a purposive devaluation of the nation of service, of doing good, of helping others in need. Even older voluntary formations which had in the past done stellar work, albeit of a conventional charity and development type, are made to appear as irrelevant, if not counter-productive. It has also led to a decline in the importance of material interventions in the lives of the poor—introducing new technologies, a focus on income generation through production—seen as only consolidating the capitalist system, helping the better-off. Most importantly all activities and organizations are sought to be judged with respect to their political role and potential (Sethi 1986).

This focus on macro political concerns is reflected in the efforts at networking and coordination. The drawing in of local social action groups into a macro political frame has meant both their rupturing from the base communities as also an increased importance of the middle class NGO interlocutors—those with the funds, contacts, language and skills to operate successfully in the new marketplace.

One implication of this new politics by new actors has been a downgrading of the already enfeebled and discredited conventional politics and political parties. Not unexpectedly, this has led to a heightened conflict with the political parties, particularly of the Left, who look upon the NGOs as fifth columnists operating on behalf of new-imperialist forces. The challenge to their monopoly over radicalism could not be tolerated (Karat 1988). The other is a shift in the perception of the government. While the subtle denunciation of political parties, particularly of the Left, is probably welcome, there is hostility towards this NGO constellation emerging as a dissenting force. Even as far back as the early eighties, the government attempted to formulate a code of conduct for voluntary agencies and impose new conditionalities governing the receipt and operation of funds, particularly foreign (Sethi & Sheth 1991).

The assumption of this new political role accompanied by radical rhetoric has created new pressures from diverse sources on the NGO sector. For a start, partly as a result of the new expectations that the NGOs have generated, there is an overloading of demands from the ground. Networking and coordination, combined with servicing grassroots groups and struggles is a complex task. The inability to satisfy these expectations has led to the trading of vilificatory charges— that NGOs have become corrupt, lazy, used to an easy lifestyle, distanced from base communities and groups—much of it unfortunately true (Hulme & Edwards 1996).

Second, the market for NGOs has become far more complex, not only because there are very many more NGOs or donors, but also because the market while expanding has redefined itself. This statement needs clarification. In the new era of liberalization, under the WB-IMF directed dispensation, there is a clear cutback in governmental expenditure, particularly in the social sectors. Equally, the focus of concern has shifted from the survival and dignity issue of the poor to global competitiveness and efficiency.

What this implies is that while conventional NGOs in the areas of social welfare, including those focusing on research, training and communication may witness a boom in their market, their role is likely to be confined to primarily carrying out base line surveys and preparing the community to accept the new development packages. Involvement of such NGOs is now the norm in all donor assisted projects, including those working through the government. The downside is that the search for credibility in the global capitalist market may lead to a crackdown on all meddlesome actors and agencies raising unnecessary issues of justice, equity, survival and sustainability—particularly by trying to organize the oppressed.[5]

It is not that the NGOs espousing a radical orientation are facing only a recessionary market. True, that the government today is far more hostile to them than it was a decade back. They have, however, got a new lifeline in the international arena. The adoption of the language of good governance by the international donor community, including the incorporation of social clauses in matters of production and trade, as also the recognition of the socially deleterious effects of liberalization and globalization, has meant that the NGO community has now become a key player in articulating social concerns in global fora.

Because national governments have today to be more appreciative of global donor concerns, NGOs have begun to use the international space to influence local policy orientations. The new global discourse on human rights, women and child issues, issues of minority identity and cultures, ecology and sustainability—much of it formed by NGOs, does serve as a check on national policies (Reddy 2000). Whether this is playing into the hands of global actors and thereby diminishing national sovereignty is a matter of debate, with NGOs more often being accused of being anti-national, what is undeniable is that local politics has now to incorporate global concerns and standards of behaviour.

A few examples may help illustrate the complex processes unleashed once local struggles/efforts tie up with international actors and attempt to make use of global fora to influence national policy while 'ensuring' relief to their client constituencies. The first relates to the linking up of anti child labour activity in the carpet industry to the global campaign to eradicate child labour by certifying whether the products sold in the global market are child labour free or not. *Rugmark* is a certification process sponsored by UNICEF and western donor organizations. Carpets which do not carry the certification can now no longer be sold in western markets. Expectedly, this has led to a closure of many carpet factories which are child labour intensive.

While, to an extent, this has forced carpet manufacturers to use adult instead of child labour, in the absence of any social security mechanisms, families earlier surviving on the incomes earned by children are now worse off. The process has also led to an increase in corruption, with manufacturers paying bribes to receive the necessary certification. Above all, the process has contributed to the ingress of social clauses into trade agreements, thereby reducing the export markets for traditional Indian handicrafts. Moreover, it has redefined the conventional understanding of childhood and work and downgraded, if not criminalized, traditional practices in artisanal families where children both worked and studies while learning skills.

The shift in India's best-known social movement, the Narmada Bachao Andolan, from demanding a just relief and rehabilitation policy for those displaced by mega-development projects to a stance insisting on 'no big dams' at any cost too can be partially traced to the global movement against big dam technology. In its long and heroic struggle, the NBA has used a mix of strategies—local level organizing, awareness campaigns through the media, putting pressure on donor agencies to stop funding such projects, questioning the fundamentals of development interventions which are both socially and ecologically unsustainable. The movement's most spectacular success has been in generating a negative image of such projects, basically abroad, leading to a drying up of external donor funds.

While at one level, this sustained campaign has forced a major reappraisal of such development projects, including the acceptance of much better relief and compensation norms, and that potential oustees have to be consulted and their concurrance taken before embarking on these projects, the NBA has also been classified as anti-national—in its denigration of the national image, of legitimizing external intervention in internal matters, and in its adopting criteria of evaluation unsuited to local contexts. Politically, the process has created a backlash against not only the NBA but other such movements, all of whom are seen as anti-development.

Impacts

Having described, albeit briefly, the internal and external environments within which the micro social action groups and the support NGOs function, we can now turn to an assessment of this phenomena, particularly on how it shapes the construction of democracy in the country.

Most analysts, even those critical of these new tendencies, would admit that these diverse struggles/efforts have been able to alter the dominant discourse on development and politics in the country. They have both placed new issues on the public political agenda as also forced rethinking about many of the old concerns. The linking up of grassroots struggles with new middle class radicalised formations, though full of pitfalls and weaknesses has revitalized the flagging democratic spirit and consciousness in the country. With many more people involved in looking at development and politics, formal structures are hopefully forced into greater accountability. Even the cooption by the state of the new language and concerns implies a process of adjustment.

The 'downside' is that the downgrading of the institutions and processes of the nation-state as a result of pressures from both above and below alongside a greater legitimacy accorded to the functioning of the market or community, as the case might be, is far too often uncritically welcomed. True, the Indian state in the past played an overwhelming role (the *mai-baap sarkar*), but its penetration was also partly to fill an institutional vacuum, as also to keep in check the local overlords. Much of what is today valorized as community and tradition is not only invented, it hides ugly inequities and oppression. Equally, external intervention is essential if societies like ours have to escape the survival trap engendered by a combination of demographic pressure, low labour productivity and technological stagnation. Third, we need to be appreciative of the need for state intervention to handle the externalities of the development process which decentralized local communities are unable or unwilling to cope with. Fourth, in today's world of giant transnational corporations and state involvement in predatory trade, a weak or loosely functioning state is at a considerable disadvantage (Bardhan 1997).

Notwithstanding the above, no worthwhile democracy can afford to let either an impersonal bureaucracy or market define the rules of the game. NGOs and other civil society organizations thus act as both buffers and filters to (hopefully) better incorporate the everyday concerns—economic, political, and moral—of the citizenry and thus help humanize both state and society.

Given the fact that social activist formations have primarily focused on the politics of issues, and foregrounded the Directive Principles of State Policy neglected by the officialdom and political parties, they have to varying degrees managed to make local formal power structures more transparent, accessible and accountable. Be it through the

Right to Information Campaign or involvement in the training of panchayat/municipality functionaries—they have tried to ensure the incursion of a new language and consciousness of rights at the base of society (Sethi 2000a).

Little of this shift at the base of society may be apparent, at least partly because our gaze is more focussed on the macro-environment where large and spectacular shifts rather than everyday resistance catch our attention. At the level of relating to and influencing macro political formations, these struggles have not been very successful. Nor have they been able to emerge as a larger nationwide political movement by forging coalitions, alliances and mergers among themselves. While this may explain the relative invisibility of their politics, or its relative inefficacy in influencing electoral behaviour, it is also that many of these groups reject the 'capture of state power' route to social transformation. For them, the long term goal of economic and political decentralization can only be achieved through changing the forms of organizations and changing people's own capabilities. Such changes, if achieved in broader society and culture, may ultimately result in a transformation of the state itself.

Does this then mean that these formations are opposed to the institutional framework of Indian democracy? Afterall, they seem to favour a 'withdrawl of legitimacy' rather than 'compete in elections' or 'engage in a revolutionary overthrow of the state' routes to constructing meaningful politics. Ideologically, they see formal democracy as a necessary but insufficient condition in the long haul towards social transformation. This, they believe, can take place if the main battle ground is shifted from mainstream politics into society and culture. Only then can further democratization be achieved—not only of political institutions, but of the family, community, the workplace—in short, of society at large.

Conclusions

We have now experienced a decade (some would argue 15 years) of a process of economic reform. Though hesistant and half-hearted, a bit like Lenin's 'One Step Forward, Two Steps Back', it is undeniable that the combination of fiscal adjustment, structural reforms, privatization and globalization of the Indian economy has fundamentally altered the landscape—both of the norms by which we live and the corresponding

discourse. And whether or not the reform process has markedly esca-
lated the growth rates of GNP per capita, or managed to 'dramatically'
reduce the proportion of the populace below the poverty line (some
argue to as low as 15–20 per cent), it is widely (though grudgingly)
accepted that the process has also resulted in a sharp escalation of inequalities—between regions, sectors, classes and communities. (Sethi
2000b: 23–26) Does this then imply that those on the receiving end of
this painful restructuring process are today worse off, even that their
changes of making a transition to a superior state are today more bleak?
It would appear so, if for no other reason than that the governing ideology of the times has become one of 'betting on the strong' rather than
'assisting the weak'.

NGOs and social movements with a self-conscious orientation towards the deprived and marginalized should theoretically thus enjoy a
greater hearing space in society. They, afterall, more than the formal
institutions of representative politics seem to be espousing the interests
of the underdogs. And yet, that is not the impression created. Nowhere
in the country have we witnessed sustained struggles against the new
policy regimen. And in the rare situations that we have, for instance the
three decade old struggle of the National Fishworkers Forum on behalf
of traditional coastal fisherfolk, the movement, despite forging internal
and external linkages with a variety of institutions and actors, has met
with extremely limited success in altering the policy governing fishing
on India's coasts (Dietrich and Nayak 2000).

Without overplaying the potential of NGOs and non-party political
formations to engender sustained processes of equitable social transformation, it does appear that a blanket oppositionism to the state and
an over-reliance on the media, courts and international actors, has
created a backlash within which such efforts, incorrectly I believe, are
seen as anti–national. Given the enhanced 'international' connections
of many local players, issues—particularly those involving conflict
with the state machinery—not only tend to be globalized even before
being nationalized, they are often painted in somewhat distorted colours.
A recent case of a health NGO, Sahyog, working on AIDS awareness
campaign in the Almora Hills, comes to mind (Sethi 2000c).

On the other hand, movements such as the Right to Information
Campaign spearheaded by the MKSS in Rajasthan or the work of the
National Slum Dweller's Federation in Mumbai seemed to have carved
out a more durable space, possibly because of a strategy of 'constructive
oppositionism'. Equally noteworthy is the success of the Kutch Mahila

Vikas Sanghatan in the border areas of Gujarat—particularly in its ability to combine the economic and the social, the private (household) domains with the public sphere. In the KMVS case, a crucial constituent of its legitimacy comes from its decision to not work with foreign funds, and to continually involve local actors—elected representatives, bureaucracy, even corporate houses—in its work. Above all, what is remarkable is the group's policy of playing a low key and supportive role with the final decision on programmes resting with organizations of base communities. I am not arguing that this process is without its conflicts or complications. Only that it offers higher chances for sustained work and not inviting premature closure (Ramachandran and Saihjee 2000).

It is as yet unclear how the 'political' NGOs will recast themselves in the years to come. What does seem evident is that efforts at social transformation need to shift focus from primarily raising 'fundamental' questions about the state and anti-development to exploring the interstices created by the political and development process and forge constructive collaboration with both the state and political parties if they, and indeed the country, has to survive as an institutional democracy.

NOTES

* This article draws heavily on two earlier papers, 'The NGO Sector in India: Historical Context and Current Discourse' (with D.L. Sheth), *Voluntas* 2(2), 1991; and 'Some Notes on Micro-Struggles, NGOs and the State', *Asian Exchange* 12(1/2), 1997.

1. There is likely to be some confusion in my using the term 'movement' to describe the activities of the micro social action groups as also the urban, support NGOs. Most analysts liken movements to large and sustained stirrings, which these activities are clearly not. Nevertheless, what is sought to be emphasized is the self-perception of these entities—as engaged in transformative politics, a desire to alter the balance of power in favour of the under-priveleged. These entities specifically demarcate themselves from conventional NGOs who they see as operating within the given rules of the game.

2. For a detailed account of the history of one such group, see Lewis (1991).

3. For a detailed description of this process, particularly the use of social action litigation, see Baxi (2000).

4. The hijacking, distortion and caricature through the imperialism of language and categories of description is rarely attended to. A hilarious account of this process is provided by novelist Tom Wolfe (1991). The account would be funnier still, if it weren't so true, though unfortunately

nothing comparable has been written on the sociology of the home-based radical chic.

A fascinating, though carricatured analysis of the functioning of the human rights groups, which emerged on the scene in a big way after the crack down on the Maoist movement in the late 1960s, is provided by Upendra Baxi. While more than commending the role of the human rights groups in keeping the 'flag flying' in the face of both massive violations of human rights by the state and a vicious campaign launched by it accusing all human rights groups as anti-national, he pointed to the disturbing prevalence of a praxis that focuses on the episodic and spectacular, almost deliberately eschewing serious and sustained work which might lead to institutional reform. He went so far as to characterize such activity as marked by a 'libidinal fascination with the pathology of state power', 'an ambivalence, if not a fear that the reform of the State would lead to a dissolving of their agendas'. As such, the actual relief that victim groups might legitimately expect from the activities of the human rights groups remains low, leading to an erosion of their faith in human rights activism.

5. Note the simultaneous wooing of NGOs in major bilateral and multilateral programmes of education, health, social forestry, even relief and rehabilitation while attacking groups like the Narmada Bachao Andolan.

REFERENCES

Bardhan, Pranab. 1997. 'The State Against Society: The Great Divide in Indian Social Science Discourse,' in Sugata Bose and Ayesha Jalal (eds), *Nationalism, Democracy and Development*. New Delhi: Oxford University Press.

Baxi, Upendra. 2000. 'The Avatars of Indian Judicial Activism: Explorations in the Geographies of (In) Justice,' in S.K. Verma and Kusum (eds), *Fifty Years of the Supreme Court in India: Its Grasp and Reach*. New Delhi: Oxford University Press.

Dietrich, Gabrielle and Nalini Nayak. 2000. 'Fishworkers' Movement in India and its Global Interactions'. Paper for Seminar on Re-inventing Social Emancipation, Coimbra, Portugal, 23–26 November.

Edwards, Michael and David Hulme. 1996. *Beyond the Magic Bullet: NGO Performance and Accountability in the Post Cold War World*. Hartcourt: Kumarian Press.

Karat, Prakash. 1988. *Foreign Funding and the Philosophy of Voluntary Organisations: A Factor in Imperialist Strategy*. New Delhi: National Book Centre.

Lewis, Primila. 1991. *Social Action and the Labouring Poor*. New Delhi: Sage Publications.

Ramachandran, Vimala and Aarti Saihjee. 2000. Flying with the Crane: Recapturing KMVS's Ten Year Journey. Mimeograph.

Reddy, C. Rammanohar. 2000. 'What Are They Protesting About?' *The Hindu Magazine*, 8 October.

Sethi, Harsh. 2000a. *Improving Citizen Access to Information*. New Delhi: UNDP.

————. 2000b. 'Rethinking Swadeshi'. Paper for Seminar on Re-inventing Social Emancipation, Coimbra, Portugal, 23–26 November.

————. 2000c. 'Civil Rights and Local Sensibilities,' *Economic and Political Weekly*, vol. 35, no. 20.

————. 1992. 'The Politics of Grassroots Movements', *Denouement*, September-October.

————. 1986. *NGOs in India: A Troubled Future*. Oslo: NORAD.

————. 1991. 'The NGO Sector in India: Historical Context and Current Discourse', *Voluntas*, vol. 2, no. 2.

Sheth, D.L. 1991. 'Politics of Social Transformation: Grassroots Movements in India'. Lecture delivered at the University of Hull, UK.

Wolfe, Tom. 1991. *Radical Chic and Mau-Mauing the Flak Catchers*. London: Cardinal, Sphere Books Ltd.

16

Creating a Public: Reinventing Democratic Citizenship

Sarah Joseph

It has commonly been maintained that there are two alternate democratic traditions in Western political theory, the liberal and the civic republican. The first is associated with philosophers writing in the individualist tradition like Locke, Bentham and Mill, the second claims inspiration from Aristotle, Machiavelli and Rousseau. (Held 1989: 23, Axtmann 1996: 46). Though distinct, both traditions have drawn on each other and provided the framework of values and concepts which have guided the evolution of democratic theory in the modern period. However, significant changes are now being introduced in democratic theory to bring it in line with new theories regarding the role of the state in a globalizing economy. The first section of the paper, briefly discusses some of these developments in democratic theory. It is argued seen that although defended as a means of strengthening and revitalizing representative democracy the developments challenge traditional democratic values like equal citizenship and accountability of governments and that this might reduce the credibility of representative democracy. In the second section the package of institutional strategies, often summed up by the phrase 'good governance' which is being devised to operationalize the new concepts of democracy and development are discussed. The claimed purpose of such reforms is to streamline the functioning of the state and to evolve partnerships between state and organized interests and citizens which would extend across the boundaries of state institutions and civil society. This partnership would, it is hoped, help to promote prosperity and social development in the post-Welfare State era. Far reaching changes are being inaugurated in state and society under the rubric of reforms and the possible effect of such changes in highly stratified and segmented societies like India needs to be critically examined.

The liberal democratic tradition has traditionally conceptualized the state as a legal-political entity and it has emphasized the importance of democratic accountability of governments to citizens who authorize and legitimize the exercise of power through the exercise of their political rights like the right to vote. Citizenship here constitutes a political identity as well as a juridical status which confers equal rights and duties in the public sphere on citizens. The republican tradition on the other hand works with a model of state as political community which stands for a notion of collective good and in which citizens are equal and active participants in the exercise of political power. Classical republican theories rejected representative democracy but contemporary neo-republican theories have adapted to it, emphasizing instead the need for active participation by citizens in the sphere of civil society as well as in formal democratic procedures.

Both these traditions have coexisted with each other in Western political theory. In recent years in particular, a strong critique of instrumental individualism, mounted from within liberal theory, has made liberal democratic theory more hospitable to republican ideals. Liberal theory has tried to develop a broader understanding of the individual as a member of different social collectivities and it has also tried to incorporate notions of political community and participation into its theory of state (Ferraro 1997). It has been hoped that this would help to create solidarity and social capital in an increasingly individualistic and market-dominated society and also contribute towards civic renewal and the re-vitalization of liberal democracy. Dissatisfaction with the passive and relatively limited role assigned to citizens in large-scale representative democracies, and the client status of citizens in the welfare state, has led liberal democratic theorists to enthusiastically support civic renewal movements in the United States and other countries. A litany of successes for citizen initiatives is cited, ranging from the defeat of apartheid to the raising of income levels in Indian villages. Following from this, as well as from the interest in civil society generated by the break up of the East European communist states, citizen initiative in civil society as the means to promote social goals has become one of the mantras of international agencies and NGOs and governments in the developing world. Citizenship is no longer seen as only a legal-political status in the public sphere but as also involving active participation in civic activities in civil society.

A similar emphasis on civic activism is also perceptible in contemporary republican theories. Neo-republican theorists in the West have raised the issue of how to restore a notion of community and common good in an increasingly fragmented and individualistic society. Political theorists have commented on the 'strange disappearance of 'civic America' (Robert Putnam) and have sought explanations. They have deplored an excessive emphasis on rights and the loss of social solidarity and hope for the creation of new forms of solidarity and social capital which will transcend fragmentation and support democracy. This has provided the context in which citizen initiatives are being celebrated in countries like the U.S. In this paper some of the implications of such agendas for developing countries like India will be examined. We need to remember that encouraging citizen initiatives and an active civil society for developing countries has been accompanied by strong advocacy of neo-liberal agendas for State and society. Neo-liberal agendas are designed to bring new life into liberal democracy without giving up its basic assumptions regarding individual autonomy and social self regulation and a limited State. Promoting an active civil society is part of the agenda and it is hoped this would not only strengthen representative democracy but also help compensate for the failures of some decades of state-led development and modernization programmes to cope with issues of poverty and slow economic growth. Moreover, for business interests and international agencies, functioning through civil society may also be viewed as a way of bypassing the corruption and bureaucratization found in many states.

Equality is a core concept of democratic theory but liberal democratic interpretations of equality have always exhibited some ambiguities. For instance, in spite of the universalistic language which they used, 19th century liberal theorists like Bentham or Mill had justified certain exclusions from the rights of citizenship. The property-less, labourers, women and non-White races constituted some of them. In general the concept of equality upheld by 19th century liberal theorists was a restricted one and it co-existed with the belief that social stratification was part of the natural order of human societies. (O'Brien and Penna 1998: 39). Even the Keynesian welfare state was designed to modify inequality rather than eliminate it. Contemporary liberal theory functions with similar assumptions but we now find that equality is no longer even described in absolute terms. The equality which is now pursued is an equality which takes into account the different circumstances and institutional locations of people along with their diverse ends and aims to develop specific capabilities in relation to them (Jaisurya 2000: 283). Moreover, the state is no longer held solely responsible for promoting equality and welfare. In terms of the new strategies being proposed, responsibility for development is to be shared with citizens, local communities, organized interests and markets functioning in partnership with the state. Stratification, thus, continues to be perceived as a part of the natural order of society.

Another area of ambiguity in liberal democratic theory has been regarding group activity in civil society. At one level, associational activity in civil society has been regarded as a sign of health of a society and democracy. Polyarchy has been celebrated although the state is still expected to function in an independent and impartial way. But the focus on group activity has led to a tendency to defend groups as positive for democracy without looking too closely into the democratic credibility of the group though there is now more awareness than before that not all groups might contribute towards building democracy (See Joseph 1998: 124ff). The experience of East European societies after the break up of communism in particular has made neo-republican theorists wary about legitimizing all groups regardless of their ideology or practices. Therefore some theorists have argued for state sponsorship of 'the right kind of groups', (Walzer, 94 Q. in Dryzek 2000: 91), while others have put in a plea for state help for associations of the poor and exploited as well. But civil society activism and groups in general are lauded as helping to socialize citizens and draw them into civic activities. This assumption also needs to be explored given the range of activities being celebrated in civil society in India today.

The dominance of neo-liberal agendas has had far reaching implications for the contemporary understanding of democracy and citizenship. Given the emphasis on good governance, which includes limiting the State, adopting new managerial techniques in administration, partnership between government and business and other important interests in society, extending the scope for markets in different spheres and the like, the older humanist conception of democracy and citizenship has had to be re-conceptualized. The demands of good governance may conflict with the earlier understanding of concepts like accountability and participation. Accountability of governments to citizens may now be translated as transparency, profitability and efficiency, with the citizen cast as consumer or end-user with the responsibility of intervening to ensure the proper functioning of State agencies. Moreover, partnerships between state, business interests and service providers (stakeholders in the current language), can blur the distinction between state and civil society and further dilute democratic accountability of governments to the body of citizens. It might also lead to the removal of a range of decisions from political decision-making in the interest of 'good governance'. Since participation is now being translated as activism not only in relation to formal democratic procedures, but also in civil society, it could include allowing business and other interests a share in governmental decision making. Such participation has acquired a new importance in many countries on account of the discredited status of political parties and representative assemblies but it is debatable whether following such strategies in deeply stratified societies like India would help to create a public which could negotiate a notion of the common good, the loss of which has been deplored in contemporary neo-republican theories.

Good Governance—New Institutional Strategies

The term governance is widely used today. It is often used interchangeably with 'government' but the implications of the term remain somewhat different. The sense in which it is used by international agencies and governments refers to the efficient, cost-effective, and democratic management of public affairs by a government. These are presented as value-neutral and universal goals which any society should wish to pursue and the success or otherwise of governance may be assessed by reference to these goals. For instance, *The World Development Report* 1997, 'The State in a Changing World', lists the political tasks of governance as electoral democracy, transparency, accountability and participation, responsiveness of governments to people, safety and security of citizens, rule of law and the like. In a chapter titled *Bringing the State Closer to People* (ch. 7), the report emphasized the need to reflect the needs of all the people in official policies, not only of the wealthy and organized. This could, as the report sees it, mean bringing the popular voice into policy making through opening up channels to civil society, and decentralization of government. Most citizens, says the report, seek voice through more than voting. They seek voice as tax payers, users of public utilities, and increasingly as members or clients of NGOs and voluntary associations. The report goes on to discuss the importance of improving institutional capacity. Where markets are not suitable, other means of ensuring popular voice should be found. However, some areas of public decision making require insulation from public pressure. In others, public-private deliberation may be possible. The authors of the report hope that by embedding the voice of powerful interest groups in such organized deliberations, the scope for opportunistic behaviour might be reduced. There is need to make arrangements by which participation of stakeholders in the design and implementation of public services can improve the rate of return on them, for example, in the areas of education and the management of natural resources. The importance of the right of information and transparency in administration is emphasized to safeguard against abuse of power. There should be as much decentralization of administration as is possible while also building horizontal links with citizens, business, NGOs and local government.

The proposals outlined in the report reflect the kind of strategies which are being adopted even by some industrialized countries like Britain, which are dismantling their welfare states. Privatizing of some services, tendering, contracting out, adopting some of the managerial practices of private business, using the profitability criteria, creating internal markets and decentralizing government functions to local levels, constitute some of them (See Rhodes 1996 and Self 2000). New devices are being used to establish direct links between citizen and different service agencies. In addition, horizontal linkages between government, business and civil society organizations are also being promoted. Such prescriptions have also become familiar of late in the discourse of states like Karnataka which have embraced the goal of modernizing administration and involving private business and civil society in the process. In fact, business has been given a leading role in the various task forces and special organizations which have been set up in the state recently. In decisions regarding the improvement of public utilities, reducing corruption in government, and developing infrastructure, a partnership between government, business and stakeholders is envisaged. Though this might mean that important areas of decision making would be removed from political discussion, a right to information ordinance has been passed and attempts are also being made to open up direct communication between citizens and government using electronic media, to hear grievances and possibly redress them. Citizen Charters are also being framed by different agencies. New technologies are being introduced to improve the efficiency of government information storage and communication. E-governance is the slogan now. The Chairman of the recently appointed Administrative Reforms Commission in the State has remarked that improving governance should be a social movement. At present however, all initiatives are coming from the state government.

Are such developments likely to bring about a more efficient and democratic government? As was mentioned above, fears have been expressed by neo-republican theorists in the West about the possibility of pressure groups coming to dominate policy-making for private gain. This is not part of their agenda for creating a public and if this happens the powerlessness of individual citizens might increase. And inevitably, it would be the more powerful and organized interests which would prevail. Instead of a reformed, democratic government becoming more effective in promoting the public interest, governments then might become victims of manipulation by different interests. In fact, the very notion of the general interest as a democratically negotiated collective interest may be excluded in such a situation and the notion of a national political community might be pre-empted by interests in civil society. (See the discussion in Self 2000). Such fears could even more justifiably be expressed in India given the structured inequalities in society and the degree of economic dependence and lack of access to information among a sizable proportion of the population and the relative power of organized interests. Neo-liberal agendas which enmesh state and civil society institutions might reduce the possibility of creating a 'public' concerned with promoting the general interest.

A major problem with state-led development in India has been the problem of corruption in government. But, increase in privatization and markets and the transferring of more decisions to them could merely increase the scale of corruption rather than eliminating the same and there are many instances of this. Nor is there evidence that e-governance would eliminate corruption. Corruption has also contributed towards the de-legitimization of democratic government. But the prescribed remedies are measures such as streamlining procedures of greater citizen alertness and activism, and opening up new avenues for communication between individual citizens and government. More basic reasons for corruption are not always considered.

A number of welfare functions are being transferred to civil society, or shared with associations and business. In education for example, not only are business interests involved in attempts to try to improve the quality of school education, local groups and communities are being invited to 'adopt' particular institutions and help to upgrade and monitor them, in addition to the responsibilities transferred to panchayats. Citizen activity to monitor government functioning or to tackle problems such as pollution and crime are also being encouraged.

With regard to problems of development and poverty eradication, empowerment is the slogan. Attempts are being made to work with local communities and religious organizations where appropriate, and NGOs, to 'empower' the poor and make them self-reliant. Self-Help Groups and micro-credit are central strategies in this regard and existing social networks of cooperation and solidarity are co-opted for the purpose along with forming new associations. These might be used to channel funds District Cooperative Banks for instance to the rural poor for income-generating schemes, and domestic urgencies from. The recovery rate is supposed to be very high, especially from women, and many success stories are cited from time to time in the press. Government and business and some of the NGOs may also provide finance, and managerial and technical expertise. The goal here would be to allow such processes to make a dent in existing hierarchies rather than to tackle inequality head on. The belief is, as Suzanne Rudolph has remarked in a recent article, that revolution in countries like India would take place through a 'slow boil', and that the effect of such micro-processes would spread out over society to change it (Rudolph 1999). If state-led development and redistribution was not very effective, such techniques, it is hoped, might have better results.

It is difficult to assess the effects of these developments as yet. But certain cautions have been sounded regarding an uncritical celebration of NGOs (Iyengar 2000). As has been pointed out in studies in other Asian countries, partnership between NGOs and governments need not always be in the interest of the poor. Some of the strategies being used to empower the poor might even have the effect of perpetuating exploitative relations in society. Relations between the poor and NGOs often tend to remain within the framework of patron-client relations and in addition, the use of existing networks of gender and caste to ensure the success of schemes like credit schemes might also serve to strengthen exploitation of women and other vulnerable groups. For instance, with regard to Bangladesh it has been held that 'domestication of development through micro-enterprises reinforces existing relations of power in private and public domains' (Fernando 1997: 76). Neo-republican theorists in the West have hoped that an active civil society would democratize society. But in deeply segmented societies like India this might not be the case. On the other hand, it could encourage greater dependence on traditional hierarchies in some cases. In any event, it is debatable how much the poor would be included into the body of citizens by such strategies. Some of them might not even find much advantage in accepting the limitations and responsibilities of democratic citizenship but may prefer to depend on existing social networks and groups even if they are exploitative in nature. It has been suggested that social movements and spontaneous associations of the poor in Latin America have not always promoted social solidarity nor helped to create a sense of a general interest. (See Reis 1997: 97). They may even have led to a narrowing of social networks in some cases. Similar consequences could occur in India too.

It has been argued by some Indian social scientists that civil society in countries like India is unlikely to follow the pattern of the largely middle class and industrialized societies of the West. Nor should we try to impose the values and institutions of the western modernity on our society. Subaltern groups cannot fit into the requirements of civil society easily and tend to continue to function in their own communitarian ways. But they may uphold values and practices which could form the basis of a new and more appropriate form of democracy than representative liberal democracy. Spontaneous communities of the poor, apparently anarchic social expressions and movements should be considered to form part of 'political society' which is concerned with democracy rather than modernization (Chatterjee 1998). But while celebrating the survival tactics of the poor, we should consider whether such activities could do more than help satisfy their survival needs. It is debatable whether they could change social structures and distribution patterns in their favour and there is no guarantee that such strategies would lead to greater inclusiveness and equality though there could be some broadening of the base of elites. The option of violence may become more attractive in such situations. The notion of indigenous and more appropriate modes of democracy is attractive but more thinking would be needed regarding its possible forms. The likelihood is that the more organized and powerful groups would continue to have a larger say in determining state policy and garnering resources unless the problem of structured inequalities is not also tackled.

Today civil society in India is in ferment with the emergence of social movements, and new groups, reactivation of community networks and redrawing of community boundaries, and the spread of markets. Many hopeful developments are taking place and remarkable examples of initiative and social concern are being shown by citizens. But it is not necessary that a strong civil society would always lead to greater equality, the strengthening of representative democracy and greater inclusiveness of citizens in democratic procedures. On the other hand, it might contribute towards the further de-legitimizing of political parties who would have to compete with NGOs and other civil society associations in their claims to represent the people. This could lead parties to try and mobilize a constituency on the basis of caste or ethnicity, or relying on populism or religious-cultural conceptions of the political community. There could be no argument for trying to go back to the past but there may be need to examine much more critically contemporary attempts to reinvent democratic citizenship in line with the demands of neo-liberal theories of state.

REFERENCES

Axtmann Roland. 1996. *Liberal Democracy into the Twenty First Century.* Manchester and New York: Manchester University Press.

Bennet, Sara and V.I. Muraleedharan. 2000. 'New Public Management and Heath Care in the Third World,' *Economic and Political Weekly,* vol. 35 no. 1, pp. 59–68.

Chatterjee, Partha. 1998. 'Community in the East,' *Economic and Political Weekly,* vol. 33, no. 6, pp. 277–81.

Dryzek, John, S. 2000. *Deliberative Democracy and Beyond.* Oxford: O.U.P.

Fernando, Jude L. 1997. 'NGOs, Micro-credit and Empowerment of Women,' *Annals of the American Academy of Political and Social Science*, vol. 554, Nov., p. 76.

Ferraro, Allessandro. 1997. 'The Paradox of Community,' *International Sociology*, vol. 12, Dec., pp. 395–408.

Held, David. 1989. *Political Theory and the Modern State.* Cambridge: Polity.

Iyengar, Sudershan. 2000. 'Role of Non-Government Organisations in Development of Gujarat,' *Economic and Political Weekly*, vol. 35, nos 35 and 36., pp. 3229–36.

Jaisurya, Kanishka. 2000. 'Capability, Freedom and the New Social Democracy,' *The Political Quarterly.*

Joseph, Sarah. 1998. *Interrogating Culture.* New Delhi: Sage.

Korten, David. C. 1992. *Getting to the 21st Century.* New Delhi: Oxford and IBH.

O'Brien, Martin and Sue Penna. 1998. *Theroising Welfare.* London: Sage.

Nauta, Lolle. 1992. 'Changing Conceptions of Citizenship,' *Praxis*, vol 12, no. 1, pp. 20–35.

Putnam, Robert D. 1995. 'Bowling Alone: America's Declining Social Captical,' *Journal of Democracy*, vol. 6, no. 1, pp. 65–78.

Reis, Elsa. 1997. Banfields Amoral Familiasm Revisted: Implications of High Inequality Structures for Civil Society,' in Jeffrey C. Alexander(ed.), *Real Civil Societies*. London: Sage.

Rhodes, R.A.W. 1996. 'The New Governance: Governing without Governments,' *Political Studies*, XLIV, pp. 652–67.

Rudolph, Suzanne, H. 2000. 'Civil Society and the Realm of Freedom,' *Economic and Political Weekly*, vol. 35, no. 20, pp. 1762–69.

Self, Peter. 2000. *Rolling Back the Market: Economic Dogma and Political Choice*. London: Macmillan.

Sen, Sidhartha. 1999. 'Some Aspects of State-N.G.O. Relationships in India in the Post-Independence Era,' *Development and Change*, vol. 30, pp. 327–55.

White, Sarah C. 1999. 'N.G.O.s, Civil Society and the State in Bangladesh: The Politics of Representing the Poor,' *Development and Change*, vol. 30. 307–26.

World Bank. 1997. *World Development Report*. New York: Oxford University Press.

About the Editors and Contributors

The Editors

Gurpreet Mahajan is Professor of Political Science at Jawaharlal Nehru University, New Delhi. She is the author of *Explanation and Understanding in the Human Sciences (1992)*, *Identities and Rights: Aspects of Liberal Democracy in India (1998)* and *The Multicultural Path: Issues of Diversity and Discrimination in Democracy (2001)*. She has also edited *Democracy, Difference and Social Justice (1998)* and co-edited *Minority Identities and the Nation-State* (with D.L. Sheth) 1999.

Helmut Reifeld is at present the Representative of the Konrad Adenauer Foundation in India. Formerly a research fellow with the German Historical Institute, London, and Bayreuth University, Germany, his co-edited works include *Pluralism and Equality* and *Women in Panchayati Raj*.

The Contributors

André Béteille has been Professor of Sociology in the Delhi School of Economics. He is a Corresponding Fellow of the British Academy, a Senior Life Associate of the National Institute of Advanced Study, and an Honorary Fellow of the Royal Anthropological Institute. His most recent publications include: *Antinomies of Society; Essays on Ideologies and Institutions and Sociology*; and *Essays on Approach and Method*.

Neera Chandhoke is Professor at the Department of Political Studies, University of Delhi. Her work centres on the overlapping areas of political theory and comparative politics. Her main publications include

Beyond Secularism: The Rights of Religious Minorities and, *State and Civil Society: Explanations in Political Theory*.

Rajeev Dhavan is a practising lawyer in the Indian Supreme Court, educated at Allahabad, Cambridge and London universities. A former academic, he has written several books and articles on law and public affairs, especially on the judiciary and the media.

Ute Frevert is Professor of Modern History at the University of Bielefeld (Germany). Her main publications in English include *Women in German History* and *Men of Honour: A Social and Cultural History of the Duel*. Her latest book is on military conscription in Germany in the 19th and the 20th century.

Dipankar Gupta is Professor at the Centre for the Study of Social Systems, Jawaharlal Nehru University, New Delhi. His recent publications are: *Culture, Space and Nation State: From Sentiment to Structure; Interrogating Caste: Understanding Hierarchy and Difference in Indian Society; Mistaken Modernity: India Between Worlds; Rivalry and Brotherhood: Politics in the Life of Farmers of North India; The Context of Ethnicity: Sikh Identity in a Comparative Setting; Political Sociology in India;* and, *Nativism in a Metropolis: The Shiv Sena in Bombay*.

Clauspeter Hill is former Representative of the Konrad Adenauer Foundation to Vietnam. A trained lawyer, he is currently in charge of the South Asia Desk in the head office of the Foundation in Germany.

L.C. Jain was a member of the National Planning Commission and has been actively engaged in the application of Gandhi's ideas to social transformation both in implementation at the grassroot level, as well as advocating policy changes in the light of field experience. He has held visiting fellowships at Harvard, Boston and Oxford Universities. He has also authored several books and papers on political decentralization and economic and social policies.

Sarah Joseph formerly taught Political Science at Lady Shriram College for Women, Delhi University. With a primary interest in contemporary political theory her publications include *Political Theory and Power* and *Interrogating Culture* in addition to several articles in journals and edited volumes.

T.N. Madan is Honorary Professor (Sociology) at the Institute of Economic Growth, Delhi. He is the author and editor of over a dozen books including *Nonrenunciation: Themes and Interpretations of Hindu*

Culture; Pathways: Approaches to the Study of Indian Society and *Modern Myths, Locked Minds: Secularism and Fundamentalism in India*. Professor Madan is currently working on a volume on religion in the modern world.

Kuldeep Mathur teaches at the Centre for Political Studies and is also currently associated with Centre for the Study of Law and Governance, Jawaharlal Nehru University, New Delhi. His research interests lie in the broad area of Public Policy Analysis and Public Administration. He has published extensively in the field of public policy processes, bureaucracy and decentralization. His recent publications include an edited volume: *Development Policy and Administration*. A forthcoming book with James W. Bjorkman is entitled *Policy, Technocracy and Development: Human Capital Policies in India and the Netherlands*.

Gail Omvedt is Senior Fellow at the Nehru Memorial Museum and Library. She is author of a number of books including: *Cultural Revolt in a Colonial Society; We Shall Smash the Prison: Indian Women in Struggle; Reinventing Revolution: India's New Social Movement; Dalit and the Democratic Revolution;* and *Dalit Visions*. She is translator of *Growing up Untouchable in India: A Dalit Autobiography*.

Margrit Pernau is a historian, affiliated with the Universities of Bielefeld and of Erfurt, Germany. She holds a Ph.D. from the South Asia Institute, Heidelberg. She has recently published *The Passing of Patrimonialism: Politics and Political Culture in Hyderabad 1911–48*. Her research interests include the history of Catholicism in Europe, cultural and social history of Indian Islam and gender history. Currently she is working on a major project on Muslim plural identities in Shahjahanabad in the 19th century.

Aswini K. Ray is Professor of International Relations and Comparative Politics, Jawaharlal Nehru University, New Delhi, and scholar and activist of the Human Rights Movement in India. His publications include *Domestic Compulsions and Foreign Policy; South Asian Regional Integration; Democratic Rights in a Post-Colonial Democracy; Global System in a Historical Perspective: A View from the Periphery;* and *Democracy and Social Capital in a Segmented Society* (forthcoming).

Arjun Sengupta is Professor at the School of International Studies, Jawaharlal Nehru University and Honorary Research Professor at the Centre for Policy Research, New Delhi. He was the former Ambassador of India to the European Union and Member Secretary of the Planning Commission. Currently he is also the Independent Expert on the Right to Development of the UN Human Rights Commission, Geneva and a Senior Visiting Fellow of the FXB Centre for Health and Human Rights, Harvard School of Public Health.

Harsh Sethi is presently Consulting Editor of *Seminar*. He has earlier worked as Acquisitions Editor, Sage Publications and has also been Fellow at the Centre for the Study of Developing Societies and Deputy Director at the Indian Council of Social Science Research. For long associated with a range of NGOs and social movements, he has co-authored and edited books on action research, human rights, participatory development and voluntary agencies.

Patricia Uberoi has taught Sociology at the Delhi School of Economics and the Jawaharlal Nehru University, New Delhi, and is now with the Institute of Economic Growth, Delhi. Prof. Uberoi has published extensively on family, gender and popular culture in both India and China.

Index

Abdul Aziz, Shah, 110
Aborigines, 45
Absolute, 251
absolutism, absolutist powers, 60–61,
    64–65, 74, 107, 120, 156, 166
accountability, 13, 18, 19, 29, 60,
    160, 171, 205, 242, 286–87, 307,
    313, 314, 316–17
accumulation, 188, 193
activism, 300, 319
adaptation, 39
administration, administrative, 164,
    171; centralism, 60; decentralized
    system, 20
Administrative Reforms Commission,
    282, 288, 319
Age of Marriage Act, 136
agnosticism, 100
Agragamee, 300
agrarian community/society, *See*
    peasant community
Aina-e-Sikander, 116
Akbar, 110, 115
alienation, 200, 202n
alim, 109
altruism, 189, 215, 216, 217, 224n
am and *khas*, 105–6
Ambedkar, B.R., 136, 137–38, 141,
    170–71
ambiguity, 316
ambivalence, 77
Amin ud Daula, 113
Ancien Régime, 74–75
Andhra Pradesh, 152
androgyny, 224n

animosity, 191
anomie politics, 244
anonymity, 142, 185
antagonism, 25
anti-caste movements, 130, 132,
    136, 137, 140–42
approbation, 197, 199
aristocracy, 37, 58, 78
Aristotle, 9–10, 13, 188, 313
art and culture, 112, 121
Aryans, 134
ashraf, 109
assimilation, 80
asymmetric behaviour, 64
Athens, *oikos* and *polis*, distinction,
    9–10; state, 17
Ati-Shudras, 134
Auckland, Lord, 116
austerity, 133
authority, 14
autonomy, 13, 24, 39, 40, 53, 165, 190,
    244, 286–88, 300
awareness, 66, 197, 316
Ayyankali, 139

backwardness, 72
Bahishkrut Bharat, 138
bandh, 54
banquet, ancient institution of, 96–97
bargaining approach, 208, 211–17, 222
behaviour, 85–86, 189, 191, 197,
    250, 305
belonging, sense of, belongingness,
    133, 134, 183, 184, 185, 188,
    189, 195, 199, 200, 202n